International Series on C

MW00963411

Series Editor:
Jing Jian Xiao
University of Rhode Island

For other titles published in this series, go to
www.springer.com/series/8358

Jean W. Bauer • Elizabeth M. Dolan
Editors

Rural Families and Work

Context and Problems

 Springer

Editors
Dr. Jean W. Bauer
Department of Family Social Science
University of Minnesota
290 McNeal Hall, 1985 Buford Avenue
St. Paul, MN 55108
USA
jbauer@umn.edu

Dr. Elizabeth M. Dolan
Department of Family Studies
University of New Hampshire
55 College Road
Durham, NH 03824
USA
e.dolan@unh.edu

ISBN 978-1-4614-0381-4   e-ISBN 978-1-4614-0382-1
DOI 10.1007/978-1-4614-0382-1
Springer New York Dordrecht Heidelberg London

Library of Congress Control Number: 2011936226

Printed on acid-free paper

Springer is part of Springer Science+Business Media (www.springer.com)

Preface

This book was created as a resource on rural families, especially low-income families. The slice of their life on which we have focused is work, and the environments and support around work. Researchers from a large multistate project sponsored by the Agricultural Experiment Stations (AES) at land-grant universities across the United States conducted research on low-income rural families and their functioning as a major policy change swept across the United States in 1996. Welfare reform influenced not only families receiving benefits, but families living in the community. In rural areas, many do not receive benefits even when they may be eligible. This book frames rural families in general, specifically what we know about low-income rural families. In addition, we use the research findings from the NC223/1011 multistate project "Rural Low-Income Families: Tracking their Well-being and Functioning in the Context of Welfare Reform" from 1998 to 2008 to provide a consistent research base and illustrate with actual voices other research concepts and findings about rural low-income families and work.

In this book, the voices of 115 mothers from the study are highlighted. All the names (including place names) are pseudonyms. Their statements illustrate the concepts presented in the chapters. The quotes you will read are taken verbatim from the transcripts of the interviews with the mothers from 1999 to 2003, when the data were collected. During this time the economic situation was changing. Chaps. 3 and 4 talk about the context of the rural situation, the variability, and employment issues for rural families.

One of our goals with this multistate research project was to bring along young researchers. Six of the authors (Bird, Katras, Lee, Manoogian, Sano, and Son) were graduate students at one point working with a RFS lead researcher. All have used the data for their dissertation and/or research that is shared in the book. Drs. Katras and Sano were research associates after they graduated and managed the work supported by National Research Initiative Cooperative Grant Program (NRICGP) funding. Six of the authors were at the first meeting of the research project in 1998, were lead researchers in their states, collected data, and have worked with graduate students using the data from the project. They are Bauer, Dolan, Lawrence, Mammen, Seiling, and Richards. Two other authors, Braun and Dyk, joined the project within the first 2 years, collected data, and supervised graduate students. Our other author, Walker, was on the project as support faculty in Maryland in the early years and has since moved to Minnesota. All of the chapters are authored by people in at least two different sites and sometimes more. This is a hallmark for cooperative work across states with the multistate research AES project.

Our goal in organizing this book is for you to learn more about the contexts in which rural families live and work: Their problems and issues with work in a changing rural environment that has been influenced by a major policy change in our nation. We happily present to you, *Rural Families and Work: Context and Problems* for your reading and as a base for future research, programs, and policy development.

Jean W. Bauer
Elizabeth M. Dolan

Acknowledgments

The idea of producing a book has been a long dream of the editors. It never would have been possible, however, without the entire Rural Families Speak (RFS) research team. In the Appendix, we share the history of the project, and identify the lead researchers and staff who worked in each state to collect the data and prepare the articles that are cited in the book. A list of the articles related to the RFS project and cited in the book is in Further Reading.

The project was funded in each state through several different sources: The states' Agricultural Experiment Stations, Cooperative Extension, grants, and/or department, college, or university research funds. Three grants for the overall support of the project were obtained from USDA, National Research Initiative Cooperative Grant Program (2001—35401-10215, 2002—35201-11591, 2004—35401-14938—J.W. Bauer, P.I.).

We are especially indebted to the mothers in our study. Over 500 were interviewed each for several hours with extensive questioning over several years. They were open and shared the reality of their lives with us—what it was like to live in a rural area as a low-income family while facing all the problems, opportunities, and joys of raising a family and making it day by day. Without them, neither the RFS nor this book would have been possible. They taught us so much about their reality, and we are now able to share their lives with you so that you can learn.

No book is possible without the assistance of others. We thank each of the chapter authors for their many hours of scholarly work to write within our constraints on the topics selected for the chapters. Other people have contributed to specific chapters and are acknowledged by the authors in that chapter. We are indebted to the reviewers for each of the chapters. Dr. Jing Xiao provided useful comments for the direction of the final manuscript. He also helped in the initial proposal to Springer Science + Business Media. This book is part of the book series on Family and Consumer Economic Issues for college students, researchers, policy makers, business practitioners, and consumers.

Individual contributions were made by a number of people: Dorothy (Dot) Kasik copy edited of all the chapters; Matty Leighton, Administrative Assistant in the

Family Studies Department at UNH, contributed technical assistance in formatting of the tables and figures; graduate students Laura Andrew (University of New Hampshire), and Chanran Seo and Samantha Zaid (University of Minnesota) helped with the preparation of tables and data retrieval, managing of the Google documents site, working with us on the references, and production of the book. Our managing Associate Editor, Jennifer Hadley, at Springer Science + Business Media was a great help in the production of the book. Thank you, Jennifer.

It was most helpful for Elizabeth to have a sabbatical leave during the early stages of the production of the book. She returned to her responsibilities as department chair of Family Studies, University of New Hampshire, which her colleagues appreciated. Jean appreciates the support of her department head, Dr. B. Jan McCulloch, in Family Social Science, University of Minnesota. Thanks go to many others, including family members for their support and helpful suggestions.

Contents

Contributors

Jean W. Bauer Department of Family Social Science, University of Minnesota, 290 McNeal Hall, 1985 Buford Avenue, St. Paul, MN 55108, USA
e-mail: jbauer@umn.edu

Bonnie Braun Department of Family and Consumer Sciences, University of Maryland, College Park, MD, USA
e-mail: bbraun@umd.edu

Carolyn L. Bird Department of 4-H Youth Development and Family and Consumer Sciences, North Carolina State University, Raleigh, NC, USA
e-mail: carolyn_bird@ncsu.edu

Elizabeth M. Dolan Department of Family Studies, University of New Hampshire, 55 College Road, Durham, NH 03824, USA
e-mail: e.dolan@unh.edu

Patricia H. Dyk Department of Community and Leadership Development, University of Kentucky, Lexington, KY, USA
e-mail: pdyk@uky.edu

Mary Jo Katras Department of Family Social Science, University of Minnesota, St. Paul, MN, USA
e-mail: mkatras@umn.edu

Frances C. Lawrence School of Human Ecology, Louisiana State University, Baton Rouge, LA, USA
e-mail: flawrence@agcenter.lsu.edu

Jaerim Lee Department of Family and Housing Studies, Yeungnam University, Daegu, South Korea
e-mail: jrlee@yu.ac.kr

Sheila Mammen Department of Resource Economics, University of Massachusetts, Amherst, MA, USA
e-mail: smammen@isenberg.umass.edu

Margaret M. Manoogian Department of Social and Public Health, Ohio University, Athens, OH, USA
e-mail: manoogia@ohio.edu

Leslie N. Richards Department of Human Development and Family Science, Oregon State University, Corvallis, OR, USA
e-mail: leslie.richards@oregonstate.edu

Yoshie Sano Department of Human Development, Washington State University, Vancouver, WA, USA
e-mail: yoshie_sano@vancouver.wsu.edu

Sharon B. Seiling Department of Consumer Sciences, Ohio State University, Columbus, OH, USA
e-mail: sseiling@ehe.osu.edu

Seohee Son Department of Family and Resource Management, Sookmyung Women's University, Seoul, South Korea
e-mail: seoheeson1@gmail.com

Susan K. Walker Family Social Science Department, University of Minnesota, Saint Paul, MN, USA
e-mail: skwalker@umn.edu

Chapter 1
Rural Families and Work Overview

Jean W. Bauer and Elizabeth M. Dolan

Introduction

Majestic mountains. Sparkling lakes. Beautiful forests. Fields of grain, corn, or cotton. Wide prairies. Small picturesque towns. Open spaces. These are some of the images that urban and suburban dwellers have of rural areas. People who live in urban areas go to rural areas to play—to ski, to boat, to fish, to hunt, to hike, to get away from the hubbub of urban life, and to relax amid the beauty and serenity. For rural residents, however, not is all idyllic. Many rural residents are working poor. In fact, rural families are much more likely to be working and poor than urban families.

This book is about rural families and work. Work includes all the things that are important for the family to be connected to paid labor. In the United States, balancing the needs of both the family and employment in rural areas takes resources, good health, social support, adequate child care, and sometimes creative strategies.

Why do we need to study rural families and their employment? The rural economy is substantially different than the urban economy. Although rural areas differ distinctly by region, some factors are true of most, if not all, rural communities. Very few rural families earn their living solely through farming—only about 6% of rural residents are full-time farmers (Johnson 2003). Other industries that have sustained rural families in the past are employing fewer people or have died out almost entirely—logging, paper mills, fishing, mining, etc. (Lichter and Jensen 2000; Johnson 2003). These heavy industry jobs paid good wages and, typically, provided various employee benefits. The industries that have moved into rural areas to replace the heavy industry jobs are often in the retail, service, hospitality, and recreational sectors that do not pay high wages nor do they provide employee benefits.

Because the heavy industry and manufacturing jobs in rural areas have declined, rural men have few options for high-paying jobs. Many women have become the

J. W. Bauer (✉)
Department of Family Social Science, University of Minnesota, 290 McNeal Hall,
1985 Buford Avenue, St. Paul, MN 55108, USA
e-mail: jbauer@umn.edu

J. W. Bauer, E. M. Dolan (eds.), *Rural Families and Work,* International Series on
Consumer Science 1,
DOI 10.1007/978-1-4614-0382-1_1, © Springer Science+Business Media, LLC 2011

family breadwinners, holding jobs in the retail or service industries at low pay and few, if any, employee benefits (Albrecht and Albrecht 2000; Johnson 2003).

Poverty has been studied using two different approaches or explanations. The first approach is to look at the community and the macrosystem. Poverty is viewed as a function of community-level variables such as the demographics of the residents and the economic structure of the community. Social problems and politics are also part of the equation (Weber et al. 2005; Cotter 2002). The second approach is to examine the contextual or individual variables that contribute to poverty. Poverty is viewed as a function of individual demographic characteristics, i.e., character or human capital flaws. This approach might also include not only the characteristics of those in poverty, but also their attitudes and behaviors as possible explanatory variables (Weber et al. 2005; Cotter 2002; Jensen et al. 2003). A part of the individual context of poverty is the "culture of poverty." Those who believe that poverty is intergenerational tend also to subscribe to the notion that children of poor parents learn certain attitudes and behaviors that perpetuate poverty, e.g., children do not have role models from whom they can learn to be industrious (Jensen et al. 2003). Cotter (2002) described the idea of "place poverty." Poverty (and wealth) is unevenly distributed across geographic locations due to local labor markets. It is the distribution of local and broader economic factors that contribute to the extent of poverty in any one locality. The types of economic activity in a rural area will shape the employment opportunities of rural workers and therefore lift the workers and their families out of poverty (or contribute to it) regardless of the workers' human capital characteristics. Each of these approaches can be helpful in understanding poverty. Rank (2004) noted that poverty may be more a function of a flawed economy than flawed individuals: There are simply not enough job opportunities for all workers to have jobs that will allow them to support their families. This is especially true in rural areas.

Rural Economic Conditions

Although farming and related agrarian industries no longer dominate rural America, the types of industries that have arisen are still less diverse than in urban areas. Furthermore, the economic boom of the 1990s did not favor rural areas. Competition from overseas manufacturers and depressed agricultural prices resulted in a lackluster rural economic situation (Lichter and Jensen 2000; Whitener et al. 2001).

How rural areas fare in recessions and boom-times relative to metropolitan areas is open to discussion. Hamrick (1997) postulated that rural areas may suffer from recession more intensely and more quickly than urban areas. Small businesses, which predominate in rural areas, would feel an economic downturn more quickly than larger businesses, and thus rural workers would experience lay-offs and reduction in hours more quickly than urban workers (Holzer 1999). Conversely, Jensen et al. (1999) found that unemployment was not a rural problem as much as underemployment, and that weakened economic conditions were less problematic for rural workers than urban workers. On the other hand, the strong economy benefited rural workers less than it did urban workers.

The underlying factor for rural residents is the types of industries available to them when they are seeking jobs. The distribution of labor markets and job opportunities are crucial to rural residents' economic well-being. In the United States, our economic well-being is largely shaped by the types of jobs we have and the money we earn from those jobs. The types of economic activity in a rural area will shape the employment opportunities of rural workers and alleviate or contribute to their poverty status and that of their families, regardless of the workers' human capital characteristics (Cotter 2002). Cotter (2002) found the odds of being in poverty to be 35% higher when living in a rural area than when living in an urban area. He concluded that the characteristics of the labor market were a powerful predictor of poverty, much more so than household-level predictors.

Employment opportunities exist in all communities whether rural or urban. The substance of this mix is the crux of the rural employment situation. Nelson and Smith (1999) described jobs as being "good jobs" or "bad jobs." Good jobs would pay decent wages, offer employee benefits, and would often likely have some flexibility which would allow employees to better balance their job and family demands. These good jobs would tend to be more stable, both in terms of employee tenure and less likely to be seasonal, leading to higher level of family financial well-being for the workers employed in good jobs. Bad jobs were the opposite, i.e., such jobs would tend to have low pay, few if any employee benefits, be less flexible, and were more likely to be seasonal. Those who held bad jobs would more likely be struggling to support their families and more likely to have more than one job in order to improve their financial well-being. The shift in the distribution of industries in rural areas over the last several decades has resulted in more "bad jobs" and fewer "good jobs" as the rural economy has become dominated by the retail, service, hospitality, and recreational industries. One of the primary repercussions of this shift is that these industries tend to employ more women than men because the jobs are low-skill and low-wage and may be seasonal or temporary. As a result, rural women may have an easier time finding employment than rural men, and, when rural men find jobs, the jobs also pay low wages (Albrecht and Albrecht 2000).

Individual Characteristics of Rural Residents

The level of education and, correspondingly, skills of rural residents have implications for employment. While rural residents tend to have lower educational levels than their urban counterparts (Jensen et al. 2003), more education does not significantly reduce the incidence of poverty for rural residents, especially for rural women (Porterfield 2001). The opportunity for education often comes in on-the-job training. So the focus is more on skills rather than formal education for many employment opportunities.

While rural women are likely to be employed, they likely earn low wages. Gender discrimination in jobs has been found to abound in rural areas. Rural culture may have rigid expectations regarding gender roles, including employment expectations (Flora et al. 1992; Larson 1978; Semyonov 1983). Although employed, rural women may be less well off than their urban counterparts. Brown and Lichter (2004) found in their comparison of rural and urban single mothers that rural single mothers had a significantly lower income-to-poverty ratio concluding that full-time employment benefited rural single mothers less than urban single mothers. Furthermore, part-time work and seasonal work are commonplace in rural areas in the industries in which rural women are employed (Gringeri 1995).

Rural workers' experience barriers to employment, especially when they are trying to balance work and family obligations. Rurality is a critical factor in health status, and health can play a critical role in the ability to maintain employment. Rural residents experience more health-related problems, both physical and mental, than urban residents. Rural residents have a higher incidence of a number of chronic health conditions, such as diabetes, hypertension, and lung disease, than urban residents (Mulder et al. 2000). Rural women, especially, have a higher incidence of mental health issues, and many rural communities have no mental health professionals (Wagenfeld et al. 1988). In fact, all types of health care services are more limited in rural areas, resulting in rural residents not accessing preventative care or receiving timely care to lessen the severity of their health problems (U. S. Department of Health and Human Services 2002).

Other barriers that impact rural workers' employment are transportation and child care. Distances between services, home, and job site can be extensive. Rural low-income families can struggle to maintain adequate transportation and have no public transportation alternative. Child care services are fewer in rural areas. If parents have jobs with nonstandard hours, which epitomize the retail, service, and hospitality industries, child care that will meet the parents' need for early morning, late night, or weekend care will be nonexistent. Many rural parents rely on relatives and/or friends to provide child care (Walker and Reschke 2004).

Consequently, several themes emerge relative to rural families as they work toward maintaining their families along with employment. These themes are availability, accessibility, acceptability, and complexity. Availability refers to whether or not the resource exists in the community or even in a nearby community. Accessibility is the ability to actually get to or access the resources. Acceptability addresses the values systems of the families as well as the local culture and how the families, and community members, see certain issues. Finally, complexity describes the lives of rural low-income families in piecing their needs together, especially when one or more of the themes are at issue.

Personal Responsibility and Work Opportunity Reconciliation Act

The Personal Responsibility and Work Opportunity Reconciliation Act of 1996 (P.L.104–193) (PRWORA) changed many things about the federal welfare system. One of the key changes administratively was the devolution of the rules to the states. Since then, rules and requirements vary among the states; however, rules and requirements do not vary by urban–rural residence. In that way, rules are still "one size fits all."

The form that PRWORA took did not arise from nothingness. How we in the US approach welfare had been evolving for years. By the 1930s, almost all states had some form of welfare. These benefits were generally called Mothers' Pension programs and were aimed at allowing mothers who had been abandoned by their husbands either through death or desertion to stay at home with their young children. Discrimination was common, with payments going primarily to white urban widows. Competing goals kept the program benefits low. While the ideal was for mothers to raise their own children, a second ideal was that parents should support their own children, plus program costs were to be kept low. Benefits were so low that most mothers needed to be employed in order for their families to survive. The legislation that created Social Security also impacted the welfare of mothers and their children. Widows and surviving minor children were covered under the new Social Security program, whereas the welfare of other mothers and children was addressed through the New Deal program of Aid to Dependent Children (ADC). During President Johnson's War on Poverty, ADC became Aid to Families with Dependent Children (AFDC) and federal rules were enacted to weed out discriminatory practices. Throughout the 1970s and 1980s, the program provided training for mothers to find employment. But the training programs were for the most part voluntary and did not appreciably contribute to the women's employability. Program cuts during the Reagan Administration increased the likelihood of mothers exiting from AFDC but through stricter rules rather than increased employment opportunities (Price 1995). While one of the focal points of PRWORA was to end welfare as an entitlement program and move welfare recipients into the labor force, only a minority of women were completely welfare dependent—only a minority received AFDC for longer than 4 years (Bane and Elwood 1983). Those who were on AFDC for longer than 8 years were likely to be younger than 25, be African-American, never married, have a child under the age of three, and likely to be in ill-health.

PRWORA was developed to address several perceived issues: To end long-term dependence of federal welfare programs; to get parents, specifically mothers, into the paid labor force so that they, not welfare, would support their families; and to involve states in making their own rules regarding welfare. The key elements of PRWORA are (Whitener et al. 2002):

- The end of AFDC and the creation of Temporary Assistance for Needy Families (TANF)

  - Whereas AFDC was an entitlement program, i.e., as long as one qualified one received benefits, TANF is not an entitlement program.

- Time limits for receiving TANF benefits

  - Federal rules established a maximum of 60 months over one's lifetime as the maximum benefit period. States were allowed to institute lower time limits.

- Fostering work became a requirement.

  - TANF clients are required to engage in work-related activities for a certain number of hours per week to get benefits. If they do not, they are sanctioned, which normally results in loss of some portion of the cash benefit.
  - Only certain types of activities could be counted as work activities.
  - TANF rules do allow married couples to receive benefits, something that was not available under AFDC rules.
  - Only a maximum of 20% of the case load per state could be exempted from engaging in work-related activities.

- Creation of a block grant to states for providing child care assistance to parents who are engaged in work activities.

Outcomes for TANF-leavers Poverty rates had been declining since the early 1990s due to the robust economy. Welfare caseloads decreased rather dramatically in the first years after the implementation of PRWORA, with case workers helping welfare recipients find jobs (Whitener et al. 2001). Early research on the effects of welfare reform found that while mothers were leaving welfare for work, they were leaving for low-wage work (e.g., Jones-DeWeever et al. 2003). Single parents who had left welfare for work were concentrated in the service, administrative support, and retail industries which paid low wages and offered few employee benefits. While families had left welfare, the overall financial well-being was not improving. A review of welfare reform by the Urban Institute revealed that by 2000, two-thirds of those who left welfare for work, and who had not returned to welfare, were employed. But the recession of the early 2000s took a toll on welfare-leavers' employment: In 2002, only 57% were employed with a median wage of $8.00/hour and only one-third had health insurance (Urban Institute 2006).

Rural Implications Rural families are more likely to be poor than urban families, and poor rural families are more likely to be two-parent families and have at least one employed parent than urban poor families (Findeis et al. 2001). These facts raised concerns about the ability of rural poor welfare recipients to find employment that would enable them to leave the federal welfare rolls. The economic boom of the late 1990s did not reach all rural areas, resulting in more limited employment options for rural residents than for their urban counterparts (Whitener et al. 2002). Employment options in rural areas are more likely to be part-time and/or seasonal in nature (Weber et al. 2001). Wage rates are typically lower in rural areas. Distances to employment opportunities, to child care, to health care, and to educational opportunities were also seen as a hindrance to rural welfare recipients successfully moving from welfare to work (Findeis et al. 2001).

Some of the mandated PRWORA policies were viewed as being disadvantageous to rural residents. The lower population density of rural communities means that services are farther apart than in urban areas, and some communities may not be able to support a full range of services, so that residents must drive to neighboring communities for some things (Whitener et al. 2001). In rural areas with few employment options, the time limits and sanction policies could severely disadvantage welfare-reliant mothers. While subsidies for child care were available to welfare-reliant mothers, if the rules required that the child care be licensed, then rural mothers were not always able to get the subsidies since licensed facilities are few and far between in rural communities, requiring mothers to rely on informal care arrangements. Finally, because tourist and recreational industries are the mainstay of many rural economies, recessions hit these communities far harder than urban areas. Underemployment and unemployment would mean that rural residents need more supports than urban residents (Weber et al. 2001).

Rural families and the rural context were not part of the PRWORA debate or subsequent rules. Thus the lack of focus has effectively increased the structural barriers for rural families' availability, accessibility, and acceptability to work and the issues related to employment. These concerns over the ability of rural low-income families to navigate the new rules regarding welfare were at the heart of the research project that has become known as Rural Families Speak (RFS).

Rural Families Speak Project

In 1997, after the enactment of the PRWORA (P.L.104–193), which emphasized employment as the pathway out of poverty to decrease reliance on government support, a group of researchers gathered to discuss the implications for rural residents, knowing that the poverty rate in rural America was greater than in urban areas. Many families in rural areas do not receive TANF, just like fewer received AFDC than were eligible. The same has been true for other food, housing, and child care programs. With a change in national policy, we wanted to study rural low-income families living the context of these policy changes.

The large multistate research group that organized the project known as RFS is described in the Appendix of the book. The research findings from the group form much of the basis for this book. To frame the environment in which our participating families lived, much of the context that will be provided will be from the late 1990s to early 2000s as this is the time period of the data collection and, hence, the findings reported in the following chapters. We focus on the rural low-income women who struggle, sometimes with their spouses or partners, to support their families.

Participants in RFS were from rural counties defined as having a Rural–Urban Continuum Code (RUCC) of 6, 7, or 8 (Butler and Beale 1994), indicating that the county had population centers ranging from 19,999 down to no more than 2,500 people. Mothers who were recruited to participate had at least one child no older than 12 years of age, and had incomes that made them eligible for food stamps or the Special Supplemental Nutrition Program for Women, Infants, and Children (WIC). Recruitment was done through programs that served the eligible families, such as WIC, Head Start, social service offices, adult education, and literacy programs. RFS was a longitudinal study comprised of three panels. Panel 1 was the largest with 14 participating states collecting data in three waves between 1999 and

2003. Panels 2 and 3 were much smaller. Panel 2 consisted of two states collecting data in two waves between 2001 and 2003, and Panel 3 consisted of one state that collected two waves of data between 2003 and 2004.[1] More details about the project and sample can be found in Appendix.

Description of the RFS Employed Participants and Their Families

Information about the participants and their families will be given in each of the chapters. The information presented here is to help provide a general picture of our rural low-income mothers and their families. Across all three panels, in Wave 1, we interviewed a total of 501 families. One of the challenges of longitudinal research is maintaining the sample. As might be expected, we lost participants in the subsequent two waves of Panel 1 interviews: In Wave 2 we had 314 participants, and in Wave 3, 265 participants. Interestingly, no families were lost in either Panels 2 or 3. The descriptive statistics provided here are of the families where the mother and/ or her partner were employed at some point during the 3 years of interviews, or the mother alone was employed if she was not partnered.

In Wave 1, participants and their spouses/partners were relatively young, but this is not surprising given that all our participating families had at least one child no older than 12 years old (Table 1.1). The number of children ranged from one to seven, with a mean of 2.4 (Table 1.1). In Wave 2, 31 Panel 1 families had new children, and in Wave 3, 26 families had new children. Six children were born between the two waves of data collection to Panels 2 and 3 families (data not shown).

More than half (55.0%) of the low-income rural mothers who were employed or had a partner who was employed were married, and 16.7% were living with their partners in Wave 1 (Table 1.1). Twenty-eight percent were not partnered, i.e., were single, divorced, or separated.

Marital status was not static over the time that we talked with these rural mothers. In Panel 1 Wave 2, 16.2% of the mothers' marital status had changed. Of these, 44.3% started living with a partner, and 25.6% married their partners. About 12% broke up with their partners and were single, another 12% separated from their husbands, and 7% got divorced (data not shown). In Panel 1 Wave 3, we found that 20% of participants had a change in marital status (data not shown). About 25% of these either married their partners or started living with a partner. The other half had relationship break-ups with 15.4% either separating or divorcing their spouses, and 18% breaking up with their live-in partner (data not shown). In Panel 2, 15.4% of the mothers indicted that their marital status had changed between the two waves of data collection. One mother got married and two started living with their partners, while the remainder was relationship break-ups. Panel 3 families were very stable

---

[1] Two states participated in Panel 3 Wave 1, but one state did not collect Waves 2/3 data, and is not included in this analysis.

Table 1.1 Characteristics of RFS participants and families at Wave 1 (Panels 1, 2, and 3) who had employment in the household ($N=371$)

Demographics	
Participant's age ($n=370$)	
Mean (*SD*)	30.2 years (7.3)
Range	17 to 59 years
Participant's ethnicity ($n=369$)	
White non-Hispanic	60.9%
Hispanic/Latina	28.5%
African-American	5.7%
Native American	1.4%
Multiracial and other	3.5%
Participant's educational level ($n=369$)	
Less than high school	32.8%
High school degree or GED	28.5%
Voc-ed or other training	12.5%
Some college or AA degree	22.0%
College graduate (BA/BS)	3.8%
Graduate work or graduate degree	0.8%
Children ($n=371$)	
Mean number of children (*SD*)	2.4 (1.3)
Range	1–7
Marital Status ($n=371$)	
Single	16.7%
Married	55.0%
Living with partner	16.4%
Divorced	7.8%
Separated	4.0%
Widowed	–
Partner's Age ($n=261$)	
Mean (*SD*)	33.3 years (8.5)
Range	17 to 68 years
Partner's ethnicity ($n=263$)	
White non-Hispanic	63.1%
Hispanic/Latina	35.7%
African-American	5.3%
Native American	0.4%
Multiracial/other	1.9%
Partner's educational level ($n=252$)	
Less than high school	39.3%
High school degree or GED	32.5%
Voc-ed or other training	9.9%
Some college or AA degree	14.3%
College graduate (BA/BS)	1.6%
Graduate work or graduate degree	0.8%

with no one indicating a change in marital status between the two waves of data collection.

The majority of participants and their spouses/partners were white, non-Hispanic. Because we had deliberately sought Hispanic participants in California, Oregon, Iowa, and Michigan, the proportion of Hispanic/Latino participants is higher than what might normally be expected. A third of the participants, and almost 40% of their spouses/partners, had less than a high school education. We asked participants if they had the opportunity to get some training or education during the preceding year: 38% of Panel 1 participants responded that they had in Wave 2 and 41% had in Wave 3. In Panels 2 and 3, 15.9% indicated they were able to get some additional training in the prior year (data not shown).

Employment for low-income rural adults changes over time. For our sample of low-income rural mothers, about two-thirds of them were employed in each of the three waves of Panel 1, and most of their partners and spouses were employed (Table 1.2). A few participant-mothers held additional jobs: In Wave 1, 18 mothers had a second job, and 3 mothers actually had a third job. In Wave 2, 15 mothers held a second job; and in Wave 3, 16 mothers worked a second job (no one had third jobs in either Wave 2 or Wave 3). A few spouses/partners also worked additional jobs: In Wave 1, six had a second job and two had a third job. Six spouses/partners had a second job in Wave 2 and five in Wave 3 (no third jobs in either Wave) (data not shown). Only two mothers in Panel 2 and one mother in Panel 3 held a second or third job, and none of their spouses or partners held multiple jobs (data not shown).

The median wage rate increased for both participants and their spouses/partners over the interview period in all three Panels, resulting in higher overall monthly income (Tables 1.2 and 1.3). Panel 1 mothers worked fewer hours on the average in Wave 3 (Table 1.2), but Panels 2 and 3 mothers worked slightly more hours. Panel 3 spouses worked fewer average hours at the second interview (Table 1.3).

Thirty-five percent of the employed families in Panel 1 and 59.6% in Panel 2 had ever relied on TANF benefits (data not shown). No one in Panel 3 indicated they had even received TANF. During the interview period, however, very few families were on TANF (Tables 1.2 and 1.3). While these families were not relying heavily on TANF, they did rely on other welfare benefits (Tables 1.2 and 1.3). Both WIC and the school lunch and breakfast program were heavily used by the families. The proportion of families using WIC dropped off most likely because children had reached their fifth birthday, making them ineligible. More families in Panels 1 and 2 were covered by Medicaid than Panel 3 families. More families in Panel 2 received Food Stamps (now called SNAP), fuel assistance (known as Low-Income Home Energy Assistance Program or LIHEAP), and housing assistance than Panel 1 families (Tables 1.2 and 1.3). Very few Panel 3 families got any benefits from these three programs (Table 1.3). More Panel 1 families were able to access child care assistance (Table 1.2) than families in either Panel 2 or Panel 3 (Table 1.3).

Transportation is the key to maintaining employment. While many families had vehicles, a small group did not (Tables 1.2 and 1.3). Furthermore, not all participant-mothers had their drivers' licenses (Table 1.2), a particular issue for Panel 3 mothers.

Table 1.2 Employment and other characteristics for Panel 1 Waves 1, 2, and 3

Per wave characteristics	Wave 1 (N=309)	Wave 2 (N=266)	Wave 3 (N=190)
Employment			
Participant employed	68.0%	66.9%	63.7%
Partner employed	95.3%	87.1%	95.1%
Participant's hourly wage			
Mean	$7.00	$8.74	$8.91
Standard Deviation	2.44	3.48	4.28
Median	$6.50	$7.44	$8.64
Range	$1.11 to $18.40	$1.00 to $27.00	$1.25 to $40.75
Partner's hourly wage			
Mean	$8.71	$10.58	$10.73
Standard Deviation	3.21	4.40	3.78
Median	$8.25	$ 9.50	$ 9.81
Range	$1.60 to $20.00	$ 4.61 to $33.48	$ 4.71 to $29.00
Participant's hours/week			
Mean	32.3	33.7	23.0
Standard Deviation	11.6	11.6	18.0
Partner's hours/week			
Mean	45.7	46.5	51.8
Standard Deviation	11.8	13.4	17.2
Income			
Monthly household income			
Mean	$1502.90	$1993.49	$2154.38
Standard Deviation	833.16	1244.36	1424.08
Government welfare benefits			
TANF	8.4%	10.5%	12.6%
Food stamps	40.5%	38.3%	38.9%
Medicaid	65.1%	66.4%	58.1%
WIC	66.3%	54.1%	41.6%
School lunch/breakfast	56.9%	62.3%	63.5%
Fuel assistance	27.2%	35.9%	35.0%
Housing assistance	15.9%	19.8%	25.0%
Child care assistance	30.0%	20.3%	23.5%
Has vehicle	92.3%	89.6%	97.3%
Participant has driver's license	81.8%	90.1%	*

*Question not asked in Wave 3

Organization of Book

Much of what appears in this volume is based on work by RFS research team members. Some original data do appear when chapter authors felt that would enhance the reader's understanding of the materials. Chapter 2 is an overview of theories and frameworks used by RFS team members. While the family ecological theory was the primary framework used by the RFS project researchers, it is not the only applicable theory. Chapter 2 brings together theories from economics, sociology,

Table 1.3 Employment and other characteristics for Panels 2 and 3, Waves 1 and 3

Per wave characteristics	Panel 2 Waves 1/2 ($N=58$)	Panel 2 Wave 3 ($N=58$)	Panel 3 Waves 1/2 ($N=30$)	Panel 3 Wave 3 ($N=31$)
Employment				
Participant employed	34.5%	42.3%	36.7%	41.9%
Partner employed	55.9%	54.8%	96.4%	54.8%
Participant's hourly wages				
Mean	$7.51	$6.80	$7.56	$10.87
Standard Deviation	5.29	1.73	3.02	3.28
Median	$6.00	$6.50	$7.80	$10.11
Range	$4.25 to $26.60	$5.15 to $11.65	$2.50 to $11.20	$ 7.75 to $23.08
Partner's hourly wages				
Mean	$9.12	$27.51	$10.53	$12.15
Standard Deviation	2.33	60.65	2.66	6.14
Median	$9.18	$8.50	$10.00	$12.15
Range	$5.15 to $14.00	$5.50 to $200.00	$ 6.93 to $18.00	$ 9.00 to $25.00
Participant's hours/week				
Mean	25.8	29.9	35.9	37.7
Standard Deviation	11.5	12.7	11.5	9.3
Partner's hours/week				
Mean	38.8	50.8	41.1	22.2
Standard Deviation	8.6	42.9	4.8	41.2
Income				
Monthly household income				
Mean	$937.69	$1231.69	$2046.67	$3006.10
Standard Deviation	701.71	1015.23	507.38	1505.49
Government welfare benefits				
TANF	10.3%	8.6%	–	–
Food stamps	74.1%	62.1%	10.0%	20.0%
Medicaid	84.5%	60.3%	56.7%	23.8%
WIC	67.2%	46.6%	70.0%	47.6%
School lunch/breakfast	69.1%	60.3%	70.0%	61.9%
Fuel assistance	58.6%	37.9%	16.7%	15.0%
Housing assistance	31.0%	24.1%	3.3%	–
Child care assistance	13.8%	10.3%	3.3%	–
Has vehicle	74.1%	79.3%	90.0%	67.7%
Participant has driver's license	74.1%	*	44.8%	*

*Question not asked in Wave 3

psychology, and family science to illustrate how each was used to answer questions about rural low-income families. Future questions are posited for many of the theories and concepts.

In Chaps. 3 through 10, chapter authors present a short review of literature on the chapter topic. They then use RFS data to help the reader fully understand the conditions and implications for rural low-income families. The voices of the mothers are heard through the use of quotations from the RFS interview transcripts. In Chap. 3, Jean Bauer, Patricia Dyk, Seohee Son, and Elizabeth Dolan help the reader become oriented to the rural milieu. While the make-up of rural low-income families is similar to that of urban low-income families, rural communities have real differences from urban communities. An overall picture of how rural low-income families manage their employment is presented by Elizabeth Dolan, Jean Bauer, and Mary Jo Katras in Chap. 4. The scope of the issues related to employment, and how these are managed by the rural families, sets the stage for the subsequent chapters about particular issues.

Chapters 5 and 6 address health of rural low-income family members and the implications for employment. In Chap. 5, Yoshie Sano and Leslie Richards acquaint the reader with the growing problem of access to health care for rural residents, including the access to health insurance. Since having enough to eat is vital to health, Sano and Richards report on food insecurity as a rural health issue. Employment can be difficult to maintain when one has mental health issues, which is the topic of Chap. 6. In this chapter, Yoshie Sano, Leslie Richards, and Jaerim Lee focus on this invisible barrier to employment. Research on urban welfare recipients has found that mental health issues and children's behavioral problems are barriers to employment. Sano, Richards, and Lee address the problems faced by the RFS families and how the mental health issues of family members impact the ability of the mothers, especially, to maintain employment.

Chapters 7 and 8 focus on some of the resources that the rural low-income families have to help them be employed. In Chap. 7, Susan Walker and Margaret Manoogian look at the resources for child care. In many rural communities, as licensed child care facilities may either not be available to low-income families due to cost or limited hours of service, Walker and Manoogian reflect on the child care choices the RFS families make. In Chap. 8, a wider scope is used to examine the resources of transportation, education, and resources to alleviate material hardship. Carolyn Bird, Elizabeth Dolan, and Sharon Seiling illustrate the abilities of the rural low-income families to creatively address transportation issues. Since education is one solution to increasing one's marketability, Bird, Dolan, and Seiling address the ability of rural low-income mothers to get more education, as well as the effects of getting more education. Finally, they review the extent to which other resources are tapped in order to make their meager incomes stretch to meet family needs. Resources are often used as compliments or substitutes for earned income.

In Chap. 9, Sharon Seiling, Margaret Manoogian, and Seohee Son look at the system of social support that helps many rural low-income families function. Social support and employment are linked for many women. The focus of Chap. 10 is the specific resource of the federal Earned Income Tax Credit (EITC). Sheila Mammen, Frances Lawrence, and Jaerim Lee help the reader understand the extent to which the EITC is claimed by the RFS participants and how the families used the EITC.

In the final two chapters, Jean Bauer, Elizabeth Dolan, and Bonnie Braun pull together the research and programmatic uses of the findings on rural low-income families, as well as the policy implications.

This book is intended to serve as a reference point on rural families and work, as well as to serve as a challenge for future endeavors. The organization is purposeful so that it can be used in a classroom.

Acknowledgment The authors would like to thank Laura Andrew, graduate student in family studies at the University of New Hampshire, for her assistance in gathering the information in the tables.

References

Albrecht, D. E., & Albrecht, S. L. (2000). Poverty in nonmetropolitan America: Impacts of industrial, employment, and family structure variables. *Rural Sociology, 65,* 87–103. doi:10.1111/j.1549-0831.2000.tb00344.x.

Bane, M., & Elwood, D. (1983). *Slipping into and out of poverty: The dynamics of spells.* (Working Paper No. 1199). National Bureau of Economic Research, Cambridge. http://www.nber.org/papers/w1199.

Brown, J. B., & Lichter, D. T. (2004). Poverty, welfare, and the livelihood strategies of nonmetropolitan single mothers. *Rural Sociology, 69,* 282–301. doi:10.1526/003601104323087615.

Butler, M. A., & Beale, C. L. (1994, September). *Rural-Urban Continuum codes for metro and nonmetro counties, 1993,* (Gov Pub A 93.44: AGES 9425). U.S. Department of Agriculture, Economic Research Service.

Cotter, D. A. (2002). Poor people in poor places: Local opportunity structures and household poverty. *Rural Sociology, 67,* 534–555. doi:10.1111/j.1549-0831.2002.tb00118.x.

Findeis, J. L., Henry, M., Hirschl, T. A., Lewis, W., Ortega-Sanchez, I., Peine, E., & Zimmerman, J. N. (2001, February 2). *Welfare reform in rural America: A review of current research.* (Report No. p2001-5). http://www.rupri.org/Forms/p2001-5.pdf/.

Flora, C. B., Flora, J., Spears, J., & Swanson, L. (1992). *Rural communities: Legacy and change.* Boulder: Westview Press.

Gringeri, C. (1995). Flexibility, the family ethic, and rural home-based work. *Affilia, 10,* 70–86. doi:10.1177/088610999501000107.

Hamrick, K. S. (1997). Rural labor markets often lead urban markets in recessions and expansions. *Rural Development Perspectives, 12*(3), 11–17 http://www.ers.usda.gov/Publications/RDP/RDP697/RDP697C.pdf.

Holzer, H. J. (1999). *Employer demand for welfare recipients and the business cycle: Evidence from recent employer surveys.* (Discussion Paper No. 1185–99). http://www.irp.wisc.edu/publications/dps/pdfs/dp118599.pdf.

Jensen, L., Findeis, J. L., Hsu, W.-L., & Schachter, J. P. (1999). Slipping into and out of underemployment: Another disadvantage for nonmetropolitan workers? *Rural Sociology, 64,* 417–438. doi:10.1111/j.1549-0831.1999.tb00360.x.

Jensen, L., McLaughlin, D. K., & Slack, T. (2003). Rural poverty: The persisting challenge. In D. L. Brown & L. E. Swanson (Eds.), *Challenges for rural America in the twenty-first century* (pp. 118–131). University Park: Pennsylvania State University Press.

Johnson, K. (2003). Unpredictable direction of rural population growth and migration. In D. L. Brown & L. E. Swanson (Eds.), *Challenges for rural America in the twenty-first century* (pp. 19–31). University Park: Pennsylvania State University Press.

Jones-DeWeever, A., Peterson, J., & Song, X. (2003). *Before and after welfare reform: The work and well-being of low-income single parent families.* http://www.iwpr.org/pdf/D454.pdf.

Larson, O. F. (1978). Values and beliefs of rural people. In T. R. Ford (Ed.), *Rural USA: Persistence and change* (pp. 91–112). Ames: Iowa State University Press.

Lichter, D. T., & Jensen, L. (2000). *Rural America in transition: Poverty and welfare at the turn of the 21st century.* (JCPR Working Paper No.187). http://www.northwestern.edu/ipr/jcpr/workingpapers/wpfiles/Lichter-Jensen.pdf.

Mulder, P. L., Kenkel, M. B., Shellenberger, S., Constantine, M. G., Streiegel, R., Sears, S. F., Hager, A. (2000). The behavioral health care needs of rural women. *American Psychological Association.* http://www.apa.org/pubs/info/reports/rural-women.pdf.

Nelson, M. K., & Smith, J. (1999). *Working hard and making do: Surviving in small town America.* Berkeley: University of California Press.

Porterfield, S. L. (2001). Economic vulnerability among rural single-mother families. *American Journal of Agricultural Economics, 83,* 1302–1311. doi:10.1111/0002-9092.00282.

Price, C. J. (1995). The effect of welfare laws on the family. *Marriage & Family Review, 21*(3/4), 217–237. doi:10.1300/J002v21n03_11.

Rank, M. R. (2004). *One nation underprivileged: Why American poverty affects us all.* New York: Oxford University Press.

Semyonov, M. (1983). Community characteristics, female employment, and occupational segregation: Small towns in a rural state. *Rural Sociology, 48*(1), 104–119. http://chla.library.cornell.edu/cgi/t/text/text-idx?c=chla;idno=5075626_4334_001.

Urban Institute. (2006, June). *A decade of welfare reform: Facts and figures.* http://www.urban.org/UPloadedPDF/900980_welfarereform.pdf.

U. S. Department of Health and Human Services. (2002). *One department serving rural America: Rural task force report to the Secretary.* http://ask.hrso.gov/detail_materials.cfm?ProdID=760.

Wagenfeld, J. O., Goldsmith, H. F., Stiles, D., & Manderscheid, R. W. (1988). Inpatient mental health services in metropolitan and non-metropolitan counties. *Journal of Rural Community Psychology, 9*(2), 13–26. http://www.marshall.edu/jrcp/v92.pdf.

Walker, S. K., & Reschke, K. L. (2004). Child care use by low-income families in rural areas: A contemporary look at the influence of women's work and partner availability. *Journal of Children and Poverty, 10,* 149–167. doi:10.1080/1796120420000271585.

Weber, B. A., Duncan, G. J., & Whitener, L. A. (2001). Welfare reform in rural America: What have we learned? *American Journal of Agricultural Economics, 83,* 1282–1292. doi:10.1111/0002-9092.00280.

Weber, B., Jensen, L., Miller, K., Mosley, J., & Fisher, M. (2005). A critical review of rural poverty literature: Is there truly a rural effect? *International Regional Science Review, 28,* 381–414. doi:10.1177/0160017605278996.

Whitener, L. A., Weber, B. A., & Duncan, G. J. (2001). Reforming welfare: Implications for rural America. *Rural America, 16*(3), 2–10. http://www.ers.usda.gov/publications/ruralamerica/ra163/ra163b.pdf.

Whitener, L. A., Weber, B. A., & Duncan, G. J. (2002). Introduction—As the dust settles: Welfare reform and rural America. In B. A. Weber, G. J. Duncan, & L. A. Whitener (Eds.), *Rural dimensions of welfare reform* (pp. 1–16). Kalamazoo: W. E. Upjohn Institute for Employment Research.

Chapter 2
Theories for Studying Rural Families and Work

Jean W. Bauer and Elizabeth M. Dolan

Introduction

Theory helps us form our research questions and therefore, in many respects, shapes our interpretation of data and our findings. Consequently, including an overview of some of the theoretical frameworks used by Rural Families Speak (RFS) is important in the exploration of the various aspects of employment. While this is not a comprehensive overview of all appropriate theories, we address the theories that can be useful in investigating rural, low-income family issues. We also present some of the unique findings to illustrate the use of the theories and frameworks.

What Is Theory?

A theory is an explanation which helps to answer the *why* and *how* questions posed by researchers (White and Klein 2008). Doherty et al. (1993) define a theory as a set of interconnected ideas that emerge from the process of theorizing which is a process of systematically formulating and organizing ideas to understand a phenomenon. In the social sciences, a theory provides a baseline for how people behave in a context. The theory can be tested with different sets of data to see if the pattern holds. A theory needs to pose definitions for its properties and categories and identify the relationships among the properties.

A theory must also have a deductive system which provides the explanation of why certain things occur (Homans 1964). White and Klein (2008) indicate that theory is connected to method. They state that "linkages between ideas and data can be organized in different ways" (p. 8). A newly developed theory, or a newly enhanced and expanded application of an existing theory, emerges when the process

J. W. Bauer (✉)
Department of Family Social Science, University of Minnesota, 290 McNeal Hall,
1985 Buford Avenue, St. Paul, MN 55108, USA
e-mail: jbauer@umn.edu

J. W. Bauer, E. M. Dolan (eds.), *Rural Families and Work,* International Series on
Consumer Science 1,
DOI 10.1007/978-1-4614-0382-1_2, © Springer Science+Business Media, LLC 2011

goes from data to ideas, i.e., an *inductive* process. If the process goes from ideas to data with the researcher starting with a theory, developing hypotheses, using data to test the hypotheses, and then discussing how well the observations fit the theory, the process is *deductive*. Both inductive and deductive uses of theory are applicable for the study of rural families. The ideas and data must fit together in a meaningful process.

In this chapter, we focus on theories and frameworks that have been used in our RFS research on rural families. The theories from various disciplines (e.g., family, economics, psychology, sociology) have been applied to our examination of rural families. The intent of this chapter is to introduce some of the theories that have been used to inform our work and posit each in relation to our findings on rural families and work. Original sources are cited so that the reader can have access to the assumptions, principles, and limitations of each theory. We also have included frameworks, some midrange theories, and ways of using theories in models. For further reading, we suggest White and Klein (2008), Chibucos et al. (2005), Boss et al. (1993), Smith and Ingoldsby (2009), and Bengtson et al. (2005).

Theories and Frameworks

Ecological Theories

Human Ecology and Family Ecology Theories Human ecology theory is concerned with the "creation, use, and management of resources for the adaption, human development, and sustainability of environments" (Bubolz and Sontag 1993, p. 419). The theory focuses on "interaction and interdependence of humans (as individuals, groups, and societies) with the environment" (Bubolz and Sontag, 1993 p. 421). Family ecology theory (Bubolz and Sontag 1993) is a general theory which uses synthesis to integrate "human development and family relationships within a family resource management framework" (p. 424) that is value-based and related to critical science. The focus is on family members as individuals, as well as the family as a whole, and is appropriate for helping to understand "…families of diverse structures and national, ethnic, or racial backgrounds, in different life stages and life circumstances" (Bubolz and Sontag, 1993 p. 424) and is also useful for policy analysis (Zimmerman 1995). The family ecological framework formed the basis of how the RFS project was conceptualized. Understanding changes among these systems was critical to understanding rural communities and rural low-income family outcomes while beginning to build evidence for strong rural communities and strong rural low-income families.

Bronfenbrenner (1986) was one of the first scientists to utilize the nested context for the four identified interdependent systems of human ecology, i.e., the micro-, meso- exo-, and macrosystems. This theoretical framing allows researchers to explore the interdependence of family and work with the exosystem of community support and networks, and the greater macrosystem that includes the values, norms, culture, and policies that influence the family and the environments.

The individual is at the center of the ecological system which Bronfenbrenner (1989) established as important, and the layers of the system influence and are influenced by the individual. The microsystem refers to the immediate environment of the individual. Although we most often consider the family system as the micro-environment, if the lens is changed to consider the individual in the work-place, the family is only part of the microsystem. Bronfenbrenner (1979, p. 22) defines the microsystem as a "...pattern of activities, roles, and interpersonal relations experienced by the...person in a given setting...." The microsystem is experienced by the individual, and the individual is then shaped by that environment. The mesosystem is the social or community environment which encompasses the individual and the microsystem. In the context of rural families, the mesosystem could be the community, the support network of the family, and the employment conditions of the parents. The exosystem is most often described as being apart from the individual and the microsystem, i.e., the individual or family does not have direct contact or interact with exosystem factors. The exosystem encompasses the events or conditions that influence the mesosystem and the microsystem. In the case of rural families, the exosystem factors could be the local economic conditions (unemployment rate, the types of jobs available, etc.); the rules regarding TANF, Food Stamps (now called SNAP—Supplemental Nutrition Assistance Program), Medicaid, State Children's Health Insurance Program (SCHIP); another family member's mesosystem; and so forth. Finally, the macrosystem consists of the cultural norms and/or beliefs that influence the other systems. Macrosystem beliefs are often the underlying framework for legislative changes (e.g., "poor people do not want to work"). Ultimately, Bronfenbrenner (1979, p. 26) hypothesized that "(A)n ecological transition occurs whenever a person's position in the ecological environment is altered as the result of a change in role, setting, or both."

RFS researchers have used the ecological framework to guide their work in various ways. Katras et al. (2004) used it to examine how rural low-income families accessed and used child-care resources to meet the needs of their families in the aftermath of welfare reform. The paper conceptualizes family and environmental interactions and relationships with an ecological system of interdependent parts in which family members affect each other, other family members, and the quality of the community. Son and Bauer (2010) framed their inquiry into rural, low-income single mothers' management of their work and family lives in family ecology theory. The single mothers had constraints and resources across the ecological system. Huddleston-Casas and Braun (2006) used the framework to illustrate the pathways that could either lead to or were barriers to employment for rural mothers across all four systems. Mammen et al. (2009b), modifying Huddleston-Casas and Braun's work, examined strategies used to cope with and manage food insecurity in both food insecure and food secure states. The microsystem was conceptualized as families and their array of resources, such as human capital and decision-making abilities. The mesosystem was the extended family members and supports, such as food pantries, and was viewed as the bridge between the microsystem and exosystem.

The macrosystem values and larger social and economic forces shaped the extent to which states were either food secure or food insecure. The ecological system of the family influenced the strategies used to cope with food insecurity. Sano et al. (2011) used the theory to investigate how low-income rural Latino, immigrant families succeed or fail to meet the family's food needs over time. Several ecological levels were found to influence the food needs of the Latino families. Sano et al. presented a table indicating how each of the levels of the ecological system linked to food security systems in the family.

The RFS project, and most papers drawn from RFS data, used the earlier versions of Bronfenbrenner's theory. He continued to develop and refine his theory, however (e.g., Bronfenbrenner 2005), adding and refining elements to consider time and historical positioning, which he labeled the chronosystem. Bronfenbrenner's theory has been used, and misused, widely (Tudge et al. 2009). Tudge et al. (2009) offered a critique illustrating both the use and misuse of the theory which may be of interest to readers. As the RFS project enters into a more mature stage, perhaps research team members will begin to use the more mature version of Bronfenbrenner's theory and consider the role of developmental time.

Family Systems Theory This theory builds on a general systems approach of interdependent parts where the parts are greater than the whole. A family can be viewed as a system in which members "interact with one another, exhibit coherent behaviors, and share some degree of interdependence" (Chibucos et al. 2005, p. 279). Family therapy scholars use this theory to guide interventions and interpret the complex relationships of individuals and their families, as well as for marital and family communications interactions (White and Klein 2008). Family systems theory allows for studies of the processes that exist in families and processes between families and their environments (Chibucos et al. 2005).

No RFS papers have used this theory explicitly for research on family and work. This theory is appropriate for work that is being done from the project on subjects that are more process oriented. Family systems theory would be useful and appropriate for investigating intrafamily communications regarding work and family issues in rural low-income families, especially when considering hypotheses about how job and economic changes of one family member impacts the family system as a whole.

Capital, Capability, and Family Economic Theories

This section frames capital and some of the ways it can be viewed from inside the family. Human capability is an expansion of the capital theories. Family economic functioning framework is a model that brings together human and social capital concepts.

Capitals Economists may focus on wealth which encompasses the assets or stock of things that can be measured. Several types of capital are present in families, including rural families.

Human Capital Theory Human capital theory was the second theory around which the RFS project was built. The development of the human capital theory is usually attributed to Becker (1975, 1993) and his colleagues at University of Chicago. Human capital theory was initially based on an economic analysis of return to education at a macro (country) level. In later years it has morphed into a microtheory for the individual. Human capital theory has been used most often in the RFS research on rural families and work.

Human capital is defined as those "...activities that influence future monetary and psychic income by increasing the resources of the people" (Becker 1975, p. 9). Human capital equals the function of the physical and mental assets of the individual, the investment in money and/or time to develop those assets, the input rate of other resources, and stocks (accumulation or amount of) that exists in the individual (Becker 1975). Investment in human capital refers to engaging in educational activities, both general and specific job training, that results in the accumulation of assets over the life cycle to increase the potential for higher levels of earnings. For example, an employee who participates in specific job training program adds more value to the employer's investment in that particular employee in addition to the potential of the employee getting a raise or promotion due to the newly acquired skills or knowledge.

Human capital theory integrates the allocation of time, household production function, and theory of choice. To measure human capital investment, the *time* related to an investment must be considered; therefore, longitudinal studies are needed to determine the actual level of investment. Becker indicated that human capital included not only investments in education and/or training, but the overall health and motivations of the individual. Household production function is the output of the work from family members in the household. The human capital of family members supports their ability to be employed, thereby increasing family well-being and psychic income. Psychic income relates to how the individual or family feels about their income. Theory of choice assumes the existence of alternatives and assumes that a person knows the rewards and costs of each alternative and decision. Grossman (1972) defined human capital as an individual's stock of knowledge that influences a person's market and nonmarket productivity (household production). While "resources" can be broadly construed in human capital theory, generally, they are considered to be such things as the individual's wealth and stock of assets including education, abilities, and experiences.

Human capital theory was the conceptual framework used in several RFS studies. Berry et al. (2008) examined job volatility among the RFS mothers by examining their employment trajectories. Among other variables, human capital was used to examine three employment groups: Stable employment, intermittent employment, and unemployed. Bird and Bauer (2009) examined the role of mothers' resources and initial human capital in their abilities to acquire additional education or training. Human capital was viewed as an asset that could be increased with education. Mammen et al. (2009a) examined satisfaction with life among rural low-income mothers over time. They defined overall capital as a "combination of physical stock, personal abilities, and access to the acquisition of various goods and services and relationships" (p. 376). Human capital was the "embodiment of individual's skills, abilities, and knowledge" (p. 376), and they used education and parental confidence as variables for human capital. Mammen et al. (2009b) used the community prosperity context to reveal a paradox in which families from states considered prosperous were persistently more food insecure than similar families from less prosperous states. Mammen et al. (2009c) examined employment decisions of those entering employment and number of hours of labor supplied. They used factors of education, risk of depression, being licensed to drive a vehicle, and life skills for human capital in modeling the labor supply decision. Simmons et al. (2007a) developed a better understanding of human capital and social support in the long-term economic well-being of rural low-income mothers. Mothers' education, knowledge of community resources, and life skills were used to frame human capital of the mothers. Using the human capital theory to examine education and training opportunities (or lack thereof) for rural low-income families enables us to understand how and when decisions are made to either pursue or to forego investments in education.

Health Capital and Personal Capital Theories Health capital theory is a variation on the human capital theory. This theory considers the demand for good health and what influences the total amount of time that can be spent in production of earned income and acquisition of various health commodities (Tomer 2003). Personal capital theory is defined by Tomer (2003) as the psychological makeup, health condition (physical), and spiritual functioning of the individual. Becker (1996) considered personal capital as the capacity that leads to satisfaction from acquisition of consumer goods, based on past consumption and personal experiences. Health capital and personal capital theories were used by Mammen et al. (2009a) to frame the satisfaction with life among rural low-income mothers over time. Health and personal capitals were measured through demographic data and objective and subjective socioeconomic circumstances of the mothers. How health and personal capital contribute to the family's economic or social well-being would enable us to have a better understanding of investments by family and society. If these capitals are influenced, as Tomer states, by the psychological makeup and spiritual functioning of the individual, then research on how to measure these concepts would add to our knowledge.

Economic Capital Theory A variation on the human capital theory is economic capital theory, sometimes referred to as socio-economic or financial capital theory (Ostrove et al. 1999; Wadsworth et al. 1999). The basic concept in this theory relates to income/earnings and occupational status. Mammen et al. (2009a) used this theory to frame the income adequacy concept for the series of capitals that a rural family has in its daily life, as part of a study on life satisfaction among rural low-income mothers.

Social Capital Theory Social capital exists in our relationships with others. The function of social capital is in the value of social structure and personal networks as resources that can be used by individuals to achieve their interests (Coleman 1988). When relationships change among people, the social capital for the individual and family also changes. Social capital, and the resources contained by the networks, can be combined in various ways to produce "different system-level behavior" (Coleman 1988, p. S101). Social capital can exist, then, at the individual and family levels as well as at the community level. A person's "actions are shaped, redirected, constrained by social context; norms, interpersonal trust, social networks, and social organizations" (Coleman 1988, p. S96). Social capital theory, therefore, encompasses the concept of relationships having value to individuals, and that value can be traded and enhanced. Social capital can help frame how rural low-income families use their social networks to access the resources they need to obtain or maintain employment, such as information to find out about job openings or more tangible resources such as childcare.

Almedom (2005) included social support, social cohesion, and social determinants of health (mental health) as part of social capital. Bradley and Corwyn (2002) used social networks as part of social capital and included occupational status as part of the social capital definition.

Several RFS researchers have used social capital theory for their theoretical framework. Simmons et al. (2007a) stated that social support is defined as the individual's satisfaction with degree of help received during a time of need (Sarason et al. 1987), presence or number of social relationships (Sanderson 2004), or care resources received from others in contact with the individual (Laakso and Paunonen-Ilmonen 2002).

Social support can come from material, informational, and emotional sources, as well as from practical help (Swanson et al. 2008). *Formal* sources of support flow from public sources, such as government or social service agencies, while *informal* sources of support come from friends, family, or other contacts. Swanson et al. (2008) used multiple indicators of program participation for formal support and various social skills as a proxy for informal support to examine food security. The need for informal support has been found to increase when any kind of hardship arises, including those that resulted from changes in policies such as what occurred with the 1996 welfare policy overhaul (Bok and Simmons 2002). Mammen et al. (2009a) also used social capital theory to frame satisfaction with life among rural low-income mothers over time through a satisfaction with social support measure. Using using social capital theory will allow RFS researchers and others to further understand the value of relationships for employed rural low-income parents.

Human Capability Theory Boulding (1985) developed a concept of human betterment as the end toward which we individually and collectively tend to strive. The *ultimate good* is the end goal toward which humans aim to better themselves, and is comprised of four universal virtues: (1) economic adequacy vs. inadequacy (riches, resources for nourishment, housing, clothing, health care, and other essentials of life); (2) justice and equality vs. injustice and inequality (for access to work, education, and health); (3) freedom vs. coercion and confinement; (4) peacefulness vs. warfare and strife.

Sen (1997) expanded Boulding's conceptualization of human capability theory, defining capability as the "ability of humans to lead lives and have reason to value and enhance the substantive choices they have" (Sen 1997, p. 1959). Sen postulated that human capital is included in the more inclusive view of human capabilities. He stated, "Capability serves as a means not only to economic production …, but also to social development" (p. 1960). Investments in human capability can lead to more overall wealth, which in turn, benefits many individuals through better health care, educational systems, and so forth, which allows people more freedom and satisfaction. The capabilities framework conceptualizes human opportunities for the good life and well-being rather than merely the accumulation of resources. The focus is more on *people* and less on *goods* (Anand et al. 2005). Most work using the capability theory has been in the field of education. Human capability theory has only recently been used in study of rural families. Son and Bauer (2009) mapped how the theory is appropriate for rural family research. Further use of this theory will help advance the understanding of the interface among individuals' personal resources, the community's resources, and the individual support systems.

Family Economic Functioning Framework Bauer et al. (2000) created the family economic functioning framework as a means of assessing families' financial self-sufficiency relative to the federal poverty line. Embedded in the model are both human capital and social support concepts. This framework is not a theory per se but a tool by which researchers, social workers, policy makers, and others could determine the extent of families' needs, and, thereby, the amount of public support (cash or in-kind) that the families would require. The family economic functioning framework plots families along a continuum based on their income and the federal poverty line. Families with incomes below the poverty level for their family size are labeled as "in-crisis." Families "at risk" have incomes between 100% and 130% of poverty. Families are considered "safe" if their incomes are between 131% and 150% of poverty, and "thriving" if their income levels are 151% to 200% of poverty. Those with incomes above 200% of poverty are termed as "sustaining." Families in crisis and at risk both rely heavily on a variety of public assistance programs. Safe families may use some programs, but generally are less dependent upon public assistance than either the in-crisis or at-risk families. Thriving families have incomes higher than most public assistance programs allow for qualification (the primary exception being Earned Income Tax Credit (EITC)), and are able to live reasonably well without the assistance. Sustaining families have achieved financial stability without need of public assistance.

This framework was used by Dolan et al. (2008) in their examination of rural mothers who got off TANF. Simmons et al. (2007b) used the framework to examine the contributions of maternal labor force participation and marital status on economic self-sufficiency over time. Simmons et al. (2007a) framed their study of the long-term economic well-being of rural low-income mothers by using the family economic functioning framework. This framework is especially useful when examining rural low-income families' use of welfare benefits and their ability to become more financially self-sufficient over time.

Resource-Based Theories

Resource management, conservation of resources, exchange, stress, and resiliency are theories focused on the resources available to individuals and families. The resources could be either their own resourcefulness or resources in the environment. Many theories that are applied to the study of rural families are based on the over-arching concept that individuals make choices, i.e., make decisions about themselves, their lives, and their families. The theories in this grouping are about resources and decisions. Some of the focus is from an economic perspective, where the rewards and costs are considered in relation to behavior. Others are from the social perspective relating to relationship and family functioning.

Family Resource Management Theory A theory that is often related to the human ecology theory is family resource management. This theory focuses on the demands placed upon a family, the resources available to the family, and the decision-making related to the use of those resources for daily living. This theory draws on concepts related to goal attainment, i.e., demands, resources, decision-making, and management by family members (Deacon and Firebaugh 1988; Hogan and Buehler 1984). The *demands* are the goals or events that require action by a family member. *Resources* can be "anything that can be used to attain desired ends or goals" (Rettig and Leichtentritt 2000, p. 160) and provide the means by which a family reaches a goal (Rettig et al. 1993). Resources can be human (individual characteristics, such as attitude or sense of humor), nonhuman (outside the individual, such as money, house, job, or material goods), community (schools, churches, parks, etc.), and/or government (cash assistance programs, educational training, food assistance, rural development and improvement, etc.). Decision-making is a process used to evaluate alternatives and make choices. The decision-making process may involve more than one person (Deacon and Firebaugh 1988). Management is how resource use is planned and implemented to meet demands (Deacon and Firebaugh 1988). Paolucci et al. (1977) built on family resource management foundations to develop an ecological framework for family decision-making. Family resource management theory defines many of the functions of daily family life that are often transparent or de facto, i.e., that are automatic or routine.

Family resource management theory was used by Powell and Bauer (2010) to investigate how families caring for children with disabilities use resources to find and keep child care and employment. Bird and Bauer (2009) used it to understand the need of low-income mothers for additional education and training. Resources and demands were discussed in Son and Bauer (2010). Because the decisions that rural low-income families make about their resources can be critical, this theory can be used to help us better understand the decisions that are made about scarce resources, and how decisions are made when scarce resources need to be spread over competing demands of family members.

Conservation of Resources Theory Another framework for viewing family and individual ability to cope with stressful situations is Hobfoll's (1989) conservation of resources theory (COR). Hobfoll contends that the resources individuals have will influence their ability to cope with stressful situations and, conversely, the stressful situations may be influenced by the resources available to individuals (Hobfoll et al. 1996). The basic premise of the COR theory is that people will want to preserve resources they already have. Stress occurs when resources are endangered, when resources are lost, and/or when resources do not develop as expected. Hobfoll categorizes different varieties of resources as possessions (assets, belongings, etc.), conditions (relationships, employment, health, etc.), personal (skills, self-esteem, etc.), and "energies" (money, credit, knowledge, etc.). Community resources can help to off-set or buffer a family or individual resource loss or, conversely, exacerbate the loss if the community does not have resources. The social networks of families and individuals can also buffer or intensify a loss, and these networks, what Hobfoll (2001) refers to as "resource caravans," develop over years. A part of an individual's or family's reaction to a loss is the feeling of control over the situation—the more control the less feeling of loss, the less control the greater feeling of loss. Hobfoll (1989) further contends that we tend to conserve and build up our resources when we are not under stress. Those who are unable, for whatever reason, to develop their resources to any extent will be less prepared to deal with a loss. Seiling (2006) used the COR theory in a case study approach to examining the ability of a small sample of low-income rural mothers to cope with stressors. Mothers with support systems and resources were better able to deal with stressors than mothers with few resources and support systems. In her Master's thesis, Piescher (2004) used the COR theory to measure the family's economic situation as an indicator of depressive symptomatology. Parenting support accounted for a significant amount of the depressive symptomatology. A combination of the perceptions of economic situation and income adequacy was found to be a better measure than either measure alone. Further use of COR will help us understand how rural low-income families use their resources to manage stressful situations, such as a job loss or reduction in hours.

Exchange Theory No single source adequately describes exchange theory. Researchers in economics, sociology, anthropology, psychology, and family studies have all developed variations on the theme of exchanges. The choices that are presented for the exchange are often labeled as utilitarian, where the rewards and costs are considered in relation to behavior. Individuals maximize utility to get what they value most. When this happens, the behavior for the motivation and the outcome (or decision) is called "rational." Family scholars call this social exchange, and they assume that behavior is goal-oriented, with elements of power and privilege in social groups. A source for the history of the various exchange theories is Turner (1991). The sources listed at the beginning of this chapter also have sections on exchange theories.

No RFS papers to date have used the exchange theory as a framework to study rural families and work. This is an appropriate theory for examining the trade-offs that families make in the interface between family and work or between workers within the family. Using the theory to study the trade-offs for childcare among family members or the decision to work or not work when paying for child care either in the marketplace or by family members would be an example of future work.

Family Stress Management Theory Boss (2002, p. 16) defined family stress as a "pressure or tension in the family system" that creates a disturbance in the stability of the family. A discrete event, or series of events, either positive or negative, can be the stressor. Boss (2002) refined the ABC-X stress model, developed by Hill (1949), by using the context of the family to analyze the family's ability to deal with stressful events. Poverty is a chronic stressor for families living with limited resources (Boss 2002). The perception (or meaning) of a stressful situation is the central focus of family stress management theory. How much a family pulls themselves together and what assets they employ is a product of the family's coping ability or strength of the family. Family stress management theory served as the guiding framework for a study of long-term employment patterns, family coping resources, and mothers' perceptions of financial well-being influence depressive symptoms among rural low-income mothers (Sano et al. 2008). They found that family resources and perceptions play vital roles in the ability to cope with stressors, and thus, support Boss' (2002) contention. A study that used the words of mothers to discuss their stress and the meaning it has to their situation would be useful for understanding low-income rural families.

Family Economic Stress Theory Family economic stress theory postulates that economic stress impacts family relationships, specifically parenting skills, i.e., parents under economic stress engage in harsher parenting methods (Conger et al. 2000; McLoyd 1990). Economic stress also has impact on perception of the quality of marriage because economic stress tends to reduce the supportive behaviors of spouses. In one study of rural couples, Whitbeck et al. (1997) reported that in addition to economic strain, fathers' working conditions also played a part in parenting and marital behaviors. For the rural mothers, only economic strain was related to parenting behaviors. While this theory has been used by others in their studies of rural families, no one on the RFS research team as yet has utilized it. The theory would be useful for looking at parent–child relationships in rural low-income families.

Family Resiliency Theory McCubbin et al. (1997) discussed the family protective and family recovery factors that play critical roles in family functioning when the family is challenged by risk factors. Risk factors emanate from a misfortune, trauma, or a transitional event that calls for a change in the family's pattern of functioning. The family's ability to withstand a risk event is often labeled as *family elasticity* or *family buoyancy* and forms the basis of the research on resilience. Most of the research using the family resiliency theory has focused on single-parent households, remarried family units, and interracial married couples, as well as longitudinal research on children, children at-risk, and inner city risk.

RFS papers that use family resiliency theory as a guide were reviewed in Braun (2009). Vandergriff-Avery's (2001) dissertation and Vandergriff-Avery et al. (2004) assessed the stress-protective and crisis recovery resources of Maryland mothers who had experienced chronic economic stressors. Waldman's (2008) thesis expanded the conceptual framework over time with a study of the strength of resources and the hidden costs of resources. When the strength of resources is not included in stress theory, the protective nature of resources may be overestimated. This theory could be useful in investigating the resiliency of the family relative to change, such as changes in parents' hours of employment, or change in family structures.

Life Perspectives

Life Course The life course perspective "incorporates temporal, contextual, and processual distinctions"…and "refers to age-graded life patterns embedded in social structures and cultures that are subject to historical change" (Elder 1996, p. 31). Elder states that life course perspective grew out of the melding of several other theoretical frameworks of social structure, individual, and social change (Giele and Elder 1998). The basic factors in the life course perspective are cultural background and social integration. The key concepts of life course perspective are time and place, human events, transitions, and trajectories. These concepts support analysis of the RFS study in which we have welfare reform issues, rural residence, where some people receive welfare while others live with the transitions of the changes around them. Elder's (1994) work identified an association between the financial difficulties of the families and family friction and depression, as well as family resources serving as key moderating factors in crises (Elder 1998). Life course perspective was used by Reschke et al. (2006) to frame the mother's perceptions of their child care arrangements and the influence of the adult daughter–older mother relational context. Life course perspective could be used to study the impact of economic differences with factors, such as unemployment, recession with the financial distress, or depression of family members over time.

Behavioral Life-Cycle Theory Proposed by Shefrin and Thaler (1988), this theory is based on how households view their assets. The basic assumption is that households do not view the various aspects of their wealth as interchangeable, and the current income will be spent most quickly and future income will be reserved, creating a life-cycle approach to saving. The theory is helpful in looking at household consumption behavior because it encompasses the factors of self-control and mental accounting. Mammen and Lawrence (2006) used this theory in their investigation of the use of the EITC refund looking at how the families planned to spend the refund and whether or not they took the refund as a lump-sum rather than as current income. Behavioral life cycle theory would be appropriate for studying rural low-income families' saving behavior, including their interest in, and use of, Individual Development Accounts (IDAs).

Employment/Output Theories

This is a group of theories have been used to examine the individual's or family's ability to generate income to support the family. These theories support work in the marketplace and work in the home. The theory of planned behavior and household production examines intentions, attitudes, and behaviors in relation to actions taken. Many of these theories use some of the concepts and theories previously mentioned. However, they were used in unique ways to study rural families and work, so they are included here.

Theory of Planned Behavior and the Household Production Theory The theory of planned behavior, developed by Ajzen (1991), frames the examination of behaviors in terms of attitudes toward that behavior, and has been well supported by research (Ajzen 1991). The basic premise is that intent can be predicted by attitudes toward a particular behavior and associated subjective norms, as well as the perceived control over the planned behavior. The individual's attitude toward the behavior is defined as the degree to which the individual has positive or negative feelings about the behavior under scrutiny. The subjective norms are defined as the amount of social pressure the individual perceives to engage in or abstain from the behavior. Finally, the perceived control is the level of ease or difficulty to actually engage in the behavior.

Goods, defined as market, household, and/or leisure time, are consumed by the household to achieve satisfaction in a maximizing manner. Households allocate time to market work, household work, and leisure to gain satisfaction. The amount of time that is allocated depends on the market wage rate, family size, and family composition (Bryant 1990). Kim et al. (2005) used both planned behavior and household production theory to study the employment and mental health of rural low-income women.

Comprehensive Employment Model Urban and Olson (2005) proposed a comprehensive employment model that includes human capital, individual, and community factors. The Comprehensive Employment Model widens the lens of examining the influences of obtaining and maintaining employment by including the barriers to the development of human capital, such as physical and mental health issues and the family environment (Urban and Olson 2005). This model is useful for thinking about unique barriers that might hamper employment in rural communities. While they found that education was key to securing and maintaining employment, low-income mothers with significant disabilities were significantly less likely to be employed. Sano et al. (2010) used this theoretical framework in their examination of low-income rural mothers who were intermittently employed over time. Their analysis found support for Urban and Olson's theory, i.e., the mothers' individual characteristics, their family circumstances, and their communities' resources all appeared to play a role in the mothers' ability to maintain employment.

Occupational Organization and Regulation of Task Performance Theory Commonly called the framework of work systems, the theory developed by Herzenberg et al. (2000) describes the factors endemic to rural low wage jobs. The theory uses the US Department of Labor's organization of production and regulation of task performance in various occupations. Four categories of work systems were identified: tightly constrained, unrationalized labor-intensive, semiautonomous, and high-skill autonomous.

Tightly constrained system jobs have very controlled work environments, high levels of supervision with low-skill-level requirements, with little training provided. Most of these jobs are fast-paced and high-stress, which result in little advancement opportunity and high turnover of workers. Tightly constrained jobs tend have low pay, and nonstandard hours of work are common. The service sector is the most common type of employment for tightly constrained jobs. Unrationalized labor-intensive system jobs are characterized by a fixed set of tasks to complete, the quality and quantity of which is difficult to measure. The job characteristics are not all that different from the tightly constrained system jobs, i.e., nonstandard hours and low pay are common. Jobs may not require many skills, and thus advancement to higher paying positions is difficult. Experienced workers, however, are desirable for employers. Unrationalized, labor-intensive jobs are those like custodians, truck drivers, and nurse's aides.

Semiautonomous system jobs require skills and training for the complex work and workers are not highly supervised. The wages are higher than the previous two categories and advancement is possible. Police officers, security guards, and hotel clerks are examples of semiautonomous jobs. Finally, high-skilled autonomous system jobs require formal training and education with screening processes for hiring. The job tasks are often complex and difficult to evaluate by supervisors. Persons in these jobs have greater advancement potential, and the cost of replacement for the employer is greater. Teachers, managers, and professional positions are examples of high-skill autonomous jobs.

This framework was used by Dolan et al. (2006) to examine the employment concerns of rural mothers in service sector jobs. Dolan et al. (2009a, b) widened the lens to couples who were both employed in all three waves of data collection, and their ability to manage both work and family when jobs offer little flexibility.

Summary

Although the RFS project was framed in the family ecology theory and human capital theory, research team members have utilized a variety of theoretical frameworks as they seek to explain the phenomena observed through our data. No one single theory is adequate to help us understand the complex lives of the rural low-income families who were RFS participants.

Some of the theories presented in this chapter will be further addressed in subsequent chapters. In other chapters, a variety of the aforementioned theories will be referenced and explained only in the context of the research findings being described.

Discussion Questions

1. Choose a research topic about rural families and work. Which theory or theories do you feel would be the most useful in the investigation of rural low-income families and work? Why?

2. How could you to use more than one theory to view the context of rural low-income families? Give an example.
3. Are there theories other than the ones listed in this chapter that could be used to study rural, low-income families and work? How would these expand our understanding of rural families?

Acknowledgments The authors would like to thank Dr. Mary Jo Katras (University of Minnesota), Dr. Jaerim Lee (Yeungnam University), Dr. Sharon Powell (University of Minnesota), Dr. Seohee Son (Sookmyung Women's University), Dr. Yoshie Sano (Washington State University, Vancouver), and Dr. Erin Hiley Sharp (University of New Hampshire) for their insightful comments that were instrumental in the development of this chapter.

References

Ajzen, I. (1991). The theory of planned behavior. *Organizational Behavior and Human Decision Processes, 50,* 179–211.

Almedom, A. M. (2005). Social capital and mental health: An interdisciplinary review of primary evidence. *Social Science & Medicine, 61,* 943–964. doi:10.1016/j.socscimed.2004.12.025.

Anand, P., Hunter, G., & Smith, R. (2005). Capabilities and well-being: Evidence based on the Sen-Nussbaum approach to welfare. *Social Indicators Research, 74,* 9–55. doi:10.1007/s11205-005-6518-z.

Bauer, J. W., Braun, B., & Olson, P. D. (2000). Welfare to well-being framework for research, education, and outreach. *Journal of Consumer Affairs, 34*(1), 62–81. doi:10.1111/j.1745-6606.2000.tb00084.x.

Becker, G. S. (1975). *Human capital: A theoretical and empirical analysis with special reference to education* (2nd ed.). New York: National Bureau of Economic Research.

Becker, G. S. (1993). *Human capital: A theoretical and empirical analysis with special reference to education* (3rd ed.). Chicago: University of Chicago Press.

Becker, G. S. (1996). *Accounting for tastes.* Cambridge: Harvard University Press.

Bengtson, V. L., Acock, A., Allen, K., Dilworth-Anderson, P., & Klein, D. (2005). *Sourcebook of family theory and research.* Thousand Oaks: Sage.

Berry, A. A., Katras, M. J., Sano, Y., Lee, J., & Bauer, J. W. (2008). Job volatility of rural, low-income mothers: A mixed methods approach. *Journal of Family and Economic Issues, 29,* 5–22. doi:10.1007/s10834-007-9096-1.

Bird, C. L., & Bauer, J. W. (2009). Understanding the factors that influence the opportunity for education and training. *Consumer Interests Annual, 55,* 83–85. http://www.consumerinterests.org/2000-2009Proceedings.php.

Bok, M., & Simmons, L. (2002). Post-welfare reform, low-income families and the dissolution of the safety net. *Journal of Family and Economic Issues, 23,* 217–238. doi:10.1023/A:1020391009561.

Boss, P. (2002). *Family stress management: A contextual approach* (2nd ed.). Thousand Oaks: Sage.

Boss, P. G., Doherty, W. J., LaRossa, R., Schumm, W. R., & Steinmetz, S. K. (1993). *Sourcebook of family theories and methods: A contextual approach.* New York: Springer.

Boulding, K. (1985). *Human Betterment.* Beverly Hills: Sage.

Bradley, R. H., & Corwyn, R. F. (2002). Socioeconomic status and child development. *Annual Review of Psychology, 53,* 371–399. doi:10.1146/annurev.psych.53.100901.135233.

Braun, B. (2009). Advancing rural family resiliency research, education, and policy. *Journal of Family & Consumer Sciences, 101*(4), 27–32.

Bronfenbrenner, U. (1979). *The ecology of human development: Experiments by nature and design.* Cambridge: Harvard University Press.

Bronfenbrenner, U. (1986). Ecology of the family as a context for human development: Research perspectives. *Developmental Psychology, 22,* 723–742. doi:10.1037/0012-1649.22.6.723.

Bronfenbrenner, U. (1989). Ecological systems theory. In R. Vasta (Ed.), *Annals of child development* (Vol. 6, pp. 187–249). Greenwich: JAI.

Bronfenbrenner, U. (2005). *Making human beings human: Bioecological perspectives on human development.* Thousand Oaks: Sage.

Bryant, K. (1990). *The economic organization of the household.* New York: Cambridge University Press.

Bubolz, M. M., & Sontag, M. S. (1993). Human ecology theory. In P. G. Boss, W. J. Doherty, R. LaRossa, W. R. Schumm, & S. K. Steinmetz (Eds.), *Sourcebook of family theories and methods: A contextual approach* (pp. 419–447). New York: Springer.

Chibucos, T. R., Leite, R. W., & Weis, D. L. (2005). *Readings in family theory.* Thousand Oaks: Sage.

Coleman, J. S. (1988). Social capital in the creation of human capital. *The American Journal of Sociology, 94,* Supplement, S95–S120.

Conger, K. J., Reuter, M. A., & Conger, R. D. (2000). The role of economic pressure in the lives of parents and their adolescents: The family stress model. In L .J. Crockett & R. K. Silbereisen (Eds.), *Negotiating adolescence in times of social change* (pp. 201–223). Cambridge: Cambridge University Press.

Deacon, R., & Firebaugh, R. (1988). *Family resource management: Principles and applications.* Boston: Allyn & Bacon.

Doherty, W. J., Boss, P. G., LaRossa, R., Schumm, W. R., & Steinmetz, S. K. (1993). Family theories and methods: A contextual approach. In P. G. Boss, W. J. Doherty, R. LaRossa, W. R., Schumm, & S. K. Steinmetz (Eds.), *Sourcebook of family theories and methods: A contextual approach* (pp. 3–30). New York: Springer.

Dolan, E. M., Seiling, S., & Glesner, T. (2006). Making it work: Rural low income women in service jobs. In B. J. Cude (Ed.), *Proceedings of the 33rd Conference of the Eastern Family Economics and Resource Management Association* (pp. 38–46). Knoxville. http://mrupured.myweb.uga.edu/conf/5.pdf.

Dolan, E. M., Braun, B., Katras, M. J., & Seiling, S. (2008). Getting off TANF: Experiences of rural mothers. *Families in Society, 89,* 456–465. doi:10.1606/1044-3894.3771.

Dolan, E. M., Seiling, S., & Harris, S. (2009a). Work constraints of rural, low income mothers and their partners. *Consumer Interests Annual, 55,* 83–85. http://www.consumerinterests.org/2000-2009Proceedings.php.

Dolan, E. M., Seiling, S., & Harris, S. (2009b, November). *Rural, low-income dual earner parents-flexibility in work/family roles.* Poster session presented at the National Council on Family Relations 71st Annual Conference, Burlingame, CA.

Elder, G. H., Jr. (1994). Time, human agency, and social change: Perspectives on the life course. *Social Psychology Quarterly, 57,* 4–15.

Elder, G. H., Jr. (1996). Human lives in changing societies: Life course and developmental insights. In R. B. Cairns, G. H. Elder, Jr., & J. Costello (Eds.), *Developmental science* (pp. 31–63). New York: Cambridge University Press.

Elder, G. H., Jr. (1998). The life course as developmental theory. *Child Development, 69,* 1–12. doi:10.1111/j.1467-8624.1998.tb06128.x.

Giele, J. Z., & Elder, G. H., Jr. (1998). Life course research: Development of a field. In J. Z. Giele & G. H. Elder, Jr (Eds.), *Methods of life course research: Qualitative and quantitative approaches* (pp. 5–27). Thousand Oaks: Sage.

Grossman, M. (1972). On the concept of health capital and the demand for health. *The Journal of Political Economy, 80*(2), 223–255. http://www.jstor.org/stable/1830580.

Herzenberg, S. A., Alic, J. A., & Wial, H. (2000). Nonstandard employment and the structure of post industrial labor markets. In F. Carre, M. A. Ferber, L. Golden, & S. A. Herzenberg (Eds.),

Nonstandard work: The nature and challenges of changing employment arrangements (pp. 399–426). Champaign: Industrial Relations Research Association.

Hill, R. (1949). *Families under stress*. New York: Harper & Brothers.

Hobfoll, S. E. (1989). Conservation of resources: A new attempt at conceptualizing stress. *The American Psychologist, 44*, 513–524. doi:10.1037/0003-066X.44.3.513.

Hobfoll, S. E. (2001). The influence of culture, community, and the nested-self in the stress process: Advancing the conservation of resource theory. *Applied Psychology: An International Review, 50*, 337–412. doi:10.1111/1464-0597.00062.

Hobfoll, S. E., Freedy, J. R., Green, B. L., & Solomon, S. D. (1996). Coping in reaction to extreme stress: The roles of resource loss and resource availability. In M. Zeidner & N. S. Endler (Eds.), *Handbook of coping: Theory, research, applications* (pp. 324–349). New York: John Wiley.

Hogan, M. J., & Buehler, C. A. (1984, November). *The concept of resources: Definition issues.* Paper session presented at the annual meeting for the National Council on Family Relations, San Francisco, CA.

Homans, G. C. (1964). Bringing men back in. *American Sociological Review, 29*, 809–818.

Huddleston-Casas, C., & Braun, B. (2006, May). *Laboring towards economic self-sufficiency: A research perspective.* (RFS Research Brief). http://www.cehd.umn.edu/fsos/assets/pdf/RuralFamSpeak/May_ResearchBrief.pdf.

Katras, M. J., Zuiker, V. S., & Bauer, J. W. (2004). Private safety net: Childcare resources from the perspective of rural low-income families. *Family Relations, 53*, 201–209. doi:10.1111/j.0022-2445.2004.00010.x.

Kim, E.-J., Seiling, S., Stafford, K., & Richards, L. (2005). Rural low-income women's employment and mental health. *Journal of Rural Community Psychology, E8*(2). http://www.marshall.edu/jrcp/8_2_Eun.htm.

Laakso, H., & Paunonen-Ilmonen, M. (2002). Mother's experience of social support following the death of a child. *Journal of Clinical Nursing, 11*(2), 176–185. doi:10.1046/j.1365-2702.2002.00611.x.

Mammen, S., & Lawrence, F. C. (2006). How rural working families use the Earned Income Tax Credit: A mixed method analysis. *Financial Counseling and Planning, 17*, 51–63. http://www1067.ssldomain.com/afcpe/doc/Vol1715.pdf.

Mammen, S., Bauer, J. W., & Lass, D. (2009a). Life satisfaction among rural low-income mothers: The influence of health, human, personal, and social capital. *Applied Research Quality of Life, 4*, 365–386. doi:10.1007/s11482-009-9086-6.

Mammen, S., Bauer, J. W., & Richards, L. (2009b). Understanding persistent food insecurity: A paradox of place and circumstance. *Social Indicators Research, 92*, 151–168. doi:10.1007/s11205-008-9294-8.

Mammen, S., Lass, D., & Seiling, S. B. (2009c). Labor force supply decisions of rural low-income mothers. *Journal of Family and Economic Issues, 30*, 67–79. doi:10.1007/s10834-008-9136-5.

McCubbin, H. I., McCubbin, M. A., Thompson, A. I., Han, S.-Y., & Allen, C. T. (1997). Families under stress: What makes them resilient. *Journal of Family and Consumer Sciences, 89*(3), 2–11.

McLoyd, V. C. (1990). The impact of economic hardship on Black families and children: Psychological distress, parenting, and socioemotional development. *Child Development, 61*, 311–346.

Ostrove, J. M., Feldman, P., & Adler, N. E. (1999). Relations among socioeconomic status indicators and health for African-Americans and Whites. *Journal of Health Psychology, 4*, 451–463.

Paolucci, B., Hall, O., Axinn, N. (1977). *Family decision making: An ecosystem approach.* New York: John Wiley.

Piescher, K. N. (2004). *Economic, social, and community factors indicating depressive symptomatology in rural, low-income mothers.* (Unpublished master's thesis). University of Minnesota, St. Paul, MN.

Powell, S. E., & Bauer, J. W. (2010). Examining resource use of rural low-income families caring for children with disabilities. *Journal of Children & Poverty, 16*(1), 67–83. doi:10.1080/10796120903575101.

Reschke, K. L., Manoogian, M. M., Richards, L. N., Walker, S. K., & Seiling, S. B. (2006). Maternal grandmothers as child care providers for rural, low-income mothers. A unique child care arrangement. *Journal of Children & Poverty, 12*(2), 159–174. doi:10.1080/10796120600879590.

Rettig, K. D., & Leichtentritt, R. (2000). Family economic issues across time. In S. J. Price, P. C. McKenry, & M. J. Murphy (Eds.), *Households across time: A life course perspective* (pp. 160–172). Los Angeles: Roxbury.

Rettig, K. D., Rossmann, M. M., & Hogan, M. J. (1993). Educating for family resource management. In M. E. Arcus, J. D. Schvaneveldt, & J. J. Moss (Eds.), *Handbook of family life education* (pp. 115–54). Newbury Park: Sage.

Sanderson, C. A. (2004). *Health psychology.* Hoboken: John Wiley.

Sano, Y., Dolan, E. M., Richards, L., Bauer, J., & Braun, B. (2008). Employment patterns, family resources, and perception: Examining depressive symptoms among rural low-income mothers. *Journal of Rural Community Psychology, E11*(1). http://www.marshall.edu/jrcp/V11%20N1/Sano.pdf.

Sano, Y., Katras, M. J., Lee, J., Bauer, J. W., & Berry, A. A. (2010). Working toward sustained employment: A closer look on intermittent employment of rural, low-income mothers. *Families in Society, 91*(4), 342–249. doi:10.1606/1044-3894.4039.

Sano, Y., Garasky, S., Greder, K., Cook, C. C., & Browder, D. E. (2011). Understanding food security among Latino immigrant families in rural America. *Journal of Family and Economic Issues, 32,* 111–123. doi:10.1007/s10834-010-9219y.

Sarason, I. G., Sarason, B. R., Shearin, E., & Pierce, G. R. (1987). A brief measure of social support: Practical and theoretical implications. *Journal of Social and Personal Relationships, 4,* 497–510.

Seiling, S. B. (2006). Changes in the lives of rural low-income mothers: Do resources play a role in stress? *Journal of Human Behavior in the Social Environment, 13,* 19–42. doi:10.1300/J137v13n01_02.

Sen, A. (1997). Editorial: Human capital and human capability. *World Development, 25,* 1959–1961.

Shefrin, H. M., & Thaler, R. H. (1988). The behavioral life-cycle hypothesis. *Economic Inquiry, 26,* 609–643.

Simmons, L. A., Braun, B., Wright, D. W., & Miller, S. R. (2007a). Human capital, social support, and economic wellbeing among rural, low-income mothers: A latent growth curve analysis. *Journal of Family and Economic Issues, 28,* 635–652. doi:10.1007/s10834-007-9079-2.

Simmons, L. A., Dolan, E. M., & Braun, B. (2007b). Rhetoric and reality of economic self-sufficiency among rural, low-income families: A longitudinal study. *Journal of Family and Economic Issues, 28,* 489–505. doi:10.1007/s10834-007-9071-x.

Smith, S. R., & Ingoldsby, B. B. (2009). *Exploring family theories* (2nd ed.). New York: Oxford University Press.

Son, S., & Bauer, J. W. (2009, November). *The capability approach for research on families in poverty.* Paper session presented at the National Council on Family Relations 71st Annual Conference, Burlingame, CA.

Son, S., & Bauer, J. W. (2010). Employed rural, low-income, single mothers' family and work over time. *Journal of Family and Economic Issues, 31,* 107–120. doi:10.1007/s10834-009-9173-8.

Swanson, J. A., Olson, C. M., Miller, E. O., & Lawrence, F. C. (2008). Rural mothers' use of formal programs and informal social supports of meet family food needs: A mixed methods study. *Journal of Family and Economic Issues, 29,* 674–690. doi:10.1007/s10834-008-9127-6.

Tomer, J. F. (2003). Personal capital and emotional intelligence: An increasingly important intangible source of economic growth. *Eastern Economic Journal, 29,* 453–470. http://www.palgrave-journals.com/eej/archive/.

Tudge, J. R. H., Mokrova, I., Hatfield, B. E., & Karnik, R. B. (2009). Uses and misuses of Bronfenbrenner's bioecological theory of human development. *Journal of Family Theory & Review, 1*(4), 198–210. doi:10.1111/j.1756-2589.2009.00026.x.

Turner, J. H. (1991). *The structure of sociological theory* (5th ed.). Belmont: Wadsworth.

Urban, J. A., & Olson, P. N. (2005). A comprehensive employment model for low-income mothers. *Journal of Family and Economic Issues, 26,* 101–122. doi:10.1007/s10834-004-1414-2.

Vandergriff-Avery, A. M. (2001). *Rural families speak: A qualitative investigation of stress protective and crisis recovery strategies utilized by rural low-income women and their families.* UMI Microform (3035864).

Vandergriff-Avery, M., Anderson, E. A., & Braun, B. (2004). Resiliency capacities among rural low-income families. *Families in Society, 85,* 562–570. doi:10.1606/1044-3894.1841.

Wadsworth, M., Montgomery, S., & Bartley, M. (1999). The persisting effect of unemployment on health and social well-being in men early in working life. *Social Science & Medicine, 48,* 1491–1499. doi:10.1016/S0277-9536(99)00052-0.

Waldman, J. (2008). *Stressor events, resources, and depressive symptoms in rural, low-income mothers.* (Unpublished master's thesis). University of Maryland, College Park, MD.

Whitbeck, L. B., Simons, R. L., Conger, R. D., Wickrama, K. A. S., Ackley, K. A., & Elder, G. H. (1997). The effects of parents' working conditions and family economic hardship on parenting behaviors and children's self-efficacy. *Social Psychology Quarterly, 60,* 291–303.

White, J. M., & Klein, D. M. (2008). *Family theories* (3rd ed.). Thousand Oaks: Sage.

Zimmerman, S. L. (1995). *Understanding family policy: Theories and application* (2nd ed.). Thousand Oaks: Sage.

Chapter 3
Rural Does Matter: Understanding the Rural Context

Jean W. Bauer, Patricia H. Dyk, Seohee Son and Elizabeth M. Dolan

Introduction

Rural low-income families face different employment barriers compared to urban low-income families because available resources or opportunities vary between rural and urban communities. Rural communities are geographically isolated, but even across and within rural settings, the opportunities vary (Duncan et al. 2002; Taylor 2001; Weber et al. 2005). Some previous studies have examined personal characteristics to explain poverty in rural areas; these include the relationships between low-income families' employment and their individual or family characteristics, such as education, skills, health, family structure, and the number of children (Berry et al. 2008; Danziger and Seefeldt 2002; Dworsky and Courtney 2007). Some researchers have claimed that the community contexts of rural families should receive special consideration (Taylor 2001; Urban and Olson 2005; Weber and Jensen 2004). Their studies report that rural residents face multiple employment barriers in their communities, such as limited employment opportunities, lack of reliable transportation, lack of child care, and geographical isolation (Katras et al. 2004; Monroe et al. 1999; Taylor 2001). Because of these factors, the reciprocal relationships of families in rural community contexts, including the opportunities and constraints, should be addressed.

Rural low-income families often experience difficulties in combining their work and family lives. Due to lower population densities, geographical isolation, and higher costs in rural areas, they are less likely than their urban counterparts to have access to formal support services to assist them while employed, such as child care, transportation, and health care services (Duncan et al. 2002). The lack of these resources makes it more difficult to manage work and family responsibilities simultaneously. To compensate for the lack of formal support, many rural low-income families rely heavily on informal social support. Previous research has reported that

J. W. Bauer (✉)
Department of Family Social Science, University of Minnesota, 290 McNeal Hall,
1985 Buford Avenue, St. Paul, MN 55108, USA
e-mail: jbauer@umn.edu

J. W. Bauer, E. M. Dolan (eds.), *Rural Families and Work,* International Series on Consumer Science 1,
DOI 10.1007/978-1-4614-0382-1_3, © Springer Science+Business Media, LLC 2011

without the appropriate informal social support, sustaining employment is difficult for rural low-income families (Dolan et al. 2006; Son and Bauer 2010).

Understanding what rural contexts are like is foundational to our discussion of rural low-income families' employment opportunities and challenges. This chapter considers four major areas from rural low-income family research including a description of rural America, an understanding of rural contexts, a listing of possible opportunities for the future, and challenges for current and future research. Some of the voices from the qualitative portion of the Rural Families Speak (RFS) study are included in these sections. They support and illustrate the issues at the individual and family level and perceptions about the rural macrosystem and community level.

Description of Rural America

What Is Rural?

Even though the nation is predominantly an urban society, most of the land in the United States is rural. Families migrated to urban centers for jobs during the rise of industrialization, producing a population shift where today, eight out of ten Americans live in an urban area. According to the US Census Bureau (2000), only 21% of Americans (approximately 59 million people) lived in rural areas in 2000; however, by 2008, 25% lived in rural areas (Reynnells 2008). While the portion of US population living in rural areas is growing slightly, few people have actual ties to rural realities, and they rely on conceptions formed through literature (e.g., Steinbeck's *Grapes of Wrath*), music (Country and Bluegrass), and visual arts (bucolic fields of grain, majestic mountains). People have images of typical rural America as being open countryside and small towns that are some distance from large urban centers. But reaching a consensus on exactly how to define "rural" or where to divide urban from rural is difficult (US Department of Agriculture [USDA] 2007, September).

The definition of rurality needs to reflect its multidimensional nature. Rural communities in the United States are as distinct from each other as they are from urban communities, each with its own economic, social, and institutional characteristics. Most definitions of rurality, however, are concerned with place characteristics and focus on key demographic indicators, including population size and/or density (Brown and Swanson 2003). Some researchers have focused on prosperity, instead, for insights into rural conditions, characteristics, and comparisons (Isserman et al. 2009). This type of definition changes the language to highlight growth and opportunity rather than rural poverty, distress, population loss, competitive disadvantage, or urban encroachment—all factors used by many researchers. An indicator of the complexity of defining rurality is that US federal agencies have more than 20 different definitions (Cromartie and Bucholtz 2008). Hence, an appropriate definition should be based on the purpose of the research (Cromartie and Bucholtz 2008). In this chapter, two definitions of rural areas are introduced: Rural-Urban Continuum Codes (RUCC) and Urban Influence Codes (UIC).

Rural-Urban Continuum Codes RUCC, sometimes referred to as Butler and Beale Codes (1994), classify all US counties onto a continuum based on population to reflect their degree of rurality and metropolitan proximity rather than to create a simple metro versus nonmetro category. The RUCC consists of nine categories with three metro and six nonmetro categories derived from the June 2003 definition of metropolitan and nonmetropolitan counties as determined by the Office of Management and Budget (OMB) (USDA 2004a). More detail on the RUCC is available on the USDA Economic Research Service website (http://www.ers.usda.gov/briefing/rurality/ruralurbcon/). The RFS project defined rural by using an earlier version with the ten categories (Butler and Beale 1994), which also used OMB data to classify the counties (Bauer 2004).

Urban Influence Codes Another way to define rurality is to use UIC, created to categorize counties by reflecting their economic opportunities instead of relying on their population size and proximity to metropolitan areas. The assumption of the UIC is that economic opportunities in smaller nonmetropolitan areas increase when they are close to larger metropolitan economies that include centers of information, communication, trade, and finance (Ghelfi and Parker 1995, as cited in Ricketts et al. 1998). The 2003 UIC were constructed based on the "metropolitan counties by size and nonmetropolitan counties by size of the largest city or town and proximity to metro and micro areas" (USDA 2007, August). The 2003 UIC classified 3,141 counties, county equivalents, and independent cities in the United States into 12 groups. Two categories (1 and 2) describe metropolitan areas, and the other ten categorize nonmetropolitan areas, with 12 representing the most remote with a population of less than 2,500 people. The decision on density is based on population per square mile. More detail on the 2003 UIC is available on the USDA Economic Research Service website (http://www.ers.usda.gov/Briefing/Rurality/urbaninf/).

These two definitions of rural areas, the RUCC and the UIC, distinguish among nonmetropolitan areas through different variables. "Rural," therefore, is not synonymous with "nonmetropolitan," despite long-term use of the terms as synonymous across many research disciplines (Isserman et al. 2009).

What Does Rural America Look Like?

Many scholars and practitioners are interested in the ways family life and opportunities for social and economic well-being compare across rural and urban places. Studies have revealed that a rural/urban gap exists in quality of life, with rural communities lagging behind urban city centers particularly with regard to infrastructure (e.g., broadband, transportation) and availability of medical and social services (Duncan et al. 2002; Hoyt et al. 1997). Although rural families share structural similarities with their urban counterparts, ties to place, poverty rates, and employment opportunities differ. In this section, the current situations in rural America are explored, including family types, rural economy, employment, and rural poverty.

Family Types Rural families are similar in type to urban families. Rural families have the same variety of family structures as are found in metropolitan areas. In 2005–2006, 66% of rural children lived in married-couple households, 16% in single-mother households, 7% in cohabitating households, 3% in single-father households, and 9% in other types of households (O'Hare et al. 2009). Interestingly, according to O'Hare et al. (2009), the percentage of rural children living in cohabitating households increased from 3% in 1995–1996 to the 7% in 2005–2006. A smaller proportion of children in rural areas lived in single-mother households than in urban areas. Except for the cohabitating and single-mother households, the family structures were similar between rural and urban areas in 2005–2006. The average size of the rural family has become smaller over the past 20 years. The average rural family size was 3.02 persons in 2000 compared to 3.27 persons in 1980 (MacTavish and Salamon 2003). The rural family size was even smaller than that of urban families (3.14 persons) in 2000. This smaller average size of rural families may reflect the aging population in rural communities (MacTavish and Salamon 2003).

These structural similarities between rural and urban families conceal important distinctions between the two, however, including social and cultural differences, poverty levels, and infrastructure deficits. Connections with family and place are identified as highly important to many rural residents, especially those with intergenerational ties to their community. Struthers and Bokemeier (2000) found that rural mothers reported living where they did because their family had always lived there, they received important social and/or economic support from family members, and/or they feared breaking family ties. Women cited family and community ties, as well as commitment to the land, as primary reasons for continuing to reside in rural areas (Tickamyer and Henderson 2003).

Changing Rural Economies Transformation is evident in rural economies. As the traditional rural industries, including agriculture, resource extraction, and manufacturing, have declined, rural industry has shifted toward the service sectors (Gibbs et al. 2005). In addition, tourism and recreational industries that take advantage of natural amenities, such as mountains, lakes, and pleasant climates, have grown (McGranahan 2003). This natural amenity-based development could be important for many rural communities in revitalizing their rural economies. Nevertheless, not every rural community has this option to exploit for their economic and community development needs (Krannich and Petrzelka 2003). Furthermore, rural communities which are overly dependent on tourism or amenity industries could experience economic instability or rural poverty due to the seasonal fluctuations of these industries (Ames et al. 2006; Krannich and Petrzelka 2003).

One of the RFS mothers talked about the options available to families in a predominately agricultural related area. Reba,[1] a 34-year-old married mother with four children, responded to the question about job opportunities.

---

[1] All names are pseudonyms.

Well there...job opportunities?...well, most of it is agriculture-related. There aren't a lot of big business in Pleasantville itself. People usually have to drive further out to find a job. And it's pretty hard for most people to make a living just by farming....But around here, as far as a lot of job opportunities you know. If farm prices were better, there wouldn't have to be so many double-income families in this area. More farm wives could stay home. They'd probably choose to. My mom's generation, a lot of them did stay home until, you know... until they were actually forced to have to go to work. 'Cause my mom was home until we were about ready to go to high school, then my mom had to work for extra income.

Mindy, a 30-year-old single mother with three children who lived in a community that was dependent upon tourism said, *"Well, I wouldn't say they're* [job prospects] *real good. During the summer is mostly when you get work. It's mostly seasonal work around here....Because of the tourist attractions, you know."*

Leatherman (2003, p. 203) defined three general characteristics of rural places that would affect access to or use of advanced information technologies (IT) which Malecki (1996) called the "rural penalty." The characteristics were:

1. the remote geography both increases costs associated with infrastructure diffusion and makes rural markets less attractive for outside investment;
2. the economic structure of rural places seems a detriment insofar as their industries are neither heavily IT-producing nor IT-using;
3. the human capital found in rural areas does not seem especially attractive either as a labor market or as a consumer market.

Employment Rural areas offer fewer job opportunities to rural residents as compared to urban residents (Duncan et al. 2002). In addition, economic restructuring, such as globalization and change in industries, has influenced the nature of work in rural areas. Employment sectors in rural areas have changed with the proportion of agricultural jobs declining considerably from 12.4% in 1976 to 6.2% in 2004 (USDA 2006, December). Growth in nonfarm employment, however, compensated for the declining farm employment. According to USDA's employment research, in 2005, 34.8% of rural counties were dependent on the manufacturing sector, 16.7% on recreation, 16.5% on retirement-destination, and 6.6% on farming. In terms of employment by occupation, 26.2% of rural people worked in professional and managerial occupations, 23.3% in sales and office occupations, 22.1% in other blue-collar occupations, 16.8% in service, 7.2% in construction and extraction, and 4.4% in farming, fishing, and forestry (USDA 2006, December).

Unemployment rates in rural areas vary around the county with the highest rates in the South (USDA 2006, December). In addition, more than 1.5 million employees in rural areas, particularly low-skill and/or less educated workers, lost their jobs between 1997 and 2003 due to industry restructuring (Glasmeier and Salant 2006). In particular, almost half the jobs in rural manufacturing industries disappeared between 2001 and 2003, compared to a 32% loss in urban areas (Glasmeier and Salant 2006). Personal characteristics of rural residents, such as lower average education level compared to urban residents and lack of job opportunities, make it harder for rural families to maintain stable employment (Duncan et al. 2002).

The RFS mothers spoke of disruptions and global issues. Jan, a 30-year-old single mother with one child said,

> There are a lot of people are losing their jobs right now. [Local manufacturer named]....
> they're sending their work to China...And it's hard, this area's really hard. People that rely
> on their work, it's a tough area to keep sustained. People here are either extremely wealthy
> or very poor... It's hard when these people work hard hours and all kinds of overtime, after
> 35 years, they've lost their jobs. 'Cause it's going to China.

Caprice, a 23-year-old married mother of four children, talked about a manufacturing company in her area.

> Jobs have gotten lot harder to find.A lot of those big companies in Westlake laid off a lot of
> people, which mean they went to the smaller places that were circled around here and they
> all most of them are full and are not hiring any more....A lot of people we know were laid
> off.Um, some of them, uh, were able to find new jobs.Some of them have not been able to
> find jobs and had to leave...My best friend,(her husband was laid off of his job), she had to
> leave the area she has grown up in to find a better job in Pleasantville...It is a bigger place
> so he [friend's husband] was able to find a job...It did not pay as good as his other did, but
> it was money.

Rural Poverty Rural residents have a higher likelihood of being poor than urban residents. High poverty counties (poverty rates of 20% or higher) and persistent-poverty counties (high poverty exists over several decades) are predominantly found in rural areas (Weber and Jensen 2004; Weber et al. 2005). The gap between rural and urban poverty rates has been persistent over time. According to USDA (2004b) research, 14.2% of the rural population was in poverty compared to 11.6% of the urban population. Statistics also indicate that poverty rates were higher for minorities than for non-Hispanic Whites in rural and urban areas. Specifically in rural areas, poverty rates were highest in 2002 for Native Americans, Black non-Hispanics, and Hispanics. In terms of rural family structure, the poverty rate for married couples was lowest, and female-headed families had a higher poverty rate compared to male-headed families.

Diversity and Disparity

New immigrant populations are changing the face of rural America. In addition, there are the wide geographic historic disparities in poverty across rural communities. In this section, we review three of these unique situations.

Growing Hispanic Population The Hispanic population has contributed significantly to population growth in rural America (Kandel and Parrado 2006). According to Kandel and Cromartie (2004), in 2000, Hispanics made up 5.5% of the rural population, indicating a growth of more than 25% during the 1990s. Furthermore, the Hispanic population has increased in rural areas outside the Southwest, including the Southeast, Midwest, and Northwest. Although Hispanics are now living in many rural communities in the United States, residential separation between Hispanics and non-Hispanic Whites is salient. Increasing numbers of Hispanic migrants in rural communities contribute to rural population growth and economic vigor. Since they have little experience with culturally diverse populations, however, many rural communities are not well prepared economically or culturally for the influx of Hispanics. The voices of the RFS mothers reflected the pressures of new people to the community and the challenging job situation. Mothers were asked "What is your opinion of job opportunities in this area?" Genoveva, a 29-year-old mother with a partner and five children, made this comment:

> I think that it's getting worse because there are more people and there is very little work, very few jobs....There was less people, there was more opportunity (because many people are moving into the area)....There was more opportunity, there was more opportunity for work. In reality because the town is small and we all want to work in one spot, where we are...

Another mother, Ededina, a 29-year-old married woman with three children, was more specific about her opinion of the type of persons who were moving into area and the job opportunities. She thought that only one place had opportunity. She said, *"Terrible. Absolutely terrible....The wages are gonna be really, really, really, really terrible. Because it's gonna be, I don't want to, I don't want to be stereotypical, it's gonna be all migrant."*

Appalachia Appalachia is a large diverse geographic region that encompasses more than 400 counties across 13 states. The Appalachian Regional Commission (ARC) boundaries are set by legislation in Congress and have changed in recent years (Thorne et al. 2004). Central Appalachia is the most remote, i.e., the farthest from urban centers, and highest in poverty. Appalachian women, especially those with young children and in female-headed households, have the highest poverty rates (Tickamyer and Henderson 2003; Tickamyer and Tickamyer 1988).

Perspectives from mothers in RFS study who live in the Appalachian area reflect the poverty and job situation. In response to the interviewer's question about what was the worst thing about where she lived, Bevin, a 40-year-old married woman with three children, said,

> The economy here. I mean there really isn't a lot of work here. And, what work is here is minimum wage or just above. And, I wonder about families where two people are working at minimum wage jobs. Two people at minimum wage jobs HERE in this village are still below the poverty level. So even if you're doing your best and working a forty-hour week, you're still looking for government support to help you get by, which is kind of crazy. It's kind of crazy....And, the five years, I guess, that we've been here we've seen a handful of ads, you know, for employment [at a local manufacturer]. So it's kind of you have to know somebody, they say in town you kind of have to know somebody to get in.

Jillian, a 40-year-old married mother with three children, gave her perception to the interviewer's question of "Do you think the job opportunities have changed very much from last year to this year?" She said,

> I think there's less, I mean, well, there's, with the factories cutting back and, the hospital, if the tax levy don't pass, it might shut down....Three hundred and sixty some people would lose their jobs. You know, so I don't know what's gonna happen. Everything's up in the air. A lot of doctors are leaving. It's kinda scary. [Interviewer: So you think the job opportunities are less now?] Yeah. For the higher quality jobs, yeah. I mean, there's plenty of McDonald's and, the lower ones.

Another mother, in the same county as Jillian, had a gallows-humor approach to the job opportunities. Kacy, a 33-year-old married woman with two children, said,

Very limited [laughing]...And there's not a real wide selection. And most of them, it's just a temporary thing, and then they, basically, I like to call it, they use you and lose you.... They bring you in for a while, and then they decide "Well, we don't need you, we'll get a different temporary."

Black Belt Another geographic designation that captures a swath of the rural South is known as the Black Belt. This social and demographic crescent of 623 counties containing higher than average percentages of black residents spans parts of Virginia, the Carolinas, Georgia, Florida, Alabama, Mississippi, Tennessee, Louisiana, Arkansas, and Texas. More poverty exists in the Black Belt—for Black and White residents—than in the area served by the Appalachian Regional Commission. Furthermore, the Black Belt matches any other region in persons who have not finished high school and challenges the other US regions in high unemployment (Wimberley and Morris 1997). The Black Belt residents are prone to persistent poverty, poor employment, low income, low education, poor health, high infant mortality, and welfare dependence.

Insights from two mothers in RFS study who live in the Black Belt region address the difficulty of finding local employment and the scarcity of those employment opportunities in their community. Jolie, a 24-year-old African American mother with an LPN degree and working as nurse, said *"They're very slim...Not for me....but I mean for everybody else though. I mean if you not in something like that. It's kind of hard to get a job around here."* Another mother, Sadira, a 32-year-old with two children, said,

It would be slim in this area. I would have to travel to Green Hill everyday.... There's nothing too much here, unless you're in the school system or you're into some type of medical. You have the prisons you know, but I don't want to do security. Um, and like the office jobs, they're pretty much people who have been there forever. You know, there's nothing here, so you would have to travel such a distance to get something.

Understanding Rural Contexts

Rural contexts are closely related to the economic well-being of rural families. Many research studies have demonstrated that rural families are more likely to be poor as compared to urban families, even after controlling for individual and community indicators, including family structure, number of children, education, and types of jobs (Cotter 2002; Snyder and McLaughlin 2004; Weber and Jensen 2004; Weber et al. 2005). In addition to the prevalence of poverty for individual rural families, rural *county* poverty rates are higher.

Perspectives on Rural Contexts

Researchers have used different perspectives to explain this economic disparity, including individual deficiencies, cultural belief systems, political-economic distortions, geographical disparities, or cumulative and circumstantial origins (Bradshaw 2007). Of these theories, two perspectives are introduced in this chapter to help explain how places are associated with families in poverty. The structuralist perspective is concerned with the systemic barriers of place, including the economic, political, and social systems which limit people's opportunities and resources (Bradshaw 2007; Weber and Jensen 2004). To be precise, structural barriers such as wages and lack of jobs or education and training opportunities in their local area prevent rural low-income families from achieving greater economic well-being. Rural low-income families usually live in poor counties and work in the lower-paying employment sectors available to them (Braun et al. 2002). These socioeconomic environments of rural low-income families, including lack of employment opportunities and living in poor communities, are critical barriers to any improvement in their economic well-being.

Another perspective poses that the characteristics of individual families and communities are interdependent in terms of poverty (Bradshaw 2007). As Glasmeier and Salant's (2006) research reported, lower-skilled and less educated workers were more likely to lose their jobs during a time of economic restructuring in rural areas compared to their urban counterparts. Therefore, opportunities and barriers that individuals and communities possess are interrelated, and both influence individual families' economic success (Cotter 2002; Wells 2002).

Rural Families Speak Context

The rural context of the RFS project is somewhat diverse. In order to understand the diverseness, we use Table 3.1 to present 2000 community level (county level, in most cases) context for the 27 counties in the study. RFS data were collected between 1999 and 2003. The median age for all people living in the county is older than our sample, a natural expectation since our participants were required to have a child under 13 at the beginning of the study (refer to Table 3.1). Median age in the RFS counties varies by almost 13 years (12.9) from the lowest median to highest median age. The age variable alone would reflect the need for the type of services that would need to be available to the respective county residents. The change in population overall was small between 2000 and 2003, but some counties lost population while others grew by more than 8% during the time we collected RFS data. Teen birth rate is a measure of a potentially low-income population and indicates a need for specialized services for health, food support, employment training, and other supports for low-income families. The RFS counties had a large range from low to high in the birth rate to teens (2.3% to 26.2%). Likewise, the variable "income less than poverty level" varied widely (4.8% to 23.1%) among the counties.

Employment of females 16 and older varied little among the RFS counties (Table 3.1). The overall unemployment rates in 2000, however, had a wide range (1.9% to 11.9%). Both "education level" and "type of jobs available in the county" indicate the diversity of the county demographic. The higher education levels typically result in larger numbers of county residents being employed in management and

Table 3.1 RFS project participants' community contexts ($N=27$)

Community Context	Range	
	Low	High
Median age	30.6	43.5
Population change from 2000–2003	−5.5%	8.4%
Persons per household (Mean)	2.33	3.18
Number of married couple families with own children under 18 years	653	63,535
Number of male householder, no wife present with own children under 18 years	55	7,463
Number of female householder, no husband present with own children under 18 years	92	18,904
Teen birth rate	2.3%	26.2%
Education—high school graduates	59.0%	88.2%
Education—B.S. degree or more	7.2%	29.1%
Housing–median value of mobile homes	$12,800	$81,800
Housing—median value of owner-occupied homes	$42,000	$135,600
Median household income	$26,018	$45,953
Persons with income less than poverty	4.8%	23.1%
Employment—females 16 and older employed	43.0%	49.1%
Unemployment rate, 2000	1.9%	11.9%
Commuting time to work in minutes	13.1	36.8
Population in management, professional, etc. occupations	20.4%	49.1%
Population in sales and office occupations	18.8.%	24.2%

Note. Data are based on 2000 information

professional-type occupations. The RFS counties have wide variations for these two variables. The RFS study was framed using the RUCC to allow comparability across the sample. The sample population, however, was diverse relative to community contexts and to the characteristics of mothers within the sample.

Understanding Rural Contexts from Other Studies

In her book *The Social Economy of Single Motherhood* (2005), Nelson interviewed a snowball sample of 68 non-Hispanic White mothers, each with at least one child under 18 years, living in rural Vermont to look at "multiple women within a single social support network" (p. 17). The social economy of the single mothers looked at the "interconnection with individuals who can provide money, goods, and help with the tasks of daily living" (p. 5).

Maintaining relationships and social networks can be challenging for rural residents. Distance between the mothers and the members of their social support networks meant that mothers had to work at maintaining their networks. Mothers wanted or needed to have exchanges with others (e.g., doing favors, sharing, and socializing), but expended much energy and time in doing so. The author contrasted her findings with those of Stack (1974) who used an urban population, by say-ing "mothers cannot simply run next door for assistance, nor can they assume that neighbors will notice their need, and if they do notice, either be available to help out or be sympathetic to the situation" (pp. 91–92). Nelson (2005) further highlight-ed the situation by stating: "The rural context helps to support an idealized vision of community where pure generosity prevails. In fact...the actual dealings single mothers have with local agencies that formally represent community, however, dif-fer significantly from that ideal" (p. 92). Nelson found that in Vermont the types of employment for women were distributed differently than for men and that most of the jobs were primarily in the service industry. While the jobs were low-paying, compared to other women in the United States, Vermont women's "earnings are high in comparison to those of their male counterparts" (p. 32). Nelson reported that her findings concerning transportation were similar to those of MacDonald and Peters (1996). The Vermont women wanted jobs that were within easy com-muting distance from home. Transportation in rural areas was a major aggravation for single mothers because it drew them into informal arrangements with others, making them dependent.

Elder and Conger (2000) interviewed 451 two-parent families in eight north-ern Iowa counties, each which had a seventh grade child, comparing those who grew up on farms and those who had not. Their focus was on ties to the land, so-cial resources, and adolescence competence and resiliency. Twenty percent of their sample farmed full-time and 10% part-time, 10% were displaced farmers who were not successful and had left farming during the 1980s, 35% were raised on a farm but no longer lived on a farm, and 25% had never lived on a farm. Full-time farm-ing families had strong ties to the land, whereas nonfarm families had weak ties. Families mattered in the lives of children, and successful families were embedded in a network of parental social ties. Elder and Conger also found that social ties in-fluenced the development of children and youth. Extended families mattered in the lives of children and their development. Social capital had been embodied by farm families for generations. Ties to the land were socially embedded in the families' local communities, churches, and schools. All of these ties provided a rich set of opportunities for the children. Elder and Conger found that farm children did more with their parents than did the nonfarm children, and farm children knew more adults in community than did nonfarm children. The nonfarm children were more involved in peer culture than were farm children. The lens and framework of gen-erational success and life course were the basis for this study.

Opportunities for the Future: Importance of Vitality

Rural areas have been undergoing substantial transitions in their economic structure. Rural manufacturing has declined, resulting in an erosion of the em-ployment base of well-paying jobs. Regional centers and outlets have replaced small town retail establishments, and services have become sparser in many areas (Walzer 2003). Economic revitalization efforts tend to promote value-added agriculture, telecommunications, and technology opportunities. Revitalization helps to redefine place for some rural families, but neither unilaterally across geographic areas nor for rural low-income families. Rural families are finding that they need to rely on jobs in nearby larger communities. When employment options are available regionally, families can remain in place, including farm families who may have to resort to nonfarm employment to supplement farm income.

The RFS mothers highlighted the inadequacy of job opportunities in their communities, the need to travel for jobs, and, in some cases, the need to move to find jobs. London, a married 23-year-old mother with one child, said,

> In this county?...I had to go to the next county over to find work. If you want a job you have to go 20 to 60 miles around here 'cuz there are no jobs here. We've got three factories. None of them hire you unless you've got your nose stuck so far up their hind end that you can't see the clouds. These fast food places, they don't pay enough. I couldn't pay my babysitter to work in fast food. There's just no jobs around here unless you want to drive 20 to 30 miles.

However, Idette, a 19-year-old single mother with one child, liked her fast-food job but saw few other opportunities.

> I'm cool at Wendy's, because it's comfortable for me, and like time-wise, like if I have to take off for a reason, I can take off. But, basically, you gotta go out of town to work.... They're jobs, but there like jobs that, you know, you gotta bust your butt for a measly whatever...and get another job just to cover your bills, so they don't pay very well, and they're like hard-working. Like most of them are warehouses and factories and they lay off every so often. Jobs suck.

Ada, a wife and 26-year-old mother of one child, talked about her family's situation and, specifically, her husband's job.

> Right now it's really hard to find a job. Um...one of the big companies that he worked at... keeps laying off people that have been there like thirty years. And all of a sudden they'll just come up to them one day and say "I'm sorry your jobs done".... So it's just been really hard on our community we know a lot of people that have been terminated and been there for a lot a lot of years and put a lot of time and effort into their job.... That and [company] is basically why people live here. And it's a little bit scary knowing that those people can't keep their jobs and then there's not a lot of other jobs either, you know, so a lot of people have to move.

Research and theoretical development emerging from the work at Iowa State and the North Central Rural Development Center focusing on community capitals (Flora and Flora 2003) have highlighted the role that rural community leaders play in identifying, assessing, and strengthening their human, social, political, built, financial, natural, and cultural capitals. Each of the capitals defined by Flora and Flora relate to those items that lead to healthy ecosystems, vibrant regional economies, and social equity and empowerment. Each capital reinforces the other in "spiraling up" the community development process (Emery and Flora 2006). Communities successfully supporting healthy, sustainable, and economically viable development are attentive to all seven types of capital. The organizational potential of rural leadership and the institutional capacity for working together, however, are often overlooked. "The quality of local institutions and their interactions are critical to creating an environment conducive to taking action that can improve community viability" (Flora and Flora 1993; Flora et al. 1997 as both cited in Leatherman 2003, p. 207).

Much of the literature around community development has policy implications for rural development. The studies are structured either to give support for development funds currently available or to advocate for additional funding for rural areas. Walzer (2003) identified the types of issues faced by communities and some innovative approaches taken in 12 Midwestern states. The issues addressed were large-scale and rarely extended to the family level. The policy lens is designed to assist state policymakers, students and scholars, and local leaders with community-wide, but not family, issues.

Lasley and Hanson (2003) addressed the changing population and other issues for rural America. Social and economic population shifts are dynamic, which lead to gains for some groups and losses for other groups. Using the UIC, Lasley and Hanson described two rural Americas, one of which is characterized as isolated. The other rural America is close to metropolitan centers and is referred to as the "urbanized rural culture," either adjacent to or within commuting distance of the metro area. Lasley and Hanson argued that for rural populations to be dispersed beyond the urbanized rural culture, opportunities beyond involvement in production agriculture must exist that will attract and maintain the rural population. Opportunities can include the way recreation is created and managed, how communities welcome newcomers such as immigrants, and how telecommunications up-grades are brought to the area. Currently, however, most rural development policy is focused on agricultural-dependent projects and conservation programs, not on economic development that will create new social, health care, and employment opportunities for rural, low-income families.

Lasley and Hanson (2003) indicated that some development policies have created full-time jobs in rural areas, but since these tend to be low-paying jobs, families still are not able to support their families and need to rely on government assistance programs. When jobs help to perpetuate poverty and/or do not lead to promotional opportunities in the long run, community decline is perpetuated, and the related social and community problems appear. Policies that rely solely on development in low-wage industries will not lead to thriving rural communities. Businesses need a local environment in which they can prosper (Walzer 2003). The rural Midwest falls behind the rest of the United States in business start-ups and prosperity. Policy that supports entrepreneurial opportunities may be a way to help communities prosper and increase support for the rural way of life and concept that rural does matter.

Challenges for Current and Future Research

Distinctive Rural Communities

The analysis using spatial data of poverty has some common challenges, regardless of whether the studies are community or contextual (Weber et al. 2005), and researchers often used a classification system to distinguish between the two (Brooks-Gunn et al. 1997; Weber et al. 2005). According to Brooks-Gunn et al. (1997), community studies examine poverty across community demographic and structural community variables. Contextual studies examine individual poverty outcomes by using individual demographic characteristics, plus community and economic characteristics. In short, community studies use county-level data to estimate county poverty based on community demographic and economic variables, while contextual studies use individual-level data to examine the likelihood that a household is in poverty in relation to relevant demographic and community factors (Weber et al. 2005). Policy variables can be included in either type of study. Poverty, however, is not equally distributed over geographic areas, and many researchers have recognized this problem. Using Census tract data for community and contextual poverty studies is limiting. Census track data works well in urban areas, but population density often creates concerns with scale and aggregations to larger areas in rural studies. The distinctiveness of rural communities could be lost in the issue of generalizability in rural research. This would be true for large county areas or aggregation across counties.

Data Sources

Data for research on rural areas come from sources such as US Department of Agriculture (Economic Research Service, National Agricultural Statistics Service), US Department of Commerce (US Bureau of Census, Bureau of Economic Analysis), US Department of Labor (Bureau of Labor Statistics), US Department of Education, and US Department of Housing and Urban Development for descriptions of conditions surrounding place of rural areas. The distinct geographic factor is an important unit of analysis in the data selection decision. The OMB data can be used for the economic and social integration around a population core (Isserman et al. 2009). Population comparisons are still limited because the OMB uses metropolitan, micropolitan, and outside core-based areas which use the US Census Bureau's definition of no urban area with 10,000 or more residents for its definition of rural.

Funding

Grants that address specific rural issues and that are focused on rural residents (rather than agriculture or development) are few. Industry-specific grants, especially related to agricultural, are more available, addressing a wide array of research topics, such as food, food production, industry generation, and so forth. Rural community development and policy-related funding are primarily focused on problems of poverty, isolation, and issues that give rise to future problems at the community, rather than family, level.

Summary and Future Directions

While the vast majority of land in the United States (97.5%) is considered rural, only 25% of the population resides there (Reynnells 2008). The demographic differences between urban and rural residents set the stage for the "rural does matter" story for rural families. Rural and urban family structures are quite similar. Rural and urban employment and unemployment rates are similar also. The rural population, however, is changing with the influx of more minorities, especially Hispanics, similar to urban populations. Differences emerge when we look at the support systems available to rural families. Fewer employment opportunities exist in rural areas, and the opportunities available often offer lower wages than might be found in urban areas. As a result, more rural families are in poverty as working poor families than urban families. Furthermore, because rural areas are quite distinct from one another, the employment options and wages will differ from one community to the next, resulting in wide variations in rates of unemployment and in poverty.

Many researchers have called for a renewed emphasis on interests such as education and training, support services for younger and older people and the places where they live rather than focusing on the social, economic, and environmental problems of rural communities. Many opportunities are available for conceptualization of how to study and understand the issues faced by rural people and their communities.

As we become more interested in the interaction between the community context and individual outcomes, we must have data on "how institutions and processes mediate the effects of living in rural areas..." (Weber et al. 2005, p. 406). We must be able to build on the rich history of others who studied rural communities and those who have studied rural families. A focus on the intersection of community and family across many disciplines of scholarship will help us understand the issues and strengths of rural low-income families.

Discussion Questions

1. What did you learn in this chapter regarding rural low-income families' lives within rural communities?
2. How do different rural community contexts influence rural low-income families' employment?

3. How do rural communities help rural low-income families to meet with their employmentneeds? What other policies would help rural low-income families facilitate employment?

References

Ames, B. D., Brosi, W. A., & Damiano-Teixeira, K. (2006). "I'm just glad my three jobs could be during the day": Women and work in rural community. *Family Relations, 55,* 119–131. doi:10.1111/j.1741-3729.2006.00361.x.

Bauer, J. W. (2004). *Basebook report: Rural Families Speak project.* http://www.ched.umn.edu/fsos/assets/centers/RuralFamiliesSpeak/pub.asp

Berry, A. A., Katras. M. J., Sano, Y., Lee, J., & Bauer, J. W. (2008). Job volatility of rural, low-income mothers: A mixed methods approach. *Journal of Family and Economic Issues, 29,* 5–22. doi:10.1007/s10834-007-9096-1.

Bradshaw, T. K. (2007). Theories of poverty and anti-poverty programs in community development. *Community Development, 38,* 7–25. doi:10.1080/15575330709490182.

Braun, B., Lawrence, F. C., Dyk, P. H., & Vandergriff-Avery, M. (2002). Southern rural family economic well-being in the context of public assistance. *Southern Rural Sociology, 18,* 259–295. http://www.ag.auburn.edu/auxiliary/srsa/pages/Articles/SRS%202002%2018%201%20259-293.pdf.

Brooks-Gunn, J., Duncan, G. J., & Aber, J. L. (Eds.). (1997). *Neighborhood poverty: Policy implications in studying neighborhoods.* New York: Sage.

Brown, D. L., & Swanson, L. E. (2003). Rural America enters in new millennium. In D. L. Brown & L. E. Swanson (Eds.), *Challenges for rural America in the twenty-first century* (pp. 1–15). University Park: Pennsylvania State University Press.

Butler, M. A., & Beale, C. L. (1994, September). *Rural-Urban Continuum codes for metro and nonmetro counties, 1993,* (Gov Pub A 93.44: AGES 9425). US Department of Agriculture, Economic Research Service.

Cotter, D. A. (2002). Poor people in poor places: Local opportunity structures and household poverty. *Rural Sociology, 67,* 534–555. doi:10.1111/j.1549-0831.2002.tb00118.x.

Cromartie, J., & Bucholtz, S. (2008). *Defining the "rural" in rural America.* http://www.ers.usda.gov/AmberWaves/June08/PDF/RuralAmerica.pdf.

Danziger, S. K., & Seefeldt, K. S. (2002). Barriers to employment and the "hard to serve": Implications for services, sanctions, and time limits. *Focus, 22,* 76–81. http://www.irp.wisc.edu/publications/focus/pdfs/foc221-part3.pdf#page=26.

Dolan, E. M., Seiling, S., & Glesner, T. (2006). Making it work: Rural low income women in service jobs. In B. J. Cude (Ed.), *Proceedings of the 33rd Conference of the Eastern Family Economics and Resource Management Association* (pp. 38–46). Knoxville. http://mrupured.myweb.uga.edu/conf/5.pdf.

Duncan, G. J., Whitener, L. A., & Weber, B. A. (2002). Lessons learned: Welfare reform and food assistance in rural America. In B. A. Weber, G. J. Duncan, & L. A. Whitener (Eds.), *Rural dimensions of welfare reform* (pp. 455–470). Kalamazoo: W. E. Upjohn Institute for Employment Research.

Dworsky, A., & Courtney, M. E. (2007). Barriers to employment among TANF applicants and their consequences for self-sufficiency. *Families in Society, 88,* 379–89. doi:10.1606/1044-3894.3647.

Elder, G. H., Jr., & Conger, R. D. (2000). *Children of the land: Adversity and success in rural America.* Chicago: University of Chicago Press.

Emery, M., & Flora, C. B. (2006). Spiraling up. *Community Development: Journal of Community Development Society, 37*(1), 19–35. http://www.highbeam.com/doc/1G1-146637132.html.

Flora, C. B., & Flora, J. L. (1993). Entrepreneurial social infrastructure: A necessary ingredient. *Annuals of the American Academy of Political and Social Science, 529,* 48–58. doi:10.1177/0 002716293529001005.

Flora, C. B., & Flora, J. L. (2003). Social capital. In D. L. Brown & L. E. Swanson (Eds.), *Challenges for rural America in the twenty-first century* (pp. 214–227). University Park: Pennsylvania State University Press.

Flora, J. L., Sharp, J., Flora, C. B., & Newlon, B. (1997). Entrepreneurial social infrastructure and locally initiated economic development in the nonmetropolitan United States. *Sociological Quarterly, 38,* 623–645. doi:10.1111/j.1533-8525.1997.tb00757.x.

Ghelfi, L. M., & Parker, T. S. (1995). *A new country-level measure of urban influence.* Rural Economy Division, Economic Research Service, US Department of Agriculture.

Gibbs, R., Kusmin, L., & Cromartie, J. (2005). *Low-skill employment and the changing economy of rural America.* http://www.ers.usda.gov/Publications/err10/err10_reportsummary.pdf.

Glasmeier, A., & Salant, P. (2006). *Low-skill workers in rural America face permanent job loss.* (Policy Brief No. 2). http://www.aecf.org/~/media/Pubs/Other/C/CarseyInstitutePolicy No2Spring2006LowSkilledW/Displaced_workers_March2006.pdf.

Hoyt, D. R., Conger, R. D., Valde, J. G., & Weihs, K. (1997). Psychological distress and help seeking in rural America. *American Journal of Community Psychology, 25,* 449–470. doi:10.1023/A:1024655521619.

Isserman, A. M., Feser, E., & Warren, D. E. (2009). Why some rural places prosper and others do not. *International Regional Science Review, 32,* 300–342. doi:10.1177/0160017609336090.

Kandel, W., & Cromartie, J. (2004). *New patterns of Hispanic settlement in rural America.* (Rural Development Research Report No. 99). http://www.ers.usda.gov/publications/rdrr99/rdrr99.pdf.

Kandel, W. A., & Parrado, E. A. (2006). Rural Hispanic population growth. In W. A. Kandel & D. L. Brown (Eds.), *Population change and rural society* (pp. 155–175). Dordrecht: Springer.

Katras, M. J., Zuiker, V. S., & Bauer, J. W. (2004). Private safety net: Childcare resources from the perspective of rural low-income families. *Family Relations, 53,* 201–209. doi:10.1111/j.0022-2445.2004.00010.x.

Krannich, R. S., & Petrzelka, P. (2003). Tourism and natural amenity development. In D. L. Brown & L. E. Swanson (Eds.), *Challenges for rural America in the twenty-first century* (pp. 190–199). University Park: Pennsylvania State University Press.

Lasley, P., & Hanson, M. (2003). The changing population of the Midwest: A reflection on opportunities. In N. Walzer (Ed.), *The American midwest: Managing change in rural transition* (pp. 16–37). Armonk: M. E. Sharpe.

Leatherman, J. C. (2003). The internet-based economy and rural economic competitiveness. In N. Walzer (Ed.), *The American midwest. Managing change in rural transition* (pp. 197–223). Armonk: M. E. Sharpe.

MacDonald, H., & Peters, A. H. (1996, October). *Distance and labor force participation: Implications for urban and rural women.* Paper session presented at the Second National Conference on Women's Travel Issues, Baltimore, MD.

MacTavish, K., & Salamon, S. (2003). What do rural families look like today? In D. L. Brown & L. E. Swanson (Eds.), *Challenges for rural America in the twenty-first century* (pp. 73–85). University Park: Pennsylvania State University Press.

Malecki, E. J. (1996). *Telecommunications technology and American rural development in the 21st century.* Paper session presented at the Tennessee Valley Authority Rural Studies Conference, Lexington, KY. http://www.rural.org/workshops/rural_telecom/.

McGranahan, D. (2003). How people make a living in rural America. In D. L. Brown & L. E. Sawnson (Eds.), *Challenges for rural America in the twenty-first century* (pp 135–151). University Park: Pennsylvania State University Press.

Monroe, P. A., Blalock, L. B., & Vlosky, R. P. (1999). Work opportunities in a non-traditional setting for women exiting welfare: A case study. *Journal of Family and Economic Issues, 20,* 35–57. doi:10.1023/A:1022115813706.

Nelson, M. K. (2005). *The social economy of single motherhood: Raising children in rural America.* New York: Routledge.

O'Hare, W., Manning, W., Porter, M., & Lyons, H. (2009). *Rural children are more likely to live in cohabitating-couple households* (Policy Brief No. 14). http://www.aecf.org/~/media/Pubs/Topics/Special%20Interest%20Areas/Rural%20Families/RuralChildrenAreMoreLikelyto LiveinCohabitatin/carseyinstitute.pdf.

Reynnells, L. (2008, September). *What is rural?* http://www.nal.usda.gov/ric/ricpubs/what_is_ rural.shtml#intro.

Ricketts, T. C., Johnson-Webb, K. D., & Taylor, P. (1998). *Definitions of rural: A handbook for health policy makers and researchers*. http://www.shepscenter.unc.edu/rural/pubs/report/ ruralit.pdf.

Snyder, A. R., & McLaughlin, D. K. (2004). Female-headed families and poverty in rural America. *Rural Sociology, 69*, 127–149. doi:10.1526/003601104322919937.

Son, S., & Bauer, J. W. (2010). Employed rural, low-income, single mothers' family and work over time. *Journal of Family and Economic Issues, 31*, 107–120. doi:10.1007/s10834-009-9173-8.

Stack, C. (1974). *All our kin: Strategies for survival in a black community*. New York: Harper & Row.

Struthers, C. B., & Bokemeier, J. L. (2000). Myths and realities of raising children and creating a family life in a rural county. *Journal of Family Issues, 21*, 17–46. doi:10.1177/019251300021001002.

Taylor, L. C. (2001). Work attitudes, employment barriers, and mental health symptoms in a sample of rural welfare recipients. *American Journal of Community Psychology, 29*, 443–463. doi:10.1023/A:1010323914202.

Thorne, D., Tickamyer, A., & Thorne, M. (2004). Poverty and income in Appalachia. *Journal of Appalachian Studies, 10*, 341–357.

Tickamyer, A., & Henderson, D. (2003). Rural women: New roles for the new century? In D. Brown & L. Swanson (Eds.), *Challenges for rural America in the twenty-first century* (pp. 109–117). University Park: Pennsylvania State University Press.

Tickamyer, A. R., & Tickamyer, C. H. (1988). Gender and poverty in Central Appalachia. *Social Science Quarterly, 69*, 874–891.

Urban, J. A., & Olson, P. N. (2005). A comprehensive employment model for low income mothers. *Journal of Family and Economic Issues, 26*, 101–122. doi:10.1007/s10834-004-1414-2.

US Census Bureau. (2000). American factfinder. http://factfinder.census.gov/home/saff/main. html.

US Department of Agriculture (2004a). *Measuring rurality: Rural-urban continuum codes*. http:// www.ers.usda.gov/Briefing/Rurality/RuralUrbCon/.

US Department of Agriculture. (2004b). *Rural poverty at a glance*. (Rural Development Research Report No. 100). http://www.ers.usda.gov/publications/rdrr100/rdrr100.pdf.

US Department of Agriculture. (2006). *Rural employment at a glance*. (Economic Information Bulletin No. 21). http://www.ers.usda.gov/publications/EIB21/EIB21.pdf.

US Department of Agriculture. (2007, August). *Measuring rurality: Urban influence codes*. http:// www.ers.usda.gov/Briefing/Rurality/urbaninf/.

US Department of Agriculture. (2007, September). *Rural definitions*. http://www.ers.usda.gov/ Data/RuralDefinitions/.

Walzer, N. (Ed.). (2003). *The American midwest: Managing change in rural transition*. Armonk: M. E. Sharpe.

Weber, B., & Jensen, L. (2004). *Poverty and place: A critical review of rural poverty literature*. (RPRC Working Paper No. 04-03). http://www.rupri.org/Forms/WP0403.pdf.

Weber, B., Jensen, L., Miller, K., Mosley, J., & Fischer, M. (2005). A critical review of rural poverty literature: Is there truly a rural effect? *International Regional Science Review, 28*, 381–414. doi:10.1177/0160017605278996.

Wells, B. (2002). Women's voices: Explaining poverty and plenty in a rural community. *Rural Sociology, 67*, 234–254. doi:10.1111/j.1549-0831.2002.tb00102.x.

Wimberley, R. C., & Morris, L. V. (1997). *The southern Black belt: A national perspective*. Lexington: TVA Rural Studies.

Chapter 4
Making Rural Employment Work

Elizabeth M. Dolan, Jean W. Bauer and Mary Jo Katras

Introduction

The purpose of this chapter is to set the stage for examining the employment is-sues of low-income rural families. Any number of studies have found that rural low-income residents have a strong work ethic, contradicting the general belief that low-income individuals do not want to work (e.g., Scott 2006; Stofferahn 2000). As addressed in Chap. 3, the rural economic situation is such that many rural residents have difficulty finding jobs that will pay wages high enough to keep their families financially self-sufficient.

Rural poverty rates have traditionally been higher than in urban areas, especially among single mothers (Porterfield 2001). While married couples are much less like-ly to be in poverty, rural married couples are more likely than urban couples to be poor (Lichter and Jensen 2000). Rural residents, even with their strong attachment to the labor force (Stofferahn 2000), are more likely than their urban counterparts to be among the working poor because the jobs that are available in rural areas are more likely to be low-wage jobs. Once an individual is employed in a low-wage job, research indicates that it is difficult to escape low-wage work, especially for women (e.g., Boushey et al. 2007; Jensen et al. 1999).

Jensen et al.'s (1999) examination of the incidence of underemployment (i.e., earning less than is needed to support one's family due to low wages, less than full-time hours, seasonal work, or a combination of these) revealed that rural workers were more likely than urban residents to slide into underemployment. Those who were single, widowed, or divorced/separated were more likely to become underem-ployed, and women were especially vulnerable. They also found that changes in the economy had less of an impact on rural workers than urban workers. In other words, rural workers were less likely to be hurt by a weakened economy but also less likely to be helped by a strengthening economy.

E. M. Dolan (✉)
Department of Family Studies, University of New Hampshire, 55 College Road, Durham, NH 03824, USA
e-mail: e.dolan@unh.edu

J. W. Bauer, E. M. Dolan (eds.), *Rural Families and Work,* International Series on Consumer Science 1,
DOI 10.1007/978-1-4614-0382-1_4, © Springer Science+Business Media, LLC 2011

Low-wage work is the mainstay of the economies of many rural communities. Women, whether rural or urban, are more apt to be low-wage earners than men (Kim 2000). This is especially true for those working in the retail and service industries. Furthermore, women who are low-wage earners are much less likely than others to receive any type of employee benefits, such as health insurance or sick days. Earning low wages, however, is only one factor that keeps employed rural residents among the working poor.

Single mothers did fare well during the robust economy of the 1990s and early 2000s, although their employment tended to be in the lowest paying industries. But the recession of 2001–2003 was hard on the employment prospects of single mothers, especially those who had less education, and those in the lowest paying industries suffered the greatest job losses (Boushey and Rosnick 2004; Levitan and Gluck 2003). Single mothers also experienced more bouts of unemployment and/ or periods of part-time employment than others (Mosisa 2003). McKernan et al. (2002) found that after welfare reform, employment rates of rural mothers were similar to those of urban mothers. Duncan et al. (2002) found that rural and urban mothers faced similar employment barriers. In a survey of urban women in 1995, almost all the women surveyed faced some sort of employment barrier, such as health issues, including depressive symptoms, or low educational attainment, but those who had more stable employment histories had fewer barriers (Polit et al. 2001). Rural mothers, however, still face barriers based on low population density, such as longer distances to services and fewer job options.

Previous research has shown that rural low-income women have similar characteristics and, therefore, share similar employment trajectories. Porterfield (2001), by using Survey of Income and Program Participation (SIPP) data, found that rural women whose family income had risen to above 150% of poverty had several common characteristics. Among other things, they worked more hours and had some post-high school education or training. College education, however, was not found to improve rural women's job and income prospects because of the lack of well-paying jobs. Rural mothers with young children appeared to have higher rates of employment than did their urban counterparts (Smith 2007). These rural mothers experienced low wages, resulting in higher rates of poverty.

Another characteristic of the working poor is the likelihood of working a nonstandard schedule (Acs et al. 2000). Nonstandard schedules include shifts that extend beyond the conventional 8:00 a.m. to 6:00 p.m. Monday through Friday schedule. Retail and hospitality industry businesses and small employers are more likely to use nonstandard work schedules and pay lower wages than larger employers in other industries. Prior research has found that nonstandard shift work has become increasingly common, especially in low-wage jobs and for female workers (Grosswald 2003; Joshi and Bogen 2007). Mothers who work nonstandard shifts may experience hardships as they strive to blend their employment and family responsibilities. "Shift-working women encounter more stress than their male peers because of the extra parental and spousal responsibilities women are usually expected to meet" (Grosswald 2003 p. 35). The combination of low wages and nonstandard scheduling results in high employee turnover rates (Andersson et al. 2003). Three-fourths of businesses paying low wages were found to experience 100% turnover rates on an annual basis, compared with a turnover rate of about 33% for higher wage paying businesses. Rural areas were found to have fewer high-wage paying firms than urban areas. Further, rural low-wage jobs are more likely to be less than full-time or part-year (e.g., seasonal) due to variability in demand (Jensen et al. 1999), and laid off workers are rarely eligible for unemployment benefits.

Jobs recently created in rural areas to replace industries that have moved out have been termed "bad jobs" (Fremstad et al. 2008; Kelly 2005). These are jobs in the service, retail, and hospitality industries that feature low pay, few job benefits, nonstandard hours, few opportunities for advancement, and little job security. The Center for Economic and Policy Research estimates, on the average, that 30% of all jobs in all states are bad jobs (Fremstad et al. 2008). Kelly (2005) termed these types of jobs as "brittle" because of the lack of flexibility in the working conditions which can result in rural mothers either quitting their jobs or being fired when they must be caretaker to a sick child or when transportation to work is unavailable. Seasonal jobs are either "feast or famine" because during the "high season," rural mothers may be required to work more than 40 hours per week with no overtime, yet during the "slow season," the workers may be relegated to only a few hours a week or laid off entirely (Kelly 2005). When rural residents are solely reliant on wages to support their families, variations in hours of work translate into substantial variations in take home pay (Jensen et al. 1999).

Job satisfaction is related to having some control over working conditions, including some flexibility to deal with family issues, working full-time, and having employer-sponsored health insurance (Scott 2006). Fewer rural respondents were satisfied with their jobs than urban respondents. Several studies have found that employers and managers themselves can have an impact on the ability of workers to maintain employment (e.g., Glass and Riley 1998). Supportive supervisors and coworkers and the flexibility to combine family and employment responsibilities have been found to be important.

Welfare Reform

The Personal Responsibility and Work Opportunity Reconciliation Act (PRWORA) of 1996 dramatically changed welfare policy. The federal entitlement system of cash assistance under Aid to Families with Dependent Children (AFDC) was eliminated, the Job Opportunities and Basic Skills (JOBS) training programs were ended, the Temporary Assistance for Needy Families (TANF) Block Grant was created, and states were allowed to design their own welfare programs within certain guidelines. Ironically, this welfare legislation did not contain specific rural provisions (US Department of Health and Human Services 2002). One of the fundamental changes enacted by the welfare reform legislation in 1996 was the requirement that most recipients of cash benefits were required to engage in work activities. Since the majority of mothers in the United States were employed, the rationale was that low-income mothers should also be employed. As a nation, however, we have mixed feelings about mothers' employment and specifically about the impact on the children (Hennessy 2009). While middle- and upper-income mothers are applauded for eschewing employment for child-raising, low-income mothers are viewed as lazy if they make this choice. Current public policy, however, does not allow welfare-reliant mothers the option to stay at home with their children. In interviews with urban low-income mothers in welfare-to-work programs, the mothers were concerned about the consequences of their employment on their children, just as higher income mothers were (Hennessy 2009). These interviews revealed that low-income mothers believed that staying home with their young children was the right thing to do and felt that women with young children should not be forced into the workplace but be allowed to choose to stay home if they desired (Hennessy 2009).

The outcomes for those leaving TANF have been examined extensively, especially among urban women. While TANF leavers either found jobs or had higher incomes compared to when they were receiving TANF, most were still earning low wages (Loprest 1999). TANF leavers were found to be employed primarily in the retail, hospitality, and clerical support sectors which pay low wages and offer little in terms of employee benefits (Scott 2006).

Much of the research on low-income families focused on the transition from welfare to work, and the obstacles faced by mothers as they endeavored to fulfill the work requirements for TANF. Weber et al. (2003) identified four major barriers for rural women moving from being welfare-dependent to being wage-dependent: Distance to job, lack of transportation resources, scarce social and educational resources, and few options for child care. Data have revealed that other variables also intervene in the ability to engage in labor force activities, variables such as family issues and concerns including health, as well as the employment environment.

Theoretical Frameworks

While Bronfenbrenner's family ecology framework (1986) is helpful in examining the many layered barriers and pathways to employment, other frameworks are also useful. Investments in human capital have long been viewed as a pathway to improving the ability to engage in labor force activities and improving wage rates. Berry et al. (2008) used human capital theory to frame their research questions. Skills are important in the employment marketplace since a more skilled worker is an asset to an employer. Kim (2000) and Monroe et al. (1999) have indicated that human capital (education and job training) are important factors for rural women in finding and keeping employment. Berry et al.'s results indicated that factors other than pure human capital were important to determining whether the Rural Families Speak (RFS) participants were employed continuously, intermittently, or not at all. Mammen et al.'s (2009) examination of labor force decisions was based in traditional economic theory, i.e., comparing the marginal utility of labor force engagement with that of leisure or the work/leisure trade-off. Their logistic regression models explained about one-third of the variance in the hours worked by the RFS mothers. The results highlighted several important factors. Jobs that provided health insurance and overtime benefits were more appealing, and the RFS mothers worked longer hours in these jobs. For rural mothers to enter the labor market, they needed support services, such as child care and transportation assistance, readily available.

Whereas lack of human capital can be a barrier to employment, other microsystem factors can also enter into the equation when investigating employment of rural low-income families. These include such things as the health of all family members and ages of children. Mesosystem variables such as the support of family and friends and the types of jobs available also are part of the dynamic. Dolan et al. (2008) used the Bauer et al. (2000) family economic functioning model to examine income-to-needs ratios to determine if families who left TANF were actually earning enough income to become financially self-sufficient (Bauer et al. 2000). The family economic functioning model is embedded in Bronfenbrenner's ecological theory—the supports that enable families to survive exist in multiple layers of the family and community environments. The family economic functioning framework mapped the dire situation of the majority of families included in the analysis. Moving off TANF did not mean that families were financially self-sufficient, nor did it mean that they were not reliant on other types of government supports. Families that did manage to improve their financial situation by and large were able to invest in their own human capital. Support systems were vitally important in enabling the families to survive especially during crises (Dolan et al. 2008).

Structural variables, such as local job market conditions, wage rates, and local unemployment rates are also important (Monroe et al. 1999) in addition to the family system variables. The Comprehensive Employment Model posited by Urban and Olson (2005) looks beyond human capital to the microsystem to predict employment. Press et al.'s (2005) model of self-sufficiency includes occupational and social obstacles to employment. Sano et al. (2010) used these two models together to further study the variables that examine the intermittent employment trajectories of the RFS mothers. They found that family circumstances, i.e., the microsystem variables, had more impact on RFS mothers' employment than did the individual characteristics. The community variables were also found to be of lesser importance.

The framework of work systems constructed by Herzenberg et al. (2000), based on the US labor market's organization of production and regulation of task performance in various occupations, has also been used (Dolan et al. 2006; Dolan et al. 2009a, b). This framework was useful in examining the phenomenon of rural low-income workers who are employed in jobs that often have the lowest pay, the least employee benefits, and the least amount of flexibility. Having some job flexibility allows parents to better mesh their work and family needs. Most of the jobs held by the RFS mothers and their spouses/partners fell into one of the first two work systems: Tightly constrained and unrationalized, labor-intensive. As described in Chap. 2, these types of jobs are low-skill, low-pay, with nonstandard shifts, and with few opportunities for advancement. RFS mothers experienced difficulties meshing their work and family lives.

RFS: How They Make It Work

The mothers interviewed for the RFS project often had characteristics which acted as barriers to employment. Health problems (their own health and that of their family members) and wanting to stay home with young children were the two reasons most frequently stated by a subsample of RFS mothers from the four eastern states who were never employed during the 3 years of interviews (Mammen and Dolan 2005).

Personal and family issues shaped the abilities of these single mothers and married couples to engage in the labor force. Building their human capital through education and training helped a number of participating mothers improve their financial conditions, even though they experienced setbacks. Personal and family concerns also kept some of these parents out of the labor force. Factors that Sano et al. (2010) found that predicted not being employed were having a young child, chronic health issues, and/or not having a car.

Mammen et al. (2009) focused on the low-income rural mothers' decisions to participate in the labor force. By using logistic regression to produce odd-ratios for each factor, they found that personal characteristics had a positive impact on the odds of being employed. Mothers who had driver's licenses, high school degrees, and child care assistance, and who were at less risk of clinical depression all had better odds of being employed than those who did not have licenses, had no child care assistance, had no high school degree, and were at greater risk for clinical depression. Also, having a spouse or partner who was employed increased the odds of the mother being employed. Having a high school degree helped to increase the odds of being employed over those without a degree, but having more than a high school degree did not change the odds of being employed. The factor that lessened the odds of being in the labor force was having income from another source, such as TANF or Supplemental Security Income (SSI). Mothers with employer-sponsored health insurance had increased odds of working more hours. The authors concluded that human capital factors were less important than other factors, and being employed may be tied to the types of jobs available in rural areas. Having a driver's license was a key factor enabling these low-income rural mothers to maintain employment. Employment of a spouse or partner had an interesting effect on the mother's employment. While increasing the odds of the mothers being employed, an employed spouse/partner reduced the number of hours the mother worked, relating to the desire to spend time raising children when possible. Health insurance was a factor in working longer hours and may be related to having to work full-time to qualify for insurance coverage (Mammen et al. 2009).

Wages and Employment

The employed RFS mothers were working primarily in the service industry (Table 4.1). Administrative support and laborers/helpers were the next largest em-

Table 4.1 RFS employed participants' mean wages and hours by industry

Employment type	Total N	Percent	Wages M (SD)	n	H Hours/week M (SD)	n
Administrative support						
Wave 1	37	12.0	$ 7.90 (2.03)	33	30.6 (10.6)	33
Wave 2	28	10.5	$ 8.98 (2.63)	26	33.2 (9.9)	25
Wave 3	14	7.4	$ 9.93 (3.02)	13	30.3 (13.2)	14
Construction						
Wave 1	–	–	–	–	–	–
Wave 2	2	0.8	$ 5.23 (7.39)	2	40	1
Wave 3	2	1.1	$13.03 (2.09)	2	55.0 (21.2)	2
Laborers and helpers						
Wave 1	38	12.3	$ 6.43 (1.55)	30	38.7 (14.2)	30
Wave 2	15	5.6	$ 6.88 (2.05)	12	37.7 (8.0)	15
Wave 3	15	7.9	$ 7.87 (1.13)	10	33.4 (11.3)	13
Management						
Wave 1	5	1.6	$ 3.87 (3.35)	3	38.8 (18.8)	4
Wave 2	5	1.9	$ 6.34 (1.85)	2	36.0 (16.8)	3
Wave 3	5	2.6	$ 8.28 (2.44)	4	32.9 (17.3)	4
Mechanics						
Wave 1	1	0.3	$ 9.80	1	–	–
Wave 2	–	–	–	–	–	–
Wave 3	–	–		–	–	–
Production						
Wave 1	13	4.2	$ 8.10 (1.29)	11	36.2 (10.8)	12
Wave2	10	3.8	$ 7.07 (1.26)	8	36.1 (8.2)	10
Wave 3	5	2.6	$14.75 (14.80)	5	40.8 (1.5)	4
Professional and technical						
Wave 1	7	2.3	$11.35 (4.16)	7	26.4 (13.6)	7
Wave 2	6	2.3	$13.43 (7.30)	6	31.9 (11.2)	6
Wave 3	8	4.2	$11.08 (3.52)	8	27.3 (15.3)	8
Sales						
Wave 1	16	5.2	$ 6.42 (1.53)	14	31.8 (7.4)	14
Wave 2	19	7.1	$18.39 (41.79)	15	30.4 (12.9)	17
Wave 3	11	5.8	$ 7.34 (2.06)	11	31.3 (7.2)	10
Service						
Wave 1	100	32.4	$ 6.46 (2.30)	88	29.2 (12.2)	86
Wave 2	87	32.7	$ 7.03 (2.65)	77	30.9 (11.8)	82
Wave 3	62	32.6	$ 8.09 (3.10)	54	29.4 (12.2)	54
Transportation						
Wave 1	1	0.3	$12.25	1	18.0	1
Wave 2	1	0.4	$12.25	1	18.0	1
Wave 3	1	0.5	$12.80	1	18.0	1

ployment categories. Wages, while averaging above the federal minimum wage ($5.15/hour from 1997 to 2006) were less than what would be needed to support a family. Only those rural mothers working in the professional/technical and trans- portation industries had mean wages above $10.00 per hour. The hours worked var- ied across the industries, but many of the mothers were working less than full-time (typically defined as working at least 35 hours per week).

Mean wages an hour for spouses/partners were higher by several dollars (Table 4.2), and the spouses/partners were employed in a wider range of industries. Those working as laborers or in sales or service jobs had the lowest mean hourly wages and averaged more hours per week than did the participants—the mean hours per week were all at or above full-time. The greatest proportion of partners was employed either as laborers/helpers or in the production industry.

Employment and TANF

Katras et al. (2009) sought to understand the factors that enabled the RFS mothers to transition off welfare versus the factors that kept them welfare dependent. Of all the working RFS families, about one-third (35.3%) had at some time received TANF benefits. Of the 62 mothers who had received TANF at some point during the three waves of interviews, only 11 were able to successfully transition off TANF and have income of at least 150% of poverty. Those who were successful in transitioning from welfare to work were more likely to be single, have fewer children, have a driver's license, have fewer depressive symptoms, receive more support from relatives, and have children with fewer health issues; that is, they had a combination of individual and microsystem factors that enhanced their employability. Those who were unable to transition off welfare typically had multiple barriers across multiple systems.

Maggie[1] is a good illustration of someone faced with the problems in the indi- vidual system and unable to transition from welfare to work during the interview period. Maggie was 35 years old at the first interview. Her older daughter was mar- ried with a toddler and her younger daughter (age 8) lived with her. Maggie had dropped out of high school when she was pregnant with her older daughter. At the second interview, she was considering getting her GED, and at the third interview she was enrolled in a GED program. Maggie did not work due to her disabilities which she described as her eyes and her nerves. Maggie's nerves made it difficult for her to do many things, including driving.

> I can't drive, it makes me too nervous. I go to Wal-Marts and I'll be so glad to get home. It's too many people. I can drive with my son-in-law and it scares me to death....I went to Wal-Mart Sunday and I was so glad to be home. I was a shakin'.

Drucilla's family is illustrative of how individual characteristics combine with fam- ily factors to influence employability. Drucilla, who was age 22 at the first inter-

---

[1] All names are pseudonyms.

Table 4.2 RFS employed partners' mean wages and hours by industry

Employment Type	Total N	Percent	Wages M (SD)	n	Hours/week M (SD)	n
Administrative support						
Wave 1	–	–	–	–	–	–
Wave 2	–	–	–	–	–	–
Wave 3	1	0.8	$10.40	1	40.0	1
Construction						
Wave 1	19	9.4	$11.81 (3.89)	12	44.8 (9.9)	12
Wave 2	7	7.6	$22.93 (10.94)	4	43.8 (4.8)	4
Wave 3	9	7.2	$14.13 (7.00)	7	43.3 (4.9)	7
Laborers and helpers						
Wave 1	62	30.7	$ 7.08 (2.44)	41	45.0 (13.7)	41
Wave 2	29	31.5	$ 9.58 (3.48)	22	49.2 (11.4)	22
Wave 3	24	19.2	$10.07 (2.86)	15	43.6 (5.9)	15
Management						
Wave 1	–	–	–	–	–	–
Wave 2	–	–	–	–	–	–
Wave 3	11	8.8	$11.22 (4.26)	7	48.9 (13.7)	7
Mechanics						
Wave 1	14	6.9	$ 9.44 (4.12)	13	45.3 (15.2)	13
Wave 2	7	7.6	$ 8.20 (2.28)	5	45.2 (14.7)	5
Wave 3	10	8.0	$ 8.80 (2.29)	9	39.8 (12.9)	9
Production						
Wave 1	47	23.3	$ 9.55 (2.52)	45	43.1 (6.3)	45
Wave 2	26	28.3	$ 9.72 (1.88)	21	43.9 (7.2)	21
Wave 3	27	21.6	$11.42 (2.99)	19	43.7 (7.8)	19
Professional and technical						
Wave 1	7	3.5	$15.60 (1.15)	3	45.0 (8.7)	3
Wave 2	3	3.3	–	–	–	–
Wave 3	9	7.2	$15.48 (4.22)	6	50.7 (17.4)	6
Sales						
Wave 1	8	4.0	$ 7.33 (1.48)	5	44.4 (8.8)	5
Wave 2	6	6.5	$ 8.47 (1.72)	5	40.3 (2.3)	5
Wave 3	7	5.6	$ 7.99 (1.77)	6	50.3 (23.4)	6
Service						
Wave 1	25	12.4	$ 7.51 (1.90)	19	40.9 (8.1)	19
Wave 2	8	8.7	$10.45 (2.56)	7	37.9 (3.7)	7
Wave 3	18	14.4	$10.64 (3.10)	13	37.1 (13.2)	13
Transportation						
Wave 1	19	9.4	$ 8.36 (3.37)	12	49.8 (18.5)	12
Wave 2	6	6.5	$ 9.78 (2.94)	6	54.2 (25.4)	6
Wave 3	9	7.2	$10.81 (2.68)	8	50.2 (13.1)	8

view, and her husband Wilfred both dropped out of high school to marry when she was pregnant with their first child, who was in kindergarten at the first interview. Her younger child was born with a brain injury, and he had several medical issues. Although Drucilla had worked while she was in high school, she was not employed during the three waves of interviews. Wilfred had worked in the lumber industry until a permanent back injury placed him on disability when he was a teenager. He often worked odd jobs for cash to supplement his disability income. Drucilla and her son both received SSI payments since she had been diagnosed with diabetes. When first interviewed, Drucilla and Wilfred had driver's licenses and had a car that was reasonably reliable. At the third interview, we discovered that Wilfred had lost his license due to a drunk-driving conviction, which limited his ability to earn extra income for the family (Katras et al. 2009).

One single mother, Jolene, whose situation was described in Dolan et al. (2008), was sanctioned off TANF. Jolene, an 18-year-old mother of a toddler and separated from her husband, often missed appointments with her case worker and was not able to fulfill the TANF work requirements because she did not have a reliable car, and the state would provide transportation assistance only if she was working. She worked sporadically at a small store within walking distance of her home, but understood that the owner did not have enough customers to hire her full-time. In Wave 3 Jolene said, *"I've got a car now. But it's not running. I just got to get help getting all the stuff fixed...I got to get a job first before I can get it all done."*

Health

Mental and physical health of family members were important factors for rural, low-income families as they sought to support their families. For many of the RFS families, personal crises were barriers to maintaining employment. For a few mothers, their own health became an issue. Taffy was a 27-year-old single mother with two young children who suffered from depression: *"I was terminated while I was in the hospital,...this one for depression, I had to end up having a nervous breakdown, and they admitted me right then and there? I wasn't allowed to call or anything."*

Flora was a 44-year-old single mother who had twins when she was 42. She was a recovering alcohol and cocaine addict, who also suffered from depression and had severe arthritis (Dolan et al. 2008). She had to give up her lucrative waitressing job for two part-time hostessing jobs due to the arthritis in her hips and had both hips replaced over the interview period. Flora was able to enroll in a Certified Nursing Assistant (CNA) program and get her certificate. Her father cosigned a loan for her so she could have a decent car, and her aunt helped with child care. Flora hoped that she could get a full-time CNA position, so she would not have to work two part-time jobs. When we talked with Flora the third time, she had suffered some setbacks. She had a car accident after she had been drinking, and the twins had been in the car with her. Both she and the children were injured. She lost her license and was in rehabilitation for several months, and her children were placed in foster care. The injuries she suffered in the accident exacerbated her physical problems and severely limited the types of jobs she would be able to do.

Because few of the tightly constrained or unrationalized, labor-intensive work system jobs (defined in Chap. 2) pay any employee benefits, health insurance coverage can be a challenge for these families. The cost of an individual family policy is prohibitively expensive, especially when a family member has an existing health issue. Brooke and Neil, a married couple with three children, provide a good example of a family struggling with the cost of health insurance. Brooke, age 43, worked two part-time jobs in town while Neil, age 45, farmed, even though he had several health conditions.

> ...(B)ut, there's no insurance. So, and that's probably our biggest...problem we're having is with health insurance. Um, my husband has his own insurance 'cause he's at high risk, so, he has no choice, and his went up to $450 a month and mine and the kids—our insurance company's pulling out of (the state), and so we're trying to find a new health insurance. ...Well, they said that they're pulling out at the end of year at the same time they raised it $150 amonth.... Well, even with my two part-time jobs, uh, my take home about covers the health insurance. And that's just awful to say that's all where it goes.

In Wave 3, Brooke mentioned that their health insurance premiums were $750 a month with a very high deductible.

Work and Family Balance

The types of jobs that low-income rural parents often have become burdensome when these parents, especially mothers, attempt to blend work and family life (Dolan et al. 2009a). For a few mothers, multiple jobs combined with nonstandard hours stretched their personal resources. Soliel, a 29-year-old mother with four children whose husband worked in a factory, was working as a disability technician and as a bartender at the time of our first interview. By the second interview, she had quit the bartending job:

> It was just too hard. I'd wake up the next day and not even spend any time with the kids 'cause I'm so tired. But you know, I wouldn't even wake up until noon, one o'clock, and then, it was hard. And then on Sundays, if I worked a Saturday, I'd have to go to work the next day. Now I just work 9:00 to 3:00 Monday through Friday, and I have the weekends off.

The strong sense of family influenced the desire and ability of many rural low-income mothers to participate in the labor force. Berry et al. (2008) found that those who worked intermittently had particular issues. For many, employment took a backseat to family, especially when a family member had a health problem, or when work and family issues collided. Oceana, for example, was a 23-year-old married mother of two, separated from her husband, and employed as a restaurant manager working 52 hours per week. She quit that job because:

> ...my job just takes too much of my time, and I hardly see my kids. I hardly spend any time with them. And so I figure I'll just get a part-time job and go to school...I'll struggle for a little bit, but, ...to better myself in the future.

Crises can impact the ability of the spouses/partners to maintain employment. For example, Brynn's husband Clark (Brynn age 27, Clark age 28, three boys) was in a car accident which left him unable to work for a couple of months (Dolan et al. 2008). Sue's (33 years old) fiancé, Quinlan (47 years old), was disabled. Sue had seven children from her prior marriage, two of whom lived with their father, and Sue and Quinlan had two children together. During the time of the first two interviews Quinlan was battling to get disability benefits. At the third interview, Sue had stopped working to take care of Quinlan: "...(B)ecause (of) Quinlan's health, and his doctor didn't feel he needed to be by himself so I stopped working...Quinlan was finally accepted for VA benefits, which meant I did not have to work" (Dolan et al. 2008).

When both spouses in a rural low-income family are employed in tightly constrained and/or unrationalized, labor-intensive work systems, the struggle to address family and work demands can be stressful. Dolan et al. (2009a, b) identified 35 couples who were employed in all three waves of interviews. Thirteen of the mothers and 17 of the spouses/partners were employed in tightly constrained work system jobs (such as food service or factory work), whereas 17 mothers and 14 spouses/partners were employed in unrationalized, labor-intensive work system jobs (such as child care, custodian, or truck driver). In only seven of the couples was one of them employed in a semiautonomous or high-skill autonomous job. The couples in the tightly constrained and unrationalized, labor-intensive types of jobs juggled working nonstandard shifts and multiple jobs with family life.

Work schedules often made family time scarce or required coordination of efforts. Marilyn, a 26-year-old married mother of two who did child care in her home, talked about why her husband, Ramsey (age 24), worked the hours that he did:

> He got a new job at...(the factory) and he works at night, midnights. He works 10:30 to 7:30 in the morning. And then he works with his dad from like 8–2 and then he comes home and goes to bed until the next night....He does not get much sleep, but we have benefits now. It is worth it to us...Ramsey's not around very much so that's hard, but I know that he has to do it in order to keep up with having money so...It's kind of a Catch 22... If he is here more, then we have less money and can't pay the bills and don't have insurance, but it would be nice if we could spend some more time together.

Chevonne, age 27, worked as a deli clerk, and her partner Sebastian, also age 27, drove a delivery truck, and they had two young children. Chevonne was accepting of their difficult schedules: "We don't, you know, get to spend as much time as we'd like to together, but we both understand we both have to work, so it's just something that we have to deal with."

Changing jobs was also used to find a better balance between work and family. Rafaela, a 45-year-old married mother of three, talked about her and her husband's problems working for different growers and the kinds of hours they needed to work. The first grower they worked for hired them for 8 weeks working only half days. Then,

> they called us from [company name] to work only at night from 5 p.m. to 3 a.m. in the morning. Then I couldn't make it because of the girl, because I was at home at 4, because you take time to punch out and then go to my house, I was at home around 4 and then the girl woke up very early...and with all this, I woke up with bad headaches...and then we started at B's and like this...we have been working like this.

Making Ends Meet

The low wages typical of the tightly constrained and unrationalized, labor-intensive work system jobs meant that many of the families we interviewed were struggling. Lynn and Liam were a young couple living together with their young son. Lynn, age 22, worked as a hospital registration clerk, and Liam, age 21, worked in a factory. Lynn was concerned about their financial situation:

> We just pay off bills and there is nothing left. Like last week I had to go to my mom's and she let me get some groceries from her house and she gave me some money to get some milk. By the time you pay the bills, there is just hardly nothing leftover. And I get paid every two weeks so if I have $40.00 bucks left, that's what I have for two weeks. If I need diapers or whatever, there is twenty bucks. And then there is the gas to get back and forth to work for those two weeks and it's gone.

Support

Support can come in several different forms. Being able to manage child care, having the help of family, and the ability to have some flexibility in one's employment situation all facilitated the ability of the RFS parents to manage employment.

Berry et al. (2008) examined job volatility in general and intermittent employment specifically, finding that those whose employment situation was stable had certain characteristics: Their employers allowed them some job flexibility which resulted in a high level of satisfaction, and they had strong support networks. Sano et al. (2010) also found social support as a critical variable to maintaining employment—mothers who had good child care were better able to maintain employment than others. One critical structural factor emerged: Employed mothers with understanding supervisors were better able to maintain employment.

When supervisors were tolerant about the struggles that their low-wage employees had with many aspects of life, and especially family life, the mothers were more able to successfully blend the two spheres. For example, Leandra, a 40-year-old divorced mother of two, described a particular situation:

> …they [employer] do more of a flex time…the little one [younger child] is going to the pumpkin farm for the first time, with Head Start, and I wanted to take off time to go to that…and they said "that's fine, if you want, you can work through your lunch and just add time on at the end, or…just come in like a half an hour early…"

Other mothers talked about the problems they had with schedules and how their supervisors helped or hindered their ability to deal with family issues. Comfort, a certified nursing assistant, and Dell, a mechanic, were married with three children. They ran into scheduling problems when Dell's job required that he stay late:

> In the wintertime when the [neighboring town] goes on snow watch, they need a mechanic there if they're out plowing in the middle of the night. And (Dell) did call, it was in January, I think it was…a couple different nights I had to call into work because he couldn't leave [neighboring town]. And I was working 11:00 to 7:00 at the time, and I just, there was no

way I could get my kids.... And there was no way I could get the kids anyplace to go to work. So I had to call in. [I: How did your supervisor react?] Actually, they were quite good about it. They completely understood.

Layla was not as fortunate as either Leandra or Comfort. Layla, who was 31 at the first interview and married, had been working in a hospital when one of her three children was hospitalized where she worked.

I got written up twice where I worked. I worked at Community Hospital, and when my son got sick he was a patient at Community Hospital. I spent the night, I spent all my time there with him, and they knew this, but they still wrote me up twice for missing work...when my son was sick and in the hospital. Not a very understanding hospital!

Lack of empathy and flexibility on the part of an employer can exacerbate the situation. Soliel experienced transportation problems at one point: *"She [supervisor] told me I had to...find another way to work or I had to take the time off. I walked or I rode my bike."* Several mothers quit their jobs because their supervisors were not tolerant of their need to care for family. When employment came up against the needs of family members, employment would give way to family needs. Eve was a 40-year-old divorced mother who worked as a cook. She had one son.

My little boy got sick and the Head Start teacher took him to the doctor and he had to take him to the hospital and the boss was really crummy about it....That is the first time I quit a job without giving them notice, but you know my kid comes first. He [boss] was not very understanding at all.

Emeline, a 28-year-old mother of two separated from her husband, quit her job in a delicatessen because she felt the demands of her family were more important:

My mother had to go into surgery. And...MacKenzie [daughter] was sick. She was on breathing treatments. And I called in and I told them that I wouldn't be there that day and that I did have to go to the hospital, my mother was having surgery, and they had a very bad attitude. And, I just I resigned...I left my job because my mother needed me and my kids needed me.

Tait was a 42-year-old diet technician in Wave 1, and her husband Theodore, age 39, was a police officer. Although Tait's manager did not hassle her about her family, he wanted her to work longer hours than she was willing to do, given that she was the mother of five. In the end, Tait decided that she needed to change jobs:

He [the manger] wanted me to give 110% of my time to my job, and I'm not saying you shouldn't do a good job, and you know, do the best you can, but I also think family's important. And he wanted me to work nights and weekends and with all of my kids, it's just (difficult).

In Wave 3, she became a licensed child care provider.

I'm home more for the kids. I don't have to worry about, 'Am I gonna get home before school's out?' 'Are they gonna let school out and I'm at work?' or... I don't have any of those worries, because I'm here, so if the school (is) out I'm (here).

Even those with more flexible jobs (semiautonomous) experienced the pull between job and family. Estela, a 30-year-old married mother of three who worked in a school resource center said:

It's been very hard...Sometimes I feel like a pressure at work, because I have to stay late for meetings, or go to trainings that I get off late, and I feel bad, because I know my kids are at home, and I'm not here to pick them up after school, or feed them when they get home... And I feel pressure that I should be home with my kids. You just got to attend the meetings, and that's part of your job description. That's all.

Child Care

Child care was a constant issue. Although child care is addressed more extensively in Chap. 7, the way that the RFS parents manage the care of their children along with their employment is important to understand. Oftentimes, a strong support system allowed these mothers to mesh work and family responsibilities.

Emiliana and Placido were a young married couple (both age 25) who had three young children. Emiliana's job with a real estate firm sometimes meant that she worked odd hours. Her mother and her aunt were her child care providers, especially for her two preschool aged children.

Rosa goes to the daycare. So she's there until 4:30 (when) my mom picks her up. ...My mom has a part-time job in the morning, so my aunt takes care of them in the morning. My aunt picks (my older daughter) up from kindergarten, and she takes care of her until my mom gets there...they're always wanted there. 'Cuz of course, it's their grandma...I've never had to worry about, oh, you know, 'my babysitter's gonna get mad 'cuz I haven't gone to go pick 'em up,' or nothing like that. 'Cuz grandma's always there.

A number of rural parents relied on extended family members to help out with child care, such as Zoe, a cashier, and her husband Willis, a forklift driver, both 28 at the first interview. Zoe's parents helped to care for their two sons, and Zoe was able to schedule her work hours when her father would be available. *"...I don't like the hours that I work, but I do that for my parents so that my dad doesn't have to have both the kids at the theatre with him in the morning."*

The problem of low wages could be off-set by having two jobs, but the cost of child care often meant that this was not a viable option, unless the extended family support system could help. Alexia, a 29-year-old married mother of two, was able to manage her two jobs in food service because she had free child care:

...Now my brother-in-law is here and he said that he would be able to watch the kids on the weekends. Before it would not benefit me to go and have to get a babysitter. It is enough with the money I earn at the (restaurant), but it really helps to get that extra money.

A strong support system can help in times of crisis. Jolie, a 24-year-old African-American single mother of two, had two auto accidents during the interview period and was severely injured in the second one. Even though she was working two jobs in the health care industry, neither offered her sick days or health insurance. Jolie had been earning enough from the two jobs to buy a house near her family. Her family helped her through her recovery by taking care of her two daughters and paying her mortgage (Dolan et al. 2008).

Comfort and Dell worked different shifts in order to minimize child care costs for their three children:

> ...I have to work evenings and weekends...and that's why I work the opposite shift as my husband, because he's home with the kids, I can't afford childcare and work too because I pay $5 an hour for my boys to be in childcare.

Working opposing shifts did minimize family time, however. Tait and Theodore worked opposite shifts to minimize child care costs for their five children:

> ...we have family time and...we work it so Theodore can stay home with the kids in the morning and I come home with them in the afternoon. Anything that needs to be done in the morning, he takes care of it, and in the afternoon I do.

For a few of the RFS mothers, the decision *not* to be employed was an economic one, especially if individual and family circumstances might make employment difficult to maintain. Jacquelyn had four daughters, was 33 years old and in the process of getting a divorce at the first interview; she stated: *"I could not possibly fit it* [employment] *in right now with four kids, and four kids with special needs and me needing a GED of my own."* Another mother, Elke, who was 23 and married with two children, explained:

> It does not pay for me to work because one of us would be just shelling out a bunch of money for day care, and it's just, it's not feasible, even though we could afford it but still, what's the point of one of us working just to pay day care?. (Mammen and Dolan 2005)

The value of family was strong among many of these mothers (Sano et al. 2010). Some mothers were able to make the choice to not be in the labor force, so that they could care for their children. Jeannette, 24 years old, married with two young children, could make this choice because her husband Garrick was able to earn enough to support their family:

> We manage okay. I had a good salary, but it was too high of a price to pay not being home at all. I didn't want someone else to raise my kids.... I am just happy to be with the kids, We'd rather do with less than have to rely on outside care.

Some mothers wanted more than just economic support from their partners when they too were employed. Liz, age 35, who married a man with several children, decided she needed to be blunt to get the help with the children and chores that she desired.

> The other day...Clifton and I were having a chat and I said, "You know, you come home from work and you take your boots off and you sit in the chair." I said, "It must be nice!" I said, "I come home, my shoes don't come off till nine o'clock at night, and I don't stop until everybody and everything is taken care of." I said, "It's time for you to contribute." He bathed the girls the other night. He did dishes while I was bowling last night. I'm like, "Thank you!"

Resources

Personal and community resources influence the ability of low-income rural families to maintain employment. Whether it is the resources that the community offers, or does not offer, or the general condition of the local economy, the mesosystem factors can make a difference in the ability to maintain employment. Community resources can contribute to the ability of individuals to develop and maintain their personal resources.

Contrary to public opinion of low-income women, the RFS mothers had a strong work ethic. "Bettering themselves" was a goal for a number of these mothers. Getting training or being in a degree program appeared to be the primary route that mothers took to improve their income earning ability. For mothers who were welfare-dependent, getting a training or degree program approved as a work experience, or being able to do the educational program along with working, was the exception (Dolan et al. 2008). Ruthanne, a divorced, 24-year-old mother of a young daughter, was enrolled in an education program at the local junior college as she completed her work requirements for TANF. She worried about not being able to find a job with wages that would lift her out of poverty:

> "I'm worried that people are only going to pay like $10 an hour, and I'm going to work from nine to five and I'm not going to be a good parent, and I'm still going to be poor." Her degree enabled her to find a job at above-poverty wages at Wave 3: "I just got a job, a good job in the public schools…Things are looking good…I will not be on welfare…I will make it. Mina [daughter] will not have to be on any kind of assistance if I have my say in it."

Jan, 30 years old and a single mother of one, was equally jubilant when she completed her dental hygiene degree and got a job:

> I was thrilled to have the help that I had. But at the same time, I couldn't wait to get off of it, and I did everything I could to get off of it as quickly as I could and not have to use it again…I was so happy [when she got her job]…I called them to tell them, you know. "Shut my case. Thank you very much. Thank you, thank you, for all your help. Goodbye."

The community can oftentimes be a resource for rural low-income working parents, but it can also sometimes be a problem. Sometimes the resources available in the community do not match the needs of the employed parents. Eve had child care challenges because of the hours that she worked: *"(The community) could upgrade their child care especially with someone like myself, I go into work at 6:00 a.m. and the day care center up town does not open until 6:00 a.m. So, you see what I'm saying, if they would open at 5:30, that would be great…"*

The type of employment options available in the community is a critical factor for low-income rural residents. Retail and hospitality industry jobs are often the most available, especially for those with little specialized training. One of the characteristics of the jobs in the tightly constrained and unrationalized, labor-intensive work systems is the irregularity and sometimes unpredictability of work schedules: Schedules and hours may change weekly, putting a burden on the family. For example, Shonda, 24 years old, worked as a cashier, and her husband Tarryl was a diet technician. They had two young children. At the first interview, Shonda was unhappy with her employment situation:

> Well, right now I'm working part-time. It's really whatever they give me…Sometimes they give me 40 (hours), sometimes they give me 20, sometimes they give me 25. Sometimes they don't even give me 20 a week…They've cut back hours. See, it's like in little spurts they give you so many hours, and then they cut back your hours so much.

Shonda had changed jobs at the second interview, working as an in-home aid for disabled persons. At the third interview, Shonda talked about their schedules and the impact on the family which had again become complicated as Tarryl was working third shift and had taken a second job as a custodian.

> It's hard…'cause sometimes I'm really tired if I have to get up early in the morning and go to work, or if I get off late at night or something like that. Being that my kids are in bed at 9:00, and they're up at 7,…and Tarryl, with him working overnight, I try to keep the kids kind of quiet for him, cause he has to work. It's hard,…just taking care of them. I do a good job, I think, but it's just hard.

Job loss and job changes are typical of low-income rural workers. About 25% of the intermittently employed RFS mothers suffered a job loss (Sano et al. 2010). Cirila, age 38, and Danel, age 35, were a fairly typical low-income married couple who worked hard to support their family. At the time of the first interview, neither Cirila nor Danel were working—Danel had been laid off but was going to begin a new job the next week. Since the youngest of their four children was 4 years old, Cirila felt that she should not work until he started school. At the second interview, Danel was working as a carpenter and earning good wages with a regular schedule, which Cirila liked. Between the second and third interviews they had moved to Texas, but they only stayed about 6 months as they felt the job opportunities were better in their home state. Danel had a new job, although he was not earning as much as before. Cirila was thinking about getting a job since their youngest child was starting school (Dolan et al. 2008).

Deferred Dreams The context of community and individual constraints came together when RFS participant mothers were asked what their ideal job would be. Seiling et al. (2005) reported on the ideal jobs of mothers who were working in the service industry. Many of these mothers dreamt of getting more education in order to obtain much better jobs in the future.

Careers in the health care field, such as nurse, medical technician or lab assistant, medical secretary, or dental assistant or hygienist were mentioned by many mothers. Other mothers dreamt of owning their own businesses, such as having a child care business, or becoming a lawyer, counselor, teacher, or marine biologist. Others were less specific in their dreams, such as wanting to work in an office environment, or they desired jobs with certain characteristics, such as working 8 a.m. to 5 p.m. Monday through Friday, getting benefits, and being paid enough to actually support their families. Only a few stated that they were currently working in their ideal jobs.

A few mothers stated that they were enrolled in training programs that would lead them to their ideal jobs. Some communities had educational services that would enable the mothers to pursue their dreams, but these mothers needed to be able to work education into their family schedules. For most, however, the ideal jobs were just dreams, with their ability to fulfill their dreams constrained by the lack of educational/training opportunities in their communities and the necessity to work to support their families.

Summary and Implications for Research

Employment does not necessarily result in financial self-sufficiency for low-income rural families. As was presented in this chapter, the road to stable employment could be bumpy and challenging. The RFS employed mothers and their spouses/partners worked, sometimes long hours, and struggled to make ends meet. Finding and maintaining employment often depended on the type of resources available to the individual and family within the community. The employment discussion in this chapter focused primarily on mother's employment patterns, options, constraints, and challenges. Future research on employment patterns for all family members would provide further insights to rural families and work. Is the employment pattern, i.e., type of jobs, hours, and benefits, the same for rural men as for rural women? Because the RFS data came solely from the mothers who were not always familiar with the details of the jobs held by their spouses/partners, interviewing mothers and fathers would provide a better picture of the stresses and strengths of rural low-income families.

We know that work varies for some families by the number of hours, weeks, or type of work available. We need more research to find out how this piecemeal work pattern influences the economic stability of the family. The confluence of rural location, nonstandard work hours, child care challenges, and low wages needs to be addressed directly. Communities and employers alike have a stake in identifying ways to facilitate how low-income rural mothers address this issue.

A goal of TANF is to move people from assistance to work. As we learned in Chap. 3, *place* does matter—rural areas are qualitatively different than urban areas. Rural low-income families face unique employment challenges, such as low wages, lack of job opportunities, and fewer resources such as child care and transportation, to help support employment. Across the board services that are successful in urban areas may not work in dispersed employment markets of rural areas. What type and level of assistance from TANF case workers will be successful for rural families on TANF?

Employment demands and family demands have received some attention in work–family research. Trying to meet the demands of family and employment can be a very complex game of "give and take." Do rural mothers have a larger conundrum than urban mothers? How does distance to work or working for employers that provide less flexibility in the work environment influence this work–family balance? The RFS project has begun the conversation around rural families' struggle with employment. Further research is needed to keep it going.

Discussion Questions

1. You are a policy maker. You have just been asked to draft new legislation that will help to support the employment of rural low-income families. List the components of your new legislation. Remember to be specific.

2. You are a job counselor in a rural social service office. A single mother with two young children comes to your office for help in finding a job. What resources will this mother need to help support her employment? How will she access these resources? What barriers may she face? How will she overcome these barriers?
3. Which theory or theories are most useful in the investigation of rural low-income families' employment? Are there other theories that could be used and how would these expand our understanding? Use the parts of the ecosystem framework (micro, meso, exo, and macro) to explain the factors that relate to employment for rural low-income mothers and their partners.
4. What are the factors that make it more difficult for rural parents to be employed or maintain employment?
5. What did you learn in this chapter that helps you understand the lived experience of rural low-income families?

Acknowledgment The authors would like to thank Ozgur Akbas and Laura Andrew, graduate students in Family Studies at the University of New Hampshire, for their work on compiling the data for the two tables.

References

Acs, G., Phillips, K. R., & McKenzie, D. (2000). Playing by the rules, but losing the game: American in low-income working families. In R. Kazis & M. S. Miller (Eds.), *Low-wage workers in the new economy* (pp. 21–44). Washington: Urban Institute.
Andersson, F., Holzer, H. J., & Lane, J. (2003, October). *Worker advancement in the low wage labor market: The importance of 'good jobs'.* http://brookings.edu/es/urban/publications/200310_Holzer.pdf.
Bauer, J. W., Braun, B., & Olson, P. D. (2000). Welfare to well-being framework for research, education, and outreach. *Journal of Consumer Affairs, 34*(1), 62–81. doi:10.1111/j.1745-6606.2000.tb00084.x.
Berry, A. A., Katras, M. J., Sano, Y., Lee, J., & Bauer, J. W. (2008). Job volatility of rural, low-income mothers: A mixed methods approach. *Journal of Family and Economic Issues, 29,* 5–22. doi:10.1007/s10834-007-9096-1.
Boushey, H., & Rosnick, D. (2004). *For welfare reform to work, jobs must be available.* http://www.cepr.net/documents/publications/welfare_reform_2004_04.pdf.
Boushey, H., Fremstad, S., Gragg, R., & Waller, M. (2007, March). *Understanding low-wage work in the United States.* http://www.inclusionist.org/files/lowwagework.pdf.
Bronfenbrenner, U. (1986). Ecology of the family as a context for human development: Research perspectives. *Developmental Psychology, 22,* 723–742. doi:10.1037/0012-1649.22.6.723.
Dolan, E. M., Seiling, S., & Glesner, T. (2006). Making it work: Rural low income women in service jobs. In B. J. Cude (Ed.), *Proceedings of the Eastern Family Economics and Resource Management Association Conference* (pp. 38–46). Knoxville. http://mrupured.myweb.uga.edu/conf/5.pdf.
Dolan, E. M., Braun, B., Katras, M. J., & Seiling, S. (2008). Getting off TANF: Experiences of rural mothers. *Families in Society, 89,* 456–465. doi:10.1606/1044-3894.3771.
Dolan, E. M., Seiling, S., & Harris, S. (2009a). Work constraints of rural, low-income mothers and their partners. *Consumer Interests Annual, 55,* 83–85. http://www.consumerinterests.org/2000-2009Proceedings.php.

Dolan, E. M., Seiling, S., & Harris, S. (2009b, November). *Rural, low-income dual earner parents—flexibility in work/family roles*. Poster session presented at the National Council on Family Relations 71st Annual Conference. Burlingame, CA.

Duncan, G. J., Whitener, L. A., & Weber, B. A. (2002). Lessons learned: Welfare reform and food assistance in rural America. In B. A. Weber, G. J. Duncan, & L. A. Whitener (Eds.), *Rural dimensions of welfare reform* (pp. 455–470). Kalamazoo: W. E. Upjohn Institute for Employment Research.

Fremstad, S., Ray, R., & Rho, H. J. (2008, May). *Working families and economic insecurity in the States: The role of job quality and work supports*. http://www.cepr.net/documents/publications/state_2008_05.pdf.

Glass, J. L., & Riley, L. (1998). Family responsive policies and employee retention following childbirth. *Social Forces, 76*, 1401–1435.

Grosswald B. (2003). Shift work and negative work-to-family spillover. *Journal of Sociology and Social Welfare, 30*(4), 31–56.

Hennessy, J. (2009). Choosing work and family: Poor and low-income mothers' work-family commitments. *Journal of Poverty, 13*, 152–172. doi:10.1080/10875540902841747.

Herzenberg, S. A., Alic, J. A., & Wial, H. (2000). Nonstandard employment and the structure of post industrial labor markets. In F. Carre, M. A. Ferber, L. Golden, & S. A. Herzenberg (Eds.), *Nonstandard work: The nature and challenges of changing employment arrangements* (pp. 399–426). Champaign: Industrial Relations Research Association.

Jensen, L., Findeis, J. L., Hsu, W.-L., & Schachter, J. P. (1999). Slipping into and out of underemployment: Another disadvantage for nonmetropolitan workers? *Rural Sociology, 64*, 417–438. doi:10.1111/j.1549-0831.1999.tb00360.x.

Joshi, P., & Bogen, K. (2007). Nonstandard schedules and young children's behavioral outcomes among working low-income families. *Journal of Marriage and Family, 69*, 139–156. doi:10.1111/j.1741-3727,206.0350x.

Katras, M. J., Dolan, E. M., Seiling, S. B., & Braun, B. (2009). The bumpy road off TANF for rural mothers. *Family Science Review, 14*(1). http://www.familyscienceassociation.org/archived%20journal%20articles/FSR_vol14_2008/1Mary%20Jo_Katras.pdf.

Kelly, E. B. (2005). Leaving and losing jobs: Resistance of rural low-income mothers. *Journal of Poverty, 9*, 83–103. doi:10.1300/J134v09n01_05.

Kim, M. (2000). Women paid low wages: Who they are and where they work. *Monthly Labor Review, 123*(9), 26–30. http://www.bls.gov/opub/mlr/2000/09/art3full.pdf.

Levitan, M., & Gluck, R. (2003, September). *Job market realities and federal welfare policy*. http://www.cssny.org/pubs/special/2003_09_fedwelfare.pdf.

Lichter, D. T., & Jensen, L. (2000). *Rural America in transition: Poverty and welfare at the turn of the 21st century*. (JCPR Working Paper No. 187). http://www.northwestern.edu/ipr/jcpr/workingpapers/wpfiles/Lichter-Jensen.PDF.

Loprest, P. (1999). *Families who left welfare: Who are they and how are they doing?* (Discussion Paper 99-0). http://www.urban.org/publications/310290.html.

Mammen, S., & Dolan, E. M. (2005). *Employment and obstacles to employment for rural, low-income mothers in the Northeast*. Paper session presented at the Rural Poverty in the Northeast: Strengthening the Regional Research Effort Conference, College Park, PA. http://nercrd.psu.edu/publications/rdppapers/rdp28.pdf.

Mammen, S., Lass, D., & Seiling, S. B. (2009). Labor force supply decisions of rural low-income mothers. *Journal of Family and Economic Issues, 30*, 67–79. doi:10.1007/s10834-008-9136-5.

McKernan, S. M., Lerman, R., Pindus, N., & Valente, J. (2002). The impact of welfare policy on the employment of single mothers living in rural and urban areas. In B. A. Weber, G. J. Duncan, & L. A. Whitener (Eds.), *Rural dimensions* (pp. 257–286). Kalamazoo: W. E. Upjohn Institute for Employment Research.

Monroe, P. A., Blalock, L., & Vlosky, R. (1999). Work opportunities in a non-traditional setting for women exiting welfare: A case study. *Journal of Family and Economic Issues, 20*, 35–60. doi:10.1023/A:1022115813706.

Mosisa, A. T. (2003) The working poor in 2001. *Monthly Labor Review, 126*(11), 13–19. http://www.bls.gov/opub/mlr/2003/11/art2full.pdf.

Polit, D. F., Widom, R., Edin, K., Bowie, S., London, A. S., Scott, E. K., & Valenzuela, A. (2001, November). *Is work enough? The experiences of current and former welfare mothers who work*. http://www.mdrc.org/Reports2001/UC-IsWorkEnough/IsWorkEnough.htm.

Porterfield, S. L. (2001). Economic vulnerability among rural single-mother families. *American Journal of Agricultural Economics, 83,* 1302–1311. doi:10.1111/0002-9092.00282.

Press, J., Johnson-Dias, J., & Fagan, J. (2005). Welfare status and child care as obstacles to full-time work for low-income mothers. *Journal of Women, Politics & Policy, 27*(3/4), 55–79. doi:10.1300/J501v27n03_05.

Sano, Y., Katras, M. J., Lee, J., Bauer, J. W., & Berry, A. A. (2010). Working towards sustained employment: A closer look on intermittent employment of rural low-income mothers. *Families in Society, 91*(4), 342–349. doi:10.1606/1044-3894.4039.

Scott, J. (2006). Job satisfaction among TANF leavers. *Journal of Sociology and Social Welfare, 33*(3), 127–149.

Seiling, S., Dolan, E. M., & Glesner, T. (2005, June). *Rural low-income women who work in service jobs tell about their lives*. Paper session presented at the Gender, Work and Organization 4th International Conference, Keele University, Staffordshire, UK.

Smith, K. (2007, Fall). *Employment rates higher among rural mothers than urban mothers*. (Fact Sheet No. 7). http://www.carseyinstitute.unh.edu/publications/FS_ruralmothers_07.pdf.

Stofferahn, C. W. (2000). Underemployment: Social fact or socially constructed reality? *Rural Sociology, 65,* 311–330. doi:10.1111/j.1549-0831.2000.tb00030.x.

Urban, J. A., & Olson, P. N. (2005). A comprehensive employment model for low-income mothers. *Journal of Family and Economic Issues, 26,* 101–122. doi:10.1007/s10834-004-1414-2.

US Department of Health & Human Services. (2002). *One department serving rural America: Rural task force report to the Secretary*. http://ask.hrso.gov/detail_materials.cfm?PropID=760.

Weber, B., Duncan, G., Whitener, L., & Miller, K. (2003, May). Still left behind, but gaining ground: Rural poverty in America. *Perspectives, 1*(1), 3–5. http://www.rupri.org/Forms/Perspectivesvol1n1.pdf.

Chapter 5
Physical Health, Food Security, and Economic Well-Being: The Rural Perspective

Yoshie Sano and Leslie N. Richards

Introduction

In the United States health and socioeconomic status are closely linked. Individuals with fewer economic resources experience higher rates of morbidity and mortality and are less likely to have access to and use health care services (Adler and Ostrove 1999; Kawachi et al. 1999; Sells and Blum 1996; Singh and Hiatt 2006; Williams 1990). Poverty is associated with a wide variety of increased health risks, including higher rates of heart disease, diabetes, obesity, hypertension, pulmonary disease, certain cancers, depression, and dental problems (Kawachi et al. 1999; Rank 2001; Seccombe 2007). Poverty has also been linked with a host of poor outcomes for children: Poorer physical health status, higher premature birth rates, lower birth weights, greater chance of prenatal exposure to alcohol and drugs, and higher likelihood of lead poisoning (McLoyd 1998; Rank 2001). Poor children paradoxically suffer higher rates of both food insecurity and obesity (Bronte-Tinkew et al. 2007), as well as higher levels of emotional and behavioral problems (McLoyd 1998) and teenage out-of-wedlock childbearing (Duncan and Brooks-Gunn 1997).

Geographical location also plays an important contextual role in family health and well-being. Rural areas present a different landscape to families than urban settings. In general, rural communities experience (a) weaker economies, meaning fewer and lower paying job opportunities, (b) more geographically disperse health care systems with fewer services being provided locally, and (c) unique social and cultural characteristics that may protect or exacerbate the health risks of certain residents. In this section, we briefly examine the impacts of weak economy and poverty in the rural context. Points (b) and (c) related to health in rural communities are addressed in the following section.

Per capita income is typically lower in rural communities than in urban areas, and rural residents are more likely to live below the poverty line. Economic disparities are especially great for minorities and children, with nearly 24% of minority chil-

Y. Sano (✉)
Department of Human Development, Washington State University, Vancouver, WA, USA
e-mail: yoshie_sano@vancouver.wsu.edu

J. W. Bauer, E. M. Dolan (eds.), *Rural Families and Work*, International Series on Consumer Science 1,
DOI 10.1007/978-1-4614-0382-1_5, © Springer Science+Business Media, LLC 2011

dren in rural areas living in poor families (National Rural Health Association 2010). Rural poverty is often more severe, more persistent, and less visible than urban poverty (Hirschl and Rank 1999; Marks et al. 1999; Rogers and Dagata 2000). Given this background, the recent decline in traditional industries such as timber, fishing, mining, and manufacturing represents a particularly troubling trend for rural communities. The higher rates of unemployment and underemployment mean lower enrollment in employer-provided private health insurance and greater reliance on public health insurance programs and an increase in the number of rural families with no health coverage at all, some despite their eligibility to receive public health insurance (US Department of Health and Human Services (USDHHS), National Advisory Committee on Rural Health 2002). Furthermore, rural residents' insurance coverage tends to be less comprehensive than their urban counterparts (Bailey 2009; Budetti et al. 1999), resulting in rural residents, on average, being responsible for a greater percentage of out-of-pocket medical expenses (Bailey et al. 2009).

The relationship between health and poverty may also work in the opposite direction, with poor health being a factor contributing to lower economic status. Health issues impacting the ability to maintain employment is a concern considering the current welfare policy, the Personal Responsibility and Work Opportunity Reconciliation Act (PRWORA) of 1996, which emphasizes transitioning to employment as a means of achieving self-sufficiency. Since passage of PRWORA, numerous studies have examined the potential obstacles that hinder individuals from transitioning to employment. These studies consistently indentify health issues of individuals and care of dependent family members with illnesses or special needs as barriers to achieving and maintaining full employment and, thereby, achieving economic self-sufficiency (Adler et al. 1999; Brunner 1997; Krieger 1999; Pincus 1994; Wilkinson 1997).

What Do We Know About Rural Health and Health Care?

Rural families are more likely to experience poor health than their urban counterparts (Hirschl and Rank 1999; Marks et al. 1999; Rogers and Dagata 2000). In fact, almost one in three adults living in rural areas report that their health is poor or fair, compared to urban counterparts (USDHHS, Agency for Healthcare Research and Quality n.d.). One reason for this regional disparity may be the changing demographic of rural communities. With the decline in employment opportunities in rural areas, many rural communities have seen *out*-migration of healthy, young adults to metropolitan areas and *in*-migration of older, less-healthy adults leaving urban areas to retire or settle in rural areas (National Organization of State Officers of Rural Health 2006). In many communities, this demographic shift has led to higher rates of chronic diseases such as arthritis, asthma, heart disease, diabetes, hypertension, and mental illness (Bailey 2009). The change in demographics alone does not entirely explain the poorer health found in rural communities, however. For example, obesity of both adults and children, which may serve as a general indicator of health given that it is associated with higher risk for a variety of other health issues including chronic disease, tends to be more prevalent in rural areas (McIntosh and Sobal 2004; Tai-Seale and Chandler 2003; US Department of Agriculture (USDA) 2009; Wright Morton et al. 2004). Thus, in addition to aging demographics, the general poorer health in rural areas can be attributed to a number of factors including weaker rural economies and lower wages leading to lower health insurance coverage, scarcity of reliable public transportation, fewer local health care services, and higher rates of food insecurity coupled with difficulty in accessing healthy food choices.

Access to Health Care Services

As previously mentioned, rural residents are less likely to be enrolled in employer-sponsored private insurance and more likely to be enrolled in public insurance, or to have no health insurance at all. Having health insurance that provides good coverage is one of the key factors determining whether a family will seek health care services. In addition, the type of health insurance can limit the choice of health service providers.

Availability of health care services, including dental and mental health, is more limited in rural areas, decreasing the likelihood that individuals will get preventative or timely care (USDHHS 2002; Wagenfeld et al. 1988). Approximately 25% of the US population live in a rural community, yet, less than 10% of physicians practice in rural areas (National Rural Health Association 2010). More than a third of rural Americans live in Health Care Professional Shortage Areas (HCPSA), of which nearly 82% are classified as medically underserved areas. The shortage of medical professionals in rural communities is predicted to worsen in the future for several reasons: Many rural doctors are reaching retirement age; fewer medical students are indicating an interest in primary care practice; more women are becoming physicians and they are less likely to practice in rural communities; and the high student debt load for a new physician means that rural practice is less financially feasible (Bailey 2009).

Many rural communities are too small to support specialists which means that patients have to choose between being treated by general practitioners (Jones et al. 2009) or traveling often substantial distances to receive specialist care at regional medical centers. Furthermore, long distances mean that travel costs are higher which leads to lower rates of follow-up care. Accessing appropriate healthcare may be particularly challenging for rural mothers and children because the number of obstetricians and pediatricians in rural communities lags far behind urban areas (O'Hare and Johnson 2004). In addition, vulnerable populations—and particularly at-risk groups, such as individuals requiring special treatments like HIV/AIDS patients or substance abusers—racial or ethnic minorities (especially those not fluent in English), and individuals with disabilities may encounter additional difficulties accessing needed services due to the lack of local service providers (USDHHS, Agency for Healthcare Research and Quality n.d.) or those who speak their language.

Health care providers in rural communities often operate under a great deal of stress. In addition to the shortage of doctors and nurses, the lack of both trained information technology (IT) professionals and broadband internet connectivity in rural communities can constrain adoption of time-saving and service-improving technologies like electronic health records, information sharing networks, and tele-medicine (Bailey 2009; Jones et al. 2009). The aging demographic of many rural communities means that a higher proportion of the population may be in poorer health, testing the capacity of the healthcare system. Lower rates of private insur-ance coverage, higher rates of public insurance coverage, and higher incidences of underinsured individuals in rural communities often mean lower reimbursements for services performed and higher reliance on expensive emergency room care in lieu of routine preventative care (Torres 2000). The resulting financial strain can prevent medical providers from making necessary investments in infrastructure and equipment.

Finally, in the context of a growing awareness of oral health as an important component of overall health and well-being, dental care for rural low-income resi-dents may be especially poor (Gamm et al. 2003). Rural residents are less likely to have dental insurance and/or fluorinated water supplies. Rural residents are more likely to have lost all their teeth or to have untreated dental decay, but are less likely to have visited a dentist in the last year than urban residents (National Organization of State Offices of Rural Health 2006). Low-income children have twice the rate of dental caries compared to higher income children, for example, 43% of Hispanic children have untreated dental caries compared to only 26% of White, non-Hispanic children (Fos and Hutchinson 2003). As with doctors, fewer dentists practice in rural areas and nearly 60% of rural counties are designated as dental shortage areas. Given the history of public health care cost controls, dentists in rural communi-ties may be unwilling to see patients with Medicaid or Medicare insurance (Bailey 2009).

Food Security and Health: The Hunger–Obesity Paradox

Obesity is particularly prevalent in rural areas and is closely related to food in-security (i.e., occasional or regular periods when a household is unable to access enough food to meet basic needs) and the availability of healthy food choices. Both hunger and obesity can have long-term adverse effects, especially on children and youth, sometimes leading to impaired cognitive abilities, inability to concentrate, behavioral problems, and difficulties in school (Center on Hunger and Poverty & Food Research and Action Center 2002). While obesity is found throughout the country, rural communities report especially high rates for both adults and chil-dren (McIntosh and Sobal 2004; Tai-Seale and Chandler 2003; USDA 2009; Wright Morton et al. 2004). Obesity is associated with higher rates of food insecurity in rural communities (Wright Morton et al. 2004), although counterintuitive on two counts. At first glance, food insecurity and obesity seem to lie on opposite ends of the spectrum. Yet in low-income populations, hunger and obesity coexist—a trend identified as the *hunger–obesity paradox* (Dietz 1995; Olson 1999). Second, high food insecurity in rural communities seems odd because, in general, many rural areas are food-producing regions.

In the first case, research indicates that families who experience food insecurity, when faced with the choice of reducing either the quality or quantity of food, often sacrifice quality before quantity (Radimer et al. 1992). In other words, families cut their food budgets by buying less expensive but more calorie-dense foods (Seccombe 2007). "Healthy" foods such as fresh fruits and vegetables may simply be too expensive, at least some of the time. Combined with the fact such foods may spoil easily, especially if a family is unable to go shopping frequently or lacks a reliable refrigerator, fresh foods may not be realistic choices. Hence, they purchase high carbohydrate and/or high fat foods such as bags of chips in lieu of the more expensive and healthier protein-rich foods.

Food choice is also related to the apparent paradox of high food insecurity in food-producing areas. Particularly challenging to rural families is the distance that they must travel to access a supermarket large enough to be stocked with a variety of fresh, healthy foods, including those produced locally. Areas that are more than ten miles from a supermarket have been described as *food deserts* or "areas where cheap nutritious food is virtually unobtainable" (Whitehead 1998, p. 189). In reality, a low-income, rural family without access to reliable transportation need not be ten miles from the grocery store to be living in what could be experienced as a food desert. Indeed, the 2009 USDA report, *Access to Affordable and Nutritious Food: Measuring and Understanding Food Deserts and Their Consequences,* notes that in small rural areas, lack of transportation infrastructure is the most defining characteristic of a food desert (compared to the racial segregation and income inequality found in urban food deserts). As a result, residents may rely on convenience stores or small local markets for their food based on proximity and not quality (Liese et al. 2007).

Other factors may also influence obesity in rural communities. These include changing employment patterns that mean fewer adults are employed in agriculture and other physically challenging occupations, strong social networks that reinforce unhealthy eating patterns, and lack of health education and fewer opportunities for physical activity in rural schools (Tai-Seale and Chandler 2003).

Impacts of Rural Community Social Structure

An individual's economic status may not simply be a function of the individual, but may also be influenced by the individual's social environment. A number of researchers have found that exposure to poverty in the neighborhood as well as in the home leads to poorer child outcomes (Duncan et al. 1998; Kerckhoff 1996; McLoyd 1998; Shonkoff and Phillips 2000). Social or cultural environment may also influence individuals in less obvious ways. In small towns, a strong social hierarchy may exist that results in a high level of trust and a sense that "everyone knows everyone." This structure is beneficial to families that are integrated into the social network (Elder and Conger 2000; Salamon 2003), but may serve as a barrier to those who have been effectively excluded (Duncan 1999). For rural, low-income or minority families who are perceptually "outside" of the supportive communi- ty, social stigmatization, as opposed to social integration, may be the daily reality (Duncan 1999; Fitchen 1981; MacTavish and Salamon 2006). Such a divided class structure hinders democratic processes, institutional support, and social, education- al, and economic options for rural low-income families (Duncan 1999) and helps to perpetuate the cycle of poverty (Wilson 1987). Thus, the health and well-being of low-income and minority individuals may depend on how the community as a whole integrates or excludes those individuals from community resources.

The Family Health and Illness Cycle Model

No single theory can provide a comprehensive understanding of family health, and many different theories can be applied to how families experience health and ill- ness. In an attempt to organize family health literature, Doherty (1991) proposed the Family Health and Illness Cycle model to describe the different aspects of families' experiences with illness. The model was based on a variety of family theories in- cluding family systems, stress and coping, and family development theories as well as symbolic interactionism and constructivism.

The Family Health and Illness Cycle model describes five domains of family health experience, all of which interact with a family's environments, includ- ing community resources and local health care systems. The first domain, *health promotion and risk reduction,* embraces a family's beliefs and behavior patterns that either promote or diminish health, including such things as dietary practices, exercise patterns, cigarette smoking, etc. The next domain, *vulnerability and dis- ease onset or relapse,* identifies events or family environments that influence susceptibility to illness such as stress level, amount of social support, and food security. The third domain, *illness appraisal,* encompasses a family's decision process regarding treatment of illness. These decisions occur in the context of availability, accessibility, and acceptability of health care options, including hav- ing quality health insurance coverage. The fourth domain, *acute response,* refers to a family's direct actions related to disease treatment. These actions are closely linked to the family's illness appraisal. The final domain, *adaptation to illness and recovery,* describes how a family adapts to the chronic illness or disability of a family member by reorganizing the family system. An example of such re- structuring would be a mother who decides to stop working and to stay home with child suffering from frequent ear infections. As described by Doherty (1991), the utility of the Family Health and Illness Cycle model lies in its use as a "beginner's map" (p. 2427) to help organize and understand the multifaceted findings related to family health.

Findings From the Rural Families Speak (RFS) Project

In recent years, one of the primary goals of research on low-income families has been to assess the impact of PRWORA enacted in 1996. In this context, one of the most important findings of the RFS project has been to demonstrate that the health challenges of family members interfere with the ability of low-income mothers to seek, obtain, and maintain employment, and ultimately to achieve self-sufficiency and improve their financial well-being. Here, we present the core findings of RFS research focusing on physical health and food insecurity of rural low-income families.

Mothers' Health and Employment in the RFS Sample

Based on 522 participants of Wave 1 (all three panels[1]) data, mothers reported zero to 22 health problems, with an average of 4.4 health problems per mother. Unemployed mothers ($n=271$) had significantly more health problems ($M=4.84$) than employed mothers ($n=251$, $M=3.83$) ($t=2.88$, df$=20$, $p<0.01$). The most common problems reported by mothers were migraines/headaches (40.6%), depression/anxiety (34.9%), tobacco use (33.7%), frequent colds/flu/sinus (30.6%), back problems (30.4%), and allergies (30.0%).

A similar pattern was observed when comparing chronic health problems of unemployed and employed mothers in Wave 1 of Panel 1. On average, mothers reported 1.7 chronic health problems including heart disease, high blood pressure, chronic pains, and arthritis (Dolan et al. 2005; Simmons and Braun 2005). Unemployed mothers reported an average of 1.9 chronic health problems while employed mothers reported an average of 1.4 chronic health problems (Simmons 2006). Simmons also reported that mothers with chronic health problems earned lower wages than those without such problems.

Approximately two-thirds of the mothers had partners. The partners reported fewer health problems, 2.6 problems per partner on average, than the mothers themselves. The most commonly reported health problems of partners differed slightly from those of mothers: Tobacco use (41.1%), back problems (23.3%), frequent colds/flu/sinus problems (23.2%), allergies (21.2%), and eye or vision problems (17.2%).

Analyzing interviews of 73 RFS mothers conducted in 1999 and 2000, Corson (2001) examined how health problems impacted economic self-sufficiency of the RFS sample. Corson found that poor health was both a direct and indirect barrier to employment, hindering job seeking and maintenance as well as efforts to gain

---

[1] Both Panel 3 states are included in this analysis.

education or training. The direct impact of health problems on ability to work is illustrated by Jane,[2] a White 25-year-old single mother of a 5-year-old son:

> I have multiple sclerosis [MS], and I get really tired if I'm working too long and it's just too much for me to sit there and get cramps in my neck. So that's not good for me to sit in there all the time…. Since I found out I had MS, I haven't worked full-time.

Another mother, Jenice, a White 31-year-old divorced mother of 6-year-old daughter, became unable to work after developing a seizure disorder:

> …I worked at a doctor's office…I was a receptionist. The only thing I did as a receptionist was to make appointments. So I was an appointment scheduler …. Started that in March of 1999 and I finished that in June of 1999. And that was due to…at the time I didn't know what was happening with my epilepsy and I was having brief memory losses and couldn't remember what day it was a lot of the times and so that really affected my job.

Poor health not only directly affects mothers' ability to work, but also indirectly impacts their potential to earn higher wages by limiting educational opportunities. Corson (2001) reported that mothers who had completed college or university had the fewest health issues, ranging from zero to two, while those with lower education suffered chronic illnesses such as asthma, allergies, diabetes, depression, etc. While the study did not examine the causal direction between poor health and lower education, the combination of poor health and lower education did appear to undermine the mothers' employability.

Children's Health and Mothers' Employment

RFS studies have consistently pointed out the importance of examining the impacts of children's health problems on mothers' ability to work (Berry et al. 2008; Corson 2001; Sano et al. 2010). Based on 522 families interviewed at Wave 1, we found that the average number of health problems of children reported by the mothers was 2.0 per child, with a range from zero to 16 problems. The most commonly reported issues were ear infections (27.6%), frequent colds/flu/sinus problems (22.6%), allergies (21.4%), asthma (13.1%), head lice (12.3%), eye or vision problems (12.0%), and behavior problems (10.5%). No significant differences were found in the number of child health problems between children with employed mothers and those with unemployed mothers.

The lack of statistical differences in the number of overall health problems of children, however, masks the challenges faced by families that have to manage serious health problems of their children. Obviously, having a child with a serious health problem is much more challenging than having a child with a few minor issues. This point is aptly illustrated by Corson's qualitative analysis (2001). Ingrid was a White, unmarried teenage mother of 1-year-old son. She talked about her son's respiratory complications immediately following his birth:

---

[2] All names are pseudonyms.

He started having problems. He was in the hospital a lot. We constantly got air-flighted to (the hospital). He's had a respirator down in with the feeding tube with things on him. He's had to be paralyzed for like a week so he couldn't pull the tube out. I mean he's gone through a lot of health problems and medical problems. You know, being in the hospitals and everything. It seems like every other week we were in there for a couple of days because of his breathing or just different things.

Now in his early childhood, Ingrid felt *"his breathing has gotten better"* but managing her son's condition was a daunting task for her. Ingrid needed to constantly carry a nebulizer, an instrument that forces medication into air passages through a fine mist to enable easier breathing. Ingrid shared:

You've got the medicine you've got to carry around. You have to remember to give him one in the morning, one at night. You have to watch out because if he does have problem breathing, you have to watch his chest...and I have to be there, because at his daycare, I can't even leave the building...I have to be there in case something happens, they won't do it. I have to be around there twenty-four, seven, because not a lot of people will take the time to learn that to do it for him. He, most of the time, has to be with me.

Ingrid's ambition to complete her GED and become a nurse had to be put on hold due to her son's medical condition. Finding a place to work while meeting the medical needs of her son would obviously be extremely difficult for her.

Even "minor" health problems can discourage mothers from seeking employment. For example, Kiersten, a White teenage mother who lived with her partner and 2-year-old daughter, found that she had to quit her job as a cashier at a local grocery store after her daughter started to get ear infections, because *"it started being a hassle with Julianna* [daughter]...*I had found where she was constantly getting ear infections, and I had to keep taking the time off from work, and it just got to be kind of a hassle."* Missing work to take care of children's health issues was a common emergent theme across many RFS studies. Previous studies identified flexible work environments that allowed for accommodation of family needs as a key factor for low-income mothers to be able to maintain employment (Berry et al. 2008; Sano et al. 2010).

Sadira, a 31-year-old single-mother of two children, was one of the few mothers who had an understanding employer. She worked for a church as a part-time employee and described how her employer's flexibility allowed her to get through a difficult financial situation:

My daughter was in the hospital for Christmas. She was back in the hospital in January. She had surgery. And actually she just got out of the hospital about two weeks ago [the interview was conducted in the middle of April]. So actually I have been off all that time. (My employer) didn't take away any of my pay. Which he could have, but he didn't. It was during the process that we were moving from (neighboring state). So the Medicaid had run out, and I had to go and reapply here, but I hadn't yet. So I took her to (the hospital). She was there for like 14 days. So when they discharged her, I still didn't have the medication. So I had all this medicine, about like $300 worth of prescriptions, and I didn't have insurance or Medicaid to pay for it. So, but because they didn't deduct from my salary, I was able to buy the medicine. Of course Medicaid is going to reimburse me, but they did not take anything away from me. I mean I was out a long time.

Children's health problems not only create obstacles for mothers' employment, they also interfere with the children's own education. Among 730 children for whom we

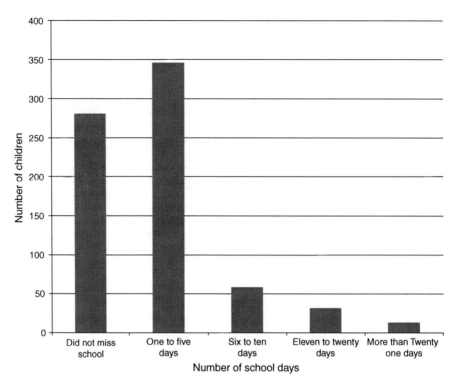

Fig. 5.1 Number of school days missed by RFS children

had data, students missed an average of three school days due to an illness or injury over the preceding year, with a range from zero to 60 days. Many children (38.4%) did not miss school at all and almost half (47.4%) only missed school between 1 to 5 days. On the other hand, 58 children (7.9%) missed between 6 and 10 days of school, 32 children (4.4%) missed between 11 and 20 days of school, and 13 children (1.8%) missed more than 21 days (Fig. 5.1). Excessive absence represents a serious disruption of a child's learning process and is a significant obstacle to the achievement of educational goals, which might prevent them from attaining reasonably well-paying jobs and possibly trap them in the cycle of generational poverty.

Oral Health

In American society, having good teeth and proper dental care is important to moving up the social ladder and obtaining higher-paying jobs (Simpler 2006). In addition, there is a growing recognition that oral health is as important as other health issues. Yet, oral health tends to be a low priority for many low-income families and dental coverage in public insurance schemes remains limited. In the RFS study, just over half of the mothers (53.9%) reported seeing a dentist in the previous year, and even fewer of their partners saw a dentist (44.0%). With respect to children in this sample, mothers reported that 55.7% had seen a dentist during the previous year. Among those children who had *not* seen a dentist in the previous year, 69.7% had *never* been to a dentist.

Simpson (2007) identified factors which contributed to the likelihood of seeking preventative dental care and treatment. Employed mothers were significantly more likely to have seen a dentist within the past year, and having high school diploma and some further education significantly increased the number of dental visits. Although no significant differences were identified by income of mothers who had seen a dentist in the previous year and those who had not (Simmons 2006), the following statements clearly indicate the linkage between the two. Belle was a 21-year-old White married mother of two children. She stated, *"We either say, do we pay our rent and have a roof over our heads? Or do we go out and get our teeth checked."* Similarly, Madeline, a White, 38-year-old, three children, cohabiting with partner, commented, *"Well, paying for dental care for me, I mean, the kids wasn't an issue because they've got Medicaid. But I need a dentist. I need it bad and I've got no money."*

One Appalachian mother, Jessalyn, also shared her frustration with the lack of dental coverage by the current welfare system. Jessalyn was a White, 37-year-old mother of four children. She stated,

> For me, I'm not satisfied in it because I think the welfare system should have a thing, especially for people, you know, that can't get the money to pay for dental work and stuff like that. I think they ought to have something, in that category. (Tatum 2006)

Access to Health Care

Both health insurance and availability of transportation play heavily into the decision of families to seek heath care services (Kim et al. 2003). The importance of health insurance is, of course, not surprising. The fact that transportation emerged as a determining factor reveals the underlying structural issue of the scarcity of local health care providers, although the RFS participants obviously do not frame their concerns in those terms. The study further revealed that having a history of emotional, physical, or sexual abuse significantly decreased the number of doctor visits, illustrating that the decision whether or not to access health care services can be complex.

Health and Dental Insurance Various RFS studies confirmed that the key determinants of accessing health care services are the presence and quality of insurance and the cost of health care (Corson 2001; Guyer 2003; Simmons and Braun 2005; Tatum 2006). Table 5.1 shows health insurance coverage by race/ethnicity of the RFS sample. Overall, 66.1% of the RFS mothers had health insurance, with two-thirds of those covered by either Medicaid or similar state insurance plans. Just over half of the mothers (51.7%) had dental insurance, with approximately three-quarters of them covered by either Medicaid or their state insurance plan. Partners' insurance coverage was even lower with only 59.6% having health insurance and 39.2% hav-

Table 5.1 Insurance Status by Race/Ethnicity ($N=518$[a])

Variables	Non-His-panic White ($n=320$) %	Hispanic/ Latino ($n=119$) %	African American ($n=37$) %	Native American ($n=26$) %	Others[b] ($n=6$) %	Total ($N=518$)%
Mothers ($N=518$)						
Health Insurance						
Yes	74.8	41.1	66.7	75.0	68.8	66.1
No	25.8	58.9	33.3	25.0	31.2	33.9
Dental Insurance						
Yes	60.1	29.4	51.5	33.3	56.3	51.7
No	39.9	70.6	48.5	66.7	43.7	48.3
Partners ($N=322$)						
Health Insurance						
Yes	61.8	41.2	64.3	62.5	100.0	56.9
No	38.2	58.8	35.7	25.0	0.0	43.1
Dental Insurance						
Yes	45.0	24.2	61.5	Not asked	54.5	39.2
No	55.0	75.8	38.5	Not asked	45.5	60.8
Children ($N=1227$[c])						
Health Insurance						
Yes	96.6	74.8	94.6	61.5	100.0	89.7
No	3.4	25.2	5.4	38.5	0.0	10.3
Dental Insurance						
Yes	83.1	63.0	91.9	19.2	86.7	75.9
No	16.9	37.0	8.1	80.8	13.3	24.1

Note: [a]Among 522 sample of Wave 1 data, four cases did not report their race/ethnicity
[b]Others include Asian, multi-racial, and other race/ethnicity
[c]Four children did not report race/ethnicity

ing dental insurance. Children were more likely to have health and dental insurance coverage than their parents. Among the 89.7% of children with health insurance, approximately 80% were covered by public health insurance (Medicaid or State Children's Health Insurance Program aka SCHIP). The majority of children (75.9%) also had dental insurance, mostly provided through public health insurance plans.

The anxiety felt by mothers without health insurance is succinctly articulated by Belle (Guyer 2003):

> My kids, I know, they're covered, health insurance-wise. But mainly it's hard for me and my husband. Because there are times when I am not able to go to the doctor just because we couldn't afford it. I think that's the hardest part, not having us covered because I worry that what if something happens to me or to my husband. If we go to the doctor we could end up with some outrageous bill. That would put us much more behind.

Often, not having health insurance is not a matter of a lack of availability of health insurance but a choice based on cost. Corson (2001) reported that many of low-income families chose not to carry insurance because they felt the cost of premium was "way too high" as indicated by Pearl's (a White, 28-year-old, married mother of one child) comment: *"...We don't even mess with insurance...We don't even go to the doctor's. Nope... 'Cause I depend on every penny I get."*

Even for families with health insurance, high co-payments were a serious concern (Corson 2001). For example, Lina, a 31-year-old, multiracial, married mother of three children, had a $45.00 co-payment to see her doctor, making her frustrated.

> Yeah, that's why we don't go…I mean unless, it's you know, an emergency…I mean like I was just, I went a couple months ago. And that's just because I had a sinus infection…. And I just, it would not go away. I mean I had it for like two weeks, and my husband goes, "Just to go to doctor." And I'm like, "But that's $45!"

Many children are covered by either Medicaid or State Children's Health Insurance Program (SCHIP), which was seen as a great help by low-income families. Magdalena (multiracial, 27-year-old, married with four children) spoke about the benefits of public insurance for her children, known as Healthy Families in her state:

> …(M)y employer would provide them insurance, but I would be paying like $72 a pay period…it adds up…my sister-in-law that has five kids introduced me to Healthy Families. So it was really a difference…I'm paying $14 a month, versus $72 a pay period…. And then I just have $5 co-pays…I mean, like with (my daughter) being sick yesterday, it would have cost me an easy—'cause they gave her penicillin shots—I'd say over a $100 visit. And with (my son) being sick this morning. I am now going to go to the pharmacy, because his prescriptions, and it's only $5.00.

Service Availability Even with Medicaid or SCHIP, rural low-income families may face challenges accessing care. Many RFS mothers spoke to the issue of doctors or dentists not accepting public health insurance. For example, Audra was a White, 40-year-old single mother of four children. She reported that

> unfortunately, (the doctor's office) sent a letter saying he was not going to accept any patients with that health program anymore. He was losing too much money. So, after all these years, you know, we've known him for…for five years. (Tatum 2006)

Guyer (2003) further elaborated how the lack of local health care providers accepting public health insurance caused mothers to travel great distances to receive routine care, as described by Keri, a Native American, 32-year-old married mother of four children:

> So I'm gonna have to be travelin' to Garden Valley and with one income, the price of gas, the way it is right now, I mean, you almost need a bank loan to get gas. You know, I'm gonna have to travel to Springfield to take my kids to the dentist and then there's no guarantee that the dentist is going to be able to see all four of them.

Other mothers spoke about the lack of specialists in rural communities. Harriet, a White, 31-year-old married mother of one child, stated:

> Being a little bit isolated from some of the benefits of the bigger city. Like, with my daughter's surgery, we had to drive clear to [nearest large city] and stay there while she had her surgery. Just not having instant access to specialists and that kind of thing.

Similarly, Eve (White, 39-year-old divorced mother of one child) shared:

> … (A)nd the medical care…his pediatrician is in Pleasantville and with gas prices you have to run to…because I have him a pediatrician because he has asthma. And it's hard when you have to run up there, but we pretty much have his asthma under control, I hope.

As evident in the previous comments, the availability of health care is closely intertwined with the issue of transportation. Similar to Kim et al. (2003), Guyer (2003) provided further evidence of the importance of transportation in seeking medical care. Maxine (White, 21-year-old, married with two children) stated:

> At first, I was getting people to take me, but then it got where they wouldn't take me any-more. So I heard about the Medivan and they've taken me over there. Usually somebody else with appointments goes with you and you have to wait for hours after they're out… you've got to walk the floors of the clinic to keep them [children] quiet. You've got to make sure you bring enough stuff to last you all day, 'cause you may be there all day, even if your appointment is only one hour.

Maxine's comment is particularly revealing because it clearly illustrates that having transportation assistance makes it easier for families to access health care, but also presents different challenges for the mother. For many mothers, taking time off from work to visit the doctor or to take their children to a doctor's appointment directly translated into a decrease in income and, potentially, the loss of a job.

Racial Disparities Between Non-Hispanic White and Hispanic Families

Data in Table 5.1 illustrate significant disparities in health and dental insurance status among racial/ethnic groups. Hispanic/Latino adults had the lowest insurance coverage compared to all other racial/ethnic groups. While health and dental insurance coverage for non-Hispanic White mothers were 74.8% and 60.1%, respectively, insurance coverage of Hispanic mothers was only 41.1% and 29.4%, respectively. Hispanic children were also less likely to be covered by health and dental insurance (74.8% health and 63.0% dental) compared to non-Hispanic White children (96.6% and 83.1%, respectively), although those percentages were still significantly higher than for Native American children (61.5% and 19.2%, respectively).

Tatum (2006) examined racial/ethnic differences related to health of the RFS sample, focusing on non-Hispanic White and Hispanic families. Neither race/ethnicity alone nor the interaction of race and insurance status predicted the number of doctor visits. Having insurance alone, however, contributed significantly to a higher number of doctor visits. Thus, for Hispanic adults and children, the lower likelihood of seeking preventative and medical treatment was related only to their significantly lower insurance coverage.

Interestingly, Tatum (2006) also discovered that the health status of Hispanic individuals was generally better than that of non-Hispanic White individuals. The average number of health problems of non-Hispanic White mothers was 5.8, while that of Hispanic mothers was 3.7. Significant differences were also found for specific health problems with non-Hispanic White mothers having a higher incidence in each case: 45% of non-Hispanic Whites vs. 2% of Hispanics used tobacco; 37% of non-Hispanic Whites vs. 7% of Hispanics had joint problems; 25% of non-Hispanic Whites vs. 7% of Hispanics had asthma; and 38% of non-Hispanic Whites vs. 20% Hispanics indicated fatigue. Similar differences were observed for the partners and children of the non-Hispanic White and Hispanic mothers. By comparing non-Hispanic White children and Hispanic children, significant differences were found in asthma (18% vs. 6%), anger management (18% vs. 6%), and migraines/headaches (13% vs. 2%). The better self-reported health status of Hispanic families may be the result of a selection bias, since many of the RFS Hispanic families were immigrants who came to the United States to engage in physical work. Having good health may have been a prerequisite for immigrating to the United States.

Despite their better health, Hispanic families face challenges in continuity of health care and communication with health care providers due to the language barrier. Tatum (2006) reported that both Hispanic adults and children were less likely than their non-Hispanic White counterparts to have a regular doctor. Individualized preventative care can be promoted by receiving continuous care by the same doctor; however, this can be particularly challenging for non-English-speaking individuals. In Tatum's study, Genoveva (Hispanic, 28-year-old married mother with five children) shared her frustrations in dealing with a translator who was not fluent in both English and Spanish: *"... (H)ere there is someone that speaks a little Spanish, and that person translates what they tell us and at times it's not the same... "* With the immigrant population an increasing proportion of the rural US population, the ability of the health care delivery system to accommodate non-English-speaking patients becomes a progressively more important factor in the promotion and maintenance of the health of rural families.

Health and Food Insecurity

Food insecurity is recognized as one of the core indicators of the nutritional state of family (Olson 2006) and functions as both a cause and consequences of an individual's health status. The USDA considers a household as being food insecure if the household experiences regular or irregular periods of time during which the family is unable to acquire enough food for all household members because of insufficient money and other resources (Nord et al. 2008). Olson (2006) looked at 316 RFS families, finding that 49.1% were considered food insecure in 1999–2000. Paradoxically, families in more affluent states experienced more persistent food insecurity than those in less affluent states, partly due to the relatively higher costs of living in those states (Mammen et al. 2009).

Factors Contributing to Food Insecurity Various RFS studies demonstrated that food insecurity is not simply the result of a lack of income. Olson (2006) identified protective factors (i.e., higher food and financial management skills, home ownership) and risk factors (i.e., maternal depression, racial/ethnic minority status, and difficulty paying for medical expenses) related to food insecurity. A particularly noteworthy association was that of food insecurity with medical expenses. Food insecure families tended to have more health problems than food secure families, and they usually had to spend money out-of-pocket to pay for medical bills, taking needed cash away from food purchases (Olson 2006).

Cultural factors can also lead to food insecurity. These include strong family obligations, lack of community acceptance, and federal immigration policies which prevent immigrant families from seeking public assistance. For example, Sano et al. (2011) found that among Hispanic immigrant families, having strong ties to their families of origin served as both protective and risk factors for Hispanic families. Extended family members provide instrumental and emotional support to their families. In return, family members, whether financially successful or not, are expected to provide financial and material assistance to other family members in the United States or back home. For example, Alexia reported food insecurity across three waves. Alexia was a 27-year-old Hispanic mother who lived in a trailer with her husband, two children, two brothers-in-law, and her own brother. Even though her household had many working adults, only her husband's wages went toward the rent and utilities. The other men sent their money to Mexico to support their families. Three years later Alexia still reported,

> We still send them money every month. It is our responsibility anyway....I try to make things last even if I have to mix rice and beans so that I can send them a little because they don't have money to go to the doctor if they need it.

Food Insecurity, Eating Patterns, and Obesity The psychological strain of risky food stretching practices often resulted in emotional eating, which Bove and Olson (2006) suggested contributed to the obesity among food insecure mothers. Mothers in food insecure families often employed dangerous food stretching strategies such as fasting, making deliberate decision to have children eat first before adults (Mammen et al. 2009); eating irregularly and sporadically; binge-like eating, alternating between near-fasting during periods of food scarcity and heavy eating during periods of food availability; and choosing low-quality, calorie-dense foods (Bove and Olson 2006). Generally, mothers in food insecure families sacrificed their own food needs for those of their children's. For example, Therica (Bove and Olson 2006), a White, 22-year-old married mother of three children, commented, *"I would make sure I fed my kids first, and then what was left I would eat."* To stretch food in the household, Therica adopted an eating pattern that consisted of alternating between eating little one day and eating a large amount the next day. Therica shared,

> I go hungry for like two days and then I'll eat...'Cause I normally don't eat, I let the kids eat, and then I go for two days without eating and then when I do eat it's big meals that I eat.

Some mothers coped with lack of solid food by drinking sugar-sweetened beverages. For instance, Steph (White, 48-year-old married mother of three children) reported consuming on the average of four 12-ounce cans of soda daily, and Lee (White, 35-year-old married mother of three children) drank 12-ounce cans of soda along with the sugar-sweetened coffee on the days when food was scarce in the house.

Lee's husband, Jarrett, described her eating as,

> She like, um, binge eats. You know, like she'll go a day where she'll just eat, eat. I mean she don't, you'll have to really fight with her to get her to stop. But then there're other days that she won't eat at all.

Further, Olson et al. (2007) discovered that RFS mothers who grew up in food insecure households tended to have obsessions with food. For example, Liz, a White, 34-year-old mother of five children, experienced poverty-associated food deprivation during childhood. She explained the long-term consequences of her behavior relating to food:

> Only because I've experienced it, and so I stock (up). I have a garden.... We have a pig butchered every year; we have a cow butchered every year. Our freezer is never empty. It's, it's just cheaper to do it that way. And, when I shop, I bargain shop and I buy lots. I will never be hungry again! I mean, I've been through it, and it's not fun!

In addition to eating behavior related to food insecurity, the likelihood of becoming overweight or obese is related to the level of physical activity. According to Bove and Olson (2006), overweight and obese women were twice as likely to report difficulties related to transportation as women who were normal or under weight. Mothers with transportation problems were more likely spend their days at home. Mothers who resided in remote areas of the countryside were generally less active than those living near town centers where mothers were able to walk to parks, shops, and employment.

Thus, the confluence of food insecurity, eating patterns, and lack of physical activity due to transportation challenges significantly increased the rate of obesity in rural low-income families. In addition to increasing the risk of other health conditions, obesity can negatively impact individuals' employability and thus their chances at achieving self-sufficiency. Olson et al. (2007) reported that obese women were less likely to be employed, as illustrated Bevin's (White, 40-year-old mother living with her partner and three children) comment:

> It [weight] affects all areas, you know! Any time we leave this house, you know, I am aware of every pound and how I look and how I measure up depending on where we're going.... Logically I can say it shouldn't be this way, but you know, for me, yeah, it's always there. So, it does, it holds me back from doing things in all areas that I'd like to do.

Summary

Findings from the RFS project clearly illustrate that rural low-income families face substantial health challenges which can interfere with their efforts to become self-sufficient. Taking the Family Health and Illness Cycle model proposed by Doherty (1991) as a guiding framework, we see that the RFS mothers were disadvantaged in all five of the model domains. First, for RFS families struggling to meet basic needs such as food, electricity, and housing, trying to improve their health seeking behavior (*health promotion and risk reduction*) was clearly not a priority. A significant number of the RFS mothers and their partners reported smoking, which was presumably a means of coping with the various stresses in their lives. Some mothers even resorted to unhealthy dietary practices and eating patterns as a means of surviving in the face of food insecurity.

The RFS studies also illustrated that low-income families live in environments which increase their susceptibility to many illnesses (*vulnerability and disease onset or relapse*). Clearly, living in poverty creates significant stress on family members. Managing the illness of family members—particularly children—hindered mothers' employability. Employment is not only important for maintaining a stable income but also provides families with access to private health insurance, which is often more comprehensive and more widely accepted than public insurance. The presence and quality of health insurance, along with transportation assistance, is one of the major determinants for a family's decisions to seek medical treatment (*illness appraisal*). Yet, one in three mothers did not have health insurance, and nearly half of them did not have dental insurance. The noninsured rates were even greater for minority families.

In order to manage health problems, many RFS mothers decided to quit jobs and remained unemployed (*acute response* and *adaptation to illness and recovery*). This has the obvious financial consequence of decreasing income, but also closes mothers off from the path toward self-sufficiency. As many RFS studies indicated, having a flexible work environment was one of the keys for mothers to be able to seek, obtain, and remain employed. When coping with illness, a family needs to evaluate the new demands on the family, assess their resources, and reorganize their family roles and functions. In this process, access to and ability to gather information regarding community resources is essential. Yet, in rural communities, getting health-related information and appropriate health care can be difficult, particularly for non-English-speaking immigrant families.

The framework of the Family Health and Illness Cycle model enables us to see the many ways that health professionals can help low-income families cope within the various domains related to health. A shortcoming of the model, as recognized by Doherty (1991), is that it does not include the interaction of families with other social groups outside of health professionals. The RFS studies highlight the vital role that can be played by community groups, social service agencies, and policymakers in promoting better family health at both the micro level of individual families and the macro level of public policy and community infrastructure. Family health can only be promoted by improving both personal actions (i.e., changing values and behaviors) and public infrastructure to support rural health. Policy implications will be discussed in greater detail in Chap. 12.

Discussion Questions

1. Family Health and Illness Cycle model was created based on various theories: family, stress and coping, and family development theories as well as symbolic interactionism and constructivism. How could each of these theories be used to explain the family health in rural low-income families?
2. What are the health factors that make it more difficult for rural families, especially mothers, to be employed or maintain employment?

3. Why is a rate of obesity higher among families with food insecurity?
4. In what way does food insecurity impact health of low-income families?
5. How can community groups, social service agencies, and policymakers promote better family health in rural communities?
6. What did you learn in this chapter that helps you understand the lived experience of rural low-income families?

Acknowledgement The authors of this chapter sincerely thank Naoyuki Ochiai for his careful reading and editing of the manuscript.

References

Adler, N. E., & Ostrove, J. M. (1999). Socioeconomic status and health: What we know and what we don't. In N. E. Adler, M. Marmot, B. S. McEwen, & J. Stewart (Eds.), *Socioeconomic status and health in industrial nations: Social, psychological, and biological pathways* (pp. 3–15). New York: New York Academy of Sciences.

Adler, N. E., Marmot, M., McEwen, B. S., & Stewart, J. (Eds.). (1999). *Socioeconomic status and health in industrial nations: Social, psychological, and biological pathways.* New York: New York Academy of Sciences.

Bailey, J. M. (2009, April). The top 10 rural issues for health care reform. *Center for Rural Affairs Newsletter,* pp. 1, 4. http://files.cfra.org/pdf/Ten-Rural-Issues-for-Health-Care-Reform.pdf.

Bailey, J., Kohn, S., & Evans, A. (2009). *Sweet the bitter drought: Why rural America needs health care reform.* (Report No. 2). http://www.communitychange.org/library/CCC-sweet-hivfin.pdf.

Berry, A. A., Katras, M. J., Sano, Y., Lee, J., & Bauer, J. W. (2008). Job volatility of rural, low-income mothers: A mixed methods approach. *Journal of Family and Economic Issue, 29,* 5–22. doi:10.1007/s10834-007-9096-1.

Bove, C. F., & Olson, C. M. (2006). Obesity in low-income rural women: Qualitative insights about physical activity and eating patterns. *Women & Health, 44*(1), 57–78. doi:10.1300/J013v44n01_04.

Bronte-Tinkew, J., Zaslow, M., Capps, R., & Horowitz, A. (2007). *Food insecurity and overweight among infants and toddlers: New insights into a troubling linkage.* (Publication No. 2007-20). http://www.childtrends.org/files/Child_Trends-2007_07_11_RB_FoodInsecurity.pdf.

Brunner, E. (1997). Socioeconomic determinants of health: Stress and the biology of inequality. *British Medical Journal, 314,* 1472–1488. http://www.jstor.org/stable/25174608.

Budetti, J., Duchon, L., Schoen C., & Shikles, J. (1999). *Can't afford to get sick: A reality for millions of working Americans.* (Publication No. 347). http://www.commonwealthfund.org/~/media/Files/Publications/Fund%20Report/1999/Sep/Cant%20Afford%20to%20Get%20Sick%20%20%20A%20Reality%20for%20Millions%20of%20Working%20Americans%20%20The%20Commonwealth%20Fund%201999%20Na/Budetti_cant_afford%20pdf.pdf.

Center on Hunger and Poverty & Food Research and Action Center. (2002). *The paradox of hunger and obesity in America.* http://www.frac.org/pdf.hungerandobesity.pdf.

Corson, C. M. (2001). *Health, well-being, and financial self-sufficiency of low-income families in the context of welfare reform.* (Unpublished master's thesis). Oregon State University, Corvallis, OR.

Dietz, W. H. (1995). Does hunger cause obesity? *Pediatrics, 95,* 766–767. http://pediatrics.aappublications.org/cgi/reprint/95/5/766.

Doherty, W. J. (1991). Family theory and family health research. *Canadian Family Physician, 37,* 2423–2428. http://www.ncbi.nlm.nih.gov/pmc/articles/PMC2145521/pdf/canfamphys00141-0115.pdf.

Dolan, E. M., Richards, L. N., Sano, Y., Bauer, J., & Braun, B. (2005). Linkages between employ-ment patterns and depression over time: The case of low-income rural mothers. *Consumer Interest Annual, 51*, 225–229. http://www.consumerinterests.org/2000-2009Proceedings.php.

Duncan, C. M. (1999). *Worlds apart: Why poverty persists in rural America*. New Haven: Yale University Press.

Duncan, G. J., & Brooks-Gunn, J. (Eds.). (1997). *Consequences of growing up poor*. New York: Sage.

Duncan, G. J., Yeung, J., Brooks-Gunn, J., & Smith, J. (1998). Does poverty affect the life chances of children? *American Sociological Review, 63*, 406–423. http://www.jstor.org/stable/2657556.

Elder, G. H., Jr., & Conger, R. D. (2000). *Children of the land: Adversity and success in rural America*. Chicago: University of Chicago Press.

Fitchen, J. M. (1981). *Poverty in rural America: A case study*. Boulder: Westview Press.

Fos, P., & Hutchinson, L. (2003). *The state of rural oral health. Rural Healthy People 2010: A Companion Document to Healthy People 2010* (Vol. 1). http://www.srph.tamhsc.edu/centers/rhp2010/10Volume1oralhealth.htm.

Gamm, L. D., Hutchinson, L. L., Dabney, B. J., & Dorsey, A. M. (Eds.). (2003). *Rural Healthy People 2010: A Companion Document to Healthy People 2010* (Vol. 2). http://srph.tamhsc.edu/centers/rhp2010/Volume2.pdf.

Guyer, A. (2003). *Depression risk: An examination of rural low-income mothers*. (Unpublished master's thesis). Oregon State University, Corvallis, OR.

Hirschl, T., & Rank, M. (1999). Community effects on welfare participation. *Sociological Forum, 14*, 155–174. doi:10.1023/A:1021653131354.

Jones, C. A., Parker, T. S., & Ahearn, M. (2009, September). Taking the pulse of rural health care. *Amber Waves, 7*(3), 10–15. http://www.ers.usda.gov/Amberwaves/September09/Features/RuralHealth.htm.

Kawachi, I., Kennedy, B., & Wilkinson, R. (1999). *The society and population health reader: Income inequality and health*. New York: New Press.

Kerckhoff, A. C. (Ed.). (1996). *Generating social stratification*. Boulder: Westview Press.

Kim, E.-J., Geistfeld, L. V., & Seiling, S. B. (2003). Factors affecting health care decisions of rural poor women. *Asian Women, 16*, 73–85.

Krieger, N. (1999). Embodying inequality: A review of concepts, measures, and methods for studying health consequences of discrimination. *International Journal of Health Services, 29*, 295–352. http://baywood.metapress.com/app/home/contribution.asp?referrer=parent&backto=issue,5,11;journal,47,160;linkingpublicationresults,1:300313,1.

Liese, A. D., Weis, K. E., Pluto, D., Smith, E., & Lawson, A. (2007). Food store types, availability, and cost of foods in a rural environment. *Journal of the American Dietetic Association, 107*, 1916–1923. doi:10.1016/j.jada.2007.08.012.

MacTavish, K., & Salamon, S. (2006). Pathways of youth development in a rural trailer park. *Family Relations, 55*, 163–174. doi:10.1111/j.1741-3729.2006.00367.x.

Mammen, S., Bauer, J. W., & Richards, L. (2009). Understanding persistent food insecurity: A paradox of place and circumstance. *Social Indicators Research, 92*, 151–168. doi:10.1007/s11205-008-9294-8.

Marks, E. L., Dewees, S., Quellette, T., & Koralek, R. (1999). *Rural welfare to work strategies: Research synthesis*. Calverton: Macro International.

McIntosh, W. A., & Sobal, J. (2004). Rural eating, diet, nutrition, and body weight. In N. Glasgow, L. Wright Morton, & N. E. Johnson (Eds.), *Critical issues in rural health* (pp. 113–124). Ames: Blackwell.

McLoyd, V. C. (1998). Socioeconomic disadvantage and child development. *American Psychologist, 53*, 185–204. doi:10.1037/0003-066X.53.2.185.

National Organization of State Offices of Rural Health. (2006). *National rural health issues*. http://www.nosorh.org/pdf/Rural_Impact_Study_States_IT.pdf.

National Rural Health Association. (2010). *What's different about rural health care?* http://www.ruralhealthweb.org/go/left/about-rural-health.

Nord, M., Andrews, M., & Carlson, S. (2008). *Household food security in the United States, 2007.* (Economic Research Report No. 66). Washington: US Department of Agriculture.

O'Hare, W. P., & Johnson, K. M. (2004). Child poverty in rural America. *Population Reference Bureau Reports on America, 4*(1), 1–19. http://www.prb.org/pdf04/ChildPovertyRural America.pdf.

Olson, C. M. (1999). Nutrition and health outcomes associated with food insecurity and hunger. *Journal of Nutrition, 129,* 521S–524S. http://jn.nutrition.org/cgi/content/full/129/2/521S.

Olson, C. M. (2006). *Food insecurity in poor rural families with children: A human capital perspective* (RFS Policy Brief). http://www.cehd.umn.edu/fsos/assets/pdf/RuralFamSpeak/RFS_ March_FoodSecurity_policy%20brief_final2.pdf.

Olson, C. M., Bove, C. F., & Miller, E. O. (2007). Growing up poor: Long-term implications for eating patterns and body weight. *Appetite, 49,* 198–207. doi:10.1016/j.appet.2007.01.012.

Pincus, T. (1994). Data confirm the social context of disease. *Advances: The Journal of Mind-Body Health, 10,* 32–35.

Radimer, K. L., Olson, C., Greene, J. C., Campbell, C. C., & Habicht, J. P. (1992). Understanding hunger and developing indicators to assess it in women and children. *Journal of Nutrition Education, 24,* 36S–45S.

Rank, M. R. (2001). The effects of poverty on America's families: Assessing our research knowledge. *Journal of Family Issues, 22*(7), 882–903. doi:10.1177/019251301022007005.

Rogers, C. C., & Dagata, E. (2000). Child poverty in nonmetro areas in the 1990's. *Rural America, 15*(1), 28–36. http://www.ers.usda.gov/publications/ruralamerica/ra151/ra151e.pdf.

Salamon, S. (2003). *Newcomers to old towns: Suburbanization of the heartland.* Chicago: University of Chicago Press.

Sano, Y., Katras, M. J., Lee, J., Bauer, J.W., & Berry, A. A. (2010). Working towards sustained employment: A closer look on intermittent employment of rural low-income mothers. *Families in Society, 91,* 342–349. doi:10.1606/1044-3894.4039.

Sano, Y., Garasky, S., Greder, K., Cook, C. C., & Browder, D. E. (2011). Understanding food security among Latino immigrant families in rural America. *Journal of Family and Economic Issues, 32.* doi:10.1007/s10834-010-9219-y.

Seccombe, K. (2007). *Families in poverty.* New York: Pearson Education.

Sells, C. W., & Blum, R. (1996). Morbidity and mortality among U.S. adolescents: An overview of data and trends. *American Journal of Public Health, 86,* 513–519. doi:10.2105/AJPH.86.4.513.

Shonkoff, J. P., & Phillips, D. A. (Eds.). (2000). *From neurons to neighborhoods.* Washington: National Academy Press.

Simmons, L. A. (2006, March). *Health: Essential to rural, low-income mothers' economic well-being* (RFS Fact Sheet). http://www.cehd.umn.edu/fsos/assets/pdf/RuralFamSpeak/March_ Health_FactSheet.pdf.

Simmons, L. A., & Braun, B. (2005). *Income matters: Understanding health in rural, low-income women.* Paper session presented at the 8th International Women's Policy Research Conference of Institute for Women's Policy Research, Washington, DC.

Simpler, D. (2006). *The working poor: Invisible in America.* New York: Knoph.

Simpson, E. (2007). *Oral health among low-income rural families: Implications for policy and programs.* Paper session presented at the Maryland Family Policy Impact Seminar. University of Maryland, College Park, MD. http://www.csrees.usda.gov/nea/food/pdfs/oral_health.pdf.

Singh, G. K., & Hiatt, R. A. (2006). Trends and disparities in socioeconomic and behavioural characteristics, life expectancy, and cause-specific mortality of native-born and foreign-born populations in the United States, 1979–2003. *International Journal of Epidemiology, 35,* 903–919. doi:10.1093/ije/dyl089.

Tai-Seale, T., & Chandler, C. (2003). Nutrition and overweight concerns in rural areas: A literature review. In L. Gamm, L. B. Dabney, & A. Dorsey (Eds.), *Rural healthy people 2010: A companion document to healthy people 2010.* Vol. 2 (pp. 115–130). http://srph.tamhsc.edu/centers/ rhp2010/Volume2.pdf.

Tatum, J. M. (2006). *Comparing the health and healthcare needs of poor rural Hispanics and non-Hispanic Whites.* (Unpublished honors thesis). Oregon State University, Corvallis, OR.

Torres, C. (2000). Emerging Latino communities: A new challenge for the rural South. *The Rural South: Preparing for the Challenges of the 21st Century, 12,* 1–7.

US Department of Agriculture, Economic Research Service. (2009). *Access to affordable and nutritious food: Measuring and understanding food deserts and their consequences.* Washington: Government Printing Office. http://www.ers.usda.gov/Publications/AP/AP036/AP036.pdf.

US Department of Health & Human Services. (2002). *One department serving rural America: Rural task force report to the Secretary.* http://ask.hrsa.gov/detail_materials.cfm?ProdID=760.

US Department of Health and Human Services, Agency for Healthcare Research and Quality. (n.d.). *Improving health care for rural populations.* http://www.ahrq.gov/research/rural.htm.

US Department of Health and Human Services, National Advisory Committee on Rural Health. (2002). *A targeted look at the rural health care safety net: A report to the Secretary.* http://www.hrsa.gov/ruralhealth/NACReportbb.pdf.

Wagenfeld, J. O., Goldsmith, H. F., Stiles, D., & Manderscheid, R. W. (1988). Inpatient mental health services in metropolitan and non-metropolitan counties. *Journal of Rural Community Psychology, 9*(2), 13–28. http://www.marshall.edu/jrcp/v92.pdf.

Whitehead, M. (1998). Food deserts: What's in a name? *Health Education Journal, 57,* 189–190. doi:10.1177/001789699805700301.

Wilkinson, R. G. (1997). Socioeconomic determinants of health: Health inequalities: Relative or absolute material standards? *British Medical Journal, 314,* 591–599. http://www.jstor.org/stable/25173857.

Williams, D. R. (1990). Socioeconomic differentials in health: A review and redirection. *Social Psychology Quarterly, 53,* 81–99. http://www.jstor.org/stable/2786672.

Wilson, W. J. (1987). *The truly disadvantaged.* Chicago: University of Chicago Press.

Wright Morton, L. M., Dreamal, H., Worthen, I., & Weatherspoon, L. J. (2004). Rural food insecurity and health. In N. Glasgow, L. Wright Morton, & N. E. Johnson (Eds.), *Critical issues in rural health* (pp. 101–112). Ames: Blackwell.

Chapter 6
Invisible Barriers to Employment: Mental and Behavioral Health Problems

Yoshie Sano, Leslie N. Richards and Jaerim Lee

Introduction

Since passage of the Personal Responsibility and Work Opportunity Reconciliation Act (PRWORA) in 1996, numerous studies have examined various barriers that hinder the transition from welfare to work. The most commonly identified employment barriers include lack of education, job skills, language proficiency, social support, community resource, child care, transportation, and poor physical health (see other chapters for details). Recognizing the importance of human capital and other resources, most states offer job assistant programs for welfare recipients to improve education and job-related skills and to provide child care and transportation assistance. Although many criticize these programs for not adequately meeting the need of the recipients, the existence of such programs indicates that the lack of human capital and resources are recognized by policy makers as barriers to self-sufficiency. What is hidden, however, are the issues of welfare recipients' mental and behavioral health problems, which can also be significant employment barriers.

Recent studies revealed that health problems, especially mental health problems and substance abuse, are highly common among welfare recipients and low-income families and constrain their ability to obtain and retain their employment (Danziger et al. 2000; Lichter and Jayakody 2001). For example, based on national samples, several studies have found that approximately 25% of welfare recipients struggle with poor mental health (Polit et al. 2001; Zedlewski and Alderson 2001) which is a significantly higher rate than for the general population (Jayakody et al. 2000). Other state-specific studies have reported that almost 50% of welfare recipients experience some mental health problems (Kalil et al. 2001a, b). Poor mental health is found to be associated with lower wages, intermittent employment, and poor job retention rates (Baron and Salzer 2002; Bray et al. 2000). A longitudinal study by Ensminger (1995) demonstrated that long-term welfare recipients were more likely to exhibit chronic health problems, poorer physical health, and higher psychologi-

Y. Sano (✉)
Department of Human Development, Washington State University, Vancouver, WA, USA
e-mail: yoshie_sano@vancouver.wsu.edu

J. W. Bauer, E. M. Dolan (eds.), *Rural Families and Work,* International Series on Consumer Science 1,
DOI 10.1007/978-1-4614-0382-1_6, © Springer Science+Business Media, LLC 2011

cal distress than the general public, indicating persistent health issues as potential causes of long-term welfare dependency.

Despite the prevalence and severity of mental and behavioral health problems, the majority of states do not systematically screen, assess, or evaluate these problems among the participants of public assistance programs. The much needed support, such as referrals and treatments, is typically not part of welfare-to-work programs. Scholarly efforts to investigate the association between health status and employment have begun to emerge only in the last few decades (O'Campo and Rojas-Smith 1998). Despite growing concerns among welfare scholars, issues of mental and behavioral health problems remain relatively invisible to policy makers, practitioners, and the general public. Addressing these important issues is imperative for poor families to successfully achieve self-sufficiency.

Background

Types of Mental Health Problems and Employment

Mental health is defined as "a range of mental and emotional conditions" (Callahan 1999, p. 8) of individuals. According to Callahan, the most common mental health problems in the United States are anxiety disorders, depressive disorders, and schizophrenia. Borrowing from Callahan's definitions of mental disorders:

> "Anxiety disorders" are characterized by severe fear or anxiety associated with particular objects or situations. They include panic disorder, phobias, obsessive-compulsive disorder, and post traumatic stress disorder. "Depressive disorders" also are known as mood disorders or affective disorders and are characterized by disturbances or change in mood, usually involving either depression or mania (elation). More women than men seem to suffer from these disorders. Seemingly fragmented thoughts and difficulty in processing information characterize "schizophrenia" (Callahan 1999, p. 8).

Among the three problems described above, anxiety disorder and depressive disorder are more prevalent than schizophrenia. Previous research revealed that generalized anxiety disorder—ranging from mild to severe anxiety—is twice as high among welfare recipients as the general population (Derr et al. 2001). The most salient mental health problem, however, is depression. Comparing depression rates of the US population in general with welfare recipients, Derr et al. (2001) found that while the rate of major depression among the general adult population was only 6.5%, that of female welfare recipients in Michigan was 26.7% and that of long-term welfare recipients in Utah was 42.3%. Given that stress is believed to activate depression in many individuals, it is not surprising that poverty is considered a common trigger. Economic problems and lower socioeconomic status have been linked to high level of stress that leads to depression (Belle 1982; Moore 2001; Simonds 2001).

Recent studies have consistently reported a strong negative association between mental health problems—particularly depression—and employment (Danziger et al. 1999; Leon and Weissman 1993; Lennon et al. 2001). For example, Danziger et al. (1999) reported that major depression significantly decreased female welfare recipients' likelihood of obtaining employment, while no association was found between employment and anxiety disorder or posttraumatic stress disorder (PTSD). Mental health problems not only impact the likelihood of entering the labor force, but also decrease the individual's ability to maintain employment (Olson and Pavetti 1996), reduce working hours and earning capacity (Johnson and Meckstroth 1998), and increase the likelihood of receiving cash assistance (Jayakody et al. 2000). Mental health problems can interfere with an individual's ability to work by diminishing her ability to function and perform even simple daily tasks, such as waking up, dressing, eating, sleeping, and communicating.

Mental Health Problems in Rural Contexts

Occurrence of mental health problems does not seem to differ between rural and urban areas. For example, using a nationally representative sample from the National Survey of Families and Households, Eggebeen and Lichter (1993) compared depressive symptoms and general sense of happiness between rural and urban populations. They found few differences between the two groups.

Rural/urban differences, however, do exist in the availability, accessibility, and acceptability of mental health care services. As described in detail in Chap. 5, health care is limited in rural areas (Findeis et al. 2001), and receiving appropriate treatment for mental health problems is particularly difficult for families with limited resources living in rural communities. Generally, the number of mental health services varies depending upon population density. Levin and Hanson (2001) documented that the most populated county offered 50 times more mental health services than the least populated county. The shortage of mental health specialists in rural areas is even more striking. In 1993, the National Advisory Committee on Rural Health reported that more than half of rural communities did not have practicing mental health specialists such as psychiatrists, psychologists, and mental health social workers. Rebhun and Hansen (2001) indicated that drug and alcohol rehabilitation facilities were also limited in rural areas. Because service demand far exceeded service availability, individuals tended to be released from treatment programs without having received sufficient treatment.

Access to mental health services is more difficult in rural areas. Hospitals are often the only place where an individual can receive general care, and often health care facilities are located at a great distance from rural communities. Fletcher et al. (2000) found that in some counties, no health care facilities accepted Medicaid, forcing many rural low-income families to travel as far as 75 miles one-way to access routine medical procedures. Furthermore, of the facilities that did accept Medicaid, services might only be available on certain days, further limiting access by individuals in rural areas. A particularly large barrier for rural low-income residents with mental health problems is the high cost of medications and treatment.

Among rural residents who have health insurance, fewer have comprehensive coverage when compared to their urban counterparts. Thus, the cost of mental health treatment is often prohibitively high for rural residents (Budetti et al. 1999).

In small communities, seeking help from mental health professionals can be stigmatizing. Acceptability—community values, attitudes, and atmosphere—is an important factor in determining an individual's willingness to seek necessary treatment. Strong emphasis on self-reliance, culturally negative beliefs toward certain mental health problems, and the lack of knowledge and education regarding mental health issues are only a few examples of acceptability challenges. In addition, in the smaller social context, the care provider may be an acquaintance, neighbor, or friend of a patient. This overlapping relationship may result in reluctance to get or provide treatment. Finally, Duncan (1999) noted that in rural communities family issues are more likely to become public issues than in urban areas, and individuals with mental health problems may not seek necessary help to avoid potential embarrassment.

Comorbidity of Mental Disorders with Substance Abuse

Past studies have found a strong linkage between mental disorders and alcohol and substance abuse/dependence (Albanese et al. 2006; Conway et al. 2006; Maremmani et al. 2006). A report by the Substance Abuse and Mental Health Services Administration (2004) estimated that between 50% and 75% of patients who received substance abuse treatment also suffered from mental illness. Both mental health problems and substance abuse are found to be associated with more sporadic employment, lower wages, and poorer job retention (Bray et al. 2000; Bryant et al. 2000). Comorbidity of substance abuse and mental illness can be a more serious issue for rural residents. Using a nationally representative sample, Simmons and Havens (2007) found that substance abuse and mental health issues are more likely to co-occur in rural areas than in urban areas, yet individuals are less likely to seek treatment. Given the smaller job market, weaker economic structure, and greater stigma attached to mental illness and substance use in rural communities, comorbidity of these problems can produce more damaging employment outcomes for rural residents.

Limitations of Previous Research

Rural low-income families with mental health problems face unique challenges in seeking, obtaining, and maintaining stable employment. Despite recent efforts to understand the relationship between mental health and employment outcomes, the literature is far from comprehensive. One limitation is the narrow focus on individuals. Many studies have approached the topic with the assumption that mental health is an individual problem. Yet, there is a growing consensus among health research scholars that health, including mental health, is the product of individual, family, community, and societal interactions. Examining health issues in the context of family and a geographic location adds a new perspective to the literature. Furthermore, most previous research focused exclusively on welfare recipients. Press et al. (2005) argued, however, that characteristics of welfare-reliant families and nonwelfare working families might not be so distinct, and thus, examining low-income families in general, rather than welfare-recipient families, might be more appropriate. Studies from the Rural Families Speak (RFS) project have sought to address these shortcomings.

Family Stress Model (FSM)

In reviewing studies on mental and behavioral health problems from the RFS project, we present the findings in the framework of FSM (Boss 2002; Conger and Elder 1994; Conger et al. 2000; Hill 1949). The original FSM (Hill 1949) has recently been expanded by researchers such as Boss (2002) and Conger and Elder (1994). While Boss focused on families' ability to manage stress, Conger and colleagues (Conger and Elder 1994; Conger et al. 2000) focused on the mediating processes between economic stress and parenting. The core of FSM, however, is to describe how environmental stressors (e.g., poverty) and internal demands (e.g., child illness) exacerbate family vulnerability (e.g., maternal depression) and exert disorganizing influences on family outcome (e.g., inability to improve economic status) while emphasizing the role of family resources and subjects' perceptions of their situation to ameliorate the negative impact of stressful environment.

Mental and Behavioral Health Measures

Due to the multidisciplinary nature of the RFS project, quantitative measures that directly assessed mental and behavioral health issues were limited. The most commonly used mental health measure by the RFS researchers was the Center for Epidemiologic Studies Depression Scale (CES-D) (Radloff 1977). The CES-D scale, containing 20 Likert-scale questions, is a widely used, standardized depression measure. Respondents are asked to rate how often they experienced specific situations or feelings in the past week. For example, one item states, "I felt that everything was an effort." Response choices are: (a) rarely or none of the time; (b) a little of the time; (c) a moderate amount of time; or (d) most or all of the time. Scores range from zero to 60, with higher scores indicating more symptoms of depression. CES-D scores of 16–26 are considered to be indicative of mild depression and scores of 27 or more are indicative of major depression (Zich et al. 1990). Cronbach's alpha for the CES-D scale for the RFS sample was .89 ($n=402$).

As a part of the Adult Health Survey and Child Health Survey, index items related to mental and behavioral problems were also included. Examples of index items included depression/anxiety; anger management; eating disorders; drug or alcohol problems; tobacco use; emotional, physical, or sexual abuse; learning disabilities; behavior problems; and attention deficit disorder (ADD)/attention deficit hyperactivity disorder (ADHD). Participants were asked if they, their partners (if applicable), or children experienced any of these problems.

Although the interview protocol did not include qualitative interview questions specifically addressing mental and behavioral issues of family members, participants often volunteered such information. The interview protocol was semistructured, and thus, participants were encouraged to freely share their experiences.

Findings from the RFS Project

A number of studies from the RFS project examined mental and behavioral health issues of rural low-income families, with the majority of those studies focusing on depressive symptoms, measured by the CES-D scale. As such, this review also centers on findings regarding depression.

Overall, approximately half (48.4%) of Panel 1 RFS participants who completed the CES-D measure ($n=386$, mean CES-D score$=17.4$, $SD=11.4$) were found to have depressive symptoms at the baseline interviews, with 29.5% indicating mild depression and 18.9% suffering major depression. The occurrence of major depression among the RFS mothers was approximately triple the 6.5% rate of the general US adult population (Derr et al. 2001). Employment status and depression rates were related. Among employed mothers ($n=196$), 39.1% reported having depressive symptoms ($M=15.7$, $SD=10.2$), with 28.1% having mild depression and 11.0% reporting major depression. For unemployed mothers ($n=190$), 51.7% had depressive symptoms (overall, $M=19.2$, $SD=12.2$), 27.1% were mild, and 24.6% were major. The difference in major depression between the two groups of mothers was striking, with twice the number of unemployed mothers indicating major depression as employed mothers. Overall depression scores by employment status was significantly different ($t=3.05$, $df=384$, $p<0.01$), consistent with the findings of previous research.

Employment Characteristics, Family Resources, and Depression

While many RFS studies confirmed the negative association between depression and employment status (e.g., Kim et al. 2005; Sano et al. 2010; and Simmons 2006), they also contributed to the knowledge base by providing more detailed examinations of depressive symptoms and employment characteristics. Simmons (2006) reported that working more hours was significantly related to fewer depressive symptoms over time; similarly, Kim et al. (2005) found that based on cross-sectional examination, fewer working hours significantly correlated with increased depression levels.

Other studies focused on employment trajectories and depression observed over the course of three waves of data (Dolan et al. 2005; Sano et al. 2008; Simmons et al. 2008). Both Dolan et al. (2005) and Sano et al. (2008) argued that dichotomizing employment into simple constructs of employment and unemployment masks the reality of irregular employment patterns experienced by low-income mothers. In general, employment of low-income women fluctuates over time due to lack of education, training, opportunities, and family situations. Dolan et al. and Sano et al. categorized long-term employment trajectories into four groups: (a) *mothers with stable employment* (those who remained employed at the same workplace over the course of the study), (b) *mothers with switching employment* (those who remained employed but changed employers), (c) *mothers with intermittent employment* (those who were employed and also unemployed for some period over the course of the study), and (d) *mothers with continuous unemployment* (those who remained unemployed over the course of the study).

Dolan et al. (2005) and Sano et al. (2008) found that various employment trajectories themselves did not significantly predict depressive symptoms at Wave 3, although depression was significantly correlated with switching employment and continuous unemployment (but not with continuous employment and intermittent employment). Family's actual income level also did not predict mothers' depressive symptoms. Instead, poor physical health and mothers' perceptions of the family's finances at Wave 1 significantly increased depression level at Wave 3. The FSM posits that family resources and perceptions of situation can play a vital role in an individual's and family's ability to cope with stressors. Simmons et al.'s (2008) findings suggested that poverty, employment status, and perception of economic situation were contributors to mental health status, but cautioned that the relationship may be circular in nature, i.e., physical and mental stressors of poverty may contribute to depression, and depression can affect the ability to engage in employment which contributes to poverty. Health, then, can be viewed as a key resource for sustaining employment and earnings (Simmons 2006). These results demonstrate that single time-point (snapshot) investigations may indicate an association between employment and depression, but may miss the underlying process(es) by which the two are linked.

Several other RFS studies have shown that stronger religious beliefs and membership in a religious community were associated with fewer depressive symptoms among rural low-income mothers (e.g., Garrison et al. 2004). Food insecurity and depression were also found to have a bidirectional relationship (Huddleston-Casas et al. 2008). Although these studies did not focus on employment outcomes, their findings indirectly support the validity of using the FSM, suggesting that factors such as good health, strong religious involvement, and high food security all influence the mental health-employment association and play a critical role in determining how families cope with chronic stress such as poverty.

Comparison Between Mothers with Low and High Depressive Symptoms

One approach to examining the role of family resources in depression is to study similarities and differences in family circumstances of mothers with greater numbers of depressive symptoms and those with fewer. Utilizing both quantitative and qualitative methods, Guyer (2003) identified, despite many similarities, several critical differences between the two groups of mothers with respect to family health and social support. The authors of this chapter also examined the impact of these two factors, i.e., family health and social support, specifically on employment outcome, using the same participants as Guyer (2003).

In these studies, mothers with low and high depressive symptoms were identified using the frequency distribution. Of 380 mothers, 15% ($n=57$) of respondents scored 6.25 and below, while another 15% ($n=59$) scored 30 and over on the CES-D measure. Based on Zich et al.'s (1990) criteria, mothers with low scores were considered as having no depression, while those with high depressive symptoms were identified as having major depression. In the following section, we briefly summarize the combined findings of the two studies by Guyer and the authors of this chapter. In addition to quantitative results, we also present the mothers' voices to illustrate the family circumstances.

Table 6.1 shows descriptive statistics of the two groups of rural mothers along with significance levels. In addition to a significant difference in income, food insecurity was higher among the mothers with major depression than those with no depression. This result is consistent with a previous RFS study (Huddleston-Casas et al. 2008). A significant association was also observed between depression and unemployment, consistent with previous research (e.g., Kim et al. 2005; Sano et al. 2010; Simmons 2006). Mothers with no depression were more likely to have a partner in their household and to have higher education.

Family Health The most noteworthy differences between the two groups were the number of health issues for the mothers, their partners, and their children (Table 6.2). The average number of health problems (both physical and psychological) was 3.4 for mothers without depression and 7.6 for mothers with major depression. Both partners and children of mothers with major depression had significantly higher number of health problems than those of mothers with no depression. For example, Belle,[1] a White 21-year-old married mother of two young children, was happy to report that her family experienced no significant health issues, including depression: *"Not that I can think of. Just, I think, one of the hard ones is dental... because that's one of those things where I know it's very important to get that checked up on."* On the other hand, Joan, a divorced 35-year-old White mother of two, described how her depression affected her day-to-day life and ability to interact with her two children. She shared:

---

[1] All names are pseudonyms.

Table 6.1 Demographic characteristics of mothers with no and major depression ($N=116$)

	No depression ($n=57$) M (SD)	Major depression ($n=59$) M (SD)	Total M (SD)
Depression scores[a]***	3.5 (1.9)	38.5 (6.5)	21.0 (18.2)
Mothers' age	30.1 (7.3)	31.2 (7.8)	30.7 (7.6)
Number of children	2.7 (1.3)	2.5 (1.6)	2.6 (1.5)
Age of youngest child in a household	2.9 (2.5)	3.7 (2.8)	3.3 (2.7)
Monthly household income*	1479.8 (804.1)	1111.3 (994.4)	1292.3 (920.9)
Food insecurity[b]***	2.2 (2.7)	6.4 (4.4)	4.2 (4.2)
	n (%)	n (%)	n (%)
Mothers' employment status*	32 (56.1%)	20 (33.9%)	52 (44.8%)
Employed	25 (43.9%)	39 (66.1%)	64 (55.2%)
Unemployed			
Presence of partner[†]			
Yes	37 (64.9%)	29 (49.2%)	66 (56.9%)
No	20 (35.1%)	30 (50.8%)	50 (43.1%)
Mothers' ethnicity			
Non-Hispanic White	34 (59.6%)	41 (69.5%)	75 (64.7%)
Hispanic/Latino	13 (22.8%)	9 (15.3%)	22 (19.0%)
African American	6 (10.5%)	6 (10.2%)	12 (10.3%)
Native American	0 (0.0)	1 (1.7%)	1 (0.9%)
Multiracial	4 (7.0%)	2 (3.4%)	6 (5.2%)
Mothers' education[†]			
8th grade or less	6 (10.5%)	2 (3.4%)	8 (6.9%)
Some high school	10 (17.5%)	14 (23.7%)	24 (20.0%)
High school or GED Specialized training	11 (19.3%)	22 (37.3%)	33 (28.4%)
After high school	11 (19.3%)	9 (15.3%)	20 (17.2%)
Some college	15 (26.3%)	11 (18.6%)	26 (22.4%)
College graduate	4 (7.2%)	0 (0.0)	4 (3.5%)
Information missing	0 (0.0)	1 (1.7%)	1 (0.9%)

[†] $p<0.10$, * $p<0.05$, ** $p<0.01$, *** $p<0.001$
[a] CES-D scores. The score ranges from 0 to 60 with higher score indicating more depressive symptoms
[b] Scores based on Food Security Module. The score ranges from 0 to 18 with higher score indicating higher food insecurity. T-tests and chi-square tests were used to examine the statistical significance of differences between compare the no depression group and the major depression group

I'm not able to have my daughters all the time. They stay quite a bit at my brother's house. Because of the kids fighting and arguing which causes a lot of stress. They are trying to figure out the right kind of medicine for me. It makes you feel groggy and want to sleep a lot. It affects me keeping up with the house and keeping the bills straight, trying to keep up with the house.

Poor family health represents an intense family demand on the mother which can exacerbate her mental disorder especially when a family member suffers from

Table 6.2 Family health problems by mothers' depressive symptoms ($N=116$)

Variable	No depression ($n=57$) M (SD)	Major depression ($n=59$) M (SD)	Total M (SD)
Number of health problems			
Mothers***	3.4 (3.0)	7.6 (5.2)	5.6 (4.7)
Partner (if applicable)*	1.8 (2.6)	3.4 (2.9)	2.5 (2.8)
Children*	4.0 (4.0)	6.8 (7.4)	5.4 (6.1)
Children's mental and behavioral problems[a]**	0.5 (1.8)	2.0 (3.4)	1.3 (2.8)
	n	n	n
Selected children's health problems			
Asthma[†]	12	27	39
Anemia**	1	15	16
Learning disability**	5	21	26
Depression*	3	16	19
Digestive problems*	2	10	12
Behavioral problems***	5	34	39
Migraines**	2	14	16

[†] $p<0.10$, * $p<0.05$, ** $p<0.01$, *** $p<0.001$

[a] Children's mental and behavioral problems included ADD/ADHD, alcohol problems, anger management problem, behavior problems, depression, drug abuse, eating disorder, fetal alcohol effects, learning disability, and tobacco use. T-tests were used to examine the statistical significance of mean differences between the no depression group ($n=57$) and the major depression group ($n=59$)

chronic illness. Paige, a White, single, 28-year-old mother of three who was in a domestic violence shelter at the time of interview, suffered from major depression, learning disability, and multiple sclerosis. Her son had seizures due to high fevers since he was a baby, one daughter had severe allergies that made it difficult for her to breathe, another daughter had sinus issues, and all three children had asthma. Paige explained that her daughter's sinus problem became worse at night. She continued, *"The only thing I can do is to put Vicks on her to get her to breathe. I tried to tell the doctor that, and it's like, all they do is to give her medicine. I gave up trying."* In her case, environmental stress, including having to live in a shelter and in poverty and internal demands of her children's chronic illnesses, along with a perceived lack of medical help, all resulted in her worsening depression.

Another mother, Keri, a Native American, 32-year-old married mother with four children, also struggled with children's chronic health issues. Keri was diagnosed as having major depression, bipolar with psychotic features, but was not taking any medication because she had to buy medications for her children. Keri's children suffered from multiple mental disorders: The first daughter was taking medication for mood swings, the second daughter was being treated with a drug for depression and anger management problems, and the third daughter was medicated for ADHD. Keri stated, *"I mean between my mental disorder and the kids' emotional disorders and, yeah, you know, our life is pretty chaotic all of the time."* When asked to describe a typical day, Keri responded:

This is going to be hard on me because typical days… I don't have typical days. I suffer from mental illness. I have times where I could go to bed at eight o'clock at night and sleep 'til twelve the next day. Then I have…like the night before last I didn't go to bed until one o'clock in the morning and I was up until two thirty trying to go to sleep. Lying in bed.

As evidenced by Keri's case, children of mothers with major depression are more likely to exhibit mental and behavioral health problems. Data presented in Table 6.2 also indicate that those children are more likely to have learning disabilities and experience depression or behavioral problems than children of mothers without depression. Furthermore, our correlation analysis indicated that there was a significant association between mothers' depressive symptoms and certain types of mental and behavioral problems among children (data not shown). Strong correlations were found between maternal depression and children's behavioral problems ($r=0.35$, $p<0.01$), children's depression ($r=0.25$, $p<0.01$), and children's learning disability ($r=0.24$, $p<0.01$). Although children may inherit susceptibility for mental illnesses from their mothers (or fathers), having to take care of children with chronic illnesses is likely to increase a mother's stress level, which exacerbates the mother's mental illness, and ultimately interferes with her ability to work. Keely, a divorced 28-year-old mother of one, commented, *"I would like to have a job. And a lot of it's my depression that keeps me in bed and not getting up and going out there. And I have no self-esteem anymore."*

Social Support Interestingly, some mothers had family members who suffered from chronic illnesses but showed few signs of depression. Closer examination revealed that the key difference for this group of mothers was the presence of positive formal and informal social support. For example, Kellan, who was 46 years old and divorced, spoke of her three of her four children as having "level 1" behavioral problems. Because their behavioral problems were quite severe, Kellan had a Personal Care Attendant (PCA) visit three times a week. The PCA assisted with daily activities and encouraged the children to do homework. She described the benefits, stating, *"Yes, I just love it. A tremendous help. 'Cause I just was drowning before she came. You know, I'd be working all day, I come home pretty much exhausted. And then I'd have to start my second job."* This comment demonstrates that receiving formal assistance can buffer the negative impact of child behavioral problems on mother's mental state.

Informal support, especially from the mother's family of origin, plays a critical role in mediating difficult family circumstances and maternal mental health. For example, Raven, who was 42 years old and single, suffered from migraines/headaches, high blood pressure, and chronic pain due to a broken rib in the previous year. Her two children had allergies and her son had anger management issues. Despite these circumstances, Raven managed to maintain a full-time job as a home visitor for Head Start. As a single mother, she relied on her own mother and grandmother for financial/material, instrumental, and emotional support—particularly for child care. Raven described her family of origin as most important to her. Raven commented, *"They're always there regardless of what the problem is, whether I want to hear what they have to say or not."* Despite various challenges, Raven perceived the challenges as a matter of life, stating *"If you don't have stress, you're not alive. You just have to be able to know how to cope with it and handle it."*

Mothers with major depression often lacked social support from their friends or family of origin. When they had support, their perceptions about receiving support were ambivalent. Asked if they go out with friends, many replied that they did not have any friends. The mothers with major depression also received a variety supports from their families of origin, particularly for child care. They seemed to be doubtful about the help they received, however, as well as expressing other negative feelings. Rashida, a young single mother with two children, relied on her mother for child care and housing and received financial support from her grandmother. Yet, she felt that she was not close to her family and did not get along with one of her sisters. She commented, *"I hope my momma treats me better. Sometimes I have a hard time with her."* Another mother, Maxine, a White, 21-year-old, married with two children who suffered from major depression, had a contentious relationship with her family of origin and had no contact with them. Maxine shared, *"I just got a job opportunity that they called me in for an interview at the factory down here. But I could not take it 'cuz I didn't have no child care."* For a mother with limited income, relying on their family members or relatives for child care is a most common survival strategy (Katras et al. 2004). Lack of social support from family of origin puts them in a more disadvantaged position and directly impacts their ability to work.

The association between maternal mental health and employment outcomes needs to be examined from a broader framework. The FSM emphasizes the importance of a variety of factors including environmental stress, family demands, family resources, and perception in determining mothers' mental health. The employment outcome is a product of organization or disorganization of all the contributing factors. Environmental stress includes not only poverty and the rural context but also domestic violence and/or contentious relationships with partners, family members, friends, or neighbors. Traumatic childhood experiences also create chronic stress. Many mothers with major depression reported having negative life experiences in their past as well as at present. They spoke of childhood abuse—physical, emotional, and sexual—sexual harassment, attempted suicides by family members, alcohol and substance abuse by parents, long-term incarceration of their partners, and family misfortunes (e.g., home burning down). In the face of environmental and chronic stress, various health-related family demands and both formal and informal social support can function as organizing/disorganizing influences on mothers' mental health.

Substance Use and Mental Health

Individuals with mental health problems are sometimes unaware of their own mental health status (Braun n.d.). Women who do have depressive symptoms may not know or may hesitate to report having depression. Simmons et al. (2007) investigated this discrepancy using health index survey data in the RFS survey protocol, which asked about the presence or absence of specific health issues, including depression. Focusing exclusively on participants who scored higher than 16 (the threshold criteria for risk of depression) on the CES-D, Simmons et al. (2007) found that just over one half (52.5%) of the mothers self-reported depression. The remaining 47.5% of mothers did not self-identify as having depression, although they exhibited symptoms of mild to major depression. According to Simmons et al. (2007), self-reporting was associated with mothers who experienced more health-related issues (e.g., illness, injuries, and permanent disability) had higher numbers of physician visits and higher rates of tobacco use. Those who did not report depression despite indicative symptoms were younger, more likely to be African-American, and more likely to have experienced pregnancy in the past 3 years.

The discrepancy between external and self-assessment of depression reported by Simmons et al. (2007) is particularly concerning because the group of non-self-identifying is less likely to seek appropriate treatments. Given the strong evidence for a correlation between mental health disorders and alcohol and substance dependence (Albanese et al. 2006; Conway et al. 2006; Maremmani et al. 2006), many undiagnosed individuals may attempt to self-medicate through tobacco, alcohol, and other substances. In a study of tobacco, alcohol, and substance use among the RFS mothers, Maring and Braun (2006) found that among 414 participants, 138 mothers (33.3%) reported smoking and 102 (24.6%) mothers reported partners' smoking. In the RFS data, the rate of alcohol and substance abuse by the mothers and their partners was less than 5%. Since those numbers are self-reported, however, we speculate that the actual number is higher. Importantly, a significant number of mothers ($n=150$, 36.2%) reported that they did not know where to find help for drug or alcohol problems, perhaps reflecting a lack of availability and access to adequate treatment.

Paige, introduced in the previous section, provides a good example. Paige was a mother with three children who was staying in a women's shelter. In addition to her own health issues, her children also experienced various health issues. Paige smoked marijuana and two packs of cigarettes a day. She claimed that smoking tobacco and marijuana helped her ease the pain that she was experiencing. She also shared that she had used other substances such as methamphetamine and Lysergic Acid Diethylamide (LSD) in the past. To support her habit of smoking two packs of cigarettes per day, Paige traveled to a neighboring state where the price of tobacco was cheaper. This expensive habit forced her to stretch her limited income from disability, welfare, and the Special Supplemental Nutrition Program for Women, Infants and Children (WIC).

Maring and Braun (2006) also tested correlations between tobacco, alcohol, and substance use and other individual factors. Significant correlations were observed between tobacco use and higher depressive symptoms, higher stress level, lower total monthly income, and poor knowledge of community resources, including the knowledge of where to find help for substance use. Alcohol use was correlated with higher depression and tobacco use. Although tobacco, alcohol, and substance use were not associated with mothers' employment status, a mother having more than one job was significantly related to all types of dependence. Maring and Braun posited that holding multiple jobs increased low-income mothers' stress level, which might result in their substance use. The authors further argued that although tobacco use was not considered as serious a substance as alcohol and other types of drugs, strong correlations with negative factors (i.e., higher depression, more stress, lower income, and lower community knowledge) should be a concern for scholars and practitioners alike.

Summary

This chapter presented various findings from the RFS project focusing on mothers' mental health, and in particular, depression. The FSM asserts that family resources and perceptions of situation jointly determine an individual's response to the environmental and chronic stress. The response, in turn, leads to successful family survival or failure. Among family resources, which range widely from formal financial support to involvement in religious community, arguably, the most important is the mothers' physical health.

Mothers with depression tend to also have physical health problems, as demonstrated by a number of RFS studies (e.g., Dolan et al. 2005; Guyer 2003; Sano et al. 2008). The co-occurring physical health problems may mask the severity of mental health issues in that health professionals and patients alike tend to focus more on "visible" physical problems than "invisible" mental problems. In addition, mothers with multiple health problems may have a harder time finding appropriate treatment, encounter greater difficulty in coordinating multiple medical appointments, and need to devote significantly more time to treating multiple health issues rather than a single health problem. Levin and Hanson (2001), thus, argued that integrating mental/behavioral health services with primary health care might be an effective strategy in rural communities. Furthermore, collaboration among primary care providers, mental health professionals, and other social services workers—including welfare-to-work counselors—could be promoted through the use of shared facilities and joint staff training.

One of the most significant RFS findings is the strong association between maternal mental health and children's health issues. Traditionally, mental health issues, such as depression, were considered problems of individuals. The RFS studies clearly demonstrated that poor maternal mental health was linked to disorganized family systems and, in particular, that maternal depression was strongly associated with children's mental and behavioral problems. Despite the similar prevalence of mental health problems between urban and rural children, however, rural children are 20% less likely to utilize mental health services due to limited availability of mental health providers and greater social stigma associated with reliance on mental health services (Lambert et al. 2009). Lambert et al. (2009) also reported that enrollment in Medicaid and State Children's Health Insurance Program (SCHIP) significantly increased rural children's mental health visits, probably because children's mental health is less likely to be covered by employment-based private insurance in rural settings. Therefore, in order to improve the delivery of mental/behavioral health services for children in rural areas, stronger support from public institutions and policy makers may be necessary such as expanding health insurance, providing health services through schools, etc.

Finally, based on RFS study findings that rural residents experience decreased availability, accessibility, and acceptability of mental health care services relative to their urban counterparts, improving the rural mental health infrastructure is imperative. In addition to integrating physical and mental health care services, as suggested above, developing rural mental health provider networks, increasing service provider efficiency, and better utilizing information technology may all help to improve the rural mental health infrastructure.

Discussion Questions

1. Which theory or theories are most useful in the investigation of rural low-income families' mental health and its relationship to employment? Are there other theories that could be used and how would these expand our understanding?
2. Why do mental health problems (e.g., depression) become barriers to stable employment?
3. Why are mental health problems often "invisible"?
4. In what way may substance abuse hinder stable employment?
5. What are the factors that may decrease the negative impact of depression on unstable employment?
6. What did you learn in this chapter that helps you understand the lived experience of rural low-income families?

References

Albanese, M. J., Clodfelter, R. C., Pardo, T. B., & Ghaemi, S. N. (2006). Underdiagnosis of bipolar disorder in men with substance use disorder. *Journal of Psychiatric Practice, 12,* 124–127. http://journals.lww.com/practicalpsychiatry/Abstract/2006/03000/Underdiagnosis_of_Bipolar_Disorder_in_Men_with.10.aspx.

Baron, R., & Salzer, M. (2002). Accounting for unemployment among people with mental illness. *Behavioral Sciences and the Law, 20,* 585–599. doi:10.1002/bsl.513.

Belle, D. (1982). *Lives in stress.* Beverly Hills: Sage.

Boss, P. (2002). *Family stress management: A contextual approach* (2nd ed.). Thousand Oaks: Sage.

Braun, B. (n.d.). *Barriers to mental health access for rural residents* (Maryland Family Policy Impact Seminar). http://www.sph.umd.edu/fmsc/fis/_docs/MentalHealthTaskForceBrief.pdf.

Bray, J., Zarkin, G., Dennis, M., & French, M. (2000). Symptoms of dependence, multiple substance use, and labor market outcomes. *American Journal of Drug and Alcohol Abuse, 26*(1), 77–95. doi:10.1081/ADA-100100592.

Bryant, R. R., Samaranyake, V. A., & Wilhite, A. (2000). The effect of drug use on wages: A human capital interpretation. *American Journal of Drug and Alcohol Abuse, 26,* 659–682. doi:10.1081/ADA-100101901.

Budetti, J., Duchon, L., Schoen, C., & Shikles, J. (1999). *Can't afford to get sick: A reality for millions of working Americans* (Publication No. 347). http://www.commonwealthfund.org/~/media/Files/Publications/Fund%20Report/1999/Sep/Cant%20Afford%20to%20Get%20Sick%20%20%20A%20Reality%20for%20Millions%20of%20Working%20Americans%20%20The%20Commonwealth%20Fund%201999%20Na/Budetti_cant_afford%20pdf.pdf.

Callahan, S. (1999). *Understanding health-status barriers that hinder the transition from welfare to work.* Washington: National Governors' Association.

Conger, R. D., & Elder, G. H., Jr. (1994). *Families in troubled times: Adopting to change in rural America* (1st ed.). New York: Aldine De Gruyter.

Conger, K. J., Reuter, M. A., & Conger, R. D. (2000). The role of economic pressure in the lives of parents and their adolescents: The family stress model. In L. J. Crockett & R. K. Silbereisen (Eds.), *Negotiating adolescence in times of social change* (pp. 201–223). Cambridge: Cambridge University Press.

Conway, K. P., Compton, W., Stinson, F. S., & Grant, B. F. (2006). Lifetime comorbidity of DSM-IV mood and anxiety disorders and specific drug disorders: Results from the National Epidemiologic Survey on Alcohol and Related Conditions. *Journal of Clinical Psychiatry, 67,* 247–257. doi:10.1001/achpsyc.61.8.807.

Danziger, S., Corcoran, M., Danziger, S., Helfin, C., Kalil, A., Levine, J., Tolman, R. (1999). Barriers to work among welfare recipients. *Focus, 20*(2), 31–35.

Danziger, S. K., Corcoran, M., Danziger, S., Heflin, C., Kalil, A., Levine, J., Tolman, R. (2000). Barriers to the employment of welfare recipients. In R. Cherry & W. Rodgers (Eds.), *Prosperity for all? The economic boom and African Americans* (pp. 239–272). New York: Sage.

Derr, M., Douglas, S., & Pavetti, L. (2001). *Providing mental health services to TANF recipients: Program design choices and implementation challenges in four states.* (MPR Reference No. 8736-403). http://aspe.hhs.gov/hsp/TANF-MH01/.

Dolan, E. M., Richards, L. N., Sano, Y., Bauer, J., & Braun, B. (2005). Linkages between employment patterns and depression over time: The case of low-income rural mothers. *Consumer Interest Annual, 51,* 225–229. http://www.consumerinterests.org/2000-2009Proceedings.php.

Duncan, C. M. (1999). *Worlds apart: Why poverty persists in rural America.* New Haven: Yale University Press.

Eggebeen, D., & Lichter, D. (1993). Health and well being among rural Americans: Variations across the life course. *Journal of Rural Health, 9,* 86–98. doi:10.111/j.1748-0361.1993.tb00501.x.

Ensminger, M. (1995). Welfare and psychological distress: A longitudinal study of African American urban mothers. *Journal of Health and Social Behavior, 36,* 346–359. http://www.jstor.org/stable/2137324.

Findeis, J. L., Henry, M., Hirschl, T. A., Lewis, W., Ortega-Sanchez, I., Peine, E., & Zimmerman, J. N. (2001). *Welfare reform in rural America: A review of current research* (Report No. p2001-5). http://www.rupri.org/Forms/p2001-5.pdf.

Fletcher, C., Flora, J., Gaddis, B., Winter, M., & Litt, J. (2000). *Small towns and welfare reform: Iowa case studies of families and communities.* Paper session presented at the Joint Center for Poverty Research Conference, Washington, DC. http://www.northwestern.edu/ipr/jcpr/workingpapers/wpfiles/Fletcher.PDF.

Garrison, M. E. B., Marks, L. D., Lawrence, F. C., & Braun, B. (2004). Religious beliefs, faith community involvement and depression: A study of rural, low-income mothers. *Women & Health, 40*(3), 51–62. doi:10.1300/J013v40n03_04.

Guyer, A. (2003). *Depression risk: An examination of rural low-income mothers.* (Unpublished master's thesis). Oregon State University, Corvallis, OR.

Hill, R. (1949). *Families under stress.* New York: Harper & Brothers.

Huddleston-Casas, C., Charnigo, R., & Simmons, L. A. (2008). Food insecurity and maternal depression in rural, low-income families: A longitudinal investigation. *Public Health Nutrition, 12,* 1133–1140. doi:10.1017/S1368980008003650.

Jayakody, R., Danziger, S., & Pollack, H. (2000). Welfare reform, substance use and mental health. *Journal of Health Politics, Policy and Law, 25,* 623–651. doi:10.1215/03616878-25-4-623.

Johnson, A., & Meckstroth, A. (1998). *Ancillary services to support welfare to work.* Princeton: Mathematica Policy Research.

Kalil, A., Born, C., Kunz, J., & Caudill, P. (2001a). Life stressors, social support, and depressive symptoms among first-time welfare recipients. *American Journal of Community Psychology, 29,* 355–369. doi:10.1023/A:1010351302196.

Kalil, A., Schweingruber, H. A., & Seefeldt, K. S. (2001b). Correlates of employment among welfare recipients: Do psychological characteristics and attitudes matter? *American Journal of Community Psychology, 29,* 701–723. doi:10.1023/A:1010413101010.

Katras, M. J., Zuiker, V. S., & Bauer, J. W. (2004). Private safety net: Childcare resources from the perspective of rural low-income families. *Family Relations, 53,* 201–209. doi:10.1111/j.0022-2445.2004.00010.x.

Kim, E.-J., Seiling, S., Stafford, K., & Richards, L. (2005). Rural low-income women's employment and mental health. *Journal of Rural Community Psychology, E8*(2). http://www.marshall.edu/jrcp/8_2_Eun.htm.

Lambert, D., Ziller, E., & Lenardson, J. D. (2009). *Rural children don't receive the mental health care they need* (Research & Policy Brief). http://muskie.usm.maine.edu/Publications/rural/pb39/Rural-Children-Mental-Health-Services.pdf.

Lennon, M. C., Blome, J., & English, K. (2001). *Depression and low-income women: Challenges for TANF and welfare-to-work policies and programs.* http://nccp.org/publications/pub_381.html.

Leon, A. C., & Weissman, M. W. (1993). *Analysis of NIMH's existing epidemiological catchment area (ECA) data on depression and other affective disorders in welfare and disabled populations: Final report.* Washington: US Department of Health and Human Services, Office of the Assistant Secretary for Planning and Evaluation.

Levin, B. L., & Hanson, A. (2001). Rural mental health service. In S. Loue & B. E. Quill (Eds.), *Handbook of rural health* (pp. 241–256). New York: Kluwer Academic/Plenum.

Lichter, D., & Jayakody, R. (2001). Welfare reform: How do we measure success? *Annual Review of Sociology, 28,* 117–141. doi:10.1146/annurev.soc.28.110601.140845.

Maremmani, I., Perugi, G., Pacini, M., & Akiskal, H. A. (2006). Toward a unitary perspective on the bipolar spectrum and substance abuse: Opiate addiction as a paradigm. *Journal of Affective Disorders, 93,* 1–12. doi:10.1016/j.jad.2006.02.022.

Maring, E. F., & Braun, B. (2006). Drug, alcohol and tobacco use in rural, low-income families: An ecological risk and resilience perspective. *Journal of Rural Community Psychology, E9*(2). http://www.marshall.edu/jrcp/Maring%20and%20Braun.pdf.

Moore, R. M. (2001). *The hidden America: Social problems in rural America for twenty-first century.* Cranbury: Associated University Press.

National Advisory Committee on Rural Health. (1993). *Sixth annual report on rural health.* Rockville: Office of Rural Health Policy, Health Resources and Services Administration, US Department of Health and Human Services.

O'Campo, P., & Rojas-Smith, L. (1998). Welfare reform and women's health: Review of the literature and implications for state policy. *Journal of Public Health Policy, 19,* 420–446. http://www.jstor.org/stable/3343075.

Olson, K. K., & Pavetti, L. (1996). *Personal and family challenges to the successful transition from welfare to work.* http://www.urban.org/publications/406850.html.

Polit, D., London, A., & Martinez, J. (2001) *The health of poor urban women: Findings from the project on devolution and urban change.* http://www.mdrc.org/publications/77/overview.html.

Press, J., Johnson-Dias, J., & Fagan, J. (2005). Welfare status and child care as obstacles to full-time work for low-income mothers. *Journal of Women, Politics & Policy, 27*(3/4), 55–79. doi:10.1300/J501v27n03_05.

Radloff, L. S. (1977). The CES-D scale: A self-report depression scale for research in the general population. *Journal of Applied Psychological Measurement, 1,* 385–401. doi:10.1177/014662167700100306.

Rebhun, L. A., & Hansen, H. (2001). Substance use. In S. Loue & B. E. Quill (Eds.), *Handbook of rural health* (pp. 257–276). New York: Kluwer Academic/Plenum.

Sano, Y., Dolan, E. M., Richards, L., Bauer, J., & Braun, B. (2008). Employment patterns, family resources, and perception: Examining depressive symptoms among rural low-income mothers. *Journal of Rural Community Psychology. E11*(1). http://www.marshall.edu/jrcp/V11%20N1/Sano.pdf.

Sano, Y., Katras, M. J., Lee, J., Bauer, J. W., & Berry, A. A. (2010). Working towards sustained employment: A closer look on intermittent employment of rural low-income mothers. *Families in Society, 91*(4), 342–349. doi:10.1606/1044-3894.4039.

Simonds, S. (2001). *Depression and women: An integrated approach.* New York: Springer.

Simmons, L. A. (2006, March). *Health: An essential resource for rural, low-income mothers' economic self-sufficiency* (RFS Policy Brief). http://www.cehd.umn.edu/fsos/assets/pdf/RuralFamSpeak/March_Health_PolicyBrief.pdf.

Simmons, L. A., & Havens, J. R. (2007). Comorbid substance and mental disorders among rural Americans: Results from the national comorbidity survey. *Journal of Affective Disorders, 99*, 265–271. doi:10.1016/j.jad.2006.08.016.

Simmons, L. A., Huddleston-Casas, C., & Berry, A. A. (2007). Low-income rural women and depression: Factors associated with self-reporting. *American Journal of Health Behavior, 31*, 657–666. http://www.atypon-link.com/PNG/doi/pdf/10.5555/ajhb.2007.31.6.657.

Simmons, L. A., Braun, B., Charnigo, R., Havens, J. R., & Wright, D. W. (2008). Depression and poverty among rural women: A relationship of social causation or social selection? *Journal of Rural Health, 24*, 292–298. doi:10.1111/j.1748-0361.2008.00171.x.

Substance Abuse and Mental Health Services Administration. (2004). *Co-occurring disorders: A guide for service providers.* (Report No. 42). Rockville, MD.

Zedlewski, S., & Alderson, D. (2001). *Families on welfare in the post-TANF era: Do they differ from their pre-TANF counterparts?* (Discussion paper no. 2000-01). http://www.urban.org/UploadedPDF/discussion01-03.pdf.

Zich, J. M., Attkisson, C. C., & Greenfield, T. K. (1990). Screening for depression in primary care clinics: The CES-D and the BDI. *International Journal of Psychiatry in Medicine, 20*, 259–277. http://baywood.metapress.com/app/home/contribution.asp?referrer=parent&backto=issue,5,9;journal,80,156;linkingpublicationresults,1:300314,1.

Chapter 7
The Challenge of Child Care for Rural Low-Income Mothers

Susan K. Walker and Margaret M. Manoogian

Introduction

Whether by choice, opportunity, economic demand, or policy expectations, mothers with young children have steadily increased their participation in the workforce during the past 40 years (Cohany and Sok 2007). As a result, the need for quality settings that provide care for children has given rise to significant and lasting social programs, such as Head Start, that offer early education and nutritious food for low-income children, federal and state policy initiatives to families pay for child care (Fuller et al. 2002), and research on the impact of care settings on children's development and learning (NICHD Early Child Care Research Network 2005). Ultimately, when working parents are satisfied with the quality of care settings for their children, their levels of personal satisfaction and the ability to maintain productive work are enhanced.

Finding quality care, however, continues to be a real challenge for families, particularly when they have limited income and/or live in areas with limited child care alternatives. Options that make economic sense for rural low-income mothers and actually facilitate their ability to work while also promoting child well-being are scarce. Program solutions for families with limited resources generally attempt to address families' structural constraints by considering the cost, location, and availability of care. A more realistic and complex picture, however, also considers mothers' attitudes and beliefs about caring for children, which, in turn, shapes their preferences for employment. Furthermore, mothers' desires to sustain strong family relationships and place their children with people they trust when other resources are uncertain influence their preferences for who cares for their children. Decisions for out of home care and education also relate to their desires for their children's learning and development. It is with this broad lens that we examine the lives of low-income rural mothers who attempt to balance their commitments for caregiving with their need to provide for their families in a limited resource environment.

S. K. Walker (✉)
Family Social Science Department, University of Minnesota, Saint Paul, MN, USA
e-mail: skwalker@umn.edu

J. W. Bauer, E. M. Dolan (eds.), *Rural Families and Work,* International Series on Consumer Science 1,
DOI 10.1007/978-1-4614-0382-1_7, © Springer Science+Business Media, LLC 2011

In this chapter, we examine the lives of rural low-income mothers, highlighting the conditions that, for most families, contribute to a work/care compromise. We first present an overview of child care in the United States and detail the necessary program and policy contexts to help understand the choices of rural families who must balance work and child care commitments. Next, we examine child care from the experiences of those rural low-income families represented in the Rural Families Speak (RFS) project. Mothers' perspectives about employment and caregiving amidst the range of options for the care of their infants and children are described. Because many rural low-income families choose and depend on care provided by family members or others familiar to the parents (also known as informal providers or kith and kin care), we also look at the benefits and relationship costs of this choice to families. We end the chapter by outlining further research needs and recommendations.

Child Care in Rural America: The Realities That Face Low-Income Families

An Ecological Perspective on the Issue of Child Care

By addressing the contextual features of child development, the ecological perspective of human development (Bronfenbrenner 1979) provides a useful lens for recognizing and understanding environmental influences when families seek care for children. This perspective identifies spatial and chronological settings or "systems" that influence development at proximal and distal locations in a child's social ecology. Child development is specific to unique biological make ups and is influenced through interactions within and between family and care settings. Child-rearing, traditionally, is provided by those in the child's microsystem, relationally and contextually closest to the child, i.e., the family. Less intimate, yet extant settings that provide potential supplemental care, education, and other service options are also situated within the microsystem. When the values for learning conveyed to a child through the family are echoed by the practices of the neighborhood child care center in which the child participates, a child's development is influenced by a reinforcement of messages within the mesosystem, or across settings. Exosystem influences on the child are not direct, but are conveyed through setting impacts on others close to the child, for example, when a mother's employment creates significant feelings of stress and this affects the quality of her parenting. In the macrosystem, development is indirectly influenced by the societal forces that shape behavior. For example, culture as a macrosystem influence may dictate family attitudes and beliefs about the ways that children should be raised and who can provide the optimum care for children. The chronosystem reflects events and transitions over the life course (Bronfenbrenner 2005). A human ecological perspective is useful in understanding how options for child care are relationally situated with proximity to the child, and how influences on parents across and within the systems affect children indirectly. Interactions across settings, such as work and home, or child care and home, are recognized as shaping developmental outcomes for the child.

Child Care Use, Selection, and Quality in the United States

Reasons for Using Child Care When parents identify and select child care, their primary motivation is to provide a safe, stimulating, and nurturing environment for their children when they are unable to do so primarily due to work commitments (Lombardi 2003). Because some care environments have the potential to support children's learning and development, parents may also choose care that promotes academic readiness and socialization and, in the case of after school care, supplements the development and learning efforts of the elementary classroom. Finding a child care setting that is trustworthy is essential to fostering mothers' employment (Henly and Lyons 2000). Because work hours and conditions vary, as do parents' own preferences for their children's care, the types of arrangements and times that care is used cover a wide range of configurations. Arrangements selected ultimately reflect parents' priorities as well as the constraints they face when making these choices.

Although the settings are diverse, a sizeable number of children in the United States are in child care. In 2010, approximately 11.3 million children under 5 years of age were in need of child care because of parents' employment, with preschool age children averaging 36 hours of care each week (National Association of Child Care Resource and Referral Agencies (NACCRRA 2010). Comparatively, in 2000, when we began collecting the RFS data, approximately 11.6 million children, or 62.9% of all children under 5 years of age, were in some type of child care arrangement (Overturf Johnson 2005). When mothers were employed, children spent an average of 36 hours each week in any type of care arrangement. If mothers were not employed, children spent an average of 18 hours per week in care (Overturf Johnson 2005).

Who Provides Care Care for children is typically provided by both formal and informal providers. Formal child care options include licensed and regulated home-based and center-based settings. These traditionally include settings for infants and toddlers, preschool age children, and afterschool settings for children between ages 5 and 12 years. Formal settings also may include those that are primarily educational or developmental in scope (e.g., Head Start, pre-K programs). Families may use these settings as the child care arrangement (considered schooling), or they may supplement custodial arrangements or other educational settings with these environments. According to the NACCRRA (2010), an estimated 18% of children under 5 years of age are in child care centers as their primary arrangement, 5% are in nursery/preschool settings, and another 7% are in family child care homes. Informal child care is generally provided by a family member, friend, or neighbor, and is unregulated. This is the most frequently used type of care for children regardless of location (Smith 2006). Care by extended family members, particularly grandmothers, is most commonly used as the primary arrangement, with 19% of children under 5 years of age in this arrangement. Other relatives or nonrelatives also provide care for 11% of children under 5 years of age (NACCRRA 2005). In 2000, 24.8% of preschool-aged children were cared for by relatives (Overturf Johnson 2005).

Depending on the needs and ages of children, families may use a variety of settings. An estimated 30% of children cared for by a grandparent and 21% of children in center care are involved in multiple arrangements (NACCRRA 2010). These settings may be a consistent combination of two or more settings, such as a child care center when a parent is at work during the day and evening care provided by a neighbor when the parent attends school. They also may include occasional, temporary, or emergency care, such as when a parent cannot take time off from work because a child is ill.

Dimensions of Quality Although multiple arrangements for children are typical across class and geography, the search for consistent quality and accessible child care among low-income families requires effort to find, secure, and pay for (Katras et al. 2004; Knox et al. 2003). A patchwork of arrangements is more likely in lower income families. In general, the difference in child care use for families based on economics and geographic location reflects the range of choices related to their preferences and needs. This difference may influence the quality of settings for children's development and contribute to an increased likelihood of piecemeal and inconsistent arrangements that may be detrimental to children's early development and their relationships with caregivers (Clarke-Stewart et al. 2002; Fuller et al. 2002; Knox et al. 2003).

Formal child care settings typically focus on the development and education of children through its professional staff who are trained and hold degrees in early childhood education and/or youth development. Adhering to state standards for licensing, these settings are subject to health and safety regulations as well as consistent staff development programs. Decades of research, evaluation, and enactment of quality standards have demonstrated the contribution of quality formal settings to children's early learning and later academic and life successes (Burchinal et al. 2000; Clarke-Stewart et al. 2002; Cost, Quality, & Outcomes Study Team 1995; Lombardi 2003). These sites, however, pose limitations for parents as they are costly, operate at traditional hours (e.g., 7:00 a.m. to 7:00 p.m.), and may be of limited availability, particularly for children under 2 years of age (Gordon and Chase-Lansdale 2001).

The Cost of Child Care In 2008, the range in cost for infant or preschool age child care in a family-provider child care home or center was reported to be between $3,582 and $15,895 annually, with the highest costs for infants in center care, and the lowest costs for 4-year-old children in family-provider child care homes (NACCRRA 2009). In 2000, the annual range of costs for a 4-year-old child in licensed care was $3,380 to $8,060, with variations by state (Schulman 2000). For example, the cost of care is often greater in metropolitan areas of the north (e.g., New York) and less costly in the south (e.g., Louisiana) (Schulman 2000). The cost of care represented on the higher end of this range exceeds the cost of tuition at many public colleges and universities and is inaccessible to most families who work (Kuhlthau and Mason 1996).

Child Care in Rural America

In rural areas, formal care is limited. Sparse populations challenge child care administrators to run profitable operations (Cochi Ficano 2006; Gordon and Chase-Landsdale 2001). Those formal care services that do exist are located in more densely populated communities. For rural families, commuting distances to employment or to child care, particularly in the absence of public transportation, may be a challenge (Colker and Dewees 2000; Fisher and Weber 2002). Limited formal care settings also restrict the number of potential slots for children, making it less likely that rural families can secure places for their children (Ghazvini et al. 1999). For example, for every child care space available in Arkansas and Oklahoma, three children were in need of care (Arkansas Advocates for Children and Families and Oklahoma Institute for Child Advocacy 2004). In some rural areas, Head Start may be the only nonparental care for young children available to rural low-income families (Colker and Dewees 2000). Most notably, organized and licensed care for infants and toddlers, as well as afterschool programs, is limited in rural areas (Beach 1997; Colker and Dewees 2000; Shoffner 1986; Smith 2006). Care for children with special needs is particularly difficult to access (Brewton et al. 2008).

For many rural low-income families, the hours of operation in formal child care settings typically do not match parental work hours. When a parent works second, third, or weekend shifts, many formal care arrangements are unavailable. In addition, when a parent works part-time or engages in occasional work (common in many rural areas that rely on seasonal tourist or agricultural economies), formal arrangements are prohibitively expensive because they require payment for full-time, year-round slots (Katras et al. 2004; Reschke and Walker 2006).

The cost of care for rural families often exceeds what is reasonable for a family budget. For those states represented in the RFS project, the average annual costs of care in 2008 for infants in a family child care home were $7,027 (ranging from $4,247 to $9,737) and $7,622 (ranging from $4,610 to $10,541) for a 4-year old in a child care center (NACCRRA 2009). In 2000, when the RFS data were collected, the costs in the same states' rural areas for infant care in a licensed child care facility averaged $4,950 (ranging from $3,570 to $7,188) (Schulman 2000) and costs for a 4-year old in licensed care averaged $4,110 (ranging from $2,556 to $5,623) (Schulman 2000). The relative dollars needed for rural child care are lower than what is required in metropolitan areas, yet rural child care is ultimately more costly for families when considering the lower overall incomes of rural households (Smith and Gozjolko 2010). To aid families, federal and state child care subsidies help cover the cost of care. These funds, however, are limited and underutilized (Schulman and Blank 2009). Less than one fifth of those families who are eligible use these subsidies, in part, because providers refuse to accept subsidies, copays are high, and/or registration is inconvenient when required to be done in person (Schulman and Blank 2009). In 2000, an estimated 15% of children living below the poverty line received federal child care subsidies, as did 10% of those living near the poverty line (Kinukawa et al. 2004).

The quality of formal arrangements may suffer in rural areas, which further limits options for care. Fewer opportunities for staff training and professional development as well as lower wages often create high turnover among center and family child care personnel (Beach 1997; Colker and Dewees 2000; National Child Care Information and Technical Assistance Center 2007). Strict standards for site licensing and accreditation are challenging to maintain in rural areas because fewer qualified child care teachers are available, and state agency licensing staff must drive longer distances to make site visits and inspections (Cost, Quality, and Child Outcomes Study Team 1995; Lombardi 2003).

With limitations for formal child care arrangements in general, and for rural low-income families specifically, many parents turn to family and friends. Informal care arrangements offer convenience and lower costs to families. Trust also weighs heavily in the decision to have children in informal care settings as it offers the advantages of keeping care within the family system and within the family's culture and language preference (Brown-Lyons et al. 2001; Porter and Kearns 2006; Uttal 1999). The unregulated nature of informal care, however, exposes children to wide variations in health and safety conditions, as well as environments and resources for learning and development (Porter and Kearns 2006). For instance, sibling care, a type of informal care that expects older children to provide care, and self-care, where children are left alone to care for themselves, may jeopardize children's safety and development. In addition, when extended family members need to be employed, child care options within the family decline. As a consequence, stress increases in the family system when needs exceed what members can accommodate (Roschelle 1997).

Reviewing the status of child care in the United States highlights the structural dilemmas faced by low-income rural families. Finding quality, trustworthy, and consistent care arrangements that are affordable and have flexible hours of operation is difficult challenge for most parents. With limited options and fewer resources, it is not surprising that rural families often rely on family and friends to patch together child care arrangements. Yet, even these arrangements can be vulnerable. Simply to provide financially for family members and to arrange suitable care for children often translates into compromise.

Understanding Child Care in Rural Low-Income Families From Theoretical Perspectives

Commitment to children, their care, and parental employment in rural low-income families has been a focus of a small group of scholars involved with the RFS project. A range of theoretical perspectives has guided their investigations into families' experiences with the selection and use of child care. Rational choice theory illuminates the choices for care that parents make amidst the options available to them (Becker 1976). Given information about the risks and benefits of each choice, parental decisions will reflect perceived optimal returns. As noted in the sections above, and will be seen specifically with the RFS families, compromises made in arranging care for children appear to reflect the delicate balance between weighing available, often limited, options with scarce and inflexible employment and transportation situations.

Role Balance and Feminist Perspectives

Women are predominantly and traditionally responsible for children's care and the selection of supplemental care for children. Scholars interested in child care as a reflection of women's lives often integrate role balance and/or feminist perspectives. Role balance theory considers the salience of a mother's role as parent and employee, highlighting how these roles influence her decisions about and experiences with child care. From this perspective, rural women have preferences for caregiving and work as it defines them as individuals, gives meaning and satisfaction to their lives, and contributes to their well-being (Marks and McDermid 1996). Their choices reflect the perceived benefits and costs to themselves, their families, and others. Reschke and Walker's (2006) examination of RFS mothers and Smith's (2002) work with mothers on public assistance identify the range of low-income mothers' commitments to work and caregiving that aligns with their notion of motherhood and how that balance shapes personal decisions and well-being. For example, when work is meaningful and their work roles have value, mothers are likely to return to work more quickly after the birth of a child (McRae 2003; Volling and Belsky 1992). More traditional views toward motherhood can affect the choice of child care, resulting in either selecting relative providers (Hock and DeMeis 1990) or preferring themselves in the caregiving role (Kuhlthau and Mason 1996). When there is incongruence between preference and reality, role theory and research suggest that personal well-being may be compromised, particularly if mothers are unable to reframe the positives of their forced situations, such as in response to the work requirements mandated by welfare reform (Hock and DeMeis 1990).

A feminist lens highlights how rural mothers' experiences with child care and employment are influenced by varying levels of structural constraints and reflect gendered expectations and behaviors within families. McRae (2003) observed that Hakim's Preference Theory (Hakim 2000)—stating that women's work and caregiving expressions reflect their preferences—should be modified to consider societal and practical restrictions. Current feminist thought underscores the subjectivity and diversity of how women express their identities and determine their lives. Feminist theory particularly is critical for the social structures of gender, race, economic class, sexuality, and work, such as those that limit women's expression and opportunities for growth (Walker 1995). Many of the RFS studies of child care and women's employment suggest the need for progressive policy and social change if rural low-income mothers are to have the same choices as those with more privilege. The additional recognition of the link between long-standing inequalities and the intersecting oppressions of gender, race, and class (Collins 1994) has relevance to an examination of rural mothers' experiences with child care and employment.

Life Course Perspective

Finally, a life course perspective is beneficial in understanding both the dimensions of child care choice and parental perceptions of the quality of child care arrangements that contribute to maintaining or dissolving arrangements. This perspective considers the contributions of life course events and early life experiences that influence individual development and behavior (Elder 1998). Temporal and social contexts of development are recognized as they promote both stability and change in individual and family development over time (see Bengtson and Allen 1993). As found in Reschke et al. (2006), a life course perspective helped to explain rural mothers' choices of their mothers as trusted and preferred care providers. Mothers' perceptions of the social capital gained from the care arrangement that could mend or sustain the mother–daughter relationship suggested added dimensions of rational choice for care beyond the practical options mothers perceive as benefits of market care.

This range of theoretical perspectives used to examine the lives of rural low-income mothers is appropriate to capture the diverse paths of women and their families regarding issues of employment and child care. To understand the lives of rural families and design effective social programs and public policies, the complex relational and contextual dynamics need to be addressed, appreciating that the energies rural low-income mothers expend in endeavoring to fulfill their dual commitments.

The RFS Project and Child Care: Implications for Families and Employment

In this section, we describe the major findings of RFS work. We highlight the complexities that rural low-income families face when negotiating their needs for financial security through employment and the care of their children when parents are working, seeking employment, pursuing education, and/or job training opportunities. Across these studies, mothers expressed concerns or identified issues they faced regarding access, quality, trustworthiness, flexibility, and affordability of child care as they worked or sought employment and educational opportunities. The results represent a range of situations. Some compromised their employment choices when care was not available. Others settled for care that was only adequate. And still other mothers, with formal or informal care options, expressed satisfaction with their work and child care situations. As Maya,[1] a 26-year-old Hispanic-American, working, partnered mother with three children, reflected on her child care provider:

> I loved her. She's great…'cause she treated the kids like I wanted them to be treated. She didn't put on a front. She treated my kids decent. Even now, they beg to go over and see her. I mean that's got to make you feel good about being a mom, knowing that your kids love going there.

Commitments to Work and Care: A Precarious Balance of Needs, Options, and Challenges

Although every family in the RFS project reported limited economic resources and concerns for child and family well-being, variations existed among families in terms of the number of working adults in the household, employment settings, hours worked, and the negotiation of child care. During interviews, mothers expressed their commitment to managing employment with the care needs of their children. If married or in committed partnerships, mothers were less likely to be working, yet, whether employed or not, they indicated their perceptions of partners' commitment to work and family. Two teams of researchers (Ko and Manoogian 2005; Reschke and Walker 2006) examined how mothers' priorities, experiences, and concerns revealed the balance between earning an income and caring for young children.

The Preference for Caregiving Over Work   In their investigation of a subsample consisting of 59 mothers living in three rural Appalachian counties, Ko and Manoogian (2005) found that despite the need to bring in more income, mothers by and large preferred not to work. Their commitment to work and family was influenced by their beliefs and adherence to traditional family models, a feature of Appalachian family life where fathers were expected to be primary breadwinners and mothers to be primary care providers when children were present in the home (Rural and Appalachian Youth and Families Consortium 1996). Mothers expressed strong preferences to raise children themselves rather than relegate the care to others. In some cases, when mothers were married or in committed relationships, they reported that their partners held similar expectations, i.e., mothers should stay home with children rather than be employed.

Ko and Manoogian's (2005) study highlighted how the rural mothers' expectations and behaviors had implications not only for their employment preferences but also their financial priorities. If mothers sought employment, they focused their search on opportunities that offered flexibility, optimizing the amount of time they were able to remain at home with children. Consider Lynnea's experience as a 33-year-old married mother with two children. She appreciated the ability to work, yet valued her role with her children.

---

[1] All names are pseudonyms.

And now if I didn't teach on the side, I don't know how we would make it. And so I'm thankful to her [Lynnea's mother] because she made me do it. So then it's the only fine line keeping me from having to leave my children. I don't have a problem working. I have a problem leaving my children.

Another mother, Juniper, 28 years old and married, described this bind of working and caring for her four children:

It is either leave your kid at school and get the protective services called on you while you need to work, or you lose your job. I just decided that my children come first. And then they had the nerve to say, "Call me if you're coming back." So, I thought and thought all night long and cried all night long about whether I was going to go back the next day, and I didn't go.

Given the costs of child care and the limited income and employment opportunities, paid work did not necessarily increase financial security. Mothers shared how they put their personal needs on hold to focus on their children, making decisions to spend their scarce resources on children. As expected, mothers desired their husbands or partners to support their families financially.

Mother's Role Preferences Related to the Use of Child Care Addressing mothers' commitments to employment and caring for children, Reschke and Walker (2006) highlighted patterns of work and child care arrangements linked to mothers' role preferences within the perspective of constrained choices. In this qualitative analysis, four patterns emerged among a subsample of 69 women living in five rural counties: (a) strong work commitment, (b) strong caregiving commitment, (c) dual work and caregiving commitment, and (d) weak commitment to work or caregiving. These emergent patterns were placed along a work care continuum of commitments, a framework that highlighted the subjective and subtle variations among mothers as to their feelings regarding paid employment and their roles as mothers/care providers to their young children.

Half of the rural mothers ($n=35$) expressed dual work and caregiving commitments and valuing work and care for children equally. No consistent pattern or type of care was used by these mothers. Twenty-seven of the 35 mothers identified using some combination of center/formal care, informal arrangements, and shared care with partners. Their narratives suggested that they were the most likely to seek strategies to balance their work and care commitments but often experienced tension as they negotiated these two domains. The analysis also examined mother's well-being through a measure of risk for depression (Center for Epidemiologic Studies Depression Scale (CES-D)) (Radloff 1977). The dual work and caregiving commitments group had the lowest reported risk for depression and the highest reported levels of life satisfaction when compared with the other groups. Although they reported some stress in finding care and negotiating their daily lives, findings suggested that these rural low-income families fared better when both care of children and income generating activities were possible.

For those families where mothers expressed strong work commitments ($n=6$), children often were cared for by kin and lived with their mothers, and in partnered situations with fathers, in multigenerational households. One important finding indicated that these mothers viewed care for children as a family commitment, not solely their individual responsibility. Because these mothers were the youngest in the sample, they likely had their children as teenagers and depended on their parents and family of origin to help them finish school, care for children, and/or provide a safe and more financially secure context for raising their children. Interestingly, these mothers' CES-D scores indicated that they had more depressive symptoms than the other mothers. These younger mothers may still be developing their identities and may be more focused on education and work than parenting (Demick 2002). Their family context may have reinforced the availability and reliance on informal care arrangements to support their desire and need to work and/or go to school.

Similar to the findings of Ko and Manoogian (2005), the mothers who indicated a strong caregiving commitment ($n=6$) presented their roles as mothers as the dominant feature of their lives. Their desire for employment was subsumed by their desire to mother and resulted in part-time work histories. Key to their motivations and experiences regarding work and family commitments, these mothers had partners who worked for wages, reported the highest level of monthly family income, and had the lowest risk for depression when compared to the other mothers. Finally, some mothers ($n=13$) had weak commitment to both work and caring for children.

Reschke and Walker (2006) identified a fifth group of mothers ($n=9$) whose life circumstances appeared to overwhelm their ability to sort out their work and caregiving expectations. Simply, their lives were so chaotic and the constraints so strong that their ability to think in terms of work or family commitments appeared to be subsumed by the stresses of their daily lives. Similarly, Brewton et al. (2008) categorized RFS mothers by their ability to cope with the stresses and demands of caring for children with special needs using the lens of the Double ABCX family stress theory (McCubbin and Patterson 1983) and the management framework for families with a chronically ill child (Knafl et al. 1996). Two groups, labeled *floundering* and *struggling,* were characterized by their inability to be self-directed and make use of resources, conveying a sense of being overwhelmed by their situations. Jocelyn's narrative illuminated how her situation influenced her ability as a single 26-year-old mother to work and care for her three children and maintains daily family routines.

> Between his appointments… he sees a psychiatrist, a family therapist, and then an individual therapist and a case manager who comes to the house. And just between the everyday stuff and his appointments, and then trying to get him taken care of at home, it just takes everything I've got.

These studies expose a variety of factors that shape rural low-income mothers' caregiving and work decisions. Some women ascribe to traditional and cultural values and when their relationship situation affords the income support, they devote their time to caregiving even though it means reduced family income. Others, perhaps influenced by personal developmental needs and/or the contextual situation of having a partner and family presence for child care support, place a value on work. The majority of mothers, however, appeared to have considered their personal needs, family contexts, employment options, child care requirements, and other resources, and struck a balance between mothering and employment. Although mothers may be identified by certain role preferences along a work care commitment continuum, external forces heavily influenced their actual decisions.

Formal and Informal Care Networks: Where Do Families Turn?

Whether by choice or by circumstance, once mothers made a commitment to seek and maintain employment, their key concern was accessing quality child care arrangements for young children or before/after school care for older children. As suggested by the picture of child care in rural areas provided earlier, the opportunities for quality, affordable, and accessible formal care settings were limited for rural families. When formal settings were present, they often existed only in the more densely populated rural towns. Not surprisingly, the RFS data revealed that while child care arrangements were varied, most families depended heavily on informal care networks (Reschke et al. 2006; Walker and Reschke 2004), termed as private safety nets, that families created to care for their children (Katras et al. 2004).

The Selection and Use of Child Care Walker and Reschke (2004) completed a comprehensive examination of child care arrangements by families in the RFS study. By using data from 11 states, they studied 323 families and 672 children under the age of 13 and documented the type, location, hours, and providers of care for each child in the family. Care arrangements varied for each child by family and community context, presenting a patchwork of care that most families utilized as they considered a multitude of factors. Care was heavily influenced by partner status, mothers' employment, and children's ages. For example, mothers who were partnered and had very young children (under 2 years old) were the least likely to be employed, providing exclusive (97.4%) care to their children. When mothers of infants worked, the majority placed their children in informal care regardless of mother's employment status (full- or part-time) and partner availability. For example, 62% of single mothers who worked part-time and 52% of those who worked full-time, and 62% of partnered mothers who worked full-time placed their children under age two in informal arrangements. Older children (3 to 4 years of age) were more likely than infants to be placed in regulated care, although informal care remained a popular primary setting. Even when mothers were unemployed, 43.5% of partnered mothers and 63.3% of single mothers reported center care as their children's primary care arrangement. When mothers worked full- or part-time, older children were likely to be in informal arrangements (e.g., 50% when a single mother worked full-time, and 42% when a partnered mother worked full-time), again indicating parents' need or preference to place their children in the homes of friends and relatives.

Secondary care arrangements, defined as care for at least 10 hours a week, also were evident. In addition to a primary arrangement of 25 hours a week or more, a greater proportion of children were in secondary care as they increased in age. For example, 41% of infants and toddlers and 75% of the preschool age children were in secondary arrangements. These secondary arrangements were necessary, for example, when a single mother worked a second job.

Fewer than 30% of RFS mothers used child care subsidies to help them place their children in formal care arrangements. Interestingly, those who reported paying for care were those who used informal arrangements. Regardless of the receipt of child care subsidies, mothers in this study reported spending 37% of their family income on child care, exceeding the cost of housing or utilities for low-income families.

The flexibility of work hours and the ability to take time off work factored heavily into the need for and selection of child care among rural low-income mothers. Mothers reported that their work had fixed hours, and many were overseen by managers who were unsympathetic to the frailties of children's health. As a result, mothers often felt caught in a bind when their children became ill. Without paid sick leave, they worried about staying home with their children for fear of losing their jobs altogether. When work shifts required that they start early or end late, rural low-income mothers had few choices about how to get their children ready for school or retrieved from child care on time.

The Experience of Finding and Using Child Care Within the Private Safety Net By using a phenomenological approach to analysis and the family ecology perspective outlined previously in this chapter, Katras et al. (2004) addressed these dilemmas by examining the child care experiences of 52 families. Their identification of private safety nets, defined as networks of informal and formal relationships, highlighted how families met their child care and other family needs in rural settings. These networks varied in terms of the structural relationships in the provision of care. In some cases, care was bartered for other services (e.g., using a car and cleaning a house). In others, monetary compensation took place at the same rate or a fraction of what professional child care providers would charge. In still others, the exchange of services was implied within the commitment and responsibilities inherent in family relationships.

Mothers used private safety nets that consisted of *trusted* relationships, enabling them and their families to access quality care that was difficult to find in their rural communities. For instance, private safety nets were utilized for child care needs that occurred during weekends, evenings, overnights, or emergencies. These mothers displayed negotiation skills when locating providers that met their distinct care needs, while at the same time fit with their network members' schedules and priorities. Cricket, a 28-year-old married mother with two daughters and a son, expressed her experience with trusted care providers within her network:

> We pretty much don't go through daycares because of that reason [only having trusted family members as care providers]. You just, you know, you've gotta watch who you're leaving your kids with now.

These networks, however, could be vulnerable when family members were unreliable, and the community lacked any child care supports. Because affordability is critical, private safety nets helped offset the child care cost burden for families. When networks were not consistent, families needed to access care that required financial resources that they might not have. When networks became fragile, mothers reported that they would forgo work and educational opportunities because children were their first priority, a theme present in other RFS studies that focused on child care (Ko and Manoogian 2005; Reschke et al. 2006).

For example, Trina, a 38-year-old single mother of one daughter, experienced chaotic and unreliable child care. When her child was injured and she was unable to find suitable child care, she compromised her work situation to be her child's care provider. She said:

> My kid got hurt and she [supervisor] told me as soon as I was done at the doctor's, to come to work. And I just like, no, I'm not doing it. I'd rather give up the job than, you know, my kid be affected from it. My kid (is) more important than money.

Informal Care Provided by Families: Finding Trusted Care With Grandmothers

Across multiple studies within the RFS project, rural mothers identified a consistent member of their social support networks—their own mothers. Grandmothers played an important role in providing both emotional and instrumental support to their families (Richards et al. 2002). Like many nonrural non-low-income families, those in the RFS study often trusted the care of their children to family of origin members, typically their children's grandmothers. Family members who lived in close proximity were the logical choice for child care when rural areas offered few formal care alternatives.

Grandmothers as Child Care Providers: Broad Impacts Utilizing a life course perspective, Reschke et al. (2006) examined how child care was experienced in the context of the long-term relationships between participants and their mothers ($n=42$). As mentioned previously, grandmother care for children offered many advantages including the flexibility needed for part-time, full-time, seasonal, and shift employment. Living close by or in households together with their daughters and families, grandmothers were quick to respond to care needs and could actively support their daughters' employment and/or educational goals by ensuring that children received care. In most cases, child care was provided free of charge, allowing mothers and their families to use their limited financial resources elsewhere.

Participants also expressed some psychological benefits of utilizing their mothers for care that helped them to feel better about working outside of the home. For instance, both Katras et al. (2004) and Ko and Manoogian (2005) found that trusted providers were essential because of the multiple ways that low-income rural families could experience marginality and oppression in the community and the workplace. Grandmother care allowed children to be in familiar environments where they were accepted and loved. In fact, these care arrangements appeared to provide, in many cases, a way to enhance the relationship between grandmothers and grandchildren, as well as grandmothers and their adult daughters.

As suggested by Katras et al. (2004), however, private safety nets built around family members could have vulnerabilities, a finding that also emerged when examining the context of grandmother care (Reschke et al. 2006). For instance, participants expressed tension when they disagreed with grandmothers on appropriate child-rearing strategies and techniques, and, at times, felt constrained in voicing these disagreements so as to not jeopardize the care they desperately needed to maintain their employment. Furthermore, mothers who may have experienced less than adequate parenting from their own mothers expressed ambivalence about grandmothers as care providers. Given that low-income families may experience limited economic resources across generations, children who have grandmothers as care providers may not be in the most optimum setting for their personal growth and development. Finally, the potentially constrained health of older grandmothers and other family care providers may present some challenges that influence the quality of care received by grandchildren and the long-term health outcomes for the grandmothers. As Tansy, a 32-year-old single mother of two children, noted:

> To be honest, I wouldn't be working if I didn't have her [mother as care provider] 'cuz I trust nobody. If one of my kids is sick, I can go to work and feel comfortable that they're being taken care of and I couldn't do that with anybody else…. But the big thing with that is, she's been in and out of the hospital and her doctors are telling her that she shouldn't over-exert herself so they're telling her to limit her hours of baby-sitting so she's not going to be able to do it this way. That's why I mentioned children care being a problem, 'cuz you just can't find it.

Rural Families, Child Care, and Employment: Program, Policy, and Future Research Needs

In this chapter, we have highlighted the situations facing rural low-income families that influence both their employment practices and child care decisions. As suggested throughout this book, rural low-income families are faced with multiple and deep challenges to make ends meet and provide for their children. Minimal, poor quality and inconsistent yet sometimes costly child care arrangements further limit the ability of rural low-income families to maintain family well-being. Like their more advantaged counterparts, low-income mothers' decisions about the child care and employment are influenced by their children's ages, with mothers staying home or working minimal hours when their children are infants and toddlers; and by the availability of a partner or family member to share in care or income generation. For families struggling financially, however, far fewer resources are available to enable them to assert personal preferences. Living in rural, isolated, and resource-limited communities may influence mother's preferences for paid employment, and her attitudes and decisions about child care. Mothers who state a commitment for staying at home to care for their children over employment may be conditioned to prefer this option from years of frustration negotiating personally unsatisfying employment settings and family and child care arrangements. They also may have witnessed the child care experiences of family and friends. Their choices may be an accommodation to their geographic location and community resources. The results of our studies reinforce feminist theory and McRae's (2003) constrained choice arguments. Clearly, rural low-income women face structural and social dynamics that greatly limit their abilities to form and assert their subjective beliefs of themselves.

Determining how much rural low-income mothers' preferences for work and caregiving are linked to cultural and/or family expectations is also difficult. Their choices may be the fulfillment of an obligation to preserve the single resource available to them, i.e., their immediate and extended family. Asking family members to provide care, paying, or bartering for this service sometimes with subsidy dollars are all ways to keep families connected. Rural low-income mothers also may choose to stay home with their children through felt and expressed commitments to upholding domestic roles that are strongly featured in rural culture and kin scripts (Stack and Burton 1993).

Whether choices are situational, learned, or culturally reinforced, options and resources that support rural low-income mothers' abilities to exercise personal and family values are severely limited. It is in this realm that public policy and program efforts as outlined in the last chapters in this volume can aid rural low-income families as they negotiate employment and care for their children.

Future Research Directions

Although the RFS data allowed us to better understand the choices, commitments, and challenges of rural low-income mothers, there is still much to learn. Research on rural low-income families and their decisions concerning work and child care must expand to ask key questions regarding the multiple challenges that face the residents of rural America. Within the multiple and interlocking contexts of culture, language, gender, and geography, families make employment and child care decisions that may or may not be influenced by their contexts. Teasing out structural conditions and constraints will better inform employment policies and tailor supportive services like transportation and child care to facilitate work. Understanding variations across families is critical to avoid a "one size fits all" response. As evident in the RFS investigations, rural low-income mothers' behaviors concerning employment varied by family structure, partner status, mother's age, and education. Employment conditions for these rural families also vary greatly. For example, Walker and Reschke's (2004) analysis included families whose child care use was affected by migrant work that took them to different states for part of a year. These barriers to care resulted in parents bringing their children with them to the fields while they worked.

As we replicate these findings and expand research questions, longitudinal investigations of child outcomes related to work caregiving configurations of rural low-income families are needed. Although much of our focus in the RFS research has been on mothers' lives and contexts that inform their care decisions, families' and society's key interest in child care quality concerns the facilitation of positive child outcomes and resilience. How are children faring with these limited care choices in the short term, and what are the impacts in young adulthood of a childhood that included low-quality/mixed setting/inconsistent child care environments? Such questions have been asked in large-scale national studies (NICHD Early Child Care Research Network 2005), but particular focus is needed in rural communities because of the unique and challenging context.

Because of the need for and great use of informal child care resources, we need a better understanding of quality in these settings, the burden on or benefit to the caregiver, and the emotional context of a nurturing environment contributing to child development, as well as the promotion of health, stimulation, and positive social skills for school success. Because grandmothers are frequently chosen or volunteer to care for their grandchildren, learning specifically how this child care arrangement enhances or thwarts personal agendas and developmental contexts for both provider and child is essential. Understanding the value of this context and evaluating this type of care on its own terms rather than from a traditional licensed care setting comparison may better help us to support children's emotional and social development as well as provide more options for families living in rural settings with limited economic resources.

Discussion Questions

1. The integration of theory and scholarly research on child care in rural low-income families is limited. Are there other theories that could be used in understanding parental decisions and experiences of child care in low-income, geographically isolated settings?
2. What are the factors related to child care that facilitate rural mothers' employment? What are the factors related to the care of children that make it more difficult to be employed or choose maintain employment?
3. Informal child care is a commonly used option for low-income families in rural areas. How could the experiences of both relative and friend care providers and children be better recognized, supported, and strengthened?
4. How would you suggest evaluating the quality of child care options ranging from formal to informal care settings? What are parents' perspectives that should be included in this assessment?
5. What are some program and policy ideas that might facilitate rural women's choices around care for their children and employment?
6. What did you learn in this chapter that helps you understand the lived experience of rural low-income families as they negotiate work and family commitments?

Acknowledgments The authors wish to acknowledge the RFS researchers who have contributed to our understanding of rural child care: Kathy Reschke, Ju-Lien Ko, Leslie Richards, Jean Bauer, Katie Brewton, Sharon Seiling, Mary Jo Katras, Carolyn Bird, and Virginia Zuiker. Our child care research builds on the work of others who are committed to child care practice, research, and policy. Finally, our work would not be possible without the efforts of the RFS focus group on child care, the state team leadership, local facilitators, and most importantly, the mothers themselves.

References

Arkansas Advocates for Children and Families & Oklahoma Institute for Child Advocacy. (2004). *Rural kids count! Sharing the stories and statistics from Oklahoma and Arkansas*. http://www.odl.state.ok.us/Kids/factbook/ruralkidscount2004/IntroPages.pdf.

Beach, B. (1997). *Perspectives on rural child care*. (ERIC Document Reproduction Service No. ED403102). http://www.ericdigests.org/1997-3/rural.html.

Becker, G. S. (1976). *The economic approach to human behavior*. Chicago: University of Chicago Press.

Bengtson, V. L., & Allen, K. R. (1993). The life course perspective applied to families over time. In P. G. Boss, W. J. Doherty, R. LaRossa, W. R. Schumm, & S. K. Steinmetz (Eds.), *Sourcebook of family theories and methods* (pp. 469–498). New York: Springer.

Brewton, K., Walker, S., & Bauer, J. (2008, November). *Stress and coping experiences of low income rural mothers raising a child with a disability*. Paper session presented at the annual conference of the National Council on Family Relations, Little Rock, AR.

Bronfenbrenner, U. (1979). *The ecology of human development: Experiments by nature and design*. Cambridge: Harvard University Press.

Bronfenbrenner, U. (2005). *Making human beings human: Bioecological perspectives on human development*. Thousand Oak: Sage.

Brown-Lyons, M., Robertson, A., & Layzer, J. (2001, May). *Kith and kin—informal child care: Highlights from recent research*. http://nccp.org/publications/pdf/text_377.pdf.

Burchinal, M. R., Roberts, J. E., Riggins, R., Zeisel, S. A., Neebe, E., & Bryant, D. (2000). Relating quality of center-based child care to early cognitive and language development longitudinally. *Child Development, 71*, 339–357. doi:10.1111/1467-8624.00149.

Clarke-Stewart, K. A., Vandell, D. L., Burchinal, M., O'Brien, M., & McCartney, K. (2002). Do regulable features of child care homes affect children's development? *Early Childhood Research Quarterly, 17*, 52–86. doi:10.1016/So885-2006(02)00133-3.

Cochi Ficano, C. K. (2006). Child care market mechanisms: Does policy affect the quantity of care? *Social Service Review, 80*, 453–484. doi:10.1086/505447.

Cohany, S. R., & Sok, E. (2007). Trends in labor force participation of married mothers of infants. *Monthly Labor Review, 130*(2), 9–16. http://www.bls.gov/opub/mlr/2007/02/art2full.pdf.

Colker, L. J., & Dewees, S. (2000). *Rural welfare issue brief: Child care for welfare participants in rural areas*. http://www.acf.hhs.gov/programs/opre/welfare_employ/rural_wtw/reports/cc_wlf_part/cc_for_welfare.pdf.

Collins, P. H. (1994). Shifting the center: Race, class, and feminist theorizing about motherhood. In D. Bassin, M. Honey, & M. M. Kaplan (Eds.), *Representations of motherhood* (pp. 56–74). New Haven: Yale University.

Cost, Quality, & Child Outcomes Study Team. (1995). *Cost, quality, and child outcomes in child care centers: Public report*. Denver: Department of Economics, University of Colorado at Denver.

Demick, J. (2002). Stages of parental development. In M. H. Bornstein (Ed.), *Handbook of parenting: Being and becoming a parent* (2nd ed., vol. 3, pp. 389–413). Mahwah: Erlbaum.

Elder, G. H., Jr. (1998). The life course as developmental theory. *Child Development, 69*, 1–12. doi:10.1111/j.1467-8624.1998.tb06128.x.

Fisher, M. G., & Weber, B. A. (2002). *The importance of place in welfare reform: Common challenges for central cities and remote rural areas*. http://www.brookings.edu/es/urban/publications/weberfull.pdf.

Fuller, B., Kagan, S. L., Caspary, G. L., & Gauthier, C. A. (2002). Welfare reform and child care options for low-income families. *The Future of Children, 12*(1), 97–119. http://www.futureof children.org/futureofchildren/publications/docs/12_01_FullJournal.pdf.

Ghazvini, A. S., Mullis, A. K., Mullis, R. L., & Park, J. J. (1999). *Child care issues impacting welfare reform in the rural south* (Information Brief No. 9). http://www.eric.ed.gov/PDFS/ ED438112.pdf.

Gordon, R. A., & Chase-Lansdale, P. L. (2001). Availability of child care in the United States: A description and analysis of data sources. *Demography, 38,* 299–316. http://muse.jhu.edu/ journals/demography/.

Hakim, C. (2000). *Work-lifestyle choices in the 21st century: Preference theory.* Oxford: Oxford University Press.

Henly, J. R., & Lyons, S. (2000). The negotiation of child care and employment demands among low-income parents. *Journal of Social Issues, 56,* 683–706. doi:10.1111/0022-4537.00191.

Hock, E., & DeMeis, D. (1990). Depression in mothers of infants: The role of maternal employment. *Developmental Psychology, 26,* 285–291. doi:10.1037/0072-1649.26.2.285.

Katras, M. J., Zuiker, V. S., & Bauer, J. W. (2004). Private safety net: Childcare resources from the perspective of rural low-income families. *Family Relations, 53,* 201–209. doi:10.1111/j.0022-2445.2004.00010.x.

Kinukawa, A., Guzman, L., & Lippman, L. (2004). *National estimates of child care and subsidy receipt for children ages 0 to 6: What can we learn from the national household education survey?* http://www.childtrends.org/Files//Child_Trends-2004_10_19_ES_NHES.pdf.

Knafl, K., Breitmayer, B., Gallo, A., & Zoeller, L. (1996). Family response to childhood chronic illness: Description of management styles. *Journal of Pediatric Nursing, 11,* 315–326. doi:10.1016/So882-5963(05)80065-x.

Knox, V. W., London, A. S., & Scott, E. K. (2003, October). *Welfare reform, work, and child care: The role of informal care in the lives of low-income women and children.* http://www.mdrc.org/ publications/353/policybrief.html.

Ko, J., & Manoogian, M. (2005, April). *Commitment to parenting and personal outcomes for rural, low-income Appalachian mothers.* Paper session presented at the annual meeting of the Ohio Association of Family and Consumer Sciences, Perrysburg, OH.

Kuhlthau, K., & Mason, K. O. (1996). Market child care versus care by relatives: Choices made by employed and nonemployed mothers. *Journal of Family Issues, 17,* 561–578. doi:10.1177/019257396017004007.

Lombardi, J. (2003). *Time to care: Redesigning child care to promote education, support families and build communities.* Philadelphia: Temple University Press.

Marks, S., & McDermid, S. (1996). Multiple roles and the self: A theory of role balance. *Journal of Marriage and the Family, 58,* 417–432. http://www.jstor.org/stable/353506.

McCubbin, H. I., & Patterson, J. M. (1983). The family stress process: The double ABCX model of adjustment and adaptation. In H. McCubbin, M. Sussman, & J. M. Patterson (Eds.), *Social stress and the family* (pp. 7–37). New York: Haworth Press.

McRae, S. (2003). Constraints and choices in mothers' employment careers: A consideration of Hakim's Preference Theory. *British Journal of Sociology, 54,* 317–338. doi:10.1111/j.1468-4446.2003.00317.x.

National Association of Child Care Resource and Referral Agencies. (2009). *2008 Price of Child Care.* Arlington: Author. http://www.naccrra.org/randd/docs/2008_Price_of_Child_Care.pdf.

National Association of Child Care Resource and Referral Agencies. (2010). *Child Care in America 2010* (State Fact Sheets). Arlington: Author. http://www.naccrra.org/publications/naccrra-publications/publications/State_Fact_Bk_2010_All_070710.pdf.

National Child Care Information and Technical Assistance Center. (2007). *Public-private partnerships supporting early care and education and after-school care.* Fairfax: Author. http://nccic. acf.hhs.gov/poptopics/public-private.html.

NICHD Early Child Care Research Network. (2005). *Child care and child development: Results from the NICHD study of early child care and youth development.* New York: Guilford.

Overturf Johnson, J. (2005). *Who's minding the kids? Child care arrangements: Winter 2002.* (Current Population Reports No. P70-101). Washington: US Census Bureau.

Porter, T., & Kearns, S. (2006). Family, friends and neighbor care: Crib notes on a complex issue. In R. Rice (Ed.), *Perspectives on family, friend and neighbor child care: Research, programs and policy.* New York: Bank Street College of Education.

Radloff, L. S. (1977). The CES-D scale: A self-report depression scale for research in the general population. *Journal of Applied Psychological Measurement, 1,* 385–401. doi:10.1177/014662167700100306.

Reschke, K. L., Manoogian, M. M., Richards, L. N., Walker, S. K., & Seiling, S. B. (2006). Maternal grandmothers as child care providers for rural, low-income mothers. A unique child care arrangement. *Journal of Children & Poverty, 12,* 159–174. doi:10.1080/10796120600879590.

Reschke, K. L., & Walker, S. K. (2006). Mothers' child caregiving and employment commitments and choices in the context of rural poverty. *Affilia: Journal of Women and Social Work, 21,* 306–319. doi:10.1177/086709906288970.

Richards, L., Manoogian, M., Seiling, S., & Bird, C. (2002, November). *Providing support and presenting challenge: Adult daughters and their mothers in rural, low-income families.* Paper session presented at the annual meeting of the National Council on Family Relations, Houston, TX.

Roschelle, A. R. (1997). *No more kin: Exploring race, class, and gender in family networks.* Thousand Oaks: Sage.

Rural and Appalachian Youth and Families Consortium. (1996). Parenting practices and interventions among marginalized families in Appalachia: Building on family strengths. *Family Relations, 45,* 387–396. http://www.jstor.org/stable/585168.

Schulman, K. (2000). *The high cost of child care puts quality care out of reach for many families* (Issue Brief No. 5). Washington: Children's Defense Fund.

Schulman, K., & Blank, H. (2009). *State child care assistance policies 2009: Most states hold the line, but some lose ground in hard times* (Issue Brief). http://www.nwlc.org/resource/state-child-care-assistance-policies-2009-most-states-hold-line-some-lose-ground-hard-times.

Shoffner, S. (1986). Child care in rural areas: Needs, attitudes, and preferences. *American Journal of Community Psychology, 14,* 521–539. doi:10.1007/BF00935.356.

Smith, J. R. (2002). Commitment to mothering and preference for employment: The voices of women on public assistance with young children. *Journal of Children & Poverty, 8,* 51–66. doi:10.1080/10796120220120386.

Smith, K. (2006). *Rural families choose home-based child care for their preschool-aged children* (Policy Brief No. 3). http://www.carseyinstitute.unh.edu/publications/PB_childcare_06.pdf.

Smith, K., & Gozjolko, K. (2010). Low income and impoverished families pay more disproportionately for childcare (Policy Brief No. 16). http://www.carseyinstitute.unh.edu/publications/PB_Smith_LowIncome-ChildCare.pdf.

Stack, C., & Burton, L. M. (1993). Kinscripts. *Journal of Comparative Family Studies, 24*(2), 157–170.

Uttal, L. (1999). Using kin for child care: Embedment in the socioeconomic networks of extended families. *Journal of Marriage and Family, 61,* 845–857. http://www.jstor.org/stable/354007.

Volling, B. L., & Belsky, J. (1992). The contribution of mother-child and father-child relationships to the quality of sibling interaction: A longitudinal study. *Child Development, 63,* 1209–1222. doi:10.1111/j.1467-8624.1992.tb01690.x.

Walker, R. (1995). *To be real: Telling the truth and changing the face of feminism.* New York: Anchor.

Walker, S. K., & Reschke, K. L. (2004). Child care use by low-income families in rural areas: A contemporary look at the influence of women's work and partner availability. *Journal of Children & Poverty, 10,* 149–167. doi:10.1080/179612042000271585.

Chapter 8
Resources as the Key to Rural Employment

Carolyn L. Bird, Elizabeth M. Dolan and Sharon B. Seiling

Introduction

Getting a job, staying employed, and earning a living wage require a variety of personal and community resources. Resources range from the general to the very specific and from emotional and subjective to tangible and objective. Defined by Hamilton as "anything people use or might want to use to achieve an end" (as cited in Moore and Asay 2008, p. 127), and by Hobfoll (1989, 2001) as goods, services, and conditions that are important or that make it possible to obtain valued items or conditions, resources come into play in many ways as low-income individuals seek and maintain gainful employment. Although Foa (1971) identified emotions and other nontangible items such as love, status, and information as resources, in this chapter, the focus will be on tangible resources in the forms of money, goods, and services. The focus in this chapter, specifically, will be on education, transportation, and other resources related to alleviating material hardship.

Theories and Frameworks for Examining Rural Employment

Success in securing and sustaining employment requires a specific combination of human capital, together with personal and community resources, to match the person with the job, meeting the needs of both employer and employee. Bronfenbrenner's (1994) ecological system frames the interrelatedness of resources contributing to employment. At the mircosystem level, human capital is a personal resource that resides in the individual and is represented through health, intelligence, knowledge, and skills (developed through education and training), and personal

C. L. Bird (✉)
Department of 4-H Youth Development and Family and Consumer Sciences,
North Carolina State University, Raleigh, NC, USA
e-mail: carolyn_bird@ncsu.edu

J. W. Bauer, E. M. Dolan (eds.), *Rural Families and Work,* International Series on Consumer Science 1,
DOI 10.1007/978-1-4614-0382-1_8, © Springer Science+Business Media, LLC 2011

factors such as motivation that enables one to apply other aspects of human capital to employment. *Human capital theory* proposes that possessing a greater amount of human capital will enable a person to get a greater return for his/her skills in the marketplace, i.e., higher wages and benefits (Grossman 1972). Furthermore, investment in one's human capital to improve one's knowledge, skills, and health will "pay off" by increasing employment opportunities, advancement, and wages. Human capital is seen as "an investment of personal resources for the production of profit" (Lin 2001a, p. 19). Becker (1975) noted that employee productivity is enhanced by personal resources, such as abilities, human capital investments on and off the job, and motivation. Personal resources may also include the means to get to one's place of employment, enough food to eat, and a home in which to live and otherwise maintain one's health. Social capital expanded neocapital theory to include social assets (Lin 2001b; Schuller et al. 2000). *Social capital theory* suggests that a person or group will gain resources through association with others in a network of mutual interest and recognition (Burt 2001; Lin 2001b). Therefore, investing one's time in relationships with friends and acquaintances can form mutual obligations that will both demand resources from and give resources to the network members. In addition to informal social capital in networks of family and friends, formal social capital operates at the organizational or community level, with trust in organizations leading to access to goods and services (MacGillivray and Walker 2000). Much of the exploration of social support and the exchange of resources within relationships can be found in Chap. 9. See also Schuller et al. 2000 for a review and critique of the development of social capital theory.

Family resource management theory, as described in Chap. 2, is focused on the demands that families face and the resources available to meet those demands. The family's environment will have bearing on the use of resources (Stafford et al. 1999). To be considered a resource, family resource management theory proposes that an object must have time, place, and form utility (Rettig 2003). Consider the scenario of attempting to make a purchase using the Electronic Benefits Transfer (EBT) card to access one's Supplemental Nutrition Assistance Program (SNAP, formerly known as food stamps) benefit in a small rural grocery store. At the moment of the purchase (time), the individual needs to have at hand in the store (place) a sufficient amount of the acceptable currency (form). Yet, the EBT card may not be a usable resource if the grocery store cannot or will not accept EBT payments. Local grocery stores in some rural areas tend to be small operations with a small customer base due to low population density (Leibtag 2005). As a result, the economies of scale may not be present to warrant investment by the store's owner in technological tools to process EBT cards. In this scenario, it does not matter how much money is available in the EBT account (a different place), or that the US government will subsequently make payment in US dollars (form) for the amount of the EBT transaction. The exchange cannot proceed with this resource, because the EBT card is not acceptable currency to this rural grocer.

Hobfoll (1989, 2001) has proposed a strong link between resources and stress. In his Conservation of Resources Theory (COR), resources are seen as goods, services, and conditions that are valued or that can be used to obtain something of value.

The theory proposes that resource losses are more powerful than resource gains and a person has to invest some of his/her resources to prevent loss, recover from loss, or gain additional resources. When resources are lost due to reduced work hours or a car accident, persons or families who have few resources may enter into a loss spiral in which more losses occur. Reduced work hours can diminish the paycheck so that the family is not able to pay the rent and utilities and, without help, they become homeless. A wrecked vehicle can lead to job loss if no alternative transportation is available.

Continuing Bronfenbrenner's Ecological Model, communities may provide public resources that encircle families at the mesosystem level with resources important to employment, such as different options for employment, child care facilities and services, schools, medical care, affordable housing stock, and public transportation systems linking residential areas to places of employment. This chapter focuses on the role of individual resources as well as public and private resources available in the community to promote and sustain the employment for rural low-income families.

Education

The ability to invest in human capital differs based on family environment, personal resources, and accessibility to educational and training programs (Becker 1975). Because of these and other reasons, low-income workers typically have lower levels of human capital, including less education and training, than their higher earning counterparts. Limited education and training is a barrier to becoming financially self-sufficient (e.g., Medley et al. 2005; Zedlewski 1999). Even those with high school or general educational development diplomas (GED) may struggle to find employment with wages sufficient to support their families (Acs et al. 2000) especially when living in rural communities. Earning a low wage also serves as a barrier to human capital acquisition since aside from discrimination and nepotism, "the most important causes of differences in opportunities are differences in the availability of funds" (Becker 1975, p. 107). Although low-wage workers have less education than mid- and high-wages workers, 73% of low-income household heads have completed high school and 35% have education or training beyond high school (Low-Income Working Families 2009).

The impact of low human capital on employment may be especially substantial for single mothers: 53.7% with less than a high school diploma were employed, compared with 75.4% with high school degrees and 89.6% with college degrees (Levitan and Gluck 2003). When women have more education, they are less likely to be low-wage workers. Kim (2000) reported that in 1998, while 50% of all female workers were low-wage workers, only one-third of those with post-high school education or training were low-wage workers. By using data from National Longitudinal Survey of Youth, Zhan (2006) reported that mothers who got more education were able to improve their financial positions over time. This was especially true for mothers whose incomes were between 100% and 200% of poverty, i.e., more education was positively related to greater financial upward mobility. The results of these studies provide continuing evidence of the fact that overtime earning power in the United States is linked to knowledge and increasingly decoupled from physical strength (Becker 1975).

Low-wage jobs, especially those without hope for advancement, are known as "bad jobs" and often trap workers in unrewarding, difficult, and unstable positions at pay below what is needed to sustain themselves and their families (Fremstad et al. 2008). Opportunities for additional training that would enable workers' advancement are rare in these jobs. As a result, low-wage workers, especially women, have a difficult time changing occupations to escape from the low-wage jobs (Andersson et al. 2002; Power and Rosenberg 1995).

The positive effect of education and training on employment success does not appear to have the expected impact for rural single mothers, however. Porterfield (2001) found that higher levels of education were less effective in raising the financial well-being of rural single mothers than for urban single mothers primarily due to the lack of employment opportunities.

A study of those who left the Temporary Assistance for Needy Families (TANF) program in South Carolina found that women who had greater human and social capital were more likely to find and maintain employment (Medley et al. 2005). Successful TANF-leavers received more assistance in finding employment from their case workers, knew more about services and transitional programs to assist them in transitioning to employment, found the welfare to work programs to be helpful, and had more help from their families than the less successful TANF-leavers.

Using the Comprehensive Child Development Program data, Urban and Olson (2005) explored the link between a low-income woman's ability to manage and her family's well-being. They found that TANF-leavers who had more effective management skills were better able to make the transition from welfare to work. Education was a key factor in predicting recidivism: Those with more education when they entered the welfare-to-work program were more likely to be employed and maintain that employment over time than those with less education. A number of the low-income mothers in their sample had traded investing in their own human capital, i.e., education, for the care of their children. Families need to adapt to time constraints and resources when mothers become employed, and low-income families have more difficulty in managing when community resources are scarce, as is the situation in many rural areas.

The opportunity for education and training beyond a high school degree or general educational development certificate (GED) is limited for TANF clients. Most state TANF programs allow only limited short-term educational opportunities, such as completing a GED or a certificate program no more than 3 months in length, based on the federal rules. GED programs and job-seeking skills courses predominate in most states. Both Banerjee (2002) and Seccombe (2000) reported that the TANF clients they interviewed expressed frustration with this approach. For many rural low-income mothers, the need to travel long distances to take college or other training courses further limited the opportunities to engage in human capital-enhancing training programs.

Transportation

Transportation is a facilitating resource. Families with access to transportation are better able to engage in activities that contribute to well-being, including work, school attendance, shopping, visiting, recreation, and so forth. Personal vehicles are used most importantly for facilitating the owners' ability to earn a living. A measure of the value of transportation is in its efficacy in fulfilling its facilitating role (Magrabi et al. 1991).

Because most people's employment is somewhere other than their places of residence, they must find ways to move between their homes and their jobs in a timely manner. The commuting distances can be quite long for those living in rural communities, making walking to work impossible for most. This *spatial mismatch,* circumstances in which suitable jobs are located in areas not accessible through public transportation or other means by potential workers, is at the heart of the transportation resource challenge for rural families (US Department of Health and Human Services, n.d.) While this mismatch often refers to the migration of employment from urban to suburban areas, it applies equally to rural areas with limited or no public transportation to connect workers to their places of employment with their homes. Lack of public options in most rural communities presents a particular challenge for low-income families who may not have access to a reliable vehicle. Thus, transportation is one of the major challenges rural low-income families encounter when seeking to obtain and maintain employment.

The ability to get from home to work is vital to sustaining employment. Multiple research studies have found that lack of transportation is a major barrier for low-income mothers' employment. The Women's Employment Study surveyed urban welfare-dependent women in Michigan and found that 47.1% of the participants indicated that they had transportation issues, compared to only 7.6% of a broad sample of women in national survey (National Center for Children in Poverty (NCCP) 2001). Meckstroth et al.(2003) reported that welfare clients in Nebraska faced problems with transportation whether they lived in rural or urban areas. Although urban welfare clients were less likely to have drivers' licenses than were rural welfare clients (26% vs. 42%, respectively), they typically had greater access to public transit. Overall, 18% of rural Nebraska welfare clients reported having transportation issues compared to 13% of their urban counterparts. Fletcher and Jensen (2000) reported that only 25% of rural TANF clients in Iowa had a registered vehicle. Similarly, Minnesota employers reported that 30% of rural TANF clients had transportation issues compared with 23% of urban TANF clients (Owen et al. 2000).

Job sites often are far from where low-income families live (Blumenberg 2002; Pindus et al. 2007). In metropolitan areas, many low-income jobs sought by welfare and former welfare clients are located in suburban areas. Since affordable housing for low-income families is not usually available in suburban areas, low-wage earners find that they have long commutes to their places of employment (Dunifon et al. 2005). Thompson (1997) reported that low-income women with complex lives were less likely to be employed when their transportation options were less reliable and more complicated, i.e., not having a reliable car and/or facing a long commute via public transit. In rural areas, too, employers may be some distance from residences, especially when located in other towns (Pindus et al. 2007).

Community and state/federal partnerships on transportation have focused on supplying public transit in metropolitan areas. The Federal Transit Authority reported that the poor are not well served by public transit in either urban or rural areas (Surface Transportation Policy Partnership, n.d.a). Even in metropolitan areas, public transportation options may be more available in suburban areas than in center city residential neighborhoods, and hours of service may not support low-wage workers with jobs that have nonstandard shifts or hours (Blumenberg 2002).

Long commutes to places of employment can be burdensome for low-income families, whether they reside in rural or urban areas. Using data from the Three-City Study, Roy et al. (2004) reported that low-income urban mothers had little control over their transportation choices, with public transit often requiring multiple transfers to get between home and job sites. The average commute time for the mothers in this study was 2 hours. Fletcher et al. (2002) reported that only 10% of their rural survey participants had access to public transportation. Having reliable transportation was statistically significantly related to being employed. Unreliable transportation had caused respondents (in the last year) to quit a job or training/education program, or to be unable to take a job or start a training/educational program. Siegel and Abbott (2007) examined the work-lives of the poor and found that transportation and inadequate employment opportunities presented the most significant barriers to employment among those who returned to the welfare rolls. Furthermore, those returning to welfare reported that they had significantly more difficulty getting to work on time than did those who had not returned to welfare.

Yet even as we focus on the transportation needs of low-income families, the employers' role in a successful transportation program should not be overlooked. To be successful, the transportation program must meet the needs of employers, including the ability to get the workers to their jobs on time. Transportation systems must also meet the needs of the workers to accomplish family-related tasks and access the resources that support employment, such as training and child care. The Chicago area study (Elliot et al. 1999) identified key principles for planning and operating employment-supportive transportation services, including route and schedule flexibility, punctual and reliable service, and service flexibility to respond to unplanned events and emergencies. These transportation characteristics correspond strongly with the stated needs of rural low-income families.

When low-income rural families' own vehicles, the cars or trucks, are often older models that require more repairs than newer ones, making them more costly to maintain. In a survey of Iowa families, many of the low-income rural respondents indicated that while they had vehicles, they were concerned about the reliability of those vehicles (Fletcher and Jensen 2000). The Children's Defense Fund found that in Mississippi, the poorest of the poor spent 42% (twice the national average) of their budget on transportation, i.e., purchase, operation, and maintenance (Surface Transportation Policy Partnership, n.d.b). For those with low incomes, whether rural or urban residents, car loans tend to be more expensive because low-income car purchasers are seen as higher credit risks and are therefore charged higher interest rates (Surface Transportation Policy Partnership, n.d.b). Reliable transportation is essential for maintaining employment, and when rural families do not have access to reliable transportation, they face more hardships than their urban counterparts.

Other Resources

Beyond education that prepares one for employment and transportation that ensures that the worker gets to the job, other resources in the community can be vital to maintaining one's place in the workforce. This is particularly true for low-income workers who struggle to find employment paying a wage that allows the worker to adequately support his or her family. Many low-income working families need support programs for help with rent and utility payments, food programs that enhance overall health as well as provide energy and strength for the job, medical care that helps maintain the health of family members, child care subsidies that enable parents of young children to work outside of home, and/or transportation programs that provide help to maintain vehicles or provide rides and cash assistance for overall support for daily living. Most of these programs are funded by the federal government but come through local county or community agencies. Being able to access these programs is often a very important skill for low-income family members to have.

When income does not allow families to have all the basics needed to sustain them, they suffer from material hardships (Mirowsky and Ross 1999). Low-income wage-earning families can have an especially difficult time because their incomes or their assets, such as their cars, may make them ineligible for many of the government support programs (Acs et al. 2000; Bok and Simmons 2002; Boushey and Gunderson 2001). Any number of studies have found material hardships to be prevalent among TANF-leavers (e.g., Bok and Simmons 2002; Edin and Lein 1997; Polit et al. 2001).

Food insecurity and housing issues are endemic among those who have material hardships. Food insecurity is defined as not having enough food for all family members to eat and/or skipping meals because there is not enough food. Housing problems include not being able to pay rent and/or utilities, being evicted, or having utilities turned off (Boushey and Gunderson 2001; Mammen et al. 2009a). Rental housing prices have risen faster than wages for low-income workers. The result is that many low-income families, whether they reside in rural or urban areas, are paying more for rent than the standard 30% of income (Bok and Simmons 2002). While families with at least one employed person have a lower incidence of material hardship than families without a worker, working does not insulate families from hardship when workers earn low wages (Boushey and Gunderson 2001).

Having assets may make low-income working families ineligible for some government programs, increasing the incidence of material hardship. For example, in the past, a vehicle that the employed person used to get to work every day could keep the family from qualifying for food stamps because the value of vehicles was counted as an asset for eligibility. In fact, Bok and Simmons (2002) reported that food stamp applicants were told to get rid of their cars in order to become eligible. Currently, SNAP eligibility rules no longer count the value of a vehicle that is used by the SNAP applicant to get to a place of employment. But the value of a vehicle could still be problematic if it is not used for work and would be considered as a countable resource (US Department of Agriculture, n.d.). Another barrier is that benefits' offices are typically open during standard business hours. If the low-income wage earner also works standard business hours, just applying for benefits may be difficult-to-impossible if the worker has to take time off from work to apply (Acs et al. 2000). Furthermore, the benefits' offices may be some distance from both the rural low-income worker's home and place of employment.

Families facing material hardships will struggle to pay for all needed expenses. The end result of "robbing Peter to pay Paul" is that some bills may not get paid. Families reported that they chose to not seek medical care in order to buy food, or to not buy food in order to get needed medical care; they paid their rent but not the utilities especially during the season when states have no-turn-off rules; and so forth. Health of family members suffers when families do not have enough to eat, forego medical care, have utilities turned off, or are evicted (Boushey 2002; Cohen et al. 2006). Fisher and Weber (2004), using Panel Study of Income Dynamics (PSID) data, found that those who lived in nonmetropolitan counties had fewer assets than those who lived in more urban counties. They concluded that the low level of assets would be a detriment to rural families because families would find it more difficult to weather and recover from income shortfalls such as reduction in hours or job loss.

Hobfoll (1989, 2001) noted that goods, services, and conditions can be important to goal accomplishment. Community services are a part of total consumption, providing services free or at minimal cost, including police protection and parks (Magrabi et al. 1991). Community services can be the condition that supports rural low-come families by bridging the personal asset deficit gap in providing resources necessary to sustain family life and employment. The ecological model (Fig. 8.1) offers a visual representation of the selection and use of nonpersonal resources to achieve goals, such as employment, satisfaction of needs, and quality of life supporting services.

Rural Families Speak (RFS) About Resources

Education

Several RFS papers have focused on the role that human capital plays in rural low-income mothers' ability to contribute to the financial well-being of their families.

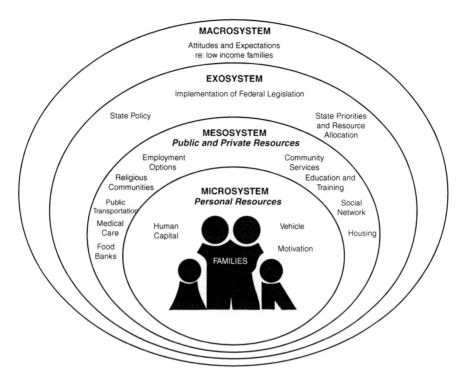

Fig. 8.1 Ecological model of nonpersonal resource selection and use

Bird and Bauer (2009) found that the rural mothers' initial educational level was important in their pursuit of additional education or training. Those with higher education initially had a greater likelihood of pursuing further education, and those with less education were less likely to improve their educational status. Furthermore, Bird and Bauer reported that having more children was associated with the mother's decreased likelihood of getting additional education, as was the presence of a partner. On the other hand, having preschool-aged children actually increased the likelihood of the rural low-income mothers improving their educational status. Mammen et al.(2009b) used Panel 1 Wave 1 data to examine the factors that were associated with the decision to be employed or to stay at home with children. They found that the odds of a mother working were 57% greater for high school graduates than those with less education. Similar to Porterfield's (2001) findings, the odds of working were not increased for those women who had training past high school. Human capital alone was not associated with employment or hours worked (Simmons et al. 2007). Social support, however, was a significant factor contributing to human capital development for these rural low-income mothers. Like others, Simmons et al. (2007) postulated that the occupational limitation of many rural communities muted the effects of educational attainment.

Dolan et al. (2008), in their examination of the mothers who were receiving welfare in Panel 1 Wave 1 but not in Waves 2 and 3, found that mothers who improved their financial position the most had some additional training post-high school that led them to jobs with higher than average wages. For example, Tana,[1] a 23-year-old single mother of 2-year-old twins, got pregnant while in college and moved back to her home town. She was able to convince her TANF case worker to count her classes toward her bachelor's degree in education toward a portion of her work requirement. In Wave 3, she had started teaching part-time.

> I teach seventh and eighth graders art in Louisville….I'm part time right now…but then in the afternoons I'm a paraprofessional for the K through 3 resource room and I help out there since I, it was just a way to make more hours…

Another mother, Ruthanne, had also been able to finish her degree program and was able to find a job.

Seiling et al. (2005) reported on the occupational dreams of the rural low-income mothers who were employed in the service industry. Contrary to the popular belief that poor people are lazy and can improve their financial situation if they just work harder, the mothers in the RFS project had aspirations to get further education that would allow them to change to a higher paying occupation. When asked what kept them from pursuing their ideal occupation, the most common response was that they could not afford to go to school, i.e., they could not afford the tuition and/or they could not afford to take time off work for classes, or their communities did not offer the kind of educational experience that they would need to have (Seiling et al. 2005).

Transportation

Transportation issues related to employment have been included in several RFS papers. Using a subsample of RFS mothers, Berry et al. (2008) reported that having a car decreased the odds of being unemployed. They also indicated that receiving transportation assistance was a predictor of both intermittent employment and unemployment. Having a valid driver's license significantly increased the odds of the RFS participant mothers being employed (Mammen et al. 2009b).

Sano et al. (2010) found that transportation and commuting distances were two of the structural variables that made maintaining employment challenging for the rural mothers. Mammen and Dolan's (2005) examination of RFS mothers living in the Northeastern states also revealed that transportation problems kept the mothers from being employed. The rural mothers who were employed were able to call on family and friends for all kinds of support, including transportation when needed. Similarly, Katras et al. (2009) qualitative analysis of 62 RFS participants who had received TANF at some point during the three waves of interviews revealed that transportation support was vital to the mothers successfully raising their incomes. For example, when Jolie, a 24-year-old single mother of three children, was in an

---

[1] All names are pseudonyms.

auto accident and was without a car, she had numerous family members upon whom she could call for help. *"My daddy's car, I use. Or my aunt's car, somebody's car, I'll call somebody."* Similarly, Jenna, a 21-year-old single mother of one, stated: *"My grandma's always available (for rides)…"* The mothers who were not successful in raising their incomes had more transportation problems. Having no vehicle and/or no driver's license was fairly common, as was having a very unreliable car. Millicent, a 21-year-old mother of one and separated from her husband, who did not work during our 3-year interview period, described her car in this way: *"Oh, it's got something wrong with it where it stalls. The brakes have needed to be changed three times…something with the engine, wires and spark plugs, a gasket."*

Older vehicles typically require more maintenance, and correspondingly, cost more to repair. Keeping a car in working condition can be an expensive proposition, and low-income families may not always have the wherewithal to deal with issues when they first arise (Dolan et al. 2006). Ruthanne, a 24-year-old divorced mother of a young daughter, was very vocal about her car problems and the struggle she had keeping it in working condition. She owned a 1995 car model that her parents had helped her buy.

> The car, the stupid car, the car problem. I put unbelievable amounts of money into the car, and I feel like I'm constantly putting money into the car. The car didn't want to start when it rained. I had to put $300 into the car. The car is a pain. So when the car goes, then the whole life goes down the tubes….It broke down a few times because I wasn't keeping up on some of the maintenance, which is another issue about being poor, you have trouble keeping up, just keeping up with things as they fall apart. The spark plugs and the spark plug wire things, they all had to be changed. So when it would rain really hard, my car would not start. It would just die.

Ruthann explained that over the last 6 months, she had invested more than $1,000 in repairing a car that had cost her $5,000. She was frustrated at the number of repairs and at how difficult it was for her to pay for the repairs. Although her parents were willing to help her out, she did not want to depend on them to pay for everything.

> Is it hard for me to get the money …? Yes, I'm pulling like one hundred things to get the money together. Most of the time my parents will say, "Just go bring it to the shop. We'll take care of it." There's always a glitch in there where I have to come up with something. I can't just come in totally empty handed.

Jenna also mentioned the difficulty of getting her car repaired, even after her financial circumstances had improved. *"The car might have to sit in the driveway for two or three days until I got paid, but yes, I (got the repairs done)."*

One solution to spending a lot of money on car repairs was to have a friend who was a mechanic. Cherilyn, a 21-year-old single mother of one, had a car that needed constant repair work. She would have been hard pressed to pay for the repairs if she had to pay full price.

> There was a period over the summer where I'd be driving down the road and the car would just shut off….And I would have to pull over, turn off the key, turn the key back on, hope the car would start, and it got to the point where the car would not restart. This went on for months. I never had any warning when it was going to happen…Fortunately, my mechanic's one of my best friends. He ended up fixing my car for me for nothing.

Having a dependable car can be empowering, especially when a mother has struggled with unreliable vehicles in the past. Lilliana, a 35-year-old divorced mother of one, worked as a certified nursing assistant. She changed jobs to work at the local hospital so that she would not have to drive so much. The hospital paid her a "signing bonus" which she used to buy a newer car. *"I just got a car that's reasonably... for the first time in my life, that's not a waiting to die. It's still under warranty, actually. I've never had a car like that. And, so I can pretty much get to everything."*

Even routine costs can add up. Ruthanne talked about the cost of gasoline for her car.

> Gas is killing me. Gas is really killing me because like I said I have to travel so far. My daughter also goes to school in Middletown. I have to travel that route in order to get to school. So now that gas prices have gone up, it's really very hard to like keep gas in my car...I burn a lot of gas.

Rural low-income mothers who do not have transportation are limited in where they can go and when they can go. Jolene, 24 years old with a young child and separated from her husband, related the problems she faced because she had no car. *"My problem is I could probably find a job, but I just don't have transportation. I've got my license and everything but I don't have a car. If I had a vehicle to get going I could find me a job."* When she was asked how she got around, she responded:

> Bum rides. Well, like to go to the store or something I have to wait until somebody comes around says we go. That's basically it, 'cuz half my family lives in another county. Well, my friend who takes me, goes to school. So I usually have to wait until she gets outa school before I can go anywhere.

Beyond being a vital resource to connect rural low-income workers to employment, transportation is critical to family maintenance activities that support the worker's ability to engage in employment. When low-income rural families have no transportation, a community transportation system that is flexible and multidimensional could be a valued resource. Sasha's story illustrates the importance of a holistic approach to community transportation. Sasha, a 43-year-old divorced mother of two children who received none of the court-ordered child support for her children, relied on a community-based transportation system. Her utilization pattern of the community transit system demonstrated key components of a responsive rural low-income worker transportation system. When asked about scheduling, Sasha responded: *"You call them a night ahead of time, tell them your schedule, what you need and what you need to have done..."*

The flexibility of the community transit system was an important support for Sasha. Sasha's community (mesosystem) provided a key resource to support rural family life. That the transportation was connected to a public assistance resource (exosystem) made it affordable. *"That's* [community transit] *the only thing that runs around town that's affordable...."* Because Sasha left for work before the school bus was scheduled to pick up her children for daycare, she relied on her work transportation to also get her children to daycare.

> They [community transit] start at 5:30 in the morning, quarter to six....From daycare and then the kids get a free ride and they go around town with the ladies, 'til daycare opens up.

> Then when daycare opens up they're usually there and I get a call from the (transit company), saying "Yep, we dropped them off." So it's kind of cool.

Katras et al. (2009) reported that mothers who successfully left TANF for work had greater transportation resources than those who were not successful, including being more likely to have a driver's license (90% vs. 66%), For Eliza, a 33-year-old African-American single mother of seven, transportation was a significant barrier to her ability to find employment as well as to access other basic needs and services. She stated:

> The main thing now would be transportation, because it wouldn't be so bad if it was just transportation to the point where I need to go and back, but with me there's dropping the kids off at childcare, picking them up, and then bringing us home, kind of thing.

The obligations of employment and daily life require rural low-income parents often to cover large amounts of territory, given the reality of rural topography. Rural low-income families, like families everywhere, need to travel places other than just between home and work: To the child care provider, to shopping, to the health care provider, etc. (Blumenburg and Walker 2003). Having reliable transportation, whether it be a personal vehicle or a community transit system, is essential not only for employment but to further family development.

Yet, adequate and responsive transportation is only one of the essential resources. Since rural employers tend to pay low wages, even when both parents are employed in full-time jobs, the total income may not be adequate to lift a rural family to a point where they are able to be financially self-sustaining.

Other Resources

Other resources are needed for rural low-income families to sustain themselves. The wages earned by rural low-income families can mean that they do not have enough income to cover all their necessities. Having critical resources in the community and knowing how to access them in times of need are vitally important for rural low-income families. The RFS participants were asked about a number of resources available in their communities. Health care is very important to all, especially workers who need to be healthy to maintain their jobs and workers who have responsibilities for caring for family members. When asked if they had easy access to grocery stores, medical care, and schools, about 10% of the RFS participants responded that they did not, and 12% responded that they "could not get to" services they needed. A majority of participants, however, appeared to be able to navigate the formal support system, stating that they knew how to access services such as assistance with utilities, housing, transportation, job training, and financial aid.

Material hardships include food insecurity and housing problems. Swanson et al. (2008) reported that among the Panel 1 RFS sample, 41.8% were food insecure. They also found that those who were food insecure were significantly less able to develop a support system and were also less likely to have supportive systems, such

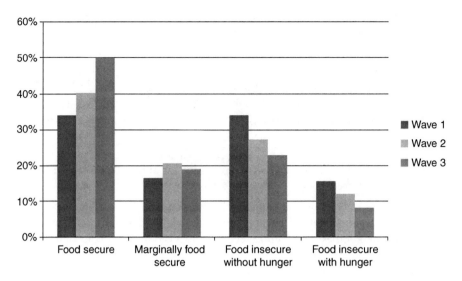

Fig. 8.2 Food security across the three waves

as a church or other organization or a supportive circle of friends. Accessing community food pantries and sharing meals with family and friends were strategies used by those who were food insecure to expand their food resources.

Among the employed Panel 1 RFS families, food insecurity declined over the 3-year interview period. Almost half indicated that they were food insecure in Wave 1 (Fig. 8.2). By Wave 3, less than 10% were food insecure with hunger, and about 70% were either food secure or marginally food secure.

In all three waves, we asked the participants if they had difficulty paying for basic needs. About 80% in Wave 1 indicated that they did, with the number of problem expenses ranging from 1 to 9 (out of 10) (data not shown). For the most part, our rural low-income families had difficulty paying for one or two items ($M=2.8$, $SD=2.3$, median$=2.0$). In Waves 2 and 3, the incidence of material hardship declined. In Wave 2, 70% indicated some problems ($M=2.3$, $SD=2.4$, median$=1.0$), and in Wave 3, only 60% indicated problems ($M=2.0$, $SD=2.5$, median$=1.0$). In Wave 2, we specifically asked if they had trouble paying their rent or mortgage with 24%, indicating that they did. In Wave 3, we specifically asked if they had trouble paying for child care: 12% indicated that they did. We also asked about car maintenance and repairs: 35% indicated that this expense was difficult for them.

Many of the families in the study used formal support resources available in their communities. Government support programs offset the incidence of material hardship by supplementing meager incomes. The largest proportion of RFS families in Panel 1 used the health insurance provided by Medicaid (Table 8.1). Next, in frequency of use were food-related programs, including Special Supplemental Nutrition Program for Women, Infants, and Children (WIC), school lunch, and SNAP (food stamps). Less than one-third of the employed families used the Low-Income Home Energy Assistance Program (LIHEAP) or child care assistance. Child care

Table 8.1 RFS Panel 1 employed families' use of welfare benefits over all three waves

Welfare benefit	Wave 1 $N=309$	Wave 2 $N=266$	Wave 3 $N=190$
TANF (% yes)	8.4%	10.5%	12.6%
Food stamps (% yes)	40.5%	38.3%	38.9%
Medicaid (% yes)	65.1%	66.4%	58.1%
WIC (% yes)	66.3%	54.1%	41.6%
School lunch/breakfast (% yes)	56.9%	62.3%	63.5%
LIHEAP (% yes)	27.2%	35.9%	35.0%
Subsidized housing (% yes)	15.9%	19.8%	25.0%
Child care assistance (% yes)	30.0%	20.3%	23.5%

assistance, especially, is important to rural low-income parents' ability to maintain employment. Few of the RFS employed families had housing assistance (Table 8.1). Panel 2 participants' use of support programs mirrored that of Panel 1 participants. Panel 3 participants, however, had lower participation rates in all programs except WIC and school lunch/breakfast (refer to Table 1.3). Participation in all of the programs differed significantly between the families with working mothers and partners and those who were not employed. Program participation was greater among the nonemployed families (data not shown).

The low wages available in rural areas often lead residents to make money in alternative endeavors. RFS participants were asked if they or their partners had ever done odd jobs for cash. Forty-one percent of participants and 46% of their partners had engaged in such activities. Participant's activities included child care/elder care, collecting cans/recycling, house cleaning, and lawn mowing. Partner's jobs were composed mainly of lawn mowing, carpentry, car repair, and recycling.

Managing the everyday needs of the family often was challenging for the RFS participants, whether they were employed, looking for work, getting additional education, or were unable to work. In Panel 1 Wave 3, 38% of the families had experienced deficiencies in their residences, 27% of which indicated that the problem had not been fixed at the time of the interview. Almost one-third (31%) said that the cost of home repairs presented some difficulty for the family. Furthermore, 18% of participants in Wave 3 lived in neighborhoods felt that they were unsafe, and 11% felt that their homes were unsafe. Forty-five percent reported problems with their cars, and 15% had missed work or training because of this in Wave 3. The cost of gasoline influenced the transportation choices of 39% of families.

Summary

Low-income families have more difficulty in managing when community resources are scarce, such as one would find in a rural area. The lack of public transit can contribute to the transportation problem because when unreliable vehicles break down, no public alternative is available (Urban and Olson 2005). Limited education resources translate into few opportunities to get employment-enhancing training.

For low-income families living in rural areas, having reliable transportation is critical. Community transportation systems are not feasible for many rural communities. When it is possible, the transit program must be affordable as well as flexible to meet the needs of the low-income families. Creating and/or expanding programs to help low-income rural families get subsidies for car repairs or help in purchasing a vehicle is vital. Some rural mothers could even need help in getting their driver's licenses.

Improving access to educational opportunities for those transitioning from welfare to work is important in improving rural low-income mothers' occupational choices. Because of the limited employment opportunities, additional training choices need to be strategic in order to command higher wages. As was illustrated in Dolan et al. (2008), certain types of educational programs (such as health- and educational-related programs) can result in employment with wages high enough for the family to thrive.

Low wages mean that many rural families need to access welfare support systems even when employed. A material hardship, such as food insecurity and not being able to pay for basic needs, was a fact of life for these low-income working families. Government welfare benefit programs were important to these rural low-income families to help them supplement their meager earnings and help alleviate some of the hardships they faced in paying for their basic necessities.

Discussion Questions

1. Which theory or theories are most useful in the investigation of rural low-income families' access to transportation and other resources and the relationship to employment? Are there other theories that could be used and how would these expand our understanding?
2. In what ways is transportation both a resource for and a barrier to employment?
3. What role does rurality play in resource availability? Are some resources readily available while others are not?
4. In what ways does community influence the ability to achieve economic self-sufficiency?
5. How would even mild material hardship influence parental choices regarding employment?
6. What did you learn in this chapter that helps you understand the lived experience of rural low-income families?

References

Acs, G., Phillips, K. R., & McKenzie, D. (2000). Playing by the rules, but losing the game: American in low-income working families. In R. Kazis & M. S. Miller (Eds.), *Low-wage workers in the new economy* (pp. 21–44). Washington, DC: Urban Institute.

Andersson, F., Holzer, H. J., & Lane, J. I. (2002). *The interactions of workers and firms in the low-wage labor market*. http://www.urban.org/UploadedPDF/410608_lowwage.pdf.

Banerjee, M. (2002). Voicing realities and recommending reform in PRWORA. *Social Work, 47*, 315–327.

Bauer, J. W., & Dolan, E. (2003). The impact of financial life skills and knowledge of community resources on food security [Abstract]. *Proceedings of the Fifth Conference of the International Society for Quality-of-Life Studies* (p. 151). Frankfurt, Germany.

Becker, G. S. (1975). *Human capital: A theoretical and empirical analysis with special reference to education* (2nd ed.). New York: National Bureau of Economic Research.

Berry, A. A., Katras, M. J., Sano, Y., Lee, J., & Bauer, J. W. (2008). Job volatility of rural, low-income mothers: A mixed methods approach. *Journal of Family and Economic Issues, 29*, 5–22. doi:10.1007/s10834-007-9096-1.

Bird, C. L., & Bauer, J. W. (2009). Understanding the factors that influence opportunity for education and training. *Consumers Interests Annual, 55*, 86. http://www.consumerinterests.org/2000-2009Proceedings.php.

Blumenberg, E. (2002). Planning for the transportation needs of welfare participants. *Journal of Planning Education and Research, 22*, 152–163. doi:10.1177/0739456X02238444.

Blumenburg, E., & Walker, M. (2003). *The long journey to work: A federal transportation policy for working families*. http://www.brookings.edu/~/media/Files/rc/reports/2003/07transportation_waller/20030801_Waller.pdf.

Bok, M., & Simmons, L. (2002). Post-welfare reform, low-income families and the dissolution of the safety net. *Journal of Family and Economic Issues, 23*, 217–238. doi:10.1023/A:1020391009561.

Boushey, H. (2002). *The needs of the working poor: Helping working families make ends meet*. Testimony before the US Senate Committee on Health, Education, Labor and Pensions, February 14, 2002. http://www.epi.org/publications/entry/webfeatures_viewpoints_boushey_testimony_20020214.html.

Boushey, H., & Gundersen, B. (2001). *When work just isn't enough: Measuring hardships faced by families after moving from welfare to work*. (EPI Briefing Paper). http://www.epi.org/publications/entry/briefingpapers_hardships.

Bronfenbrenner, U. (1994). Ecological models of human development. In M. Gauvain & M. Cole (Eds.), *Readings on the development of children* (2nd ed., pp. 37–43). New York: Freeman. (Reprinted from *International encyclopedia of education*, Vol. 3, 2nd ed., Oxford: Elsevier.)

Bubolz, M. M., & Sontag, M. S. (1993). Human ecology theory. In P. G. Boss, W. J. Doherty, R. LaRossa, W. R. Schumm, & S. K. Steinmetz (Eds.), *Sourcebook of family theories and methods: A contextual approach* (pp. 419–450). New York: Springer.

Burt, R. S. (2001). Structural holes versus network closure as social capital. In N. Lin, K. Cook, & R. S. Burt (Eds.), *Social capital: Theory and research* (pp. 31–56). New Brunswick: Transaction Publishers.

Cohen, R., Kim, M., & Ohls, J. (2006). *Hunger in America: National report prepared for America's Second Harvest*. http://feedingamerica.org/our-network/~/media/Files/A2HNationalReport.ashx?.pdf.

Dolan, E. M., Braun, B., Prochaska-Cue, K., & Varcoe, K. P. (2002). Conceptualizing the interface among family, community and labor force participation for rural limited resource families. Paper session presented at the 42nd Annual Workshop, National Association for Welfare Research and Statistics, Albuquerque, NM. http://www.nawrs.org/NewMexico/papers/t5b1.pdf.

Dolan, E. M., Katras, M. J., Braun, B., & Seiling, S. (2006). *Rural TANF recipients: How do they fare overtime?* Paper presented at the Welfare Research and Evaluation Conference, Crystal City, VA.

Dolan, E. M., Braun, B., Katras, M. J., & Seiling, S. (2008). Getting off TANF: Experiences of rural mothers. *Families in Society, 89*, 456–465. doi:10.1606/1044-3894.3771.

Dunifon, R., Kalil, A., & Bajracharya, A. (2005). Maternal working conditions and child well-being in welfare-leaving families. *Developmental Psychology, 41*, 851–859. doi:10.1037/0012-1649.41.6.851.

Edin, K., & Lein, L. (1997). *Making ends meet*. New York: Russell Sage Foundation.

Elliot, M., Palubinsky, B., & Tierney, J. (1999, September/October). Overcoming roadblocks on the way to work. *Urban Research Monitor, 4*(4). http://www.huduser.org/periodicals/urm/1099/urmintro.html.

Fisher, M. G., & Weber, B. A. (2004). *Does economic vulnerability depend on place of residence? Asset poverty across the rural-urban continuum* (Working Paper No. 04-01). http://www.rupri.org/Forms/WP0401.pdf.

Fletcher, C. N., & Jensen, H. (2000). *Iowa rural welfare to work strategies project: Final report to the Iowa Department of Human Services.* Ames: Iowa State University.

Fletcher, C. N., Garasky, S., & Jensen, H. H. (2002). Transiting from welfare to work: No bus, no car, no way. Paper session presented at the Hard-to-Employ and Welfare Reform Conference, Washington, DC. http://www.northwestern.edu/ipr/jcpr/workingpapers/wpfiles/fletcher_garasky_jensen_SRI2001.pdf.

Foa, U. G. (1971). Interpersonal and resource economics. *Science, 171*(3969), 345–351. doi:10.1126/science.171.3969.345.

Fremstad, S., Ray, R., & Rho, H. J. (2008). *Working families and economic insecurity in the States: The role of job quality and work supports.* http://www.cepr.net/documents/publications/state_2008_05.pdf.

Grossman, M. (1972). On the concept of health capital and the demand for health. *The Journal of Political Economy, 80*(2), 223–255. http://www.jstor.org/stable/1830580.

Hobfoll, S. E. (1989). Conservation of resources: A new attempt at conceptualizing stress. *American Psychologist, 44,* 513–524. doi:10.1037/0003-066X.44.3.513.

Hobfoll, S. E. (2001). The influence of culture, community, and the nested-self in the stress process: Advancing the conservation of resource theory. *Applied Psychology: An International Review, 50,* 337–412. doi:10.1111/1464-0597.00062.

Hsueh, J., & Yoshikawa, H. (2007). Working nonstandard schedules and variable shifts in low-income families: Association with parental psychological well-being, family functioning, and child well-being. *Developmental Psychology, 43,* 620–632. doi:10.1037/0012-1649.43.3.620.

Katras, M. J., Dolan, E. M., Seiling, S. B., & Braun, B. (2009). The bumpy road off TANF for rural mothers. *Family Science Review, 14*(1). http://familyscienceassociation.org/archived%20journal%20articles/FSR_vol14_2008/1Mary%20Jo_Katras.pdf.

Kim, M. (2000). Women paid low wages: Who they are and where they work. *Monthly Labor Review, 123*(9), 26–30. http://www.bls.gov/opub/mlr/2000/09/art3full.pdf.

Leibtag, E. (2005). Where you shop matters: Store formats drive variation in retail food prices. *Amber Waves, 3*(5), 12–18. http://www.ers.usda.gov/AmberWaves/November05/pdf/FullIssueNovember2005.pdf.

Levitan, M., & Gluck, R. (2003, September). *Job market realities and federal welfare policy.* http://www.cssny.org/pubs/special/2003_09_fedwelfare.pdf.

Lin, N. (2001a). Building a network theory of social capital. In N. Lin, K. Cook, & R. S. Burt (Eds.), *Social capital: Theory and research* (pp. 3–29). New Brunswick: Transaction.

Lin, N. (2001b). *Social capital: A theory of social structure and action.* Cambridge: Cambridge University Press.

Low-Income Working Families. (2009). *Updated facts and figures* (LIWF Fact Sheet). http://www.urban.org/publications/411900.html.

MacGillivray, A., & Walker, P. (2000). Local social capital: Making it work on the ground. In S. Baron, J. Field, & T. Schuller (Eds.), *Social capital: Critical perspectives* (pp. 197–211). New York: Oxford University Press.

Magrabi, F. M., Chung, Y. S., Cha, S. S., & Yang, S. (1991). *The economics of household consumption.* New York: Praeger.

Mammen, S., & Dolan, E. M. (2005). *Employment and obstacles to employment for rural, low-income mothers in the Northeast.* Paper session presented at the Rural Poverty in the Northeast: Strengthening the Regional Research Effort Conference, College Park, MD. http://nercrd.psu.edu/publications/rdppapers/rdp28.pdf.

Mammen, S., Bauer, J. W., & Richards, L. N. (2009a). Understanding persistent food insecurity: A paradox of place and circumstance. *Social Indicators Research, 92,* 151–168. doi:10.1007/s11205-008-9294-8.

Mammen, S., Lass, D., & Seiling, S. B. (2009b). Labor force supply decisions of rural low-income mothers. *Journal of Family and Economic Issues, 30,* 67–79. doi:10.1007/s10834-008-9136-5.

Meckstroth, A., Ponza, M., & Derr, M. (2003). Employment obstacles in rural areas. *Perspectives, 1*(1), 1011. http://www.rupri.org/Forms/Perspectivesvol1n1.pdf.

Medley, B. C., Edelhock, M., Liu, Q., & Martin, L. S. (2005). Success after welfare: What makes the difference? An ethnographic study of welfare leavers in South Carolina. *Journal of Poverty, 9,* 45–63. doi:10.1300/J134v09n01_03.

Mirowsky, J., & Ross, C. E. (1999). Economic hardship across the life course. *American Sociological Review, 64,* 548–569. http://www.jstor.org/stable/2657257.

Moore, T. J., & Asay, S. M. (2008). *Family resource management.* Thousand Oaks: Sage.

Morris, J. E., & Coley, R. L. (2004). Maternal, family, and work correlates of role strain in low-income mothers. *Journal of Family Psychology, 18,* 424–432. doi:10.1037/0893-3200.18.3.424.

National Center for Children in Poverty (NCCP). (2001). Why some women fail to achieve economic security: Low job skills and mental health problems are key barriers. *The Forum, 4*(2), 1–3. http://www.researchforum.org/media/forum42.pdf.

Owen, G., Shelton, E., Stevens, A. B., Nelson-Christinedaughter, J. N., Roy, C., & Heineman, J. (2000). *Whose job is it? Employers' views on welfare reform.* http://www.northwestern.edu/ipr/jcpr/workingpapers/wpfiles/Owen_Shelton.pdf.

Pindus, N., Theodos, B., & Kingsley, G. T. (2007). *Place matters: Employers, low-income workers, and regional economic development.* http://www.urban.org/UploadedPDF/411534_place_matters.pdf.

Polit, D. F., Widom, R., Edin, K., Bowie, S., London, A. S., Scott, E. K., & Valenzuela, A. (2001). *Is work enough? The experiences of current and former welfare mothers who work.* http://www.mdrc.org/publications/74/full.pdf.

Porterfield, S. L. (2001). Economic vulnerability among rural single-mother families. *American Journal of Agricultural Economics, 83,* 1302–1311. doi:10.1111/0002-9092.00282.

Power, M., & Rosenberg, R. (1995). Race, class, and occupational mobility: Black and white women in service work in the United States. *Feminist Economics, 1*(3), 40–59. doi:10.1080/714042248.

Rettig, K. D. (2003). Family Resource Management. In D. Bredehoft & M. Walcheski (Eds.), *Family life education: Integrating theory and practice* (pp. 101–109). Minneapolis: National Council on Family Relations.

Roy, K. M., Tubbs, C. Y., & Burton, L. M. (2004). Don't have no time: Daily rhythms and the organization of time for low-income families. *Family Relations, 53,* 168–178. doi:10.1111/j.0022-2445.2004.00007.x.

Sano, Y., Katras, M. J., Lee, J., Bauer, J. W., & Berry, A. A. (2010). Working towards sustained employment: A closer look at intermittent employment of rural low-income mothers. *Families in Society, 91,* 342–349. doi:10.1606/1044-3894.4039.

Schuller, T., Baron, S., & Field, J. (2000). Social capital: A review and critique. In S. Baron, J. Field, & T. Schuller (Eds.), *Social capital: Critical perspectives* (pp. 1–38). New York: Oxford University Press.

Seccombe, K. (2000). Families in poverty in the 1990s: Trends, causes, consequences, and lessons learned. *Journal of Marriage and Family, 62,* 1094–1113. doi:10.1111/j.1741-3737.2000.01094.x.

Seiling, S. B. (2006). Changes in the lives of rural low-income mothers: Do resources play a role in stress? *Journal of Human Behavior in the Social Environment, 13,* 19–42. doi:10.1300/J137v13n01_02.

Seiling, S., Dolan, E. M., & Glesner, T. (2005). *Rural low-income women who work in service jobs tell about their lives.* Paper session presented at the Gender, Work and Organization 4th International Conference, Keele University, Staffordshire, UK.

Siegel, D. I., & Abbott, A. A. (2007). The work lives of low-income welfare poor. *Families in Society, 88*(3), 401–412. doi:10.1606/1044-3894.3649.

Simmons, L. A., Braun, B., Wright, D. W., & Miller, S. R. (2007). Human capital, social support and economic well-being among rural low-income mothers: A latent growth curve analysis. *Journal of Family and Economic Issues, 28,* 636–652. doi:10.1007/s10834-007-9079-2.

Stafford, K., Duncan, K. A., Dane (sic), S., & Winter, M. (1999). A research model of sustainable family businesses. *Family Business Review, 12,* 197–208. doi:10.1111/j1741-6248.1999.00197.x.

Surface Transportation Policy Partnership. (n.d.a). *Transportation and jobs.* (Fact sheet). http://www.transact.org/factsheets/jobs.asp.

Surface Transportation Policy Partnership. (n.d.b) *Transportation and poverty alleviation.* (Fact sheet). http://www.transact.org/factsheets/poverty.asp.

Swanson, J. A., Olson, C. M., Miller, E. O., & Lawrence, F. C. (2008). Rural mothers' use of formal programs and informal social support to meet family food needs: A mixed methods study. *Journal of Family and Economic Issues, 29,* 674–690. doi:10.1007/s10834-008-9127-6.

Thompson, M. A. (1997). The impact of spatial mismatch on female labor force participation. *Economic Development Quarterly, 11*(2), 138–145. doi:10.1177/089124249701100203.

Urban, J. A., & Olson, P. N. (2005). A comprehensive employment model for low-income mothers. *Journal of Family and Economic Issues, 26,* 101–122. doi:10.1007/s10834-004-1414-2.

US Department of Agriculture. (n.d.) *Supplemental nutrition assistance program.* http://www.fns.usda.gov/snap/applicant_recipients/eligibility.htm.

US Department of Health and Human Services. (n.d.). *Inadequate transportation. A report by the US Department of Health and Human Services.* http://aspe.hhs.gov/hsp/isp/ancillary/transp.htm.

Zedlewski, S. R. (1999, September). *Work activity and obstacles to work among TANF Recipients.* (New Federalism, Series B, No. B-2). http://www.urban.org/UploadedPDF/anf_b2.pdf.

Zhan, M. (2006). Economic mobility of single mothers: The role of assets and human capital development. *Journal of Sociology & Social Welfare, 33*(4), 127–150.

Chapter 9
"I Don't Know How We Would Make It"—
Social Support in Rural Low-Income Families

Sharon B. Seiling, Margaret M. Manoogian and Seohee Son

Introduction

> We'd either eat here, or go to somebody else's house *[laughs]*. Yeah, go to a friend's, or whatever. Like, you know, I can feed my kids but if I don't have any, anything, I'll call a friend, "Donna, did you cook anything?" She goes, "Oh, yeah." "Do you have any left-overs?" "Well, yeah." "Can I get some?" "Sure." So you know…. We kind of help each other like that…. Three or four times a year, five times…and we just go back and forth, try and help each other.

As illustrated by Savannah,[1] a 35-year-old Hispanic single mother of four, help from others influences daily experiences and family well-being. The amount and types of help individuals and families offer and receive varies by context and temporality. Most families access informal (aid provided by friends, neighbors, and family) and formal (aid provided by service providers and agencies) sources of social support (Domínguez and Watkins 2003; Greder et al. 2008). For rural, low-income families, informal social support may include some or all of the following: Instrumental support such as child care, transportation, and financial aid; informational support such as advice, job leads, and access to resources; and emotional support such as companionship, encouragement, and empathy (Hogan et al. 1993; Miller and Darlington 2002; Plickert et al. 2007). Formal social support resources may include cash assistance, such as Temporary Assistance for Needy Families (TANF), Supplemental Security Income (SSI), and the Earned Income Tax Credit (EITC); Medicaid; food programs such as food stamps (now known as the Supplemental Nutrition Assistance Program or SNAP), Special Supplemental Nutrition Program for Women, Infants, and Children (WIC), school lunch, and emergency food assistance; housing assistance and the Low-Income Home Energy Assistance Program (LIHEAP); employment and education assistance; child care subsidies; and/or emo-

---

[1] All names are pseudonyms.

S. B. Seiling (✉)
Department of Consumer Sciences, Ohio State University, Columbus, OH, USA
e-mail: sseiling@ehe.osu.edu

J. W. Bauer, E. M. Dolan (eds.), *Rural Families and Work,* International Series on Consumer Science 1,
DOI 10.1007/978-1-4614-0382-1_9, © Springer Science+Business Media, LLC 2011

tional support from human service providers, such as mental health counseling and compassionate conversation (Domínguez and Watkins 2003; Swanson et al. 2004). Most individuals receive support from a variety of sources, with a majority of supporters providing specialized assistance (Miller and Darlington 2002; Wellman and Wortley 1990). Because of geographic distance from many services and limited household incomes, most rural low-income families obtain goods and services informally from family and friends through their network connections (Duncan et al. 2002; Taylor 2001).

In this chapter, we first present an overview of social support as it pertains to low-income families residing in rural areas. We define social support, note relevant theoretical perspectives, and highlight related literature that aids our understanding as to how informal networks exchange support when needs are high and resources are few. Next, we examine the types, strengths, and constraints of social support that emerged from the narratives of the rural, low-income mothers who participated in the Rural Families Speak (RFS) project. We conclude by outlining further research needs and strategies for aiding positive employment and family well-being outcomes for rural low-income families.

Understanding Social Support in Rural Low-Income Families

Support exchanges provide a mechanism through which resources are obtained and retained, enabling individuals and families to survive both physically and psychologically (Hobfoll 2009). Interaction within a social network also establishes and reinforces one's identity and defines one's roles within a social system (Burleson 2003; Hobfoll 2009; Hobfoll et al. 1990; Magdol 2000). These network relationships foster norms of social exchange (Acock and Hurlbert 1990; Pearlin 1985) that facilitate and protect resource flows (Hobfoll et al. 1990). They also establish coping norms that guide members' actions in managing stressful situations (Pearlin 1985).

How individuals offer and receive support in families has generally been addressed through the perspectives of altruism and reciprocity (Altonji et al. 1997; McGarry 2000). From the perspective of *altruism,* individuals express their concern for their family members' well-being by perceiving needs and sharing resources (Jayakody 1998), most often within the context of the parent–child relationship (Rossi and Rossi 1990). In families, these altruistic behaviors often stem from a parental concern for future generations and reflect parental income levels when compared with the financial resources of other family members (Lee and Aytac 1998). For instance, an older parent may offer financial help and coresidence to an adult child and her family so that educational goals may be met and grandchildren receive better care.

Most people accept the norm of *reciprocity* in the provision of support, which means repaying the support given with the same or equivalent resources within a fairly short period of time (Nelson 2000; Phan et al. 2009). For families facing ongoing financial constraints, reciprocity may be critical to sustainability of the network, especially when exchanging with nonkin. For some, just knowing that friends or family *would* return the favor is reassuring emotional support (Dunkel-Schetter and Bennett 1990). Acts of reciprocity vary by the relative resource richness of the parties in the exchange, the relationship between the giver and receiver, the duration of the relationship, and the location or environment within which the exchange occurs (Amato 1993; Curley 2009; Nelson 2000; Phan et al. 2009; Plickert et al. 2007). Family members also may exchange support in order to motivate reciprocal actions (Hogan et al. 1993), even in relationships between intimate partners (Iida et al. 2008). Not all forms of support are expected to be repaid, or the reciprocity rules may be relaxed for support exchanged with kin (Amato 1993; Phan et al. 2009; Plickert et al. 2007). The parent–adult child relationship is the most likely context in which the provision of help occurs without an expectation for repayment in kind (Plickert et al. 2007). Repayment may be postponed for a long time, repaid in services that require time but little or no financial investment, or exchanged with emotional support or other intangible resources (Nelson 2000; Plickert et al. 2007) "…where value is measured by gratitude, bonding, or the development of a sense of mutual obligation" (Levitan and Feldman 1991, p. 151). For instance, an older, low-income grandmother may offer to provide care to grandchildren with the hope and expectation that her daily needs of meals and housing will be met by her adult child's family. Parents' support for their adult children often comes with expectations for behavior or achievement of certain goals (Nelson 2000), with norms of behavior being enforced in the exchange.

Families facing financial strain may lose their enthusiasm for and ability to participate in social networks (Bauman and Downs 2000; Moos and Mitchell 1982; Nelson and Smith 1999). The economic strains imposed by socioeconomic conditions may limit low-income families' ability to reciprocate support, increasing discord within the network which, in turn, impedes engagement in their networks (Dominguez and Watkins 2003). In addition to having fewer resources to exchange, the concomitant economic stress and strain can reduce one's ability to participate in social networks (Hogan et al. 1993). Orthner et al. (2004) found that fewer than half of low-income families thought that they would have support when they needed help. Unfortunately, the neediest support seekers often are the least able to obtain informal assistance due to the resource scarcity of their networks (Bauman and Downs 2000; Cohen 2002; Hogan et al. 1993).

The *Conservation of Resources* (COR) theoretical perspective provides a useful framework for understanding social network participation by families facing economic constraints and related stress. According to this theory, individuals and families seek to obtain and protect important resources, such as goods, services, and conditions that are important or that make possible the acquisition of valued items or conditions (Hobfoll 1989, 2001). Resource loss is the major factor in creating stress (Hobfoll 2001). The two basic principles of COR are (a) people react more powerfully to loss of resources than to gains, and (b) people must invest some of their resources to protect what they have, recover from loss, and/or gain resources

(Hobfoll 2001). One can see this operating in family networks with members investing time, money, and tangible resources for protection against loss (paying rent or utilities to prevent homelessness), recovery from loss (paying a hospital bill or helping with court costs after divorce), or gain (buying a car or paying for education that builds human capital) of other members. As mentioned above, support by older, more resource-rich members may be motivated by altruism or by investing for a future return of support by younger members that can limit or ameliorate their losses in old age. Resources tend to be linked in what Hobfoll (2001) calls "resource caravans," in which investments build up over generations and through network connections. Individuals in resource-scarce networks can experience loss spirals, however, when investments do not bring the hoped for gain or recovery from loss (Hobfoll 2001). The loss of one resource (an affordable child care provider, for example) can lead to the loss of other resources (loss of job and its related income and benefits) for both individuals and families (Lein et al. 2005). A loss spiral can ensue, leaving the family unit more stressed, more dependent on network support, and less able or willing to reciprocate in the near term (Hobfoll 2001; Seiling 2006). An example of scarce resources limiting exchanges was discovered by Smith (2005) in her study of inner city job seekers. She found that employees who were in vulnerable positions were unwilling to risk their reputations by recommending friends as co-workers for fear that the persons seeking jobs would not be well received by their employers and, consequently, putting their own jobs at risk.

Informal social support varies across the life course as family networks typically provide essential aid and support to ensure the well-being of members (Rossi and Rossi 1990), particularly those who have the greatest needs, such as young children, older family members, or those who experience health constraints or economic troubles. For instance, family members provide most of the financial support transferred within networks (Hao 1996). Antonucci and Akiyama (1995) depicted the active exchange of social support across the life span in their *convoy model*. In this model, individuals have a convoy of support members who stay consistent or change over time as needs and relationships shift. The support that parents provide to children over many years is a reflection of this life course perspective. For instance, the most common exchange for financial support flows across generations from parents to children (Rosenzweig and Wolpin 1993, 1994) with adult children typically providing less financial assistance to older parents (McGarry and Schoeni 1995).

As generational position may influence the nature and extent of support in families (Freedman et al. 1991), so too may gender (Lye 1996; Marks and McLanahan 1993), with evidence suggesting that gendered family relationships may be more or less typical contexts for the exchange of social support (Rossi and Rossi 1990). How support is shared within kin networks also may be motivated by focused and deliberate strategies related to current and future security and access to resources. For instance, women's security, emotional well-being, and personal survival may be linked to the work they do in families, reflected through *kinkeeping,* the maintenance of strong networks that offer dense and needed support exchanges (di Leonardo 1987).

Social Support Within the Context of Family Relationships

Obtaining informal social support inevitably involves interacting with one or more network members and, through these connections, relationships are created or amended. In fact, social support is an important quality of social relationships (House et al.1988). The process of exchanging support with another person builds the bonds between them (Plickert et al. 2007), including enhancing the relationships of intimate partners (Gleason et al. 2008). What may begin as a purely instrumental exchange can transform a relationship or network into an "expressive object" through an affective process (Lawler 2001, p. 349). Relationship quality, particularly provider expressiveness, also is related to the quality of support received (Hill 1997). The relationships among network members serve as lenses through which they interpret the support provided (Moos and Mitchell 1982), basing its value, in part, on who is providing the support (Hogan et al. 1993). Women tend to be more responsive than men to both positive and negative interactions with network members, indicating that relationship quality may be more salient for women in both providing and receiving support (Durden et al. 2007; Schuster et al. 1990).

Emotionally intimate relationships are key to informal social support regardless of income level (Hobfoll 2009), with most support coming from partners and close family and friends (Mickelson and Kubzansky 2003; Thoits 1995). Immediate kin, particularly parents, are counted on for emotional support by most people (Agneessens et al. 2006; Miller and Darlington 2002). The closeness expressed in these relationships may lead to a greater feeling of commitment to others in the network, especially among family members. Low-income families typically receive support from extensive kin dominated networks (Schoeni 1992). Therefore, maintaining good relationships with family members is critical for sustaining the flow of support. The type of relational tie may influence informal social support in different ways. Family ties are more enduring and tend to have more obligation or filial features, whereas friendship ties are voluntary, and these relationships tend to be more volatile (Phan et al. 2009; Thoits 1995). Most people report that family members are the persons from whom they would seek support (perceived) or from whom they obtain (received) the most help (Ahluwalia et al. 1998; Amato 1993; Miller and Darlington 2002). Support from family members is usually more satisfying than that coming from nonkin, except for companionship, which is mostly provided by friends (Wan et al. 1996).

The provision of social support in families also may have implications for managing emotional well-being, critical in families with high levels of stress, such as those struggling with limited economic resources. Schuster et al. (1990) found that supportive interactions often reduced distress-producing effects of negative interactions with relatives. From the perspective of support exchanges across generations of family members, Connidis and McMullin (2002) highlighted how developmental transitions such as children reaching adulthood may result in ambivalence and tension. For example, parents may have different feelings about providing certain support to children once they leave home and/or are expected to become full-time wage earners. As a result, young adults may experience both support and scrutiny by interconnected older family members as they begin to make their own choices (Widmer 2006). Life course changes, such as leaving the parental home or changing marital status, can cause turnover in support network composition (Wellman et al. 1997). Development of ambivalence in relationships with parents may foster the expansion of these new networks.

Due to the complexities of social interactions and support (Rhodes et al. 1994), seeking and receiving social support requires skill in building and maintaining relationships (Levitan and Feldman 1991; Nelson 2000; Vangelisti 2009). Green and Rodgers (2001) found that when network members were unable to create positive emotional relationships with others, they were less likely to obtain instrumental as well as emotional support.

Costs of Receiving and Giving Support

Although generally thought of as positive, exchange of social support also may have negative effects on members within support networks (Curley 2009; Rook 1990). Much previous research on social support has emphasized the benefits obtained by the recipient, particularly through relief from stress and provision of tangible resources (Thoits 1995). In recent years, more has been learned about the potential negative features of social support. Not all individuals wish to receive support. Vangelisti (2009) identified several reasons why social support may not be welcome. First, the costs may outweigh the benefits of the good or service provided. For example, the need for assistance may put or keep the receiver in a problematic relationship. Second, the process could be "embarrassing, stigmatizing, or distasteful" (Vangelisti 2009, p. 42), particularly if it is made public. Also, the support given may not be helpful, such as when attempts by an incompetent provider may worsen the situation (Dunkel-Schetter and Bennett 1990). The receiver's self-efficacy may be put into question. Other negative aspects of support provision may include emphasis on the unfortunate circumstances, ongoing dependence by the receiver, and unwanted indebtedness, including demands to reciprocate (Curley 2009; Vangelisti 2009).

Social support can be especially negative if the support provider is a person who is disliked or distrusted. The provision of support depends on the trust established between individuals in the network that often requires a shared history (Magdol and Bessel 2003). When trust is not experienced in the support exchange, constraints to the flow of needed resources may occur. Researchers have found that disadvantaged populations, including low-income mothers, developed distrust and withdraw from network members after experiencing emotional drama or gossip and/or moving into a new life stage or location (Bidart and Lavenu 2005; Curley 2009). Distrust beliefs lead to distrustful actions (Hobfoll 2009), resulting in smaller networks and less social support, while conversely, individuals who believe that they are loved and supported will act in ways to advance this state (Hobfoll 2009; Pearlin 1985). The support provider also may find that exchanges have a negative impact. For instance, offering help to others is costly in time, effort, and resources when creating and reinforcing support networks (Levitan and Feldman 1991). Simply, provision of resources by some members of the network to others means that those resources come at the expense of the providers (Portes and Landolt 1996). Individuals at the center of a support network may find themselves drained by the needs of network members, especially when a stressful event involves multiple people in the network (Hobfoll 2009; Thoits 1995). Persons connected to the member experiencing a stressful life event, additionally, may feel threatened by the same crisis and be unable or unwilling to provide support due to fear of being affected (Thoits 1995; Turner 1994). This "stress contagion" can exhaust resources and result in withdrawal of support. Psychological distress also can hinder development of perceived support as individuals move into new social settings (Lakey and Dickinson 1994). Caregivers' physical and/or mental health and economic well-being can be threatened when too much is demanded by adult children, parents, or others seeking assistance. Wakabayashi and Donato (2006) found that women who provided care for their elderly parents were more likely to be in poverty later in life than those who did not, even after holding employment and health constant. A longer-term chronic stressor, additionally, can lead a needy member of a disadvantaged network to "overdraw" from the supply of instrumental and emotional support resources and lose his/her ability to tap them when needed again (Hobfoll 2009; Mickelson and Kubzansky 2003; Nelson and Smith 1999). A study by Turner (1994) revealed that while women have social ties that are more likely than those of men to promote emotional support exchanges, they also suffer from more negative interactions with network members.

Supportive relationships can increase the perceived value of support resources and ameliorate emotional demands (Durden et al. 2007), whereas negative relationships can cause a person to be wary of the support offered. Relationship problems can exacerbate economic strain and increase stress (Rhodes et al. 1994) among those who have few resources. Furthermore, stress may erode one's supportive relationships (Green and Rodgers 2001), putting the network resources at risk.

Being part of a support community (or network) means that members must conform to the rules and norms of the group (Portes and Landolt 1996). Demands of family and friends can be challenging to manage (Acock and Hurlburt 1990), can drain resources (Kana'iaupuni et al. 2005), and can undermine a low-income individual's attempt to rise above his/her economic circumstances (Portes and Landolt 1996). These dense networks provide strong binding capital but they may be detrimental to getting along without reliance on the family (Widmer 2006).

Social Support: The Influence of Proximity, Contact, and Rural Location

Proximity among network members has a powerful effect on support exchanges (Domínguez and Watkins 2003; Magdol and Bessel 2003). Not only does provision of services decrease with distance, but other types of support diminish as well (Curley 2009; Hogan et al. 1993; Lee et al. 1994; Martin and Yeung 2006). For example, researchers found that in addition to providing less child care, grandparents gave less parenting advice and less financial support when they were at greater distances from their adult children and grandchildren (Hogan et al. 1993). Life transitions, with their concomitant relocation, often lead to changes in networks and in needs for support (Bidart and Lavenu 2005; Wellman et al. 1997). Proximity to social support resources appears to matter a great deal to an individual's close friendships. Martin and Yeung (2006) were surprised to find that moving away from close friends was more likely to sever those relationships than weaker ties. Even relatively short distance moves can reduce or eliminate interaction with network members. For instance, two years after being relocated from public housing, the social support ties among a group of low-income mothers were lost or greatly weakened (Curley 2009).

Members of support networks range widely in contact frequency. Many individuals in dense family networks see each other daily. Others have no face-to-face contact because of distance or type of relationship, with varying occurrence of interaction by phone or internet. Proximity has a big influence on frequency of interaction, and the ability to interact often enhances network members' relationships and support quality (Hill 1997; Hogan et al. 1993).

High levels of contact typically are experienced when kin and/or nonkin members share a household. Coresidence provides much support to low-income families, especially among single mothers who pursue employment and educational opportunities. Although sharing a home brings relationship challenges, it provides varied and flexible resources including services such as child care and transportation, as well as financial support, information/advice, and emotional support (Henly 2002; Hogan et al. 1990). Coresidence varies by ethnicity with African-American mothers more likely than Whites to live with, or close to, kin (Hogan et al. 1990).

Living in a rural location has implications for social support as well. The more relaxed nature of support reciprocity in rural areas (Amato 1993; Mickelson and Kubzansky 2003; Phan et al. 2009) may be due to the longevity and multifaceted nature of many interpersonal relationships in rural communities. Phan et al. (2009) speculated that, rather than expecting no reciprocation, people in rural areas have relationships that accept longer-term returns than are typically examined in academic studies. Rural residents also typically have more extensive and stronger networks than city dwellers, brought on partly by the relative scarcity of formal services (Duncan et al. 2002), and they exhibit a preference for family support over that of friends (Amato 1993). Among low-income rural families, the convergence of lack of mobility in rural areas, dense family networks, and an elevated need for support may lead to lessened enforcement of balanced exchanges of services in the *near term*. The greater reliance on kin support by rural families tends to hold them in communities with a dearth of high-paying jobs with benefits. Limited employment opportunities keep family incomes low and require greater support from network members. The system can work well, but it leaves many low-income families with scarce resources and few options.

Social Support and the RFS Project: Implications for Family Well-Being and Employment

Working groups of scholars have focused on both informal and formal social support networks in the RFS project. In this section, we first describe our sample in terms of how the rural, low-income mothers and their families accessed needed resources and support that helped them to make ends meet and provide for their families. Next, we highlight the findings that have emerged across multiple studies that focus on the exchange of social support, particularly those that involve informal support sources, the most visible type of support evident in these families. Finally, we outline implications and recommendations for research and policy as we seek ways to best support rural, low-income families.

Frequency, Types, and Need: Social Support and Rural, Low-Income Families' Well-Being

RFS participants in Wave 3 (N=311) were asked about the kinds of support, the frequency of support, and their perceptions of this help regarding their informal support networks. Overall, most participants reported receiving support from relatives (84.4%) and friends/neighbors (75.8%). Almost half (47.1%) received help *often* from kin over the most recent month, compared to about one-third (33.9%) receiving assistance *often* from friends or neighbors. When asked about how many people they could turn to for help, only four (1.3%) said they had no one. The largest proportion (37.6%, n=117) reported they had three to five people, with about one-fourth (25.8%, n=77) indicating they had ten or more support providers in their network.

The quantitative data indicated additional evidence of Hobfoll's (2001) *resource caravans,* linking individual's social and human capital. Size of the support network was strongly linked to level of education. Participants with larger networks were more likely to have completed high school and post secondary education (Fig. 9.1). Of participants who reported that they had ten or more members in their support networks, 13% had less than high school education, 26% were high school graduates, and 61% had completed some type of post secondary education (χ^2=27.48, p=.001). As expected, those with the larger networks were more likely to have provided frequent support in the past month. Also, participants who had received assistance *often* from relatives were more likely to have received help *often* or *sometimes* from friends as well (Table 9.1). Size of the network also was linked with level of poverty (Table 9.2). Although their need was greater, families with lower incomes had fewer people from whom they could obtain other resources. Employed mothers had greater frequency of support received from relatives than did their non-employed counterparts (89.2% and 79.3%, respectively; χ^2=5.63; p<.02). No difference was found between employment status and support received from friends.

Fig. 9.1 Relationship between level of education and size of perceived informal network

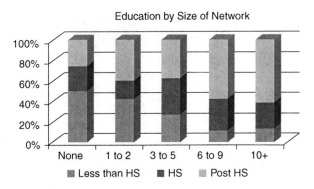

Education by Size of Network

Table 9.1 Relationship between Frequency of Support Received from Relatives and from Friends (N=311)

Received support from friends	Received support from relatives (%)			
	Never	Rarely	Sometimes	Often
Never	46.8	17.8	20.0	20.4
Rarely	17.0	20.0	8.6	13.4
Sometimes	17.0	44.4	41.4	20.4
Often	19.1	17.8	30.0	45.8

$\chi^2 = 41.47; p < .001$

Table 9.2 Size of Perceived Support Network by Level of Poverty ($N = 311$)

	Mean % of poverty line	N
None	77.0	4
1 to 2	92.0	65
3 to 5	121.3	117
6 to 9	122.2	48
10+	133.9	77

$F = 2.37; p = .05$

Living with a partner provided an additional source of income and extension of the social network. In the RFS study, the size of the support network, however, was not significantly related to whether the participant lived with a partner. On the other hand, frequency of support received from both friends and family was significantly related to partner status. Specifically, 82% of unpartnered, compared to 72% of partnered, mothers received support from friends ($\chi^2 = 3.99; p < .05$); whereas, 91% of partnered and 80% of unpartnered mothers received assistance from relatives ($\chi^2 = 6.62; p = .01$).

Rural, low-income mothers and their children received considerable social support from their family members, friends, workplace supervisors, and/or community agencies, including child care, transportation, financial help, food, and housing (Dolan et al. 2006; Greder et al. 2008; Seiling et al. 2006; Swanson et al. 2004). Many rural, low-income families have relied on these social support networks to meet their basic needs, such as food and housing (Greder et al. 2008; Swanson et al. 2004). Rural, low-income mothers usually mentioned that their mothers, parents, or grandmothers often gave food or provided financial support to buy food, and they frequently used shared meals with their parents, other family members, or friends to stretch their food resources. They planned for and used food assistance resources frequently for their families' food security instead of using it for occasional relief (Swanson et al. 2004). This pattern was illustrated in the quote by Savannah at the beginning of the chapter.

Greder and colleagues (2008) studied 48 Latina mothers in two states. Social support played a key role in helping rural low-income, immigrant Latino families to achieve economic well-being and adjust to US society. Most Latina mothers reported that they could obtain some form of social support from their networks including family members, friends, or community agencies to meet their needs for food and housing. In addition, most Latina mothers had first lived with their extended families when they immigrated to the United States. In this way, relatives often helped them adjust to US society and meet their immediate needs. Mothers also depended on cash transactions from family members rather than formal subsidies.

RFS investigations additionally have explored the ways in which level of need mobilized support networks and the receipt of information. For instance, the types, amounts, and sources of social support differed for RFS participants depending on family food security and/or income levels (Greder et al. 2008; Seiling et al. 2006). Greder et al. (2008) reported that food secure and food insecure Latina mothers differed in types and sources of support. Food insecure Latina mothers had more financial support from family members, whereas, food secure mothers obtained more tangible support from community agencies. Most immigrant Latina mothers, however, used community support only rarely for housing, relying rather on their informal support networks.

Another study examined the relationship between social support and poverty level (Seiling et al. 2006). Using cluster analysis, researchers found that mothers who reported having the fewest financial resources were the most likely to receive both informal and formal support compared to those who had higher incomes. Families with the most financial need also were the most likely to receive emotional support and obtain material resources when compared to families with more financial resources. No differences were found among families regarding receipt of support from parents and other family members or the size of their networks, however.

The Role of Social Support in Bolstering Financial Resources and Human Capital

Social support was especially important for rural, low-income mothers to maintain employment since these mothers had few available resources to accommodate their work and family responsibilities (Son and Bauer 2010). Dolan et al. (2006) explored how social support helped rural, low-income mothers in service sector jobs manage their work and family responsibilities. Their jobs were classified into four work systems that were tightly constrained, unrationalized labor intensive, semiautonomous, and high-skill autonomous. These mothers needed different types and levels of social support depending upon the types of jobs they had. Because they were more likely to work erratic schedules with little flexibility, mothers who were in tightly constrained work systems often needed more social support in order to take care of their family's needs, especially child care. Informal supervisor support was especially important for these women. When these mothers had supervisors who were flexible and understood their situations, they were much better able to manage their work and family responsibilities simultaneously and stay employed. Researchers also found that availability of informal support could influence these mothers' work patterns. That is, changing jobs was one of the strategies rural, low-income mothers used to accommodate their incompatible work and family responsibilities when adequate social support was not available (Seiling et al. 2005). For example, Chara, a 21-year-old single mother of a young son, began working as a security officer at the local courthouse because her living situation had changed. She had been living with her aunt and uncle and delivering the morning newspaper. When her aunt and uncle asked her to move out, delivering the morning paper became untenable.

> The newspaper route was good money, but ... I couldn't depend on it...And the hours, they worked if we lived with my aunt and uncle, but I went to work about 3:00 a.m. and that wouldn't be possible when it's just Max [son] and me. I would have to wake him up and take him with me...So we needed to move and I looked for another job.

Informal Social Support: Negotiating Family Relationships When Support Is Needed

After the first wave of data collection, research team members on the *RFS* project identified a recurrent theme. Most often, rural mothers identified their mothers as primary providers of social support to their families. At the same time, it was not uncommon for participants to identify their mothers as the person who made life more difficult for them. Noting the complexities of social support when structural constraints are severe, investigators focused on participants' family of origin relationships and the exchange of informal social support in the context of these long-term kin ties.

Richards et al. (2002) recognized that the adult daughter-older mother tie is particularly salient and provides an important source of support between generations across all stages of adult life (Rossi and Rossi 1990; Silverstein and Bengtson 1997). Using feminist and life course perspectives, they focused on the exchange of support within these relationships. In addition, they examined mothers' narratives regarding the nature of these relationships when structural constraints were present. Wave 1 interviews with 375 married and unmarried mothers, who reported that their mothers were still living, were used for this analysis. Results illuminated how daughters received support from and provided support to their mothers and, in some cases, rejected relying on their mothers as a strategy for survival. The flow of support and the complexities of these relationships, when family needs were critical, influenced the ability of those rural, low-income families to meet daily needs and secure employment.

Not surprisingly, most of the women (70%) in the RFS project grew up in poor families. Poverty during childhood resulted from marital disruption, substance abuse, low-wage work, and/or periods of unemployment among parents. The RFS mothers' early family experiences were marked by their parents' struggles to make ends meet. Perhaps because of this long-term family need for support, most participants lived close to their families of origin: Two-thirds of mothers lived less than an hour away from their own mothers, including 36 women who coresided with their mothers. Typically living close to mom was viewed as positive, in part because of the assistance provided by mothers. For example, Keely, a 28-year-old mother of one, emphasized, *"I'll never move away from my mom...we'll always stay by each other."*

Participants' mothers seemed to be particularly important providers of a complementary array of emotional and instrumental support. Participants relied on their mothers for emotional care, support of parenting, and empathy when daily living brought challenges. As Keely explained, *"Whenever I have just broken down, I can't take things any more, she's* [mother] *always there to call."*

Due to economic hardships, low-income mothers frequently have problems accessing just about all the necessities of life: Adequate housing, utilities, child care, food, clothing, and transportation. Rural locations tend to exacerbate the struggle of these mothers and their families to work and make ends meet due to the lack of community support systems. Most rural communities, for instance, have little, if any, public transportation. As with emotional support, persons most often identified as providing instrumental support to the RFS families were participants' mothers. The mothers helped pay bills, provided child care, bought clothing for their daughters' families, offered transportation when needed, and fed their daughters and their families. For instance, when finding herself without a ride due to her unreliable vehicle, Alexandria, a single mother with two children, stated, *"I'm 36 years old and I call my mom."* In addition, these adult daughter–mother relationships appeared to feature reciprocity, particularly in the provision of emotional support. A number of participants (47%) reported talking to their mothers every day by phone or in person.

The depth of these relationships had implications for participant families in terms of employment and education. For instance, many of the mothers detailed their desires to stay in rural areas despite the lack of employment and educational opportunities in their communities. In some cases, participants felt the pull of helping family members that needed support. Shakira, a 47-year-old African-American mother of four, shared, *"Well, I would love to live in town again. But my mother's here, and she's ill, and my uncle's not very well at times."* Another participant commented that she refused to move, despite her husband's request and desire to find employment with higher wages.

Ambivalent Relationships: Implications for Personal Autonomy and Family Well-Being

Depending on family of origin members for help with child care, transportation, and other types of support needed to maintain educational and employment opportunities could bring tension and frustration. Crissy, a 31-year-old mother of two, reported having a lot of contact with her grandparents, who lived near her. She described her relationship with them as close, but also complicated.

> Because they're old and they did things differently and they just think…I don't know if they just think everything's easier now. I mean, their way of solving things were to spank the kids on the butt, teach 'em a lesson. You don't do that anymore, you know, 'cause they're always saying, "Oh, Isaiah just needs a good spanking and he'll straighten out." That's not true, you know, so they make it harder because if you have a problem, they're pretty supportive of helping you out. But they'll say, "Well, you got yourself into that mess, if you did this differently, it wouldn't have happened." But I love them to death, but they're the hardest.

Wanting to further understand those relationships in which mothers reported mixed emotions or ambivalence about their relationships with their mothers and the constraints that emerged through the need for instrumental support, Manoogian et al. (2003) identified a sample of 52 participants who described their relationships with their own mothers as ambivalent. In these cases, participants appeared to experience both psychological and sociological levels of intergenerational ambivalence (Connidis and McMullin 2002; Lüscher and Pillemer 1998). Psychological ambivalence occurs when individuals, such as the women in the RFS project, express simultaneous and contradictory emotions about their mothers. Linked to psychological ambivalence, sociological ambivalence emerges when individuals attempt to meet societal expectations which may result in conflicting or contradictory messages about performance of roles and responsibilities. These relationships are of particular importance as future flows of support may be severed if the needs become too great, if the relationships become too difficult to negotiate, and/or if the provider is unable to maintain needed levels of support. For the RFS mothers with children, the goal of seeking and maintaining employment promoted dependence on others for child care, transportation, and material support. Yet, the dependence on these relationships for all kinds of support could have implications for personal autonomy, emotional well-being, and child/family outcomes.

In their examination of these relationships, Manoogian et al. (2003) found evidence of intergenerational ambivalence in these rural, low-income families. A common response from mothers in this sample was reflected in 23-year-old Jadad's description of both the help and the conflict in her relationship with her mother. Jadad, a single mother of one who lived with her mother, explained: *"She gives us a roof and transportation, where I can keep my money and use it for us or whatever. The negatives are my mom. She's like…I don't know how to explain it. She just drives me crazy sometimes."*

From their narratives, it was apparent that earlier childhood experiences shaped participants' current relationships with mothers. These antecedents to ambivalence appeared as participants primarily grew up in poor families and their childhoods were marked by hardship, chaos, and challenge, all of which have been shown to have potentially poor outcomes for children (Duncan and Brooks-Gunn 1997). Because effective parenting often suffers in economically vulnerable families (Conger et al. 1994), and may contribute to maternal depression and well-being (Ahluwalia et al. 2001), a number of participants grew up in households that were vulnerable. Many reported that due to family of origin experiences earlier in life, they were unable to develop the types of relationships they desired with their mothers. At the same time, they were forced to stay connected to their mothers and depend on these relationships because of their limited economic resources.

As families of origin were expected to ease the strain produced by limited resources, participants also depended on high levels of support, including coresidence, a living situation that greatly circumscribed their sense of independence and autonomy. For instance, Lysette, aged 18 and a divorced mother of one, explained her frustrations about living in her childhood home with her current partner and child: "*You can't have two women in the house and a child can't have two mothers, not at the same time.*" In addition, their mothers' criticisms of their parenting and partnership decisions were of particular concern to a number of participants. Maire, a 22-year-old single mother of one, shared her frustration with her mother's criticism about how she was performing her roles as mother and responsible adult.

> She'll go and tell my sister little things. Like she's disappointed how I'm raising Jack and how I'm doing moneywise. But it's none of her business. The only reason why she's disappointed I'm raising Jack is the fact that she wants it her way.

Tension between participants' mothers and their partners often put the participants in a difficult spot. Nineteen-year-old Annabel, mother of one, commented on her dilemma:

> My partner and I were talking about getting married, but my mom did not like it and she got mad at us for a while, because my partner is so much older than me *[age 37]*, but we decided no. We were talking about getting married, but we decided not to.

Rather than being a boon, coresidence sometimes interfered with a family's economic well-being and employment. In one case, Florence, a 30-year-old mother of two, was operating a child care business out of her home. Her mother and brother moved in with her.

> Last year *[her mother]* was living with me at different times. And she was living with me, but she wasn't invited. She just kind of moved in. Well, I decided that I wasn't going to have that, because I was working out of my home and, um, people would be bringing their children and she and my brother *[who is in his twenties]* just got out of prison, which I was not happy with…and she wouldn't go look for work and he wouldn't go look for work and I decided I had enough so I changed the locks on my door and she has not been talking to me since. It's not very good.

In order for RFS participants to gain needed education and training as well as obtain and maintain employment, their mothers were key members of the informal support networks. Participants, who felt ambivalent about their mothers as parents or that their mothers' support had been unreliable or undesirable when they were young, still needed help from this critical family relationship. When participants' mothers provided support such as child care, food or transportation, an incentive was created to focus on the flow of support, and to overlook the personal costs of ambivalence in these relationships. Participants potentially risked the support they received if they desired to change their current relationships with their mothers. In some cases, participants were able to renegotiate these relationships. A few others were able to ensure that other informal support sources were in place before making the decision to cut off the relationship with their mothers. In all cases, however, the viability of this relationship and the flow of support were critically needed for the participant-mothers and their families.

Maintaining the relationship with a partner could be another challenge for these RFS participants. Fighting with or breaking off the relationship could lead to loss of their child care provider and the resulting loss of employment. Vera, a 41-year-old mother with two children, found that her former partner caused problems at her place of employment, stemming from issues in their interpersonal relationship.

> He'd be coming by all the time to my building where I worked, causing problems. He threatened to go for custody because I was working nights. I ended up giving my notice and told them my reason why. *[Prior to their break-up, he would stay with the children when she worked nights but used it against her when the relationship fell apart.]* I broke it off and that really set him off. So, I ended up getting done there. I went on leave.

Formal Support Services and Rural Low-Income Families: Ambivalence About Access

As indicated earlier, the families in the RFS project tended to rely on family, friends, and neighbors to help meet their critical needs. Their use of informal social support, however, did not preclude accessing and utilizing formal social support resources in their communities, as indicated by Table 8.1 in the previous chapter. By accessing formal support, the families in RFS demonstrated their ability to make use of a wide variety of resources on a daily basis and to negotiate systems that could be difficult to understand and that require skills to meet qualification standards. As Seccombe (2007) suggested, community resources, social policies, as well as local, regional, and federal programs, are critical for developing and strengthening families with limited financial resources. Food stamps (SNAP), TANF, Head Start, and WIC are just a few of the formal social support resources that RFS families needed and used.

In other parts of this volume, researchers have focused attention on particular types of formal support resources (i.e., Chap. 7 on child care by Walker and Manoogian and Chap. 8 on other resources by Bird et al.) that are critical to helping families access and maintain employment. In this section, we highlight ways in which mothers in the RFS project engaged with a variety of formal social support providers in order to help their families meet daily needs and maintain both employment and family responsibilities. Interpersonal competence and management skills, in addition to persistence, are needed to qualify for and receive formal support resources from agencies and organizations. Having access to the required information often is critical in gaining assistance. Mona, a 34-year-old single mother of three, tried unsuccessfully to get information about child support payments over the phone.

> If you wanna know something that's going on with your case, all you get is a recording; if you wanna know anything about your case, write a letter. Well, I'm sorry; I don't have time to write a letter, I need to know right now... "I'm sorry, I don't have a number and I don't have my pin number." *[The agency responded]* "Well, we can't help you then."

With the intent of aiding the delivery of services among community agencies, Waybright et al. (2004) investigated the use of formal support sources among 59 RFS families across three counties in northern Appalachia. Generally, mothers' narratives reported mixed feelings and responses regarding both the access and receipt of support from their local programs and agencies. Some mothers ($n = 19$) reported that they were satisfied with both the delivery and the amount of support provided by formal support sources, while others ($n = 15$) detailed largely negative reactions to formal support in their communities. The remaining mothers ($n = 15$) expressed mixed responses to services based on the type of organization, their perceptions of treatment from service-providers, and the impact of the resource specifically connected to child well-being. Mixed responses also were linked to perceived deficits in the provision of aid. For instance, LIHEAP usually was available to these rural low-income families, but "keeping a car running and insured" was another matter.

Scholars who have specifically investigated individuals and families in the Appalachian region have suggested that Appalachian identity is strongly linked to faith, kin relationships, and community culture (Coyne et al. 2006; Reiter et al. 2009). Related to these findings, RFS mothers in this region largely reported receiving formal support from faith-based organizations, typically churches. Due to familiarity and accessibility, participants appeared to feel comfortable in approaching churches or church-sponsored programs that provided such necessities as food and clothing. They expressed more hesitancy in approaching formal agencies and program providers such as the Department of Health and Human Resources, Job and Family Resources, or Community Resources. Their selection of services may be reflective of the treatment they reported receiving when they sought support rather than the organization itself. For instance, Lexie, a 27-year-old married mother of one, shared that the person working at a secular agency "...*made me cry. That woman up there was totally mean about it.*" Mimi, age 51, who was living with her partner and three pre-teen and teenaged children (one of whom had a terminal illness), shared her painful experience with one agency. Regarding the treatment she received, Mimi reported that she felt, "*Like you're beneath them. And that is very insulting to you, because you wouldn't go unless you're desperate.*" Kissane (2007) found that low-income women largely viewed secular and religion-based organizations similarly, valuing the resources they received over the types of relationships developed with service-providers. Nola, age 36, married, with three children, reported that she was treated well when she accessed services. "*Most of the time they* [secular organization] *are nice and polite. I have never been to* [faith-based agency]. *They are not overly friendly, but they are not nasty or mean. Just down to business."*

Often times, a personal relationship with an agency employee fostered the support available, especially in an emergency situation. For instance, a need for emergency housing was solved for a mother named Charity, age 26, and her three children because the mother knew someone who could help.

> When we was evicted...my husband had just went to jail, and I had three kids, and five days to be out, so I was going nuts... We was inches away from being put on the street. And nobody would tell me what to do, and I knew the head honcho in Community Action. I called (him) and I told him, "And now I have five days to have a place to live and the only thing that anybody's telling me is the (domestic violence shelter), and that's not an option with my kids"...and two days later he called, and he said "We got you a place. Don't worry about it." So if I wouldn't have known to call (him), instead of messing around with everybody else, I don't think I would have got it.

Mothers also appeared to endorse those agencies and programs that made a distinct difference for their children, such as WIC, free and reduced lunch programs, and Head Start. As reported elsewhere in Ko and Manoogian (2005), mothers in this subsample of the RFS project expressed strong commitments to their children and valued their roles as mothers within traditional family frameworks. Related to this, participants felt most positive about those programs that helped children obtain enough food to thwart hunger and provide adequate nutrition. Simply, mothers reported that if it had not been for their children, they would not have sought formal support because as Linnea, a 19-year-old mother who was married and had one child, shared, *"I don't like going to ask for help. I just have so much pride."* Many people in rural communities endorsed the idea that asking for help was not behavior to be encouraged, even when they worked for organizations that were established to help families in need. In some agencies or organizations, individual workers might be criticized when they go beyond the narrow confines of the job assignment. Charity told this story:

> And then (a worker) from Head Start, any time I need to go grocery shoppin' (she takes me). They used to jump onto her about it, because, you know, she was spending too much time with me. But then whenever the state came in and everything telling what the transitionalist *[sic]* should do for a family and help a family out with, then they started praising her. You know, like "That is so good. You took Charity grocery shopping" and everything. They jumped her one day and loved her up the next.

One critical area of formal support mentioned by most of the women in the sample focused on medical care. Mothers reported that medical personnel were moving away from the area, leaving the community with few options for care. In addition, several mothers in one county commented on the only mental health care provider available to them for their children. The mothers stated that this practitioner was not meeting the needs of their children and that they "won't go to him." As a consequence, families were stressed to find adequate care for their children's psychological and emotional health that was within driving distance of their rural homes.

Most participants reported that they received a medical card (Medicaid) for their children, but had no insurance for themselves. A few mothers focused on the stigma that they thought was attached to having a medical card. Hadley, a 31-year-old married mother of two young sons, stated, *"Now, I think sometimes like the emergency room, if they saw that the kids had a medical card or something, maybe it was my imagination or maybe it wasn't that I thought they were kind of treated as second-class citizens."* A 28-year-old mother of five, Nova, revealed that her primary care physician was leaving her community. As a consequence, the free samples that were often given to her by her physician as a means to manage her diabetes and finances would soon disappear. When asked about her plan for managing her diabetes, this recent widow shared that she was too embarrassed to talk to the new physician about her financial situation, indicating that she would cut back on both medication and routine testing. Establishing the same level of trust with her new physician would take time.

In addition to the ways that mothers perceived the treatment they received from formal support providers, the mothers' comments also suggested that receiving help from formal support providers outside of trusted kin and friend networks influenced their personal identities and emotional well-being. For instance, Fern's comments reflected her personal comparisons to others and how she viewed those who received priority in obtaining formal support. According to this 27-year-old single mother with a young daughter, *"Yeah, I was down there today trying to get food stamps. Start shooting some babies out and maybe they'll give me something. Drink and do drugs, maybe they'll carry me. Give me a crazy check."* As a consequence, many mothers reported how they negotiated the type of contact and times they approached agencies in hopes of receiving help from a specific individual who treated them well. One mother demonstrated how the development of trust and relationship with her caseworker had changed over time, allowing her to feel better about the support she received. Tansy stated that her caseworker had been "mean," but that she had gotten "nicer" the longer she had known her. This 32-year-old divorced mother of two wondered if these professionals were trained to put on a mean persona when in the agency and explained, *"She's been in Wal-Mart a few times since then, and every time she comes through my line purposely to tell me how proud of me she is."* According to Tansy, her caseworker was "nicer" when she was not in the office. Observing Tansy at her job may have changed her opinion of her worthiness for receiving agency support. As seen in the comments of Tansy and Charity, small rural communities can provide opportunities to develop relationships and/or have contact outside of the service-provider venue, which may enhance or detract from the formal support exchange.

Managing Resources in Ways that Create Gains and/or Reduce Losses: Implications for Low-Income Rural Families

Rural low-income families often live in a world constrained by scarce community resources, providing few opportunities for them to earn enough from employment to meet all of their needs and enable them to save for emergencies or for the future.

When limited community assets are coupled with a deficit of individual and family skills, families can be hard pressed to obtain and retain adequate resources; even a small crisis can propel them into a loss spiral. Often their management skills (Olson et al. 2004) and their interpersonal skills (Burleson 2003; Hill 1997; Plickert et al. 2007; Vangelisti 2009) determine their well-being. Families that have social networks with substantial "resource caravans" from kin, friends, social agencies and organizations can thrive in circumstances that would push others over the brink into chaos, hunger, and homelessness (Hobfoll 2001; Seiling 2006). As indicated earlier, many of the families in our study chose to stay near their parents or other network members in order to maintain their connections to these sources of assistance. Not all of them, however, were able to negotiate a position of self-efficacy and positive mental health while enmeshed within their dense networks (Manoogian et al. 2003). Because they were dependent on others for tangible resources, and unable to establish positive interpersonal relationships, many participants were not able to establish workable boundaries and resource exchanges. Complex family forms, such as those containing children with different fathers (and related extended families), those sharing a residence with parents of the adult child, and those with children living outside the household with another parent or grandparent, are especially liable to experience boundary ambiguity, i.e., being uncertain who is part of the family (Sarkisian 2006), possibly leading to unstable or ineffective support networks. Unsuccessful or inadequate support networks, sometimes called *private safety nets,* can leave many low-income single mothers with no place to turn but to the welfare safety net (Harknett 2006).

Although moving through the life course often builds skills, some low-income parents do not have the human or social capital to access formal support, manage their income, parent their children, or provide care for other family members. Social service providers are quite varied in their guidance of those seeking assistance. Many RFS mothers had inadequate management and interpersonal skills to successfully navigate the formal support system. Helping families keep adequate records and appointment schedules would enable them to obtain needed services. Social service providers who model positive interpersonal skills in their interactions with clientele and treat them with respect could also facilitate their clients' access to resources. Providing family counseling and mental health services to low-income families in rural communities could help them interact positively with family and friends to build and maintain their social networks. Social agencies or organizations should consider establishing funds to provide small grants of cash that could stop loss spirals from occurring when negative life events threaten a family's stability. Examples of need for such cash grants are automobile repair or replacement, medical or dental bills, attorney fees, home repairs, and child care. Flexibility in working arrangements such as sick leave, or the ability to change work hours or days might forestall a mother's choosing to terminate employment in order to care for a sick child or parent.

Utilizing an intergenerational family-focused approach to helping rural, low-income families could also strengthen family resiliency and support better child and family outcomes. Because so much of the informal social support received by the mothers and families in the RFS project came from the family of origin, particularly from the mothers of participants, creating and offering programs that include multiple family members would be important. Specifically, if grandmothers are the most likely providers of child care to working mothers and their families, perhaps creating multi-session educational programs for all family members would be beneficial. These programs could allow for multigenerational exchanges, plans for providing care, and focused agreements as to how child care could be performed within family contexts that undergird child well-being and enable both mothers and grandmothers to express confidence in their negotiated roles. While living with extended family members is a common strategy among rural, low-income families, these living contexts, as suggested by families in the RFS project, appear to promote stress among family members. Information and skill development sessions for multigenerational coresidential families could also help families conserve and manage resources while promoting a positive exchange of instrumental and emotional support in the context of these family relationships. Training in anger management and nonviolent communication could facilitate more positive interaction among members of a household or network. Furthermore, intergenerational family-focused educational programs could help families to understand together how to navigate formal support services and access needed aid for all members.

Local employers or organizations such as community foundations, the YMCA, or Cooperative Extension might consider sponsoring low-cost family activities such as a Family Fun Day at the county fair or a weekend camp for children and their mothers or grandmothers with opportunities for skill-building as well as fun in a different setting. Local organizations also could provide scholarship funds to buy athletic uniforms and band instruments and pay for field trips and other fees to enable low-income children to participate in extra-curricular activities. Transportation may be an issue for some of these families, so rethinking the bus schedule to allow low-income children to stay for such activities after school would be in order. Supporting healthy activities for all family members could enhance not only their physical health and combat rising rates of obesity in rural communities (National Advisory Committee on Rural Health and Human Services 2005), but also foster positive mental health in multiple generations.

Future studies are needed to continue collecting information from rural families who face a different set of challenges and opportunities than families in urban areas. The investigation of social support should be approached by interviewing multiple members of the networks. In this way, issues such as cost of support exchanges and ambivalence in relationships could be more thoroughly understood. Although the RFS study did collect data on use of formal support systems, a purposive approach to understanding the interaction between those and families' informal networks was not included. A more thorough examination of the support choices that families make and the thoughts they have about staying in their home communities versus moving to better employment opportunities would be valuable. RFS researchers did investigate the reception that participants had when applying for assistance from government and nonprofit agencies. Suggestions for related policy changes are included in a later chapter. Many of the mothers in our study had young children, and those with wage-earning partners tended to express interest in staying home to care for their children until they reached school age (data not shown). A follow-up study or a long-term longitudinal study that revisited mothers after their children got older might yield different results with regard to employment and the concomitant support needs.

Discussion Questions

1. Which theory or theories are most useful in the investigation of rural low-income families' social support and its relationship to employment? Are there other theories that could be used and how would these expand our understanding?
2. How do relationships with network members influence the assistance available from the network?
3. How might a low-income mother's assistance from her informal network collide with her employment demands?
4. How can social support networks facilitate employment?
5. What are the negative aspects of social support especially for rural, low-income families?
6. How do resource constraints of rural, low-income families influence the levels of social support?
7. How can social support networks make it more difficult to be employed or maintain employment?
8. What did you learn in this chapter that helps you understand the lived experience of rural low-income families?
9. What other programs or policies would help enhance rural, low-income mothers' management and interpersonal skills?

References

Acock, A. C., & Hurlbert, J. S. (1990). Social network analysis: A structural perspective for family studies. *Journal of Social and Personal Relationships, 7,* 245–264. doi:10.1177/0265407590072006.

Agneessens, F., Waege, H., & Lievens, J. (2006). Diversity in social support by role relations: A typology. *Social Networks, 28,* 427–441. doi:101016/j.socnet.2005.10.001.

Ahluwalia, I. B., Dodds, J. M., & Baligh, M. (1998). Social support and coping behaviors of low-income families experiencing food insufficiency in North Carolina. *Health Education Behavior, 25,* 599–612. doi:10.1177/109019819802500507.

Ahluwalia, S. K., McGroder, S. M., Zaslow, M. J., & Hair, E. C. (2001). *Symptoms of depression among welfare recipients: A concern for two generations.*http://www.childtrends.org/Files/Research_Brief_Depression.pdf.

Altonji, J. G., Hayashi, F., & Kotlikoff, L. (1997). Parental altruism and inter vivos transfers: Theory and evidence. *Journal of Political Economy, 105,* 1121–1166. http://www.jstor.org/stable/10.1086/516388.

Amato, P. R. (1993). Urban-rural differences in helping friends and family members. *Social Psychology Quarterly, 56,* 249–262. http://www.jstor.org/stable/2786662.

Antonucci, T. C., & Akiyama, H. (1995). Convoys of social relations: Family and friendships within a life span context. In R. Blieszner & V. H. Bedford (Eds.), *Handbook of aging and the family* (pp. 355–372). Westport: Greenwood Press.

Bauman, K. J., & Downs, B. A. (2000). Measures of help available to households in need: Their relation to well-being, welfare, and work (Working Paper Series No. 42). http://www.census.gov/population/www/documentation/twps0042/twps0042.html.

Bidart, C., & Lavenu, D. (2005). Evolutions of personal networks and life events. *Social Networks, 27,* 359–376. doi:10.1016/j.socnet.2004.11.003.

Burleson, B. R. (2003). The experience and effects of emotional support: What the study of cultural and gender differences can tell us about close relationships, emotion and interpersonal communication. *Personal Relationships, 10,* 1–23. doi:10.1111/1475-6811.00033.

Cohen, P. N. (2002). Extended households at work: Living arrangements and inequality in single mothers' employment. *Sociological Forum, 17,* 445–463. http://www.jstor.org/stable/3070350.

Conger, R., Ge, S., & Elder, G. (1994). Economic stress, coercive family process and developmental problems of adolescents. *Child Development, 65,* 541–561. http://www.jstor.org/stable/1131401.

Connidis, I. A., & McMullin, J. A. (2002). Sociological ambivalence and family ties: A critical perspective. *Journal of Marriage and Family, 64,* 558–567. doi:10.1111/j.1741-3737.2002.00558.x.

Coyne, C. A., Demian-Popescu, C., & Friend, D. (2006). Social and cultural factors influencing health in southern West Virginia: A qualitative study, *Preventing Chronic Disease, 3,* A124. http://www.cdc.gov/pcd/issues/2006/oct/06_0030.htm.

Curley, A. M. (2009). Draining or gaining? The social networks of public housing movers in Boston. *Journal of Social and Personal Relationships, 26,* 227–247. doi:10.1177/0265407509106716.

di Leonardo, M. (1987). The female world of cards and holidays: Women, families, and the work of kinship. *Signs, 12,* 440–453. http://www.jstor.org/stable/3174331.

Dolan, E. M., Seiling, S., & Glesner, T. (2006). Making it work: Rural low income women in service jobs. In B. J. Cude (Ed.), *Proceedings of the Eastern Family Economics and Resource Management Association Conference* (pp. 38–46). Knoxville. http://mrupured.myweb.uga.edu/conf/5.pdf.

Domínguez, S., & Watkins, C. (2003). Creating networks for survival and mobility: Social capital among African-American and Latin-American low-income mothers. *Social Problems, 50,* 111–135. http://www.jstor.org/stable/3096825.

Duncan, G. J., & Brooks-Gunn, J (Eds.) (1997). *Consequences of growing up poor.* New York: Russell Sage Foundation Press.

Duncan, G. J., Whitener, L. A., & Weber, B. A. (2002). Lessons learned: Welfare reform and food assistance in rural America. In B. A. Weber, G. J. Duncan, & L. A. Whitener (Eds.), *Rural dimensions of welfare reform* (pp. 455–470). Kalamazoo: W. E. Upjohn Institute for Employment Research.

Dunkel-Schetter, C., & Bennett, T. L. (1990). Differentiating the cognitive and behavioral aspects of social support. In B. R. Sarason, I. G. Sarason, & G. R. Pierce (Eds.), *Social support: An interactional view* (pp. 267–318). New York: John Wiley.

Durden, E. D., Hill, T. D., & Angel, R. J. (2007). Social demands, social supports, psychological distress among low-income women. *Journal of Social and Personal Relationships, 24,* 343-361. doi:10.1177/0265407507077226.

Freedman, V. A., Wolf, D, A., Soldo, B. J., & Stephen, E. H. (1991). Intergenerational transfers: A question of perspective. *The Gerontologist, 31,* 640–647. doi:10.1093/geront/31.5.640.

Gleason, M. E. J., Iida, M., Shrout, P. E., & Bolger, N. (2008). Receiving support as a mixed blessing: Evidence for dual effects of support on psychological outcomes. *Journal of Personality and Social Psychology, 94,* 824–838. doi:10.1037/0022-3514.94.5.824.

Greder, K., Cook, C., Garasky, S., Sano, Y., & Randall, B. (2008). Rural Latino immigrant families: Hunger, housing, and social support. In R. L. Dalla, J. DeFrain, J. Johnson, & D. A. Abbott

(Eds.), *Strengths and challenges of new immigrant families: Implications for research, policy, education and service* (pp. 345–367). Lanham: Lexington Books.

Green, B. L., & Rodgers, A. (2001). Determinants of social support among low income mothers: A longitudinal analysis. *American Journal of Community Psychology, 29*, 419–441. doi:10.1023/A:1010371830131.

Hao, L. (1996). Family structure, private transfers, and the economic well-being of families with children. *Social Forces, 75*, 269–292. http://www.jstor.org/stable/2580765.

Harknett, K. (2006). The relationship between private safety nets and economic outcomes among single mothers. *Journal of Marriage and Family, 68*, 172–191. doi:10.1111/j.1741-3737.2006.00250.x.

Henly, J. R. (2002). Informal support networks and the maintenance of low-wage jobs. In F. Munger (Ed.), *Laboring below the line: The new ethnography of poverty, low-wage work and survival in the global economy* (pp. 197–203). New York: Russell Sage Foundation.

Hill, C. A. (1997). Relationship of expressive and affiliative personality dispositions to perceptions of social support. *Basic and Applied Social Psychology, 19*, 133–161. doi:10.1207/s15324834basp1902_1.

Hobfoll, S. E. (1989). Conservation of resources: A new attempt at conceptualizing stress. *American Psychologist, 44*, 513–524. doi:10.1037/0003-066X.44.3.513.

Hobfoll, S. E. (2001). The influence of culture, community, and the nested-self in the stress process: Advancing the conservation of resource theory. *Applied Psychology: An International Review, 50*, 337–412. doi:10.1111/1464-0597.00062.

Hobfoll, S. E. (2009). Social support: The movie. *Journal of Social and Personal Relationships, 26*, 93–101. doi:10.1177/0265407509105524.

Hobfoll, S. E., Freedy, J., Lane, C., & Geller, P. (1990). Conservation of social resources: Social support resource theory. *Journal of Social and Personal Relationships, 7*, 465–478. doi:10.1177/0265407590074004.

Hogan, D. P., Hao, L. X., & Parish, W. L. (1990). Race, kin networks, and assistance to mother-headed families. *Social Forces, 68*, 797–812. http://www.jstor.org/stable/2579354.

Hogan, D., Eggebeen, D., & Clogg, C. (1993). The structure of intergenerational exchanges in American families. *American Journal of Sociology, 98*, 1428–1458. http://www.jstor.org/stable/2781826.

House, J. S., Umberson, D., & Landis, K. R. (1988). Structures and processes of social support. *Annual Review of Sociology, 14*, 293–318. http://www.jstor.org/stable/2083320.

Iida, M., Seidman, G., Shrout, P. E., Fujita, K., & Bolger, N. (2008). Modeling support provision in intimate relationships. *Journal of Personality and Social Psychology, 94*, 460–478. doi:10.1037/0022-3514.94.3.460.

Jayakody, R. (1998). Race differences in intergenerational financial assistance: The needs of children and the resources of parents. *Journal of Family Issues, 19*, 508–533. doi:10.1177/019251398019005002.

Kanaʻiaupuni, S. M., Donato, K. M., Thompson-Colon, T., & Stainback, M. (2005). Counting on kin: Social networks, social support, and child health status. *Social Forces, 83*, 1137–1164. doi:10.1353/sof.20050036.

Kissane, R. J. (2007). How do faith-based organizations compare to secular providers? Nonprofit directors' and poor women's assessments of FBOs. *Journal of Poverty, 11*, 91–115. doi:10.13001/J134v11n04_05.

Ko, J., & Manoogian, M. (2005, April). *Commitment to parenting and personal outcomes for rural, low-income Appalachian mothers*. Paper session presented at the annual meeting of the Ohio Association of Family and Consumer Sciences, Perrysburg, OH.

Lakey, B., & Dickinson, L. G. (1994). Antecedents of perceived support: Is perceived family environment generalized to new social relationships? *Cognitive Therapy and Research, 18*, 39–53. doi:10.1007/BF02359394.

Lawler, E. J. (2001). An affect theory of social exchange. *The American Journal of Sociology, 107*, 321–352. doi:10.1086/324071.

Lee, Y., & Aytac, I. (1998). Intergenerational financial support among White, African American, and Latinos. *Journal of Marriage and the Family, 60,* 426–441. http://www.jstor.org/stable/353859.

Lee, G. R., Netzer, J. K., & Coward, R. T. (1994). Filial responsibility expectations and patterns of intergenerational assistance. *Journal of Marriage and the Family, 56,* 559–565. http://www.jstor.org/stable/352867.

Lein, L., Benjamin, A. F., McManus, M., & Roy, K. (2005). Economic roulette: When is a job not a job? *Community, Work & Family, 8,* 359–378. doi:10.1080/13668800500262752.

Levitan, L., & Feldman, S. (1991). For love or money: Nonmonetary economic arrangements among rural households in central New York. In D. C. Clay & H. K. Schwarzweller (Eds.), *Household strategies* (pp. 149–172). Greenwich: JAI Press.

Lüscher, K., & Pillemer, K. (1998). Intergenerational ambivalence: A new approach to the study of parent-child relations in later life. *Journal of Marriage and the Family, 60,* 413–425. http://www.jstor.org/stable/353858.

Lye, D. (1996). Adult-child-parent relationships. *Annual Review of Sociology, 22,* 79–102. http://www.jstor.org/stable/2083425.

Magdol, L. (2000). The people you know: The impact of residential mobility on mothers' social network ties. *Journal of Social and Personal Relationships, 17,* 183–204. doi:10.1146/annurev.soc.22.1.79.

Magdol, L., & Bessel, D. R. (2003). Social capital, social currency, and portable assets: The impact of residential mobility on exchanges of social support. *Personal Relationships, 10,* 149–169. doi:10.1177/0265407500172002.

Manoogian, M., Richards, L., & Peters, C. (2003, November). *Negotiating poverty and family ties: Adult daughters' ambivalent relationships with mothers in rural, low-income families.* Symposium paper presented at annual meeting of National Council on Family Relations, Vancouver, Canada.

Marks, N. F., & McLanahan, S. S. (1993). Gender, family structure, and social support among parents. *Journal of Marriage and the Family, 55,* 481–493. http://www.jstor.org/stable/352817.

Martin, J. L., & Yeung, K. T. (2006). Persistence of close personal ties over a 12-year period. *Social Networks, 28,* 331–362. doi:10.1016/j.socnet.2005.07.008.

McGarry, K. (2000). *Testing parental altruism: Implications of a dynamic model* (NBER Working Paper No. W7593). http://www.nber.org/papers/w7593.

McGarry, K., & Schoeni, R. F. (1995). Transfer behavior in the health and retirement study: Measurement and the redistribution of resources within the family. *Journal of Human Resources, 30,* 184–226. http://www.jstor.org/stable/146283.

Mickelson, K. D., & Kubzansky, L. D. (2003). Social distribution of social support: The mediating role of life events. *American Journal of Community Psychology, 32,* 265–281. doi:10.1023/B:AJCP.0000004747.99099.7e.

Miller, R. J., & Darlington, Y. (2002). Who supports? The providers of social support to dual-parent families caring for young children. *Journal of Community Psychology, 30,* 461–473. doi:10.1002/jcop.10023.

Moos, R. H., & Mitchell, R. E. (1982). Social network resources and adaptation: A conceptual framework. In T. A. Wills (Ed.), *Basic processes in helping relationships* (pp. 213–232). New York: Academic Press.

National Advisory Committee on Rural Health and Human Services (NACRHHS). (2005). *The 2005 Report to the Secretary: Rural health and human service issue.* Washington, DC: Author.

Nelson, M. K. (2000). Single mothers and social support: The commitment to, and retreat from, reciprocity. *Qualitative Sociology, 23,* 291–317. doi:10.1023?A:1005567910606.

Nelson, M. K., & Smith, J. (1999). *Working hard and making do: Surviving in small town America.* Berkeley: University of California Press.

Olson, C. M., Anderson, K., Kiss, E., Lawrence, F. C., & Seiling, S. B. (2004). Factors protecting against and contributing to food insecurity among rural families. *Family Economics and Nutrition Review, 16*(1), 12–20. http://www.cnpp.usda.gov/Publications/FENR/V16N1/FENRV16N1.pdf.

Orthner, D. K., Jones-Sanpei, H., & Williamson, S. (2004). The resilience and strengths of low-income families. *Family Relations, 53,* 159–167. doi:10.1111/j.0022-2445.2004.0006.x.

Pearlin, L. I. (1985). The sociological study of stress. *Journal of Health and Social Behavior, 30,* 241–256. http://www.jstor.org/stable/2136956.

Phan, M. B., Blumer, N., & Demaiter, E. L. (2009). Helping hands: Neighborhood diversity, deprivation, and reciprocity of support in non-kin networks. *Journal of Social and Personal Relationships, 26,* 899–918. doi:10.1177/0265407509345655.

Plickert, G., Coté, R. R., & Wellman, B. (2007). It's not who you know, it's how you know them: Who exchanges what with whom? *Social Networks, 29,* 405–429. doi:10.1016/j.socnet.2007.01.007.

Portes, A., & Landolt, P. (1996). The downside of social capital. *The American Prospect, 26,* 18–23. http://www.lexisnexis.com/hottopics/lnacademic/?verb=sr&csi=161341.

Reiter, P. L., Katz, M. L., Ferkitich, A. K., Ruffin, M. T., & Paskett, E. D. (2009). Appalachian self-identity among women in Ohio Appalachia. *Journal of Rural Community Psychology, E12*(1). http://www.marshall.edu/jrcp/VE12%20N1/Reiter%20JRCP.pdf.

Rhodes, J. E., Ebert, L., & Meyers, A. B. (1994). Social support, relationship problems and the psychological functioning of young African-American mothers. *Journal of Social and Personal Relationship, 11,* 587–599. doi:10.1177/0265407594114006.

Richards, L., Manoogian, M., Seiling, S., & Bird, C. (2002, November). *Providing support and presenting challenge: Adult daughters and their mothers in rural, low-income families.* Paper session presented at the annual meeting of the National Council on Family Relations, Houston, TX.

Rook, K. S. (1990). Detrimental aspects of social relationships: Taking stock of an emerging literature. In H. O. F. Veiel & U. Baumann (Eds.), *The meaning and measurement of social support* (pp. 157–180). New York: Hemisphere.

Rosenzweig, M. R., & Wolpin, K. I. (1993). Intergenerational support and the life-cycle incomes of young men and their parents: Human capital, investments, coresidence, and intergenerational financial transfers. *Journal of Labor Economics, 11,* 84–112. http://www.jstor.org/stable/2535185.

Rosenzweig, M. R., & Wolpin, K. I. (1994). Parental and public transfers to young women and their children. *The American Economic Review, 84,* 1195–1212. http://www.jstor.org/stable2117768.

Rossi, A., & Rossi, P. (1990). *Of human bonding: Parent-child relations across the life course.* Hawthorne: Aldine de Gruyter.

Sarkisian, N. (2006). "Doing family ambivalence": Nuclear and extended families in single mothers' lives. *Journal of Marriage and Family, 68,* 804–811. doi:10.111/j.1741-3737.2006.00295.x.

Schoeni, R. F. (1992). *Another leak in the bucket? Public transfer income and private family support* (Research Report No. 92-249). Ann Arbor, MI: University of Michigan Population Studies Center.

Schuster, T. L., Kessler, R. C., & Aseltine, R. H. (1990). Supportive interactions, negative interactions, and depressed mood. *American Journal of Community Psychology, 18,* 423–438. doi:10.1007/BF00938116.

Seccombe, K. (2007). *Families in poverty.* New York: Pearson Education.

Seiling, S. B. (2006). Changes in the lives of rural low-income mothers: Do resources play a role in stress? *Journal of Human Behavior in the Social Environment, 13,* 19–42. doi:10.1300/J137v13n01-02.

Seiling, S. B., Dolan, E. M., & Glesner, T. (2005, June). *Rural low-income women who work in service jobs tell about their lives.* Paper session presented at the Gender, Work and Organization 4th International Conference, Keele University, Staffordshire, UK.

Seiling, S. B., Stafford, K., McCabe, S., & Reschke, K. (2006). Social support as a means to well-being for rural low-income mothers. In B. J. Cude (Ed.), *Proceedings of the Eastern Family Economics and Resource Management Association Conference* (pp. 88–100). Knoxville. http://mrupured.myweb.uga.edu/conf/20.pdf.

Silverstein, M., & Bengtson, V. (1997). Intergenerational solidarity and the structure of adult child-parent relationships in American families. *American Journal of Sociology, 103*, 429–460. doi:10.1086/231213.

Smith, S. S. (2005). "Don't put my name on it": Social capital activation and job-finding assistance among the black urban poor. *American Journal of Sociology, 111*, 1–57. doi:10.1086/428814.

Son, S., & Bauer, J. W. (2010). Employed rural, low-income, single mothers' family and work over time. *Journal of Family and Economic Issues, 31*, 107–120. doi:.1007/s10834-009-9173-8.

Swanson, J., Lawrence, F., Anderson, K., & Olson, C. M. (2004). Low-income rural families: How formal and informal supports address food needs. In J. Fox (Ed.), *Proceedings of the Eastern Family Economics-Resource Management Association Conference* (pp. 27–29). Tampa.

Taylor, L. C. (2001). Work attitudes, employment barriers, and mental health symptoms in a sample of rural welfare recipients. *American Journal of Community Psychology, 29*, 443–463. doi:10.1023/A:1010323914202.

Thoits, P. A. (1995). Stress, coping, and social support processes: Where are we? What next? *Journal of Health & Social Behavior (Extra issue)*, 53–79. http://www.jstor.org/stable/2626957.

Turner, H. A. (1994). Gender and social support: Taking the bad with the good? *Sex Roles, 30*, 521–541. doi:10.1007/BF01420800.

Vangelisti, A. L. (2009). Challenges in conceptualizing social support. *Journal of Social and Personal Relationships, 26*, 39–51. doi:10.1177/0265407509105520.

Wakabayashi, C., & Donato, K. M. (2006). Does caregiving increase poverty among women in later life? Evidence from the Health and Retirement Survey. *Journal of Health and Social Behavior, 47*, 258–274. doi:10.1177/002214650604700305.

Wan, C. K., Jacard, J., & Ramey, S. L. (1996). The relationship between social support and life satisfaction as a function of family structure. *Journal of Marriage and the Family, 54*, 502–513. http://www.jstor.org/stable/353513.

Waybright, L., Morrison, P., Seiling, S., Meek, J., & Manoogian, M. (2004, October). *The informal and formal support networks of rural, low-income Appalachian families.* Paper session presented at the annual conference of the National Association of Extension Family and Consumer Sciences, Nashville, TN.

Wellman, B., & Wortley, S. (1990). Different strokes from different folks: Community ties and social support. *American Journal of Sociology, 96*, 558–588. doi:10.2307/2781064.

Wellman, B., Wong, R. Y., Tindall, D., & Nazer, N. (1997). A decade of network change: Turnover, persistence and stability in personal communities. *Social Networks, 19*, 27–50. doi:10.1016/S0378-8733(96)00289-4.

Widmer, E. D. (2006). Who are my family members? Bridging and binding social capital in family configurations. *Journal of Social and Personal Relationships, 23*, 979–998. doi:10.117/0265407506070482.

Chapter 10
The Earned Income Tax Credit:
An Incentive to Rural Employment

Sheila Mammen, Frances C. Lawrence and Jaerim Lee

Introduction

The federal Earned Income Tax Credit (EITC) was enacted in 1975 to help offset the Social Security taxes of low-income families with children. The EITC was also meant to provide those taxpayers with an increased incentive to work. As a refundable tax credit, the EITC can reduce a taxpayers' tax liability to below zero. A refund will be given for any balance left. In other words, the EITC can be used as payment towards a taxpayers' tax debt, and if the payment exceeds the debt, a refund will be given for the "overpayment." Some families are eligible even if they owe no taxes, making the entire credit refundable. This, in turn, allows eligible taxpayers to receive the full amount for which they qualify, regardless of their tax liability.

Originally, the EITC was meant to be temporary, small, and only for the 1975 calendar year. The tax credit, however, was made permanent by the Revenue Act of 1978 and has grown tremendously over the years. By 2007, $48 billion had been claimed by 24 million eligible working families (US Internal Revenue Service 2009). Today, it is the largest federal aid program targeted towards low-income families (Wancheck 2008). Due to the success of the federal EITC, 23 states and the District of Columbia have enacted state EITC programs as well (Levitis and Koulish 2008).

Benefits of the EITC

The tax credit provides significant benefits to low-income working families and the communities in which they live. As a source of additional income, the EITC has helped to lift many low-income families out of poverty (Scholz 1994), reduced welfare caseloads (Dowd 2005; Holt 2006), and reduced income inequality (Ber-

S. Mammen (✉)
Department of Resource Economics, University of Massachusetts, Amherst, MA, USA
e-mail: smammen@isenberg.umass.edu

J. W. Bauer, E. M. Dolan (eds.), *Rural Families and Work,* International Series on Consumer Science 1,
DOI 10.1007/978-1-4614-0382-1_10, © Springer Science+Business Media, LLC 2011

ube and Forman 2001). Berube (2000, cited in Holt 2006) reported that the credit provided a 13% boost in the community average family income in some urban and rural places. Compared to all other federal programs, the EITC is credited as the single program most responsible for reducing child poverty (Blank 1999; Greenstein and Shapiro 1998; Johnson et al. 2003); about half of all Hispanic children and almost half of all children in the South face less hardship because their families receive the tax credit (Greenstein and Shapiro 1998). Combined, the federal EITC and the refundable state EITCs have lifted more families out of poverty than any other public assistance program (Johnson et al. 2003).

The EITC has contributed to an increase in low-income families' employment and income, especially among single mothers (Grogger 2003; Holtzblatt et al. 1994; Noonan et al. 2007). For single mothers, the EITC is a strong incentive to remain in the labor force (Ellwood 2000; Hotz and Scholz 2003; Mammen et al. 2009; Meyer and Rosenbaum 2001). According to Neumark and Wascher (2001), the state EITC is considered even more useful than the minimum wage because the state EITC appears to incentivize adults to enter the labor force.

The EITC has a positive impact on the economy of local communities. The ripple effect on retail markets in poor neighborhoods is even greater than that of the federal income tax returns since working families in these communities are more likely to receive the tax credit (Berube and Forman 2001; Edwards 2004). Ultimately, increased consumption may lead to additional benefits as more jobs may be created, giving families greater access to goods and services. A final benefit of the federal EITC program is the bipartisan political support that it has enjoyed over the years due to the fact that the tax credit is given only to those who worked the previous year and because it acts as an incentive to remain in the labor force (Mammen et al. 2009).

Eligibility for the EITC

To receive the EITC, families or individuals must meet certain requirements. They must (a) have a valid social security number, (b) have earned income from the previous year, (c) be a US citizen or meet citizenship or resident alien requirements, and (d) file an income tax return with an EITC worksheet. When filing taxes for the previous year, applicants cannot use the married-but-filing-separately status, be the qualifying child of another person, or file forms 2555 or 2555-EZ, both of which are for foreign earned income.

Adjusted gross income must be within certain income ranges. For the 2010 filing year, for a family with one qualifying child, income could not exceed $35,535, or $40,545 if married filing jointly. For a family with two qualifying children, income could not exceed $40,363, or $45,373 if married filing jointly. And for a family with three or more qualifying children, income could not exceed $43,352, or $48,362 if married filing jointly. For families, the maximum tax credit for the 2010 tax year was $3,050 with one qualifying child, $5,036 with two qualifying children, and $5,666 with three or more qualifying children[1] (US Internal Revenue Service 2010).

The amount of the credit received is based on family earned income for the tax year. Those families whose total earned income is nearest the middle of the eligible income distribution benefit the most from the tax credit. The income supplement steadily increases up to a certain level of earned income. Eventually, a plateau is reached in the middle of the income spectrum. Families at this middle or plateau level receive the maximum amount of credit. As families' income become larger, they receive incrementally less of the credit.

Families who are eligible for the EITC, in the past, could receive their funds in one of two ways. Most families, upon filing their federal income tax forms, received a lump sum payment in addition to any other tax refund. Families could also receive the EITC as advanced monthly payments in their paychecks, provided their employers were supportive of this. As of January 2011, however, the advanced EITC option was discontinued as a result of the Education, Jobs, and Medical Assistance Act enacted in 2010.

Review of Related Literature and Theory

A number of studies have been conducted on the EITC covering a variety of topics. Key research questions have been: (a) what are the differences between those families who take advantage of the EITC and those who are eligible but do not file for the credit, (b) how do families receive the credit, and (c) how do families use the credit. In addition to the Rural Families Speak (RFS) project, various data sets, such as the National Longitudinal Survey of Youth, the National Survey of America's Families, the Survey of Income Program Participation, and researcher self-prepared surveys, have been used to answer these questions.

Characteristics of Those Who Filed for the EITC and Those Who Did Not

Caputo (2006) reported that about half of the EITC eligible tax filers filed tax returns and received the credit. The EITC filers were more likely to be younger, female, less educated, born in the United States, separated/divorced/widowed, past recipients of food stamps and/or Temporary Assistance for Needy Families (TANF), live in poor families for a greater number of years, and work fewer weeks per year

---

[1] The American Recovery and Reinvestment Act of 2009 (ARRA) established a temporary increase in the EITC for families with three or more children. In addition, ARRA increased the beginning point of the phase-out range for the tax credit for all married couples filing a joint return, regardless of the number of children. These changes applied to the 2009 and 2010 tax years only.

on average than those who did not file but were eligible. In an earlier study, Scholz (1994) found the EITC participation rate of those eligible to be between 80% and 86%. Those who received the tax credit were more likely to report higher incomes, receive a larger EITC payment, and live in states with state income taxes. Berube and Tiffany (2004) reported that families in large cities were the most likely to receive the EITC, followed closely by families in rural areas, while those in smaller metro areas and large suburbs were less likely.

Researchers have reported that families whose primary language is something other than English were less likely to receive the credit (Berube and Forman 2001; Maag 2005; Phillips 2001b; Varcoe et al. 2004). These families were reported to be generally less aware of the credit or to experience difficulties in filing taxes, indicating a possibility that language barriers may decrease EITC participation. In particular, Hispanics have been identified as less likely than other ethnicities to receive the credit. Varcoe et al. (2004), using RFS data, found that only 36% of eligible rural Hispanic families in California received the credit. Hispanic families appeared to possess inaccurate understanding of the tax credit and/or were unaware of its existence. Berube and Forman (2001), Maag (2005), and Phillips (2001b) also reported that Hispanic households had very little understanding of the EITC.

The effect of education on EITC participation has been studied by several researchers, yielding mixed results. Phillips (2001a) found that parents who finished high school or had at least some college education were more likely to know about and receive the EITC than those with less than a high school education. Caputo (2006), on the other hand, found that less educated mothers were more likely to claim the credit.

Similarly, the effect of participation in public assistance programs on participation rates showed mixed results. Scholz (1994) reported that EITC nonparticipants were more likely to receive public assistance. In more recent studies, Caputo (2006) and Phillips (2001a) found that those who received public assistance, including TANF or food stamps, were more likely to file for the EITC since they were more likely to have been informed of the credit.

In addition, the literature is unclear on how marital status affects the participation rates. Caputo (2006), Dowd (2005), and Phillips (2001a) indicated that married, low-income parents were less likely than single parents to report receiving the credit, while Blumenthal et al. (2005) and Scholz (1994) indicated that married parents were more likely to claim the credit.[2]

Tax preparation is another salient topic in the EITC literature. Berube et al. (2002) found that approximately two-thirds (68%) of the EITC recipients relied on

---

[2] Married couples must use the married, filing jointly option when filing their income taxes if they are to be considered eligible for the EITC. If the combined income moves the family into the mid range level of the credit, where they would receive the largest benefit, filing jointly is an advantage.But this can be a disadvantage if the combined incomes decrease their benefits or make them ineligible for the credit.Cohabiters must file as individuals. Some cohabiting couples who file separately may have the same, or larger combined household income than some married couples, and still receive the full amount of the credit if the parent or guardian who claims the credit earns the qualifying income.

professional assistance with tax filing. Blumenthal et al. (2005) reported that 60% of all the EITC participants used outside assistance, both paid and unpaid, to file their tax returns. Mammen and Lawrence (2006) and O'Hare and Johnson (2004) expressed concern that the high fees charged by some tax preparers reduced the tax credit received by rural families. Furthermore, reliance on outside tax preparers appeared to eliminate the families' need to understand the tax credit. Interestingly, some eligible families did not claim the EITC even when using a professional tax preparer (US Government Accountability Office 2003).

How Families Receive the EITC

Families who qualify for the EITC previously were able to choose between advance payments and a lump sum payment. If families received the credit as advance payments, household income flow and utility was increased. More than 98% of recipients, however, reported receiving a lump sum payment (McCubbin 2000; Olson and Davis 1994; Romich and Weisner 2000; Scholz 1994). Families may prefer the lump sum form of payment so that they can purchase consumer durables or bigger ticket items (Barrow and McGranahan 1999). A large lump sum may have a positive psychological effect and may be used more judiciously than regular, smaller amounts of money.

How Families Use the EITC

Savings was frequently mentioned as a way that the EITC was used (Beverly et al. 2000; Romich and Weisner 2000; Smeeding et al. 2000). Smeeding et al. (2000) found that about half of their respondents stated that they saved some or all of their refund for future uses such as paying bills, purchasing consumer durables, and making educational investments in themselves or their children. Beverly et al. (2000) reported about a fifth (21%) of the respondents used the EITC for savings and indicated that their first priority was to establish precautionary savings.

Other uses included paying bills, purchasing large-ticket consumer goods, and accumulating assets (Romich and Weisner 2000; Smeeding et al. 2000). For almost half of the respondents in their study, Smeeding et al. (2000) reported that paying a bill was the highest priority, whereas making consumer purchases was the second priority. Romich and Weisner (2000) reported respondents using the tax credit to purchase large-ticket consumer goods and accumulate assets. In the same study, they found expenditures on children and making improvements in transportation and housing situation were also priority uses. Smeeding et al. found that the EITC played an important role in improving the social mobility of recipients through the purchase or repair of a car, paying for education, or relocating.

The Behavioral Life-Cycle Theory

The behavioral life-cycle theory (BLCT) proposed by Shefrin and Thaler (1988) provides a useful framework to examine household consumption behavior as it relates to the EITC benefits. One of the merits of the BLCT is the inclusion of self-control, mental accounting, and framing to the life-cycle theory of saving.[3] Self-control may be costly to families, which may lead them to practice no self-control and avoid decision-making. If this were the case, families' preferences would be to receive the entire EITC at once, i.e., as a lump sum as opposed to receiving it as an advance with their monthly pay checks throughout the year. Unlike the large infusion of funds that families may receive when they opt for the lump sum payment, the advance was a smaller amount of cash. Therefore, the advance method required families to plan and exercise some degree of self-control, particularly if they were interested in using the tax credit for savings or for making large purchases.

According to the BLCT, *wealth* may be categorized into three mental accounts: Current assets, current income, and future income. Families are most likely to be tempted to spend current income and are least likely to spend future income (Graham and Issac 2002). This implies that, relative to the EITC, families may prefer to receive the credit as a lump sum payment which, consequently, may enable them to better manage how and when they spend the funds. Shefrin and Thaler (1988) opine that a one-time cash infusion may be "framed" differently or may be given a different value than regular family income. This occurs in spite of the fact that the EITC, a form of windfall income, is anticipated. As a consequence, household marginal propensity to save the lump sum EITC would be greater.

Findings from the RFS Project

The findings from the various studies mentioned above have informed our analyses of the RFS data and the understanding of the impact of the EITC on rural low-income families. In the rest of the chapter, we present the obstacles that eligible, working, rural families face in their participation in the EITC, profiles of those families who received the tax credit, the impact of the income supplement on their consumption patterns and asset behavior and, finally, the relationship between EITC nonparticipation and financial distress.

---

[3] According to the life-cycle theory of saving (Fisher 1930; Modigliani and Brumberg 1954), individuals will fully consume their lifetime incomes by spreading their consumption evenly over earning and retirement years. By first saving and then dissaving, their net worth is never negative.

What Are the Obstacles to Participation in the EITC?

In Panel 1 Wave 2 of the RFS study, about one-third of the 237 eligible,[4] rural low-income families did *not* receive the EITC (Mammen and Lawrence 2006). All mothers, regardless of whether or not their families qualified for the tax credit, were asked, "Did you receive the Earned Income Tax Credit since our last interview (conducted a year ago). If so, how much?" It was evident from the responses that some of them recognized the EITC and were able to provide an estimate of the amount that their family received, while others were confused. Their responses were examined systematically for patterns and themes that identified obstacles to participation in the EITC. Four types of obstacles, which were not mutually exclusive, emerged: (a) unawareness of the existence of the program, (b) misconceptions of the EITC, (c) problems related to assistance with tax preparation, and (d) irrational economic behavior.

Unawareness of the Program   Many of the rural mothers appeared to be unaware of the tax credit that could provide a much needed boost to their household income. For example, Annabel[5], a single, White, 20-year-old mother of one who was eligible for the tax credit asked, *"What is that? ...I have not heard of it. Am I supposed to get it?"* Maeve was similarly confused. She was White, 41-year-old, and married with four children. Although Maeve was eligible for the tax credit, she wanted to know, *"Would that be figured in your income tax?...I guess. I don't know. Is that an option for who—what kind of people?"*

When Theda, a 19-year-old, White mother of one, separated from her husband, was asked if she participated in the tax credit, she inquired, *"What was that?"* If Theda had been aware of the existence and the benefits of the tax credit, she would probably not have allowed her mother to claim her in return for $200 from her mother: *"'Cause I let her* [mother] *cover me. 'Cause I did work enough to send it* [tax form] *in but I didn't. 'Cause I don't think you have to, do you? 'Cause that's really giving, I don't know."*

A total lack of awareness of the EITC was also clear in the case of Paige, a White, 29-year-old mother of three. When asked if she received the EITC, she replied emphatically, *"I don't do credit cards."*

Misconceptions About the EITC   The rural mothers had numerous misconceptions about the EITC. Some of them were not sure if they qualified for it or if they received it, or they were generally confused by the tax credit and were unable to distinguish it from the regular tax refund and the child tax credit. Such misconceptions are evident in the examples that follow.

---

[4] To determine eligibility and participation in the EITC program, we (a) checked the respondent's and/or spouse's employment status for the previous year; (b) examined the previous year's household income, in relation to the number of children, to assess if the family qualified for the EITC; (c) analyzed the qualitative responses systematically to confirm that the respondent filed taxes, requested the tax credit, and obtained the EITC; and (d) used the size of the reported refunds to verify if the EITC was received.

[5] All names are pseudonyms.

Although she worked during the previous year, Estella, a 37-year-old, married, Hispanic mother of three responded, *"No, we didn't qualify, oh, did we qualify? I don't know if we qualified for that."* Had Joanne, a 25-year-old, White mother of three, and her husband better understood the EITC and its benefits, they may have known what they were foregoing:

> We didn't make enough to even file taxes last year. His boss would not take out taxes last year. It took me to the beginning of the year to fight him, and I threatened him with a bunch of stuff that we know that's going on…just under the table, and you know. To finally get him to take taxes out this year. So we couldn't file this year.

Other mothers simply did not know whether or not they received the EITC. This response from Constance, a 20-year-old, White mother, living with a child and a partner, was typical: *"I don't know. No, I don't think we did. Maybe we did. I don't know. Did we get the…no, we didn't. I think we have to be both 21 or even over 21 it said."* Constance's employment from the previous year had qualified them for the tax credit.

Problems Related to Assistance with Tax Preparation Although the respondents were not asked specifically if they had sought assistance in filing their taxes, this issue was raised by them. Such assistance, while helpful to those who are unfamiliar or uncomfortable with tax forms, may also discharge them of the need to have knowledge of the EITC since they are handing over the responsibility to the "expert." This idea of disassociating themselves from their taxes appeared to be the case with several of the respondents who relied on various family members as well as professional tax preparers.

The family of Lina, a 32-year-old, multiracial, married mother of three, was qualified for the EITC because her husband was employed the previous year. Yet, when asked if their tax refund included the EITC, Lina confessed, *"I don't do the taxes, so I don't know (if the EITC is received)."* Perhaps the reason why Estelle, who has been cited previously, may not have understood the EITC program was because, as she reported, *"Earned income credit, it's some, they do for…each, for the taxes. I don't know, because I didn't do my taxes, my bookkeeper took care of that."*

Several mothers turned over the tax filing to other family members and, therefore, knew little about the tax credit. This was true of Tia, a White, 18-year-old mother of one. She relied on her husband to do the taxes: *"I get taxes back, but I don't know what. I've never had to file taxes myself."* Laurel was 33 years old with a partner and two children. She was eligible for the EITC as she was employed during the previous year. Interestingly, Laurel entrusted her mother with tax filing: *"No, I, I'm, not sure how much (EITC was received), my mum did my income tax."*

Irrational Economic Behavior The EITC is an income supplement available to all eligible families, however, many of the rural families failed to take advantage of it. Such behavior may be considered irrational since they were not acting in their own economic self-interest, often for reasons that were inexplicable. Although Kylie was eligible for the EITC, when asked how much EITC she received, this White, married, 22-year-old mother of two replied, *"No, I didn't, I stay away from that, it confuses me."* Similarly, other respondents qualified for the EITC based on their eligibility status but did not receive it. Ellema, a 37-year-old Hispanic mother of one, asked incredulously, *"Why open a can of worms? I only worked three months, ten hours a week. They can keep it…"*

The behavior of some families appears to defy logic because, in part, they do not have the necessary support to file their taxes. For example, Rhoda, a mother with two children who was 33-year old and living with a partner, confessed, *"I have not done my taxes for two years. But we qualify (for the EITC)…"*

Who Receives the EITC?

To examine the characteristics of EITC participants and their families, we conducted binary logistic regressions using a sample of 314 mothers who were interviewed at both the first and second waves of Panel 1 of the RFS project (Gudmunson et al. 2010). The dependent variable was EITC participation (1 = yes, 0 = no) at Wave 1 and Wave 2. The independent variables were family earned income, earned income squared, the mother's age, marital status (married vs. no partner, cohabiting vs. no partner), number of children, education level, interview language (1 = Non-English, 0 = English), number of public assistance programs in which they participated (i.e., Special Supplemental Nutrition Program for Women, Infants, and Children (WIC), housing assistance, Low-Income Home Energy Assistance Program (LIHEAP), school lunch programs, child care assistance, transportation assistance, and Medicaid), and ability to prepare one's own taxes (1 = yes, 0 = no). Data from Wave 1 and Wave 2 were analyzed separately.

Table 10.1 shows the results of logistic regressions. Both family earned income ($OR_{Wave1} = 1.055$, $p < 0.01$; $OR_{Wave2} = 1.063$, $p < 0.001$) and earned income squared ($OR_{Wave1} = 0.995$, $p < 0.001$; $OR_{Wave2} = 0.998$, $p < 0.001$) were significantly associated with the odds of EITC participation, revealing a curvilinear relation between family income and the EITC participation in each year. This finding is consistent with previous studies that reported a positive relation between EITC participation and earned income or the size of estimated EITC benefits based on income (Blumenthal et al. 2005; Phillips 2001a). We further plotted the relation between income and EITC participation and found an inverted U-shaped curve, which indicated that the EITC participation was the highest near the middle of the income spectrum. This finding implies that having the middle level of earned income within the eligible income range may be an incentive to participate in the EITC, given greater benefits in the plateau range. Families with the lowest levels of earnings, then, are less likely to claim the EITC, although the credit could boost their family income. These families may decide to avoid dealing with hassles related to filing taxes due to their very low income, without really knowing the potential amount of the EITC benefits.

Table 10.1 Summary of Logistic Regression Analysis Predicting EITC Participation (N = 314)

Predictor	Wave 1 1999–2000			Wave 2 2000–2001		
	B	SE B	OR	B	SE B	OR
Income[a]	0.053	0.017	1.055**	0.061	0.015	1.063***
Income squared[a]	−0.005	0.001	0.995***	−0.002	0.000	0.998***
Age	0.027	0.020	1.027	0.004	0.019	1.004
Marital status[c]						
Married	−0.633	0.350	0.531†	−0.058	0.372	0.944
Cohabiting	−0.039	0.403	0.961	−0.204	0.411	0.816
Number of children	0.072	0.125	1.075	0.110	0.121	1.116
Education[b]	0.068	0.108	1.071	0.292	0.113	1.339*
Non-English interview	−3.557	1.061	0.029**	−2.431	0.539	0.088***
Number of programs	0.190	0.103	1.209†	0.202	0.097	1.224*
Can prepare own taxes	0.618	0.301	1.855*	−0.290	0.322	0.748
Intercept	−1.894	0.756	0.150*	−1.824	0.736	0.161*
Cox & Snell R^2	0.211			0.208		
-2 Log Likelihood	350.783			354.037		

Note: OR = Odds Ratio

[a] Measures of family earned income were in thousands of dollars

[b] Education achieved in the first year was used in all equations and was measured on a scale of 1 to 8

[c] The comparison group for marital status was *no partner*.

†$p < 0.10$, *$p < 0.05$, **$p < 0.01$, ***$p < 0.001$

Adapted from Table 2 in "EITC Participation and Association With Financial Distress Among Rural Low-Income Families," by C.G. Gudmunson, S. Son, J. Lee, and J.W. Bauer, 2010. *Family Relations, 59*, p. 375. Copyright 2010 by National Council of Family Relations

Among the demographic variables, marital status, education, and interview language were significant predictors of EITC participation. Specifically, married mothers at Wave 1 were 47% less likely to participate in the EITC than those who were living without a partner ($OR_{Wave1} = 0.531$, $p < 0.10$). This result is in line with earlier research that found lower EITC participation among married parents compared to single parents (Caputo 2006; Phillips 2001a). The lower participation rate among married mothers might indicate marriage penalties associated with the EITC because married couples could be placed in the phase-out range or could become ineligible if their earned income is too high as a result of the requirement to file taxes jointly.

The mother's higher education level was also associated with a greater likelihood of receiving the EITC at Wave 2 ($OR_{Wave2} = 1.339$, $p < 0.05$), as Phillips (2001a) reported. We also found a strong association between interview language and EITC participation both at Wave 1 and Wave 2 ($OR_{Wave1} = 0.029$, $p < 0.01$; $OR_{Wave2} = 0.088$, $p < 0.001$). Mothers who were interviewed in a language other than English were much less likely to participate in the EITC, compared to those who were interviewed in English. This result suggests that limited English competency can be a major barrier to EITC participation, since low-income workers whose first language is not English may lack access to information about the EITC program or may find it difficult to file taxes (Berube and Forman 2001; Varcoe et al. 2004).

Families who participated in other public assistance programs were more likely to receive the EITC as well ($OR_{Wave1} = 1.209$, $p < 0.10$; $OR_{Wave2} = 1.224$, $p < 0.05$). Participation in one more program was associated with 21% higher odds of EITC participation at Wave 1 and 22% higher odds at Wave 2. This finding implies that those who receive other types of public assistance may be more informed or knowledgeable of the EITC (Caputo 2006; Phillips 2001a). Being able to file taxes without assistance was also related to an 86% higher likelihood of EITC participation at Wave 2 ($OR_{Wave2} = 1.855$, $p < 0.05$). Related to our earlier discussion that many rural low-income families ask others, often their extended family members, to help them file taxes, these families are less likely to receive the EITC funds unless the assisting individual is aware of the EITC program.

How Do Nonparticipating Rural Families Differ from Participating Families?

Other differences were found between participating and nonparticipating families in Panel 1 Wave 2 through bivariate analyses using the Pearson chi-square statistic and difference of means (Mammen et al. 2011) When mothers' statements regarding the EITC were examined, the receipt of the EITC was found to be strongly associated with having some knowledge about it, with 84% of participants having a fair understanding but only 52% of nonparticipants having a fair understanding of the

EITC. The rest (48%) had little or no understanding of the EITC. This disparity between the lack of understanding and participation in the EITC is corroborated in the findings of Berube and Foreman (2001), Maag (2005), Phillips (2001a), and Varcoe et al. (2004).

Hispanic families (14%) were, overwhelmingly, less likely to receive the EITC when compared to White families (73%), perhaps due to language barriers (Gudmunson et al. 2010). Such a lop-sided result, indicating a strong relationship between ethnicity and EITC participation, has been reported by others as well (Berube and Foreman 2001; Caputo 2006; Maag 2005; Phillips 2001a; Varcoe et al. 2004). Nonparticipating families were likely to be larger (53% had three or more children, 47% had one or two children), a finding that initially appears incongruous. This relationship, also reported by Scholz (1994), may be due to the fact that a larger EITC benefit tier[6] had not been developed for larger families when the data for previous studies, including the RFS data, were collected (Greenstein 2000).

Families who participated in the EITC were more likely to be food secure[7] (65%) than food insecure (36%). The reverse was true of the nonparticipating families, i.e., they were more likely to be food insecure (54%) than food secure (46%). This finding may be considered an affirmation of the positive impact that the tax credit has on the well-being of rural families. A similar conclusion may be made from the finding that families who did not receive the EITC income supplement were more likely to consider their income as being inadequate[8] (38%) when compared to those who received EITC (25%). Receipt of the EITC may also have an effect on the satisfaction with life[9] with those who received the EITC more likely to express greater life satisfaction ($M=4.0$) than those who did not ($M=3.7$) (Mammen et al. 2009).

EITC eligible families, in the RFS study, lived across multiple states in numerous counties that varied in how rural they were. Using the Index of Relative Rurality,[10] we found that nonparticipating families were likely to live in more rural counties ($M=0.52$) than participating families ($M=0.47$). This may be the result of

---

[6] This was temporarily established through the ARRA of 2009. See footnote 1.

[7] A family that has consistent and reliable access to sufficient food in order to maintain an active and healthy life is considered food secure (Nord et al. 2005).

[8] The adequacy of respondents' income was gauged by asking "To what extent do you think your income is enough for you to live on?" Respondents selected from (a) not at all, (b) can meet necessities only, (c) can afford some of the things we want but not all we want, (d) can afford about everything we want, or (e) can afford about everything we want and still save money.

[9] Satisfaction with life was ascertained by asking, "Overall, how satisfied are you with your life right now?" Respondents selected from (a) very dissatisfied, (b) dissatisfied, (c) mixed feelings, (d) satisfied, or (e) very satisfied.

[10] The Index of Relative Rurality (IRR) is a continuous, multidimensional measure that incorporates four dimensions: Population size, population density, extent of area that is urbanized, and the distance to the nearest metropolitan area (Waldorf 2007). The IRR is scaled from 0 to 1, with 0 being the most urban and 1 being the most rural.

having few or no outside tax preparation services in counties that are more rural, compounding the problem of a lack of knowledge that these families already face.

How Does the EITC Affect Consumption Patterns and Asset Behavior?

The 147 mothers in Wave 2 who received the EITC were asked how they used their refund[11] (Mammen and Lawrence 2006). From their responses, seven categories were established that revealed the consumption patterns and asset behavior of rural families: (a) pay bills and loans, (b) improve access to transportation, (c) purchase consumer nondurables, (d) establish savings and build assets, (e) purchase consumer durables, (f) enjoy windfall income, and (g) increase human capital (Fig. 10.1). This pattern of EITC usage suggests that the families, by treating the tax credit as "wealth," are behaving as predicted by the Behavioral Life-Cycle Theory.

Pay Bills and Loans Rural low-income families found the infusion of cash from the EITC to be extremely useful and used it to pay off their bills and loans, much like their urban counterparts (Smeeding et al. 2000). Almost 44% of the mothers reported that they used all or part of the EITC to pay bills such as utilities, cable, and credit cards as well as to repay loans from family members and others. For Cora, a divorced mother of three, paying her bills was a priority: *"Paid bills. Bought a little bit of extra food for the house. I had thought about getting a car, but, at the time, I found the bills and stuff were more important to pay."* Maryann, a 26-year-old mother of two children, used her tax credit to pay off a loan that was extended to her by her father.

> Um, I paid off all the stuff that I borrowed for school. I paid…I fixed my car, actually, this year, is what I did. This last year. 'Cause I borrowed some money from my dad to fix it while it wasn't working and then…I got my check and he said, "Aha!" *[she had to repay the loan.]*

Improve Access to Transportation About 24% of the families used their tax credit on various transportation-related expenses such as to purchase or repair a vehicle, purchase tires, renew their licenses, and pay for car insurance. Most rural residents do not have access to public transportation, and the lack of a reliable vehicle makes it particularly difficult for them to engage in essential activities such as going to work, getting groceries, or visiting the doctor. London, a 22-year-old divorced, Hispanic mother with one child, revealed how she planned to use the EITC.

> But we're goin' to paint the truck with it this year. Because the truck we bought, it's not brand new. It's a '94 model. The rocker panels on the bed have got to be fixed, they're rustin'. But we're gonna paint it and put that fiberglass in there.

---

[11] The respondents were not asked how much they spent on each item or in each category. Respondents could also have purchased items in any number of categories.

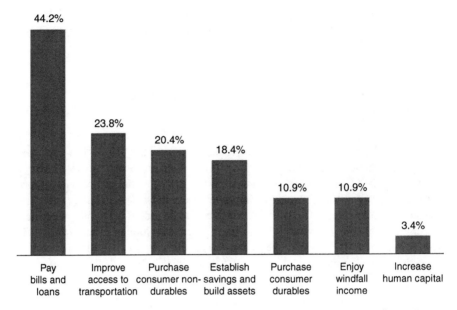

Note. Families could have used the tax credit to purchase items in more than one expenditure category.

Fig. 10.1 EITC usage of rural families

Purchase Consumer Nondurables The EITC helped 20% of the families to purchase numerous consumer nondurables including child-specific items (clothes, toys, and school supplies), clothes for adults, food, and several other minor items. The tax credit was used overwhelmingly to address one particular need, that is, to buy children's clothing. The reason for such expenditure was clear in Enid's remarks, *"...Oh my goodness did I spend money on clothing. Spent like six hundred bucks on clothing just for my daughter. Then she outgrew it all already. It's like, man, I can't win for nothing."* Enid was a 29-year-old single White mother with four children.

Establish Savings and Build Assets About one-fifth (18%) of the families used the extra income from the EITC to create savings and to help build assets. Some saved it for their future living expenses as illustrated by Lida, a 24-year-old single White mother of one. She reported that she used the EITC *"to keep afloat."* She explained further, *"I lived off of it. I was out of work for a month and a half so lived off of it (and that's how I paid all the bills)."* Others considered the EITC as a revenue source to build assets, including the purchase, maintenance, or repairs of a house and ownership of a business. Of the 21% who were home owners, 30% of them had saved their tax credit to be used for house-related expenses such as roof repairs, carpeting and tiling, homeowners insurance and property taxes, or down payment on a house. This is illustrated in the response from Sue, a 34-year-old White mother of six: *"I used it for my wedding, and I paid $1,600 on his* [husband's] *house and property* [tax] *so he didn't lose it."*

The rural families had many unmet financial demands for which they used the EITC. The value of saving these funds, however, was not entirely lost on them. This sentiment may be gleaned from Ruthanne, a 25-year-old divorced mother of one, who received $2,000 from the tax credit.

> What did I do with that? I paid off my credit card. I paid $1,400 to my credit card. I think I took care of a lot of odds and ends things. I needed a new rug, so I bought the new rug. I bought a VCR that I needed in here. Then I think I spent the rest of it. I might have done something constructive, but most of the time I plan all my money right to the end.

Purchase Consumer Durables The average tax credit of $2,294 is a significant amount of additional income to rural families whose median monthly income was $1,500 in Wave 1 (refer to Table 1.2). In addition, receiving the amount as a lump sum payment makes it easier for them to purchase big-ticket consumer goods. Other studies have reported that 60% of urban families use the tax credit to purchase consumer durables (e.g., Romich and Weisner 2000), however, only 11% of the RFS families did so. They purchased home furniture, household appliances, and entertainment equipment. The most commonly purchased items were beds for the children. The families' increased purchasing power due to the EITC and its consequent multiplier effect cannot be understated. Darlene, a 20-year-old mother living with her partner and one child, reported that she used her tax credit to purchase a *"washing machine, espresso maker, kitchen table, couch, bedroom set, DVD player."*

Enjoy Windfall Income The lump sum payment from the EITC was treated by 11% of the families as if it were windfall income. This is evident in their spending pattern. Much like middle-income families, low-income families also take the opportunity to "splurge" a little when they receive a large sum of money that is not from a regular source. The majority (87%) spent their EITC on a vacation and to visit family and friends. Several mothers planned special activities for their children. For example, Fiona, a 26-year-old married mother of two, reported that she *"paid some bills off. Gave the kids nice birthday party, 'cause they never had a birthday party. They could invite all their friends in their class, so we took them to a local Burger King and had a big old party."*

Increase Human Capital Human capital was another expenditure category, albeit made by the least number of families (3%). The vast majority of them (60%) used their tax credit to purchase a computer while the rest used it to pay off their student loans. The small number of families who made this investment might be indicative of the type of jobs available in rural areas which provide little incentive to invest in human capital.

EITC Nonparticipation and Financial Distress

Being eligible for but not participating in the EITC may have a negative influence on financial stress[12] among rural low-income families, when receiving the credit could

---

[12] Financial stress refers to the rural low-income mother's perception of the family's economic situation or change.

ease their financial stress by lowering economic hardship or by increasing savings or assets. In order to examine whether or not eligible nonparticipation in the EITC was associated with financial stress, we conducted three sets of OLS regressions using a sample of 314 RFS participants of the first two waves of data collection (Gudmunson et al. 2010). The dependent variables were three forms of financial distress: (a) income inadequacy,[13] (b) economic loss,[14] and (c) financial pressure.[15] The independent or control variables in the three regression models were tax-related predictors, including eligible nonparticipation of the EITC, the proportion of received EITC funds to family earned income, time passed since the tax season, tax preparation ability, and other demographic predictors, such as family earned income, the mother's age, marital status, number of children, education level, and interview language. The results based on Wave 2 data are presented in Table 10.2.

Not participating in the EITC, despite being eligible, was associated with a greater level of perceived income inadequacy ($\beta=0.179$, $p<0.01$) and economic loss ($\beta=0.225$, $p<0.01$). This result shows that participating in the EITC could reduce financial stress in rural low-income families. Having a larger proportion of the EITC to family income, however, was associated with a higher sense of income inadequacy ($\beta=0.126$, $p<0.05$) and economic loss ($\beta=0.145$, $p<0.05$). When we combined these two effects together, we found evidence that the positive role of EITC participation in reducing financial distress could be counterbalanced in some families where the amount of EITC funds received was a substantial portion of their earned income.

In addition to EITC-related variables, family earned income itself was a strong predictor of financial distress. Specifically, lower family income was significantly associated with higher sense of income inadequacy ($\beta=-0.291, p<0.001$), was significantly related to greater economic loss ($\beta=-0.240, p<0.01$), and was marginally associated with more frequent experience of financial pressure ($\beta=-0.148, p<0.10$). This result suggests that low earned income is the key driver of financial stress in rural low-income families.

Conclusion

The RFS study has provided new insights on the impact of the EITC on rural working families. The EITC provides a powerful boost to these families' economic well-being by not only encouraging employment but by increasing their purchasing

---

[13] For measurement of income adequacy, see footnote 8.

[14] Economic loss was assessed by respondents' level of agreement with a statement, "Compared to two years ago, would you say your family's economic situation has" from 1 (*improve a lot*) to 5 (*gone down a lot*).

[15] Financial pressure was measured by asking whether there was a time when the respondent had a hard time making ends meet or paying for necessities in terms of seven family expenses. Summed scores from the seven items were used to indicate the financial pressure.

Table 10.2 Summary of OLS Regressions Predicting Financial Distress in the Second Year ($N=314$)

Variable	Income inadequacy			Economic loss			Financial pressure		
	B	SE B	B	B	SE B	B	B	SE B	B
Income[a]	-0.018	0.005	-0.291***	-0.019	0.006	-0.240**	-0.018	0.009	-0.148†
Age	-0.009	0.007	-0.074	-0.002	0.009	-0.015	0.021	0.014	0.088
Marital Status[b]									
Married	-0.006	0.140	-0.003	0.104	0.179	0.044	0.157	0.279	0.045
Cohabiting	0.109	0.157	0.045	0.279	0.201	0.091	0.286	0.312	0.063
Number of children	0.071	0.043	0.103	0.167	0.055	0.192**	0.110	0.086	0.085
Education	0.081	0.043	0.122†	0.061	0.055	0.074	0.207	0.086	0.167*
Non-English interview	0.293	0.181	0.102	-0.066	0.231	-0.018	0.233	0.360	0.044
Number of programs	0.016	0.039	0.024	-0.059	0.050	-0.068	0.042	0.078	0.033
Can prepare own taxes	-0.046	0.122	-0.021	0.068	0.156	0.025	-0.134	0.243	-0.033
EITC									
Eligible non-participation	0.343	0.128	0.179**	0.544	0.163	0.225**	0.092	0.253	0.026
Amount as % of income	0.567	0.285	0.126*	0.825	0.363	0.145*	0.052	0.566	0.006
Time since tax season	0.017	0.017	0.057	0.022	0.021	0.057	0.048	0.033	0.084
Intercept	2.987***	0.317	—	1.960***	0.405	—	0.121	0.630	—
R^2	0.167			0.147			0.058		

[a] Based on family earned income listed in thousands of dollars
[b] The comparison group for marital status was *no partner*.
†$p<10$, *$p<0.05$, **$p<0.01$, ***$p<0.001$

Adapted from Table 3 in "EITC Participation and Association With Financial Distress Among Rural Low-Income Families," by C.G. Gudmunson, S. Son, J. Lee, and J.W. Bauer, 2010. *Family Relations, 59,* p. 378. Copyright 2010 by National Council of Family Relations power and their ability to save, as well as by reducing their financial distress. Often short of money and with little or no access to credit, the opportunity cost of nonparticipation is very high for rural families, yet, many forego this income supplement. Compared to families who do not receive the tax credit, those who do receive it are less likely to experience financial distress and more likely to express greater life satisfaction. Reasons for nonparticipation include misconceptions about the EITC, lack of assistance with tax filing, as well as simple irrational behavior.

The primary reason why eligible families do not receive the EITC is their failure to file income taxes and claim the credit, overwhelmingly, the result of having little or no knowledge about it. The lack of understanding is exacerbated by individual and familial characteristics. The end result is that the rural families who are the least informed about the income supplement are also the most vulnerable. These include families with very low income, who are less educated, have more children, and who are minorities facing difficulties with the English language (Gudmunson et al. 2010; Mammen and Lawrence 2006; Varcoe et al. 2004). Outreach activities directed towards these families must emphasize a thoughtful approach including identifying respected community leaders, such as local family educators, and appropriate local networks, such as doctors' offices and schools, where information could be distributed. Another reason why families did not participate in the EITC is because they could not get the needed assistance with tax preparation (Mammen and Lawrence 2006; Varcoe et al. 2004).

Through the American Reinvestment and Recovery Act of 2009, families with three or more children were provided a temporary increase in the EITC. Working families benefit the most when they receive the federal EITC along with the refundable earned income tax credit that some states provide (Johnson et al. 2003; Neumark and Wascher 2001).

The Behavioral Life-Cycle Theory may be used to explain rural families' usage of the EITC. By separating their income into mental accounts, these families are able to exert greater self-control over what they have framed as current income (regular paycheck income) and wealth (lump sum EITC) (Mammen and Lawrence 2006). As a result, they use the EITC for short-term savings, to pay bills, and to purchase a variety of consumer durables and nondurables.

Discussion Questions

1. Use the parts of the eco-system framework (micro-, meso-, exo-, and macrosystems) to address the impact that the EITC has on rural low-income mothers and their families.
2. How can the Behavioral Life-Cycle Theory be applied to consumption patterns among the rural low-income families who choose to receive the EITC as a lump sum payment?
3. What are the ways in which the EITC enhances the economic well-being of low-income working families?

4. What are the opportunity costs of foregoing the EITC to eligible rural low-income families and to the communities in which they live?
5. How do the findings presented in this chapter compare to other research studies that you may have read related to EITC or use of EITC?
6. What marketing techniques would you suggest be used to encourage eligible families to file for EITC benefits?
7. What are the barriers, presented in this chapter, that are related to nonparticipation in the EITC among low-income working families? Among these barriers, what may be the unique obstacles that contribute to the lower participation in the EITC among rural low-income families as opposed to their urban counterparts?
8. What did you learn in this chapter that helps you understand the lived experiences of rural low-income families? Relate your learning to how you would use it for social work, in-classroom teaching, early childhood education, advocacy for specific groups in a nonprofit organization; or policy development in schools, community, or at a national level. Choose one approach and discuss.

Acknowledgments The authors would like to thank Clinton G. Gudmunson, Seohee Son, and Jean W. Bauer for their committed work on the Earned Income Tax Credit in rural families and communities.

References

Barrow, L., & McGranahan, L. M. (1999). *The Earned Income Tax Credit and durable goods purchase* (JCPR Working Paper No. 144). http://ideas.repec.org/p/wop/jopovw/144.html.

Berube, A., & Forman, B. (2001). *A local ladder for the working poor: The impact of the Earned Income Tax Credit in US metropolitan areas.* http://www.brookings.edu/es/urban/eitc/eitcnationalexsum.htm.

Berube, A., & Tiffany, T. (2004). *The "state" of low-wage workers: How the EITC benefits urban and rural communities in the 50 states.* http://www.brookings.edu/~/media/Files/rc/reports/2004/02childrenfamilies_berube/20040203_berube.pdf.

Berube, A., Kim, A., Forman, B., & Burns, M. (2002). *The price of paying taxes: How tax preparation and refund loan fees erode the benefits of the EITC* (Survey Series). http://www.brookings.edu/ES/urban/publications/berubekimeitc.pdf.

Beverly, S. G., Tescher, J., & Marzahl, D. (2000). *Linking tax refunds and low-cost bank accounts.* (Center for Social Development Working Paper No. 00-19). Symposium presentation on Asset Building Policies, Washington University, St. Louis, MO.

Blank, R. (1999, February). *What public policy research should we be doing?* Lecture presented at the Institute for Policy Research, Northwestern University, Evanston, IL.

Blumenthal, M., Erard, B., & Ho, C. (2005). Participation and compliance with the Earned Income Tax Credit. *National Tax Journal, 58,* 189–213. http://ntj.tax.org.

Caputo, R. K. (2006). The Earned Income Tax Credit: A study of eligible participants vs. non-participants. *Journal of Sociology and Social Welfare, 33,* 9–29.

Dowd, T. (2005). Distinguishing between short-term and long-term recipients of the earned income tax credit. *National Tax Journal, 58,* 807–828. http://ntj.tax.org.

Edwards, R. D. (2004). Macroeconomic implications of the earned income tax credit. *National Tax Journal, 57,* 45–65. http://ntj.tax.org.

Ellwood, D. T. (2000). *The impact of the earned income tax credit and social policy reforms on work, marriage and living arrangements* (JCPR Working Paper 124). http://www.northwestern. edu/ipr/jcpr/workingpapers/wpfiles/ellwood_eitc99_update.PDF.

Fisher, I. (1930). *The theory of interest as determined by impatience to spend income and opportunity to invest it.* New York: Macmillan.

Graham, F., & Isaac, A. G. (2002). The behavioral life-cycle theory of consumer behavior: Survey evidence. *Journal of Economic Behavior and Organization, 48,* 391–401. doi:10.1016/S0167-2681(01)00242-6.

Greenstein, R. (2000). *Should EITC benefits be enlarged for families with 3 or more children?* http://www.cbpp.org/3-14-00tax.pdf.

Greenstein, R., & Shapiro, I. (1998). *New research findings on the effects of EITC.* http://www. cbpp.org/cms/index.cfm?fa=view&id=1649.

Grogger, J. (2003). The effects of time limits, the EITC, and other policy changes on welfare use, work, and income among female-headed families. *The Review of Economics and Statistics, 85,* 394–408. doi:10.1162/003465303765299891.

Gudmunson, C. G., Son, S., Lee, J., & Bauer, J. W. (2010). EITC participation and association with financial distress among rural low-income families. *Family Relations, 59,* 369–382. doi:10.1111/j.1741-3729.2010.00609x.

Holt, S. (2006). *The Earned Income Tax Credit at age 30: What we know.* http://www.brookings. edu/~/media/Files/rc/reports/2006/02childrenfamilies_holt/20060209_Holt.pdf.

Hotz, J., & Scholz. J. (2003). The Earned Income Tax Credit. In R. A. Moffitt (Ed.), *Means-tested transfer programs in the United States* (pp. 141–198). Chicago: University of Chicago Press.

Holtzblatt, J., McCubbin, J., & Gillette, R. (1994). Promoting work through the EITC. *National Tax Journal, 47,* 591–607. http://ntj.tax.org.

Johnson, N., Llobrera, J., & Zahradnik, B. (2003). *A hand up: How state earned income tax credits help working families escape poverty in 2003.* http://www.cbpp.org/3-3-03sfp.htm.

Levitis, J., & Koulish, J. (2008). *State earned income tax credits: 2008 legislative update.* http:// www.cbpp.org/6-6-06sfp.pdf.

Maag, E. (2005). *Paying the price? Low-income parents and the use of paid tax preparers* (Series Report No. B-64). http://www.urban.org/UploadedPDF/411145_B-64.pdf.

Mammen, S., & Lawrence, F. C. (2006). How rural working families use the Earned Income Tax Credit: A mixed method analysis. *Financial Counseling and Planning, 17,* 51–63. https:// www1067.ssldomain.com/afcpe/doc/Vol1715.pdf.

Mammen, S., Lass, D., & Seiling, S. B. (2009). Labor force supply decisions of rural low-income mothers. *Journal of Family and Economic Issues, 30,* 67–79. doi:.1007/s10834-008-9136-5.

Mammen, S., Lawrence, F. C., St. Marie, P., Berry, A. A., & Knight, S. E. (2011). The earned income tax credit and rural families: Differences between non-participants and participants. *Journal of Family and Economic Issues, 32,* 461–472. doi:10.1007/s10834-010-9238-8.

McCubbin, J. (2000). EITC noncompliance: The determinants of the misreporting of children. *National Tax Journal, LIII,* 1135–1164. http://ntj.tax.org.

Meyer, B. D., & Rosenbaum, D. T. (2001). Welfare, the earned income tax credit, and the labor supply of single mothers on welfare. *Quarterly Journal of Economics, 116,* 1063–1114. doi:10.1162/00335530152466313.

Modigliani, F., & Brumberg, R. (1954). Utility analysis and the consumption function: An interpretation of cross section data. In K. K. Kurihara (Ed.), *Post Keynesian economics* (pp. 388–436). New Brunswick: Rutgers University Press.

Neumark, D., & Wascher, W. (2001). Using the EITC to help poor families: New evidence and a comparison with the minimum wage. *National Tax Journal, 54,* 281–317. http://ntj.tax.org.

Noonan, M. C., Smith, S. S., & Corcoran, M. E. (2007). Examining the impact of welfare reform, labor market conditions, and the earned income tax credit on the employment of black and white single mothers. *Social Science Research, 36,* 95–130. doi:10.1016/j.ssresearch.2005.09.004.

Nord, M., Andrews, M., & Carlson, S. (2005). *Household food security in the United States, 2005.* (Economic Research Report No. 29). http://www.ers.usda.gov/Publications/ERR29/.

O'Hare, W. P., & Johnson, K. M. (2004). Child poverty in rural America. *Population Reference Bureau Reports on America, 4*(1), 1–19. http://www.prb.org/pdf04/ChildPovertyRural America.pdf.

Olson, L. M., & Davis, A. (1994). *The earned income tax credit: Views from the street level.* Institute for Policy Research (Working Paper No. 94-01). Evanston, IL,Northwestern University.

Phillips, K. R. (2001a). The earned income tax credit: Knowledge is money. *Political Science Quarterly, 116,* 413–424. http://www.jstor.org/stable/798023.

Phillips, K. R. (2001b). *Who knows about the earned income tax credit?* (New Federalism No.B-27). http://www.urban.org/url.cfm?ID=310035.

Romich, J. L., & Weisner, T. (2000). How families view and use the EITC: Advance payment versus lump sum delivery. *National Tax Journal, 53,* 1245–1265. http://ntj.tax.org/.

Scholz, J. K. (1994). The earned income tax credit: Participation, complication, and antipoverty effectiveness. *National Tax Journal, 47,* 64–85. http://ntj.tax.org/.

Shefrin, H. M., & Thaler, R. H. (1988). The behavioral life-cycle hypothesis. *Economic Inquiry, 26,* 609–643. doi:10.111/j.1465-7295.1988.tb01520.x.

Smeeding, T. M., Phillips, K. R., & O'Connor, M. (2000). The EITC: Expectation, knowledge, use and economic and social mobility. *National Tax Journal, 53,* 1187–1210. http://ntj.tax.org/.

US Government Accountability Office (GAO). (2003). *Tax administration: Most taxpayers believe they benefit from paid tax preparers, but oversight for IRS is a challenge* (Report No. GAO-04-70). http://www.gao.gov/new.items/d0470.pdf.

US Internal Revenue Service. (2009). *EITC thresholds and tax law updates.* http://www.eitc.irs.gov/central/main/.

US Internal Revenue Service. (2010). *EITC thresholds and tax law updates.* http://www.eitc.irs.gov/central/main/.

Varcoe, K. P., Lees, N. B., & López, M. L. (2004). Rural Latino families in California are missing earned income tax benefits. *California Agriculture, 58,* 24–27. doi:10.3733/ca.v058n01p24.

Waldorf, B. (2007). Measuring rurality. *In Context, 8*(1), 5–8. http://www.incontext.indiana.edu/2007/january/2.asp.

Wancheck, J. (2008). *Earned income tax credit.* http://www.nlihc.org/detail/article.cfm?article_id=5205&id=46.

Chapter 11
Applications for the RFS Findings: Programs and Future Research

Jean W. Bauer, Elizabeth M. Dolan and Bonnie Braun

Introduction

With the passage of welfare reform, opportunities arose not only for research but for the application of research as well. The Rural Families Speak (RFS) study demonstrates Boyer's (1990) concept of the scholarship of engagement through discovery and application of knowledge. The Temporary Assistance for Needy Families (TANF) rules, implemented in 1997, provided a platform for research and development of community-based programs through the nationwide land-grant universities and US Department of Agriculture (USDA) system (Braun and Bauer 1998). The outcome of the legislation not only influenced those who were direct recipients, but also families living in similar situations with low incomes but not receiving benefits. This was the contextual setting for many of the rural families described in Chap. 3. In this chapter, we address applications of the research-based knowledge to initiatives targeting individuals, families, and communities, as well as further research initiatives. This chapter also provides examples of programs that are based directly on RFS research findings. We then address ideas for future research. Together, the examples answer the questions of what can be done with research-based knowledge.

Boyer (1996) stated that the "scholarship of engagement means connecting the rich resources of the university and research to our most pressing social, civic, and ethical problems [of today]" (p. 32). The manner in which he approaches the scholarship of integration in the larger context of connecting research and engagement within and across disciplines to solve problems is exactly what the RFS team has been trying to do with issues around rural families and work. Boyer states that the discovery, i.e., research, is only part of the process. Integration across disciplines, combined with sharing of the scholarship and application, also needs to take place (Boyer 1990). The bulk of this book has reported on the discovery and integration across the disciplines of the scholarship around rural, low-income

J. W. Bauer (✉)
Department of Family Social Science, University of Minnesota, St. Paul, MN, USA
e-mail: jbauer@umn.ed

J. W. Bauer, E. M. Dolan (eds.), *Rural Families and Work,* International Series on Consumer Science 1,
DOI 10.1007/978-1-4614-0382-1_11, © Springer Science+Business Media, LLC 2011

families and work. These last two chapters will begin a dialogue about the research, programs, and policy potentials. The purpose is to make connections that contribute to the most pressing social, civic, and ethical problems for families in rural America.

Community-Based Applications

The RFS study informed some initiatives and suggested others, targeting individuals, families, and communities. Members of the RFS team related emerging findings at numerous professional meetings so that the study could inform professional practice. Some of the community-based applications of findings were intended to improve skills of mothers, others to improve the quality of living of whole families, and still others to address the community environments in which the families lived and worked. RFS team members also conducted three webinars as part of continuing education of the workforce (available at http://www.cehd.umn.edu/fsos/Centers/RuralFamiliesSpeak/breezeWebcast.asp#details).

Cooperative Extension Programs

The nationwide Cooperative Extension system mobilized its resources to address welfare reform. A welfare-to-work survey (Braun and Philogene 2001) commissioned by the National Association of State Universities and Land-Grant Universities found evidence of extensive involvement by Cooperative Extension in this arena (Braun and Benning 2001). In many states, state extension specialists and county educators obtained funds through the TANF block grants to support their direct programming to mothers. Through this work, mothers were mentored and curricula were developed and taught on many topics related to the transition to work. Public policy education was conducted to inform policy makers and engage citizens. The Food Stamp Nutrition Education Program (FSNEP) expanded to meet needs of people eligible for, or receiving, food stamps (now called Supplemental Nutrition Assistance Program or SNAP). In Maryland, Ohio, and other states, findings of the RFS study were used as the rationale for creation of a food resource management component to the program, as well as to modify other components of the program. These helped mothers to expand the use of their food resources for their families.

In Iowa, members of the RFS team focused on listening to the voices of marginalized families, specifically in the Hispanic community, and engaged them in public policy decisions (Greder et al. 2004). In Maryland, with funding from the Charles F. Kettering Foundation, RFS team members also focused on previously unheard voices by investigating the conditions under which low-income women could and would engage in public policy deliberations (Braun and Waldman 2006).

In Maryland, county commissioners were taught the value of both the Earned Income Tax Credit (EITC) and food stamps to address family and community economic well-being. They learned of the economic impact on their counties when those funds flow first to families then to the local community through purchases. One county began encouraging citizens to apply for both. Also, in Maryland, the RFS findings were used to obtain funds from a foundation to conduct family financial educational programs tied to the EITC and Individual Development Accounts (IDAs).

Since only some of the RFS families actually received the EITC, efforts to increase the numbers in both rural and urban areas were seen as having economic benefit to individuals, families, and the communities by a number of RFS Cooperative Extension team members. In New Hampshire, RFS data were the impetus behind creating a coalition to train volunteers through the Volunteer Income Tax Assistance (VITA) program with specific information on the EITC (New Hampshire Statewide Earned Income Tax Credit Alliance n.d.). The Alliance members represent family support agencies, educational institutions, community action programs, and financial institutions, as well as Cooperative Extension and several foundations. The New Hampshire Alliance's efforts have been focused on the rural areas of the state, although the Alliance also operates in several of the state's urban areas. California, too, has used the RFS data regarding the EITC to promote awareness in rural communities. The University of Minnesota Extension has led a tax education coalition (MNTEC) of more than 50 members composed of community professionals from state and federal agencies, human services, community agencies, legislative staff, faith-based groups, and others with the purpose of promoting tax education and financial literacy to working Minnesotans with limited resources. They also support free tax consultants and taxpayer advocacy efforts. Finally, the coalition helps members maintain awareness of tax and financial resource policy issues to assist families throughout the state. The coalition distributes materials in several languages to support the needs of Minnesota workers.

A number of other RFS team members worked in their states to incorporate findings in a variety of programs. For example, in California, RFS data were used to help develop a financial literacy curriculum, "Making Every Dollar Count" (Varcoe et al. 2008) for limited resource audiences. In New Hampshire, findings were used to inform revisions in a welfare-to-work curriculum for TANF clients. Kentucky team members created a health-related blog for women and an educational series to raise awareness of depression. RFS findings were integrated into the Cornell Community and Rural Development Institute's programming on the future of rural New York. In Oregon, a community gardening initiative was instituted to promote physical exercise and to enhance healthy eating.

Taken together, these few examples of application of the RFS research findings to programs are evidence that the research study has utilitarian value. The RFS findings, as well as other research on rural families, can be utilized to create appropriate programs for rural families. The RFS project, however, should be seen as only a first step in research about rural low-income families. RFS findings have answered some questions, but have raised other ones.

Research Applications

Chapter authors raised questions regarding further work to better understand rural low-income families. In this section, we first address the additional work that has already flowed from the initial RFS project, and then we address the questions raised but not yet answered.

RFS-Initiated Research

Additional research studies emerged from the findings of the initial RFS investigations. Several RFS research team members instituted smaller research studies based on our RFS data. The initiative in Iowa, focused on the Hispanic community and their housing issues, goes beyond the scope of RFS. Similarly, research on Appalachian families and intergenerational families has emerged. In New Hampshire, the RFS data spawned a small investigation into TANF clients' choices around child care. In Minnesota, two graduate students working on the RFS project conducted a community context study with the local Extension Educator in one of the counties of data collection. They interviewed the providers of services to understand the perspective of the providers and the context in which services for low-income families were presented. A community forum resulted from the project. Finally, the findings on the significance of health have evolved into another multistate project.

In 2008, the RFS research team launched our current project (NC 1171 RFS about Health (RFS–H)) which continues through 2013. The team chose to focus on both physical and mental health as vital to understanding well-being of rural families when health emerged as a prime impediment to the ability of rural low-income mothers to secure and maintain employment. Other studies may emerge, and still others are needed to more thoroughly understand the lives of rural families.

Recently, a study using the RFS data centered on measurement of poverty and depression symptomatology (Frazer 2011), suggesting that the manner in which we design TANF and other employment programs can be supported by what we know about poverty and depression. Whether to get people into work program first or to heal people before work has long been a long-term question (Simmons et al. 2008). While research findings support both approaches, findings appear to be connected to the focus of the research study: Research focused on the work-first concept has tended to support the value of getting TANF clients into the workforce, while research focused on the mental health/depression issues of TANF clients finds that addressing these issues first is more beneficial. Frazer (2011) reframes the debate by outlining policy implications and solutions that address both employment and depression simultaneously.

Suggestions for Future Research

Much more research exists on the issues and concerns of urban residents than rural residents, probably because more people reside in urban areas and finding research participants is therefore easier. The rural context, however, presents a number of socioeconomic challenges for those who reside there as described in Chap. 3.

Rural employment options have been referred to as "brittle" (Kelly 2005) and as "bad jobs" (Fremstad et al. 2008). The jobs are *brittle* because they offer little incentive to form long-lasting relationships between employee and employer, i.e., the bonds are easily broken. The jobs are *bad* because they offer low wages, few if any employee benefits, little job security, and limited to no advancement opportunities, and they often require that employees work nonstandard schedules. The RFS research just touched the surface of how the brittle, bad jobs affect rural families. Because the RFS respondents were the mothers, we have only limited information on the employment issues of the fathers, and what we do have is from the mothers' perspective. The point of view of rural low-income fathers is needed to form a more complete picture of the family situation.

The RFS study, while not focused on TANF-reliant families, did find that some reported difficulties in fulfilling the requirements to maintain their TANF grants. Only 17% of the mothers received TANF at Wave 1, with fewer receiving it in subsequent waves. A more detailed investigation is needed to identify the key elements, which enable rural TANF clients to move from welfare to work. Because TANF case workers appear to have great influence on how well a rural client does, the case workers need to be an integral part of the research framework. This is another example of the engaged scholarship framework.

The care of children while parents are employed is a prime focus for rural parents. We know that family and friends offer a source of low cost, often no cost, care for financially strapped rural parents. Figuring out the decision factors behind child care choices was beyond the scope of the RFS study. Still to answer are such questions as: (a) what are the factors related to personal preferences of the parents, especially the mothers, or to cultural norms, or family expectations, and/or simple expediency; and (b) what are the implications for the children in the long-term relative to those child care choices? Johnson et al.(2010) addressed the implications for children of urban mothers' low-wage work. Using the Women's Employment study data based on current and former TANF clients living in an urban area, they determined that employment in general did not have a deleterious effect on the children. Urban mothers can face long commutes, especially on public transit, and have issues with nonstandard work schedules. Rural mothers, on the other hand, face these issues with fewer child care choices to keep their children safe and often have unreliable transportation. Outcomes for children of rural low-income parents are a topic ripe for investigation, as well as researching options for alternative transportation.

A more purposeful approach to investigating support networks and resources of rural low-income families is needed. This knowledge would provide a more complete picture of rural family life and inform community leaders on how best to direct community resources to fit the needs of their least prosperous residents.

The research found that health was a prime factor keeping the rural mothers from seeking and maintaining employment. A number of the rural mothers who were reliant on TANF had health problems or members of their families had health problems. At least two studies used a sample with families who had a child with disabilities (Brewton 2008; Powell and Bauer 2010). In general, mothers can qualify for TANF much more easily than for disability benefits (state or federal). While not presented in this volume, RFS data indicated that rural mothers did not have an easy time getting disability benefits. We need to understand the intersection between health and benefits for both adults and children, especially qualifying for disability benefits, and when the disability is mental rather than physical, among rural families. The RFS study has just scratched the surface of what is reality for rural low-income families. Integration of scholarship and application to address the problems facing rural families in general, and low-income rural families in particular, does not end here. To help other scholars begin thinking in this holistic way, Table 11.1 presents two parts of Boyer's (1996) engaged scholarship model to give a few examples of future research and the application of knowledge for programs or policy.

Summary

As these examples suggest, the RFS findings can both inform programs and future research. The findings can help customize the programs to fit the environment and needs of rural, low-income families. Findings can be used to convince potential funders of the needs of rural residents. Programs developed for urban areas are not likely to be easily translated for rural communities. The geospatial issues and low population densities often mean that the programs would be too expensive to implement or too difficult for rural residents to get to. The unique characteristics of the rural community must be considered, which requires rural community leaders and others, such as Cooperative Extension specialists and educators, to "think outside the box" of urban-centric programs and policies.

The same can be said of research—so frequently based on urban populations. Because only about 25% of the US population lives in designated rural areas, rural families can be viewed as an underserved minority on which research should be focused. The diversity of rural areas, economies, and populations make rural-focused studies fertile ground for future research. All of the published articles from the RFS team recommend additional studies and should be considered by student and faculty researchers.

Engaged scholarship, and the involvement of community educators such as Cooperative Extension specialists, provides a pathway for bringing the findings of research to enhance the lives of rural low-income families. Getting research translated into messages the public, students, and decision-makers can understand was a challenge undertaken by the RFS team. Many of the team's findings were presented in

Table 11.1 Research question examples and their use in an engaged scholarship approach

Question	Who could use the knowledge?	How this knowledge could affect programs or policy?
What is the relationship between family ties to the community and the social support networks?	School administrators Faith based communities Social agencies Child care centers/ workers Health care providers	Using Ecological lens to understand the relationships within the family, to their near environments will influence the way the opportunities are viewed Strength of the boundaries, upon which to build support networks that could change the resiliency of the family and members in the labor market, school place, or community
How do families feel about the job prospects in the community?	Workers Employers Policy makers Community development professionals	Family's feelings about job prospect are not isolated. Each member of the family will have a different view. Opportunities for communities are based in understanding of context of jobs and how employers and communities can support healthy families to make community thrive
Many jobs in the rural areas are shift work and non-standard hours. What is the impact on family functioning, health, and dynamics?	Employers School administrators Child care providers Health care providers	Effect of non-standard work schedules on community services Use ecological lens to discuss issues and potential solutions to enable families involved in changing shift work and non-standard hours to balance employment and family demands
How does pre-2014 health insurance coverage issues predict post-2014 health insurance coverage in relation to cost, availability, accessibility, regional differences for health insurance in rural families?	Health professionals and providers Employers Family members Post secondary schools (those with 26 year old students and employees) Policy advocates Insurance industry	Knowledge of current health insurance situation can inform policy for 2014 implementation

the form of research and/or policy briefs. More creative means can also be effective. One such tool developed by a member of the team is a three-act play designed to engage the audience in the production grounded in the findings and often using the words of the mothers interviewed. "Livin' on the Byways: Rural Families Speak" (Braun 2007) has been performed in several contexts and is available on the web.

Research into the lives of rural low-income families, as well as other types of families, is important as our lives become more complicated. While *knowing* is important for those who work directly with families in various contexts, *translating* the knowledge into programs that will directly help families is similar circumstances is vitally important. Program development that increases the literacy of families' abilities in everyday life is critical. Programs and research are two of three areas of application of RFS findings. In the next chapter, the authors focus on the application to public policy.

Discussion Questions

1. Engaged scholarship is the connection of the resources of the university with pressing social, civic, and ethical problems. Develop a list of research questions that faculty and graduate students in your department are working on, and that have the potential to contribute to the well-being of rural families. Why are the questions important?
2. What are some examples of community-based applications where you work or go to school? How can you at this point in your life see yourself making a contribution?
3. Develop a new research question about rural families and suggest who could use the knowledge and how the knowledge could be applied. See Table 11.1 as an example.
4. What are the limitations of using research to inform practice?

Acknowledgments The authors of this chapter want to acknowledge the work that Nanci De Felippe, Ph.D. graduate student at the University of Minnesota, did for us on the background literature for this chapter.

References

Boyer, E. L. (1990). *Scholarship reconsidered: The Carnegie Foundation for the Advancement of Teaching.* San Francisco: Jossey-Bass

Boyer, E. L. (1996). The scholarship of engagement. *Bulleting of the American Academy of Arts and Sciences, 49*(7), 18–33. http://www.jstor.org/stable/3824459.

Braun, B. (2007). *Livin' on the byways—Rural families speak.* [Dramatization]. http://www.sph. umd.edu/fmsc/people/documents/LivinOnLifesByWays11-15-07.pdf.

Braun, B., & Bauer, J. (1998). Welfare reform: An opportunity to engage universities in community and economic development. *Journal of Public Service and Outreach, 3,* 33–37.

Braun, B., & Benning, L. (2001). Welfare reform 4 years later: The mobilization of the land-grant system. *Journal of Extension, 39*(3). http://www.joe.org/joe/2001june/comm1.php.

Braun, B., & Philogene, M. (2001). *Employability task force welfare to work survey.* Washington: National Association of State Universities and Land-Grant Colleges.

Braun, B., & Waldman, J. (2006). *Engaging unheard voices.* Final Report to the Kettering Foundation. http://www.sph.umd.edu/fmsc/fis/_docs/Engaging_Unheard_Voices.pdf.

Brewton, K. E. (2008). *Qualitative analysis of the stress and coping experiences of low-income rural mothers raising a child with a disability.* (Unpublished master's thesis). University of Minnesota, St. Paul, MN.

Frazer, M. S. (2011). *Poverty measurement and depression symptomatology in the context of welfare reform.* (Unpublished doctoral dissertation). University of Minnesota, St. Paul, MN.

Fremstad, S., Ray, R., & Rho, H. J. (2008, May). *Working families and economic insecurity in the States: The role of job quality and work supports.* http://www.cepr.org/documents/publications/state_2008_05.pdf.

Greder, K., Brotherson, M. J., & Garasky, S. (2004). Listening to the voices of marginalized families. In C. L. Anderson (Ed.), *Family and community policy: Strategies for civic engagement* (pp. 95–116). Alexandria: American Association of Family and Consumer Sciences.

Johnson, R. C., Kalil, A., & Dunifon, R. E. (2010). *Mother's work and children's lives: Low-income families after welfare reform.* Kalamazoo: W. E Upjohn Institute for Employment Research.

Kelly, E. B. (2005). Leaving and losing jobs: Resistance of rural low-income mothers. *Journal of Poverty, 9,* 83–103. doi:10.1300/J134v09n01_05.

New Hampshire Statewide Earned Income Tax Credit Alliance. (n.d.). *New Hampshire Earned Income Tax Credit.* http://www.nheitc.org/home.htm.

Powell, S. E., & Bauer, J. W. (2010). Examining the resource use of low-income families caring for children with disabilities. *Journal of Children & Poverty, 16*(1), 67–83. doi:10.1080/10796120903575101.

Simmons, L. A., Braun, B., Carnigo, R., Havens, J. R., & Wright, D. W. (2008). Depression and poverty among rural women: A relationship of social causation or social selection? *Journal of Rural Health, 24,* 292–298. doi:10.1111/j.1748-0361.2008.00171.x.

Varcoe, K. P., Peterson, S. S., Johns, M., Grajales-Hall, M., Costello, C., & Breyer, K. (2008). *Making every dollar count/Haga. render su dinero.* (ANR Publication 3519). Oakland: University of California Regents.

Chapter 12
Policy Issues and Applications: Rural Concerns

Elizabeth M. Dolan, Jean W. Bauer and Bonnie Braun

Importance of Policy

As we have repeatedly stated, the rural economy is different from the urban economy. The industries that dominate many rural communities are small ones. Not only does this mean that residents have fewer options for employment than do urban residents, but also small businesses often do not offer employee benefits. Rural communities also tend to provide fewer formal support services for families, including health care, and those that are available may be some distance away. As a result, rural low-income families struggle to support their families. Relying on an array of public benefits may be the only way that rural low-income families manage to support their families. In this chapter, we look at policies related to welfare and other low-income-related programs with a lens on some of the issues that may arise in rural areas. Like programs discussed in the previous chapter, a one-size-fits-all approach to policy may not benefit rural residents.

During debates about welfare, limited attention was given to rural–urban differences. One key player stated that sufficient evidence of differences did not exist (Haskins 2004). Weber et al. (2001) and others compared rural–urban differences after passage of the act.

Weber et al.'s (2004) comparison of outcomes 5 years after the implementation of the Personal Responsibility and Work Opportunity Reconciliation Act (PRWO-RA) of 1996 (P.L. 104–193) revealed few differences between urban and rural single mothers. Both rural and urban single mothers had made gains in employment. When demographic factors were controlled, they found that poverty rates for single mothers had not declined, however. They concluded that rural residents were not disadvantaged by the change in rules brought about by PRWORA, but the progress of single mothers was stymied by their limited education opportunities, age, and ethnicity.

E. M. Dolan (✉)
Department of Family Studies, University of New Hampshire, 55 College Road, Durham, NH 03824, USA
e-mail: e.dolan@unh.edu

J. W. Bauer, E. M. Dolan (eds.), *Rural Families and Work,* International Series on Consumer Science 1,
DOI 10.1007/978-1-4614-0382-1_12, © Springer Science+Business Media, LLC 2011

Framing Policy

Before discussing ideas about policies to enhance the lives of rural low-income families, we need to look at the system of addressing social policy, i.e., how does policy get framed? Chambers (2000) provided a framework for social policy analysis, as analyzing policy requires a unique lens to frame the issue. The components of an issue that needs to be addressed are several: The problem needs to be defined; the causes, antecedents, and consequences need to be indentified; ideologies and values of the various viewpoints need to be understood; and, finally, an analysis is needed of who will gain, and what will be gained, from the policy as well as who will lose and what will be lost.

Definition of the problem is the key component in social policy analysis. People may "know" what they see or experience as the problem, but not everyone will experience the problem in the same way. A well-defined problem will help with identifying what is causing the problem, what has come before "now" that influences the problem, and what are the consequences or outcomes currently of the problem. The ideologies or differences of opinion of those who will be addressing this problem are similarly very important to identify. This is especially true when elected officials, be they federal, state, or local, are going to vote on the ultimate resolution. Conservatives and liberals may not even agree that a problem exists, much less on how to resolve a problem. By identifying the various viewpoints, advocates can address each one in proposing solutions to the problem. Finally, analyzing who will be the gainers and losers is vitally important (Chambers 2000). Both direct and indirect cost-benefit analyses help advocates not only identify the solutions, but also understand what any unintended consequences will be. Benefits of new policies are rarely universal for the effected people.

Social policy reflects society's desire, or attempt, to manage scarce resources (consider the debate on providing health care coverage for all in the United States that occurred during the spring and summer of 2010). The competing and conflicting demands of those who have an interest in the outcome of a change in policy shape the final outcome of the policy. Chambers (2000, p. 72) states that the goal of social welfare policy is "about selection and rationing, in an attempt to correct injustice."

Events and attitudes often coalesce to bring about social change (e.g., courts may consider a certain law suit "ripe" for a decision because of a change in social attitudes). What attitudes and events brought about the 1996 Personal Responsibility and Work Opportunity Reconciliation Act (PRWORA)? Was the problem of wanting mothers to work in exchange for benefits new? What had changed? Was this a new variation or a drastic change? Why was society receptive to this change? Referencing Bronfenbrenner's ecological framework, several macrosystem factors influenced the design of PRWORA. Aid to Families with Dependent Children (AFDC) was under fire because of the feeling that AFDC encouraged the poor to remain welfare-dependent by undermining the work ethic and that AFDC did not promote traditional married families since benefits were not paid to married couples. The popular perception of AFDC recipients was that these mothers were lazy, promiscuous, and lived well at the public's expense. Furthermore, the fathers of the AFDC-recipient children were seen as dead-beats who did not want to support their own children. Finally, there was a perception that "too much" was spent on welfare programs and that spending should be reduced (Haskins 2009a, b; Reese 2007).

How well has PRWORA done in achieving its goals of reducing spending, reducing the number of people on welfare, and promoting family? The answer to this question depends on who is answering and when the question is being answered. In the boom years of the late 1990s, and even into the early 2000s, the Temporary Assistance for Needy Families (TANF) case loads dropped (except for the recession period in 2001–2002). But, in her study of the causes and consequences of welfare reform, Reese (2007, p. 50) concluded that: "(D)espite proponents' emphasis on promoting self-sufficiency and marriage, PRWORA failed to reduce poverty or to shift family formation patterns among low-income families; instead, this new welfare law created highly destructive consequences by denying low-income families access to greatly needed income and social services." Reese's analysis, however, did not focus on rural concerns.

Finally, the values that are held by those who will be impacted by the policy need to be considered. In this case, the values that are held by welfare recipients are another important component underlying policy. Leichtentritt and Rettig (2001) state that values "influence perceptions, decisions, and actions and as a result, affect the welfare of individuals, their family members, and the community" (p. 150). Lee et al. (2010) found that seven main values emerged from rural welfare recipients' comments regarding their experiences with the welfare system and welfare reform. These values are self-esteem, autonomy, uniqueness, advancement, security, independence, and fairness relating to the economic and social-psychological well-being of the mothers and their children. The values revealed how these rural mothers perceived their environments, made important decisions, and why they behaved in certain ways.

Proposals

Reauthorization Proposals

The Rural Families Speak (RFS) research team took on the challenge of better understanding the conditions affecting rural low-income families as a response to the context of welfare reform. The study was intended to provide evidence of the well-being of families in the wake of reform. The findings from the longitudinal study raise questions and suggest policy and program options going forward as the legislation is reauthorized in 2010 and 2015.

Policy-makers, especially, have considered welfare and welfare reform from the individual deficit perspective, i.e., individuals who are poor are lacking something that prevents them from adequately supporting their families (Huber and Kossek 1999). Although PRWORA has allowed states to modify the welfare rules to fit the needs of the state, for the most part, little has been done to address the differences between rural and urban economies. Assessing the efficacy of various policies is, then, an important exercise.

In a book that describes a 7-year overtime situation for 753 welfare-reliant single mothers and the well-being of their children, Johnson et al. (2010) frame the welfare reform debate that forms the context for these mothers. The same context exists for the rural mothers in our RFS study. The original PRWORA legislation is described in Chap. 1 of this volume. Proposals were made in the reauthorization legislation to create more ways to support the work component, but little has changed for the context in which mothers, whether rural or urban, find themselves. Blank and Haskins (2001) of the Brookings Institution made extensive proposals relative to the first reauthorization of PRWORA which was slated for 2001. For a variety of reasons, PRWORA reauthorization was not enacted until 2006. The second reauthorization was slated for 2010, but not yet considered at the point this is being written. Haskins (2009a) again suggested changes, although only a few of the proposals would directly benefit rural families.

The 2006 reauthorization legislation increased the work requirements for those who were TANF-reliant and increased the penalties for noncompliance. While we have no direct evidence of these rules causing hardship in rural areas, given what we know of the rural economy, more flexibility would undoubtedly benefit rural TANF recipients. Allowing more educational activities to count toward the work requirement would also benefit rural families. As Weber et al. (2004) found, low educational attainment among rural single mothers was impeding their ability to find employment that would pay them enough to support their families.

Haskins (2009a) proposed a special provision for so-called floundering mothers who have serious difficulties and are unable to sustain employment. Creating special programs to help these mothers to address their issues has only been proposed at this point in time. Rural TANF clients would more than likely benefit from such programs as we found many RFS families had serious issues that kept them out of the labor force (Katras et al. 2009).

Focusing on fathers, and helping fathers increase income, could directly help rural families. One proposal suggests substantially increasing the Earned Income Tax Credit (EITC) for single persons with no dependents. Having a larger EITC would provide more incentive for unmarried fathers to work and pay child support.

Marriage promotion has been a part of PRWORA since its onset. Simmons et al. (2007) found that marriage did not increase the financial well-being of the RFS families, in and of itself. Working more hours and having a partner (married or not) who was employed were the key elements to increasing financial well-being. As rural low-income families are more likely to be married than urban low-income families, promoting marriage has only limited impact on rural low-income families.

Proposals to Support Rural Low-Income Families

Researchers who have focused on the well-being of rural low-income families generally concur that TANF rules could be modified to better serve the rural populace (e.g., Huber and Kossek 1999; Weber et al. 2001; Whitener 2005). As we have repeatedly stressed in previous chapters of this volume, rural communities either lack or have greatly reduced options for supporting working families, whether they are low-income or not. The local rural economic conditions may mean that while parents are employed, they are not employed at wages and/or have enough hours of employment to allow them to support their families without continued assistance from some federal assistance programs (Weber et al. 2001). While many of the proposals would also have benefits for urban low-income families, the focus is on rural impacts.

An example of the difficulty in providing assistance in rural areas is the USDA Summer Food Service Program designed to provide meals to school-aged children who get the School Lunch and Breakfast Programs during the academic year. The sparse rural population has resulted in many rural school districts not qualifying for the summer program. Changes were made in the eligibility requirements to address this issue in order to reach rural children, but the results have been mixed at best (Wauchope and Stracuzzi 2010). Delivering meals to children's homes was costly, providing meals at specific sites was not cost-effective due to too few children at any one site, and children often lacked the transportation to get to these sites and/or had to travel long distances to get to the sites. Furthermore, many rural areas could not find an organization that had the interest and/or capacity to produce the meals. Administrators are searching to find solutions that will increase the availability of food programs for rural low-income school children during the summer. Some of the suggestions are to work on increasing parental awareness of the program, mandating school district participation, providing free transportation to all eligible children, providing mobile site (like the bookmobile concept), providing a free meal to an accompanying parent, and increasing staff salaries and resources (Wauchope and Stracuzzi 2010).

Employment Rules on time limits and sanctions could be made community- or county-specific to address the issue of fewer job opportunities and support services, and the absence of public transportation options in those areas (Weber et al. 2001). Rural low-income single mothers in particular may have a difficult time complying with work requirements if child care and transportation are not available. For example, one of the RFS mothers, Jolene,[1] was sanctioned off TANF because she did not have transportation, could not find a job in her community within walking distance that provided her with enough hours, nor could she get to her appointments with her TANF case worker. In her state, she could only get transportation assistance if she was complying with all the work requirements (Dolan et al. 2008).

---

[1] All names are pseudonyms.

Most demonstration programs have been done in urban settings, but the concepts should hold true for rural areas also although more community and other supports may be required. So-called "mixed strategies" have proven to be successful. In Portland, Oregon, e.g., the welfare-to-work program provided a range of activities for clients to improve their skills and tailored programs to meet the needs of the individual TANF clients. "The Portland program also helped more recipients earn both a GED and an occupational certificate than any other program yet studied" (Martinson and Strawn 2003, p. 3). Those participating in this program were typically in more than one activity at any one time.

The New Hope project in Milwaukee, Wisconsin, provided an earnings supplement, subsidized child care, and subsidized health insurance to low-income parents working at least 30 hours a week (Zedlewski et al. 2006). Compared with a control group not receiving the subsidies, the New Hope parents were found to work more and therefore earn more, had greater awareness of community supports, and were more likely to use formal center-based care for their children (Duncan et al. 2008).

In Cleveland, Ohio, the Achieve Program placed case workers at employment sites with the aim of reducing turnover of low-income earners by increasing supports for the employees. Case management actions included counseling, referrals, information about community resources, and assistance for emergency needs such as transportation and last-minute child care. The Achieve Program resulted in a significant reduction in employee turnover (Zedlewski et al. 2006).

The state of Maine also has worked on increasing access to work supports for low-income working families. The state administrators focus on delivering services and programs to their TANF and other low-income working clients in a more flexible, user-friendly manner, especially relative to enrollment and retention. Maine offers interpreters so that language is not a barrier to enrollment and has eliminated the need for face-to-face recertification interviews. This approach has kept TANF case loads relatively low while improving participation rates in both SNAP and Medicaid (Zedlewski et al. 2006).

Communities/states should take advantage of the provisions of the 1998 Workforce Investment Act (WIA) which allows for federal job training to reflect local employment needs to match job seekers with jobs (Whitener et al. 2001). As several of the demonstration projects have illustrated, low-income workers, and especially rural low-income workers, may need more flexibility in their jobs in order to juggle work and family. When employers are mindful of the problems that their low-wage employees may encounter and make accommodations, the employees are more loyal and turnover is reduced. When low-income rural parents have no flexibility, no sick or personal days, and no vacation days, when child/family issues arise, parents will sacrifice work to take care of the family issue. The working parents, then, may be viewed as unreliable and could be terminated. Two programs have been working with employers to address this issue. When employers are interested in offering their employees flex-time, the US Department of Labor's Flex-Options Project provides free assistance over the telephone to help employers resolve their flex-time issues. The second program is sponsored by the A. P. Sloan Foundation, the Institute for a Competitive Workforce, and the Twiga Foundation, called the "When Work

Works" initiative. This initiative gives awards to employers who meet the initiative's criteria for fostering a flexible working environment so that employees can combine their work and family obligations (Dolan 2009).

Communities could encourage and help local employers to become more flexible in order to be able to accommodate the work/family issues of their employees. Resulting programs could address transportation, since getting to places of employment, as was reported in Chap. 8, is an issue affecting both workers and employers. To subsidize transportation for workers from many communities within a region, employers could use a school-bus model to pick employees up at predetermined locations (Pindus et al. 2007). Vans or small buses picking employees up from park-and-ride areas would reduce the wear-and-tear on the employees' personal vehicles, could save on costs, and would also allow a one-car family to have that car available to the other spouse/partner to get to employment or to run family errands.

Health and Health Care Health (physical and mental) of TANF applicants and family members should be considered as barriers to full employment. Pathways or access to disability benefits need to be created when physical and/or mental health considerations of applicants or the applicants' family members indicate that employment would be difficult. Low-income rural families currently move in and out of health care systems as their incomes rise and fall. The Patient Protection and Affordable Care Act (PPACA) of 2010 (P.L. 111–148) has potential for improving the access to health care for rural low-income parents. Those who do not have insurance will be able to purchase health care insurance through state-based exchanges starting in 2014 (Jackson and Nolen 2010). Families and individuals who make between 100% and 400% of poverty will have their premiums subsidized, with a cap on how much they will have to pay based on their income levels. People will be eligible for Medicaid up to 133% of poverty, including single adults with no children. Benefiting rural low-income families especially is the requirement that coverage cannot be denied for preexisting conditions. Other changes in the health care delivery systems will occur as a result of the PPACA. What these are will be determined as the Health Exchanges get developed in each state.

Currently, however, in a number of states families with children insured through the State Children's Health Insurance Program (SCHIP) find that their children become disqualified for coverage when they get a pay raise. A few states have "steps" allowing parents to pay into the program with higher premiums as their incomes rise. More states should contemplate this type of framework to benefit the health of children.

While not having insurance to pay for care was a substantial barrier for RFS families, not having health care practitioners available to them was another issue. When rural health care providers do not accept Medicaid, the problem of access is exacerbated. Having access to medical facilities as well as medical personnel, especially specialists, is increasingly difficult in many rural communities. As reported in Chaps. 5 and 6, the shortage of health care professionals in rural areas is acute. A paper in the Journal of the American Medical Association (Rosenblatt et al. 2006) reported that rural community health centers had more vacancies and vacancies were open longer than comparable urban health centers. The major barriers to filling positions were low salaries, isolation, inferior school districts, and few employment opportunities for spouses. The PPACA of 2010 contained provisions for loan forgiveness as a means to attract practitioners to rural areas. Some states and counties have already begun loan repayments or provision of housing to attract physicians and other health care providers to low population-density areas.

Small communities, struggling to support a full-service hospital, turn to regional community health centers as an increasingly common model for delivery of services. These regional health centers, while efficient relative to economies of scale, can be substantial distances from the communities served. One solution has been to provide transportation to the regional health center from the outlying communities. While the "medi-van" concept, i.e., a van/bus that will pick up residents from a central location to take them to the regional health center, presents one option for getting health care, it is not without problems. As Maxine was quoted in Chap. 5, taking the medi-van typically results in a doctor's appointment becoming an all-day affair.

Another model brings medical personnel and facilities to the community, much like the bookmobile concept used by libraries. A bus is outfitted with basic medical needs and travels from community to community on a regular basis. The traveling medical facility could also have mental health professionals as part of the team. In some respects, this type of model could help ameliorate the stigma of visiting a mental health professional identified in the RFS study. No one would know if the patient was seeing a medical professional or a mental health professional since the two would be in one spot. This model could help not only build the human capital of the community (a healthier population), but also increase social networks. More remote communities would benefit by having the medical facility come to the community.

Child Care Child care is a critical support for low-income families. Rural low-income families have the complication of not having a wide variety of child care services at their disposal. Low-income parents may find that the cost of child care exceeds their take-home wages, especially when more than one child needs care and/or an infant needs care. Rural low-income families are less likely for several reasons to use child care subsidies. Rural low-income parents may not be able to find a child care provider who will take the subsidy. Many rural parents use family or friends as care providers. Some of these providers may not want payment, but others may want to be paid in cash, or not want the trouble of dealing with the state requirements necessary to qualify for the subsidies. Increasing the funding for the child care subsidies would still benefit rural low-income families, however. Allowing working parents with incomes up to 200% of poverty to qualify for subsidies would help reduce the burden of child care when center-based care is used (Cauthen 2007; Dolan 2009). The Economic Policy Institute has proposed making child care free for those whose incomes are below the federal poverty guidelines, and capping copays for higher earning families at no more than 20% of a family's income (Cauthen 2007).

The Child and Dependent Care Tax Credit (CDCTC), which covers not only care of children less than age 13 but also other dependent family members of any age, offers only limited assistance to rural low-income families. The CDCTC is calculated based on the family's income, amount of taxes owed, and the amount paid for child or dependent care. For the tax years 2009 and 2010, the CDCTC was temporarily expanded by lowering the qualifying income from $12,500 to $3,000 so that more low-income families would qualify for the credit (Purmort 2010).

The Economic Policy Institute has recommended eliminating the CDCTC and putting the funds toward free child care and child care subsidies for families with income up to 200% of poverty (Cauthen 2007). Others (Campbell et al. 2006) propose making the CDCTC a refundable tax credit similar to the EITC. Either of these two possibilities would ease the burden of the cost of child care for rural low-income families, although neither is without some issues.

Few options for child care are as much an issue for rural low-income families as the cost of child care. While rural mothers may rely on relatives out of choice to care for their children, this may be their only option. Nonstandard work schedules almost guarantee that the working parents must rely on kin-care for their children. Especially in rural areas, licensed center-based care options do not operate on weekends, late nights, or on holidays, and/or the center-based care options may be too far away to be viable alternatives. For the rural parents working in the retail and hospitality industries, nonstandard hours are the norm. Communities where the tourist-related industries are the mainstay of the economy could work with local employers to develop child care options for those who are required to work the nonstandard hours. Furthermore, before- and after-school programs would serve the needs of rural low-income working parents. While low-income parents may not fully trust on center-based care for their young children, they do trust Head Start (Dolan 2009). Expansion of Head Start and Early Head Start programs in rural areas could be beneficial.

Since finding child care providers is one of the problems identified by RFS mothers, communities could find ways to make appropriate care available and affordable. Children need care-providers who are skilled and knowledgeable about child development, and they need to be presented with opportunities to grow intellectually, socially, and physically. The extent to which children receive adequate care will affect their human capital throughout their lives. Not only could quality programs help the children, but workforce preparation programs could help low-income rural mothers, and fathers, find employment. If communities have access to child development programs though local community colleges, the entire community could be enhanced by helping low-income rural parents gain degrees and/or certifications needed for running a licensed care facility. Not only would the owner of the facility need to receive the appropriate education, but the workers hired would also need their degrees and/or certifications. The assistance could be provided through microenterprise loans that would help with college tuition as well as with setting up the facility itself. If existing suitable space is available in a central location, i.e., one having ample access to outdoor areas, kitchen facilities, and restrooms that could be retrofitted for children, as well as having parking for staff and parents, then the possibility of opening a child care center would be facilitated. The more building and retrofitting a location needs, however, the more expensive the enterprise becomes.

Other Resources Access to reliable transportation is a critical factor for rural low-income families. The programs that have been developed for urban areas are focused on public, mass transportation which does not translate well in rural communities. Programs like the Federal Job Access and Reverse Commute Initiative (Surface Transportation Policy Project, n.d.) focus on assessing transportation needs to make employment options more accessible for low-income households without personal cars by providing transit service where low-income families live to get them to where they work. Low population densities in rural communities make this approach impractical. In rural communities, the most helpful transportation assistance would focus on providing low-income families with subsidies to buy or repair personal vehicles and buy insurance. Programs like More Than Wheels help low-income individuals and those with damaged credit to buy new cars. This particular program guarantees loans so that interest rates are lower. The program also provides counseling, budgeting, and car purchase negotiation assistance (More Than Wheels, n.d.). Other programs accept donations of previously owned vehicles, rehab the donations, and give or sell the rehabbed vehicles to low-income individuals at low cost. Facilitating transportation not only eases the burden of long commutes to places of employment, but also helps rural low-income families get access to other essential services. Finally, as we found with our RFS participants, some rural low-income mothers may even need help in getting their drivers' licenses.

In their study of the RFS mothers who got off and stayed off TANF, Dolan et al. (2008) found that education and training appeared to be key factors for the few mothers who were able to become wage-reliant and earn high enough wages so that they and their families were thriving. TANF rules around education and training became more restrictive in the 2006 reauthorization legislation. TANF rules discourage states from allowing TANF clients from investing in their own human capital by restricting educational experiences to short-term ones (Center for Law and Social Policy (CLASP) 2010; Martinson and Strawn 2003). Job training programs have proved to be successful in assisting TANF clients in finding and keeping higher paying jobs than they might normally have found. Rural TANF clients may have fewer skills and more barriers than their urban counterparts, so are in need of extended times to complete education and training programs, more time than currently is allowed under TANF rules (Martinson and Strawn 2003).

Adults are not the only rural residents who have educational issues. Because many low-income families move frequently, their children's school records may not follow them in a timely manner from school to school or district to district. The residential mobility typically involves short distances within one school district or into a neighboring district. School officials should be encouraged to collaborate with regard to students' records so that the children's learning would be supported and their chances of completing high school would be maximized.

Low-income families, whether they are rural or urban residents, face what can be called an implicit tax on their incomes as their incomes rise and lose all or part of various support programs (Romich et al. 2007). The so-called tax rate depends on the program: SNAP (food stamps) ends when family income reaches 130% of poverty, housing subsidies are based on percentage of median income for the community, child care subsidies continue up to 200% of poverty, and so forth. While many of these benefits are reduced gradually as family income rises, low-income families can see dramatic reductions when all subsidies are reduced simultaneously in response to a pay raise. For someone whose earnings are near the top of the eligibility ceiling, a small increase in wages can result in loss of subsidies from potentially more than one program, leaving the family worse off than before the raise. Loss of eligibility for SNAP, housing subsidies, and child care subsidies may well deter low-income mothers from accepting a raise or applying for a better paying job. Romich et al. (2007, p. 424) state that the "current system fails by denying the working poor a chance at economic mobility." Better coordination among programs would benefit all low-income families.

Other possibilities have been proposed. Several years ago, US Representative Bob Filner (D-CA) proposed a refundable tax credit of $2,000 for each adult and $1,000 for qualified dependents to all those who do not itemize deductions on their federal income tax forms (Caputo 2007). A more radical proposal was made by Murray (2006) to provide a guaranteed income of $10,000 per year to each adult. Earned income over $25,000 would reduce the income grant. The grant would be phased out when earned income reached $50,000 per year. This program would replace all other benefits programs.

Earned Income Tax Credit In 2009, the American Recovery and Reinvestment Act (ARRA) expanded the federal EITC to include families with three or more children, and increased the ceilings on adjusted gross incomes for all household categories. The changes, however, applied only to the 2009 and 2010 tax years. The Tax Relief, Unemployment Insurance Reauthorization, and Job Creation Act of 2010 extended the EITC expansion to tax years 2011 and 2012. This expansion should be made permanent, however. As illustrated in Chap. 10, the federal EITC provides a needed income boost for rural low-income families. Evidence indicates that the EITC raises the employment rates of single mothers (Eissa and Hoynes 2006). To further support low-income working families, states with income taxes should consider instituting state EITCs. In 2009, 23 states and the District of Columbia already had a state version of the EITC with all but two states having refundable credits that mirrored the federal credit.

Community/state coalitions need to expand the Volunteer Income Tax Assistance (VITA) programs into rural areas so that more families will be able to take advantage of the federal (and state if applicable) EITC. Tax preparation assistance will allow low-income families to keep more money in their pockets by not paying for tax preparation services.

Rural Communities Employees, especially rural employees, need to have some flexibility in their work arrangements, especially for parents of children at home. Research has found that some job flexibility increases employee commitment, reduces absenteeism, and reduces employee turnover. Sometimes, it does not take very much flexibility for a worker to be helped. The proximity of the employment to the needs of the family often determines the amount of flexibility needed. Small employers have more difficulty offering employees this flexibility even though work/family issues crop up frequently for their employees. Neither the Fair Labor

Standards Act (FLSA) nor the Family and Medical Leave Act (FMLA) is helpful in this regard (Kornbluh et al. 2004). Finding ways of structuring employment, however, would allow supervisors and other employees to be supportive of one another by covering if/when an employee needed some flexibility.

Conclusions

The rural economy is different from the urban economy. Rural communities tend to provide fewer formal support services for families, including health care and other well-being care. This chapter has highlighted some of the policies that were in the original welfare reform legislation in 1996 and changes in the subsequent re-authorization legislation. The chapter gives some of the few policy differences that researchers and policy experts, who understand the rural context, have offered as suggestions for the future. While many of the low-income families who are in the RFS project were not receiving TANF, they were receiving other support services and programs that helped them to continue to work and care for their families.

In this chapter, we have described some of the problems that are endemic for rural low-income families, and we have proposed some alternatives for dealing with them. We have attempted to craft our suggestions to appeal to a broad spectrum of political beliefs. We have not, however, done any cost-benefit analyses on any of the policy suggestions. Our suggestions can be viewed as policy issues that are ripe for debate. Further research is needed to understand the complexities that are presented by the suggestions made in this chapter. The contexts and problems that face rural families add to the complexity.

The themes of availability, accessibility, acceptability, and complexity were raised in Chap. 1. These issues have been addressed throughout this volume. Resources (e.g., child care, social support, educational opportunities, employment opportunities, etc.) are not particularly *available* when it does not exist in the community or a nearby community. Resources are not *accessible* when rural family members do not have reliable transportation. The value systems of families as well as the local culture and how the families, and community members, see certain issues will influence the *acceptability* of certain resources and options. Rural low-income families' lives can be exceedingly *complex* as they piece together the resources they have to maintain employment and successfully support their families.

Discussion Questions

1. Apply Chambers' theoretical model of policy analysis to a current policy proposal focusing on the implications for rural low-income families. Will this proposal help facilitate the employment for rural low-income parents?
2. Which policies facilitate employment? What revisions could be made in existing policy to better address rural issues?

3. What are the policies that make it more difficult to be employed or maintain employment?
4. What did you learn in this chapter that helps you understand the lived experience of rural low-income families?

Acknowledgment The authors want to thank Nanci De Felippe, a Ph.D. graduate student at the University of Minnesota, for her work on background literature for this chapter.

References

Blank, R., & Haskins, R. (Eds). (2001). *The new world of welfare*. Washington, DC: Brookings Institution.

Campbell, N. D., Entmacher, J., Matsui, A. K., Firvida, C. M., & Love, C. (2006). *Making care less taxing: Improving state child and dependent care tax provisions*. http://www.nwlc.org/sites/default/files/pdfs/MakingCareLessTaxing2006.pdf.

Caputo, R. K. (2007). Working and poor: A panel study of maturing adults in the U.S. *Families in Society, 88*, 351–359. doi:10.1606/1044-3894.3644.

Cauthen, N. K. (2007, October). *Improving work supports closing the financial gap for low-wage workers and their families* (Economic Policy Institute Briefing Paper No. 198). http://www.sharedprosperity.org/bp198/bp198.pdf.

Center for Law and Social Policy (CLASP). (2010). *Funding career pathways and career pathway bridges*. http://www.clasp.org/admin/site/publications/files/FundingCareerPathwaysFederal PolicyToolkitforStates.pdf.

Chambers, D. E. (2000). *Social policy and social programs: A method for the practical public policy analyst*. Needham Heights: Allyn & Bacon.

Dolan, E. M. (2009). Policy implications. *Consumer Interests Annual, 55*, 91–92. http://www.consumerinterests.org/2000-2009Proceedings.php.

Dolan, E. M., Braun, B., Katras, M. J., & Seiling, S. (2008). Getting off TANF: Experiences of rural mothers. *Families in Society, 89*, 456–465. doi:10.1606/1044-3894.3771.

Duncan, G. J., Huston, A. C., & Weisner, T. S. (2008). *Higher ground: New hope for the working poor and their children*. New York: Russell Sage Foundation.

Eissa, N., & Hoynes, H. W. (2006). Behavioral responses to taxes: Lessons from the EITC and labor supply. In J. M. Poterba (Ed.), *Tax policy and the economy* (pp. 73–110). Cambridge: MIT Press.

Haskins, R. (2004). Welfare reform: Success with troubled spots. *Eastern Economic Journal, 30*(1), 125–134. http://www.jstor.org/stable/40325438.

Haskins, R. (2009a, December). *The 2010 reauthorization of welfare reform could result in important changes*. http://www.brookings.edu/~/media/Files/rc/papers/2009/1218_welfare_reform_haskins/1218_welfare_reform_haskins.pdf.

Haskins, R. (2009b). What works is work: Welfare reform and poverty reduction. *Northwestern Journal of Law and Social Policy, 4*(1). http://www.law.northwestern.edu/journals/njlsp/v4/n1/3.

Huber, M. S., & Kossek, E. E. (1999). Community distress predicting welfare exits: The under-examined factor for families in the United States. *Community, Work & Family, 2*, 173–186.

Jackson, J., & Nolen, J. (2010, May 24). *Health care reform bill summary: A look at what's in the bill*. http://www.cbsnews.com/8301-503544_162-20000846-503544.html.

Johnson, R. C., Kalil, A., & Dunifon, R. E. (2010). *Mother's work and children's lives: Low-income families after welfare reform*. Kalamazoo: W. E. Upjohn Institute for Employment Research.

Katras, M. J., Dolan, E. M., Seiling, S. B., & Braun, B. (2009). The bumpy road off TANF for rural mothers. *Family Science Review, 14*(1). http://familyscienceassociation.org/archived%20 journal%20articles/FSR_vol14_2008/1Mary%20Jo_Katras.pdf.

Kornbluh, K., Isaacs, K., & Boots, S. W. (2004, May). *Workplace flexibility: A policy problem* (Work & Family Program Issue Brief No. 1). http://www.newamerica.net/Download_Docs/pdfs/Pub_File_1584_1.pdf.

Lee, J., Katras, M. J., & Bauer, J. W. (2010). Values underlying U. S. low-income mothers' voices about welfare and welfare reform: An inductive analysis. *International Journal of Human Ecology, 11*(2), 63–75.

Leichtentritt, R. D., & Rettig, K. D. (2001). Values underlying end-of-life decisions: A qualitative approach. *Health & Social Work, 26,* 150–159.

Martinson, K., & Strawn, J. (2003, April). *Built to last: Why skills matter for long-run success in welfare reform* (Workforce Development Series Policy Brief No. 1). http://www.clasp.org/publications/BTL_brief.pdf.

More Than Wheels. (n.d.). *Organization details.* http://www.morethanwheels.org/about.

Murray, C. (2006). *In our own hands: A plan to replace the welfare state.* Washington, DC: AEI Press.

Pindus, N., Theodos, B., & Kingsley, G. T. (2007). *Place matters: Employers, low-income workers, and regional economic development.* http://www.urban.org/UploadedPDF/411534_place_matters.pdf

Purmort, J. (2010). *Making work supports work: A picture of low-wage workers in America.* http://www.nccp.org/publications/pdf/text_914.pdf.

Reese, E. (2007). The causes and consequences of U. S. welfare retrenchment. *Journal of Poverty, 11*(3), 47–63. doi:10.1300/J134v11n03_05.

Romich, J. L., Simmelink, J., & Holt, S. D. (2007). When working harder does not pay: Low-income working families, tax liabilities, and benefit reductions. *Families in Society, 88,* 418–426. doi:10.1606/1044-3894.3651.

Rosenblatt, R. A., Andrilla, C. H. H., Curtin, T., & Hart, L. G. (2006). Shortages of medical personnel at Community Health Centers: Implications for planned expansion. *Journal of the American Medical Association, 295*(9), 1042–1049.

Simmons, L. A., Dolan, E. M., & Braun, B. (2007). Rhetoric and reality of economic self-sufficiency among rural, low-income families: A longitudinal study. *Journal of Family and Economic Issues, 28,* 489–505. doi:10.1007/s10834-007-9071-x.

Surface Transportation Policy Partnership. (n.d). Transportation and poverty alleviation. (Fact sheet). http://www.transact.org/factsheets/poverty.asp.

Wauchope, B., & Stracuzzi, N. (2010, Spring). *Challenges in serving rural American children through the summer food service program* (Issue Brief No. 13). http://www.carseyinstitute.unh.edu/publications/IB_Wauchope_SFSP.pdf.

Weber, B. A., Duncan, G. J., & Whitener, L. A. (2001). Welfare reform in rural America: What have we learned? *American Journal of Agricultural Economics, 83,* 1282–1292. doi:10.1111/0002-9092.00280.

Weber, B., Edwards, M., & Duncan, G. (2004). Single mother work and poverty under welfare reform: Are policy impacts different in rural areas? *Eastern Economic Journal, 30*(1), 31–51. http://www.jstor.org/stable/40325434.

Whitener, L. A. (2005). Policy options for a changing rural America. *Amber Waves, 3*(2). http://www.ers.usda.gov/AmberWaves/April05/Features/PolicyOptions.htm.

Whitener, L. A., Weber, B. A., & Duncan, G. J. (2001). Reforming welfare: Implication for rural America. *Rural America, 16*(3), 2–10. http://www.ers.usda.gov/publications/ruralamerica/ra163/ra163b.pdf.

Zedlewski, S., Adams, G., Dubay, L., & Kenney, G. (2006). *Is there a system support low-income working families?* (Low-Income Working Family Paper No. 4). http://www.urban.org/UploadedPDF/311282_lowincome_families.pdf.

Appendix

A Brief History of Rural Families Speak Project

In 1997, a group of researchers predominately associated with the Agricultural Experiment Station (AES) Research in 34 states met in St. Louis to discuss a new multistate research project. The Personal Responsibility and Work Opportunity Reconciliation Act (P.L. 104-193) had been signed into law in August 1996. The researchers knew that as policy changes, so do the lives of the people closely affected by the policy. The newly initiated research on welfare reform was being conducted mostly in urban areas. Little focus was being placed on rural areas and thus on rural families. In early 1998, a proposal was sent to the North Central Agricultural Experiment Station Directors. The writing team was composed of researchers from Michigan, Minnesota, Missouri, Nebraska, Oregon, and Indiana. This proposal was accepted mid 1998 as a five year project (October 1998 through September 2003): NC-223 "Rural Low-Income Families: Tracking their Well-Being and Functioning in the Context of Welfare Reform," hereafter commonly called "Rural Families Speak." At the first official meeting of the project, 15 states agreed to be participants (California, Idaho, Kentucky, Louisiana, Massachusetts, Michigan, Minnesota, Missouri, Nebraska, New Hampshire, New York, Ohio, Oregon, Utah, and Wyoming). Another five states were interested, but did not have official approval to be part of the project (Colorado, Indiana, Iowa, South Dakota, and Wisconsin). During the first year, Idaho, Missouri, and Utah dropped out of the project; Colorado and Indiana officially joined the project. Maryland joined the project in 2000 in time to collect data. Wyoming dropped out of the project in 2001 after Wave 1 data collection. Colorado continued with the project, but never collected data. All of these states formed Panel 1 for this project. A graduate student on the project in Oregon joined the faculty at Ohio University and worked with the lead researcher in Ohio and with extension faculty in West Virginia to collect data in West Virginia toward the end of the project. Ohio collected data at a second site in Ohio and with the data from West Virginia, forming Panel 2. These counties with some of the original counties formed a geographical subsample of Appalachia families for the study. In 2003, the NC-223 project was extended for another five years and given a new number: NC-1011. Two more states, Iowa and South Dakota, joined the project. They collected data using the same methodology as in Panel 2, forming Panel 3. The complex methodology and data collection are explained later.

J. W. Bauer, E. M. Dolan (eds.), *Rural Families and Work,* International Series on Consumer Science 1,
DOI 10.1007/978-1-4614-0382-1, © Springer Science+Business Media, LLC 2011

The target sample for the research project was rural low-income families. The criteria to be included were at least one child less than 13-year old who resided in the household, and an income of less than 200% of poverty level for the family size. Families with young children were desired because these were the families with most of the concerns that were being addressed by the legislation. Thus, researchers focused on recruiting families with children younger than 5 years of age. Several issues were of concern as the research team commenced identifying the sample population: The lack of consistent rural definitions, access to central telephone directories (in 1999), spatial distances, and funding. Community programs that targeted low-income families were the sources that the researchers used to get initial contacts with the mothers fitting the criteria for the project.

A common protocol was developed, and used, by the participating states. States had the freedom to add questions, but not to remove any from the common protocol. The Agricultural Experiment Station (AES) structure in each cooperating state allowed for one face-to-face research team meeting per year. The work on multistate project was accomplished electronically, though teleconferencing, or as an add-on to other meetings that team members attended.

The first round of data collection, Wave 1, was purposively focused on obtaining qualitative data. In addition to factual information, we wanted to understand the lived experiences of these rural low-income mothers. Thus we asked them about their feelings and attitudes about a number of factors. This resulted in a multi-method and quasi-structured protocol. Many of the researchers on the team were trained as quantitative researchers, not qualitative, and because we needed to have a consistent interview methodology across all the states, training for interviewers was conducted by a team member who regularly taught qualitative research methods. Dr. Leslie Richards at Oregon State University, along with her graduate students did the distant education training. Pilot data of two cases for the protocol were collected in California, Indiana, Louisiana, Massachusetts, Minnesota, Missouri, Nebraska, New Hampshire, Ohio, and Utah, in 1999. There were 14 useable cases that met all the inclusion criteria and were complete. The protocol required between one and three hours of interviewing. Wave 1 data were collected in 14 states (25 counties) over a period of time from 1999 to 2001. After data cleaning 413 mothers were included in the Panel 1, Wave 1.

The Wave 2 was developed as follow-up to help track family experiences of the functioning in the context of the welfare reform implementation. This protocol was used by 13 state research teams (23 counties) in Panel 1 between 2001 and 2002. Attrition is a concern with any longitudinal study. The population of low-income families who move often and have many barriers was a problem, making it difficult to keep in touch with all the Wave 1 participants. Several methods were used to keep in contact, but in the end only 315 mothers were found and agreed to continue with the study, a retention rate of 76.3% of the participants.

The Wave 3 protocol was developed as a more quantitative instrument with only a few open-ended questions for the mothers. Thirteen state research teams collected data in 23 counties between 2002 and 2003. Further attrition resulted in 265 mothers being interviewed at this wave with for a total 64.1% retention rate for the sample.

In the time that the Panel 1 (Wave 1, 2, 3), data were being collected the second Panel was developed. Panel 2 used a combination of Wave1 and Wave 2 protocols to collect the data and get synchronized with the timing for Wave 3 data collection resulting in only two points of data rather than three. Panel 2 data collection involved two states and three counties. Panel 3 started in 2004 with the addition of two more states to overall project. They used the protocol developed for Panel 2 (the combined Wave 1 and 2 protocols) for the initial data collection, and then followed a year later with the Wave 3 protocol. Data collection was in two states (three counties) for Wave 1/2, but only one state collected data in Wave 3.

The intent of longitudinal aspect of data collection was to study the mothers' context over time. The longitudinal data set has been used for much of the work reported in this book. The longitudinal sample with three panels of data consists of 501 mothers in 15 states from 27 counties. States included are: California, Indiana, Iowa, Kentucky, Louisiana, Maryland, Massachusetts, Michigan, Minnesota, Nebraska, New Hampshire, New York, Ohio, Oregon, and West Virginia. Four states purposely focused on collecting data from their large Latina population (California, Iowa, Michigan, and Oregon). Four states have at least one of their sites in the Appalachian Regional Commission boundaries (Kentucky, New York, Ohio, and West Virginia).

This book is centered on rural families and work, however, the mothers were asked about many other topics that related to their daily lives and the context in which they lived during the early years of the twenty-first century. The overall goal of the RFS project was to track the well-being of mothers and their functioning over time by including the individual and family circumstances, the changing welfare policy environment, and the community context in which the families functioned. The topics included: Household composition (adults and children and movement in and out); health (physical for adults and children and mental for mothers (CES-D)); economics (employment and current work, including benefits, sources of income, employment history); housing (utilities, condition, moving patterns, homelessness); child care (sources, barriers); family functioning (parenting, child support, social support, personal well-being); transportation, government benefits, life skills, life satisfaction; family of origin characteristics such as education, employment, moving, and welfare receipt; community resources; and scales to assess family food security (Food Security Module), income adequacy, and material hardship. The qualitative questions focused on the mother's daily life, her interactions with her support systems, her perceptions on topics related to economic well-being, community, personal safety, and her goals and hopes for herself, family, and children in the future. Finally a community contextual data set for 2000 was compiled for consistent, comparable data for all the counties in which data were collected. If the data were not available for all counties, the information was not included in the data set.

The multistate, multidisciplinary approach allowed for a better understanding of the many facets and complexities faced by rural low-income families within the context of their communities. The multistate research team consisted of family scientists, family economists, nutritional scientists, psychologists, and sociologists. A number of Cooperative Extension specialists were either project leaders or

Table A.1 Structure and persons involved with NC-223/1011 research project

State University panel of study	Researchers and chairs of project	Graduate students	Undergraduate students
California			
University of California-Riverside and Davis Panel 1	Karen Varcoe (PI) Martha Lopez Nancy Lees (left in 2003) Lenna Ontai	Holly Pong	
Colorado			
Colorado State University (left in 2003)	Carole J. Makela (PI)		
Indiana			
Purdue University (left in 2005) Panel 1	Elizabeth Kiss (PI) Flora L. Williams (PI) (retired in 2001) Jeanne Contras	Rebecca Sero-Lyn[a]	
Iowa			
Iowa State University (joined in 2003) Panel 3	Steven Garasky (PI) Christine Cook (PI) Kim Greder (PI)	Bruce Randall Lizmelia Ortiz Dawn Browder[a] Andrea Bentzinger[b] Moises Perales Laura Seversion	
Kentucky			
University of Kentucky Panel 1	Patricia Hyjer Dyk (PI) Leigh Ann Simmons (joined 2004)	Debra Kershaw Sarah Frank Amanda Brody Jennifer Holz Esther Edwards Derek Feldman Jessica Kropczynski	
Louisiana			
Louisiana State University Panel 1	Frances C. Lawrence (PI) Ann Berry Vicky Tiller	Ann Berry[a] Jennifer Burczyk-Brown	
Maryland			
University of Maryland Panel 1	Bonnie Braun (PI) Elaine Anderson Susan Walker Jinhee Kim Connie Barnett Cindy Tuttle Julie Kohler	Maria Vandergriff-Avery[a] Crystal Tyler Melissa Rudd[b] Marni Duitch Johnel Hector Lisa Benson, Stephanie Grutzmacher[b] Orville Grimes Megan Fitzgerald Taryn Desfulan Sarah Kaye Marta McClintock-Comeaux	Julianna Plumb[c] Emma Simson Joanna Waldman Ruth Bowler Hannah Bennett Marjorie Strachman Ingrid Lofgren Regina Mohammad Shannon Thompson

Table A.1 (continued)

State University panel of study	Researchers and chairs of project	Graduate students	Undergraduate students
		Elisabeth Frost Maring Leigh Ann Simmons-Wescott[a] (University of Georgia) Linda Oraveca Jokena Smith Islam[b] Rose Marghi[b] Joanna B. Waldman[b]	
Massachusetts University of Massachusetts-Amherst Panel 1	Sheila Mammen(PI) Gretchen May Shirley Mietlicki	Michael Salemme Kim Wilson Michelle Woodford[b] Swetha Valluri	Caleb Mills Megan Dolan Peter St. Marie Thomas Martin Michael Mead Robert Young
Michigan Michigan State University Panel 1	David Imig (PI) Dennis Keefe (PI) (retired in 2002) Barbara Ames (PI)	E. Brooke Kelly[a] Laurie A. Bulock[a,b] Mary McDonald	
Minnesota University of Minnesota, St. Paul Panel 1	Jean W. Bauer (PI) (Chair NC223, 2000–2002) Mary Jo Katras (NRIGCP Grant Research Associate)	Sharon Powell[a] Mary Jo Bartl Katras[a] Carolyn Bird[a,b] Szu-Yi Peng Kristine Piescher[b] Jenet Jacob Jaerim Lee Seohee Son Clinton Gudmunson Katherine Brewton[b] Chanran Seo Tisa Thomas Samantha Zaid Nanci De Felippe Shuling Peng Monica Frazer[a]	Kelly Andrews Tonya Miller Lance Terwedo Jessica Ovel Michelle Kodet Tara Colby Brooke Jenkins Jessica Thompson Jenna Olson Kerrie Skinner Scott Ploehm Erin Steva Marissa Frazier
Missouri University of Missouri (left in 1999)	Ed Metzen (PI) (Chair NC223, 1998–1999) Lucy Shraeder		
Nebraska University of Nebraska, Lincoln Panel 1	Kathleen Prochaska-Cue (PI) (Chair NC223, 1999–2000) Susan Churchill (PI) Kathy Bosch Vicki Plano Clark Catherine Huddleston-Casas (joined 2006)	Pam Oltman[b] Busisiwe Nkosi Carrie Doll Maleah Woodward Becky Stefanski Christina Higgins Toni Hill-Menson Tiffany Wigington Autumn Howard	Amanda Cue Kimberly Uber Jamie Frost Tylinn Lewis

Table A.1 (continued)

State University panel of study	Researchers and chairs of project	Graduate students	Undergraduate students
New Hampshire			
University of New Hampshire Panel 1	Elizabeth Dolan (PI) (Chair NC1011, 2004–2008) Suzann Enzian Knight (PI)	Jessica Murphy Roclyn Carey Gregory Kovacs Talia Glesner[b] Laura Andrew Christopher Mausolff Kara Campbell Sabrina Harris Ozgur Akbas	Francesca Devaney[c]
New York			
Cornell University Panel 1	Christine Olson (PI) Josephine Swanson (PI) Caron Bove Kenda Anderson	Ellen Muraca	Megan Lent[c] Lindsay Petrovic[c] Emily Miller
Ohio			
Ohio State University Panels 1 and 2	Sharon B. Seiling (PI) (Chair NC223/NC1011, 2002–2004) Kathryn Stafford Kathy Reschke Chester Bowling William Grunkemeyer	Eun-Jin Kim Jing Zhao Jiwon Seo Jonghee Lee Christina Hermsdorfer Susan McCabe Margaret Hart[a]	
Oregon			
Oregon State University[d] Panel 1	Leslie Richards (PI) Sally Bowman (PI) (left in 2003) Yoshie Sano, (NRICGP Research Associate)	Margaret Manoogian Yoshie Sano[a] Beth Hilberg Corinne Corson[b] Sireesha Pamulapti Martha Hotchkiss SoYoung Lee, Marina Merrill Sarah Feeney[b] Amy Guyer[b] Robin Ozretich[b] Carrie Farris Amanda Taylor Isaac Washburn Devora Shamah Rica Amity Talya Abel[b] Verna Ourada Kate Behan Molly Trauten Doris Cancel Tirado Jody Alaniz Yu-Jin Jeong Michaella Sektnan	J.M. Tatum[c] Phillis Annoh Renee Arreola Emielle Centrella Ariana Chavarria Vesna Cogurik Nicole Dobbins Jorge Dorantes Leslie Eleveld Jared Englund Nini Graham Erin Harrington Meagan Hogle Arkeema Hollins Amy Kim John Kim Holland LaRue Angela Lewis Emily Morris Rosa Munoz Tiffany Odell Silvia Ortiz Sarah Pieren Simon Sei

Table A.1 (continued)

State University panel of study	Researchers and chairs of project	Graduate students	Undergraduate students
			Zachary Tharp
			Matt Thomas
			Rachel Thompson
			Teresa Vazquez
			Reid Yamashiro
South Dakota			
South Dakota State University (joined in 2003) Panel 3	Donna Hess, (PI) Don Arwood (PI)	Joshua Turner Tricia Wek-Visker[a] Cynthia Wasberg[a] Saileza Khatiwada	
West Virginia			
University of West Virginia and University of Ohio (joined in 2000) Panel 2	Margaret Manoo-gian (PI) (Ohio University) Linda Waybright Patty Morrison	Jessie Meek Kristen Hamler Cara Luce[b] K.P. Shih[b]	Ju-Lien Ko[c]
Wyoming			
University of Wyo-ming (left in 2001) Panel 1	Bernita Quoss (PI)	Gena Sandberg	
AES administrator	Janet Bokemeier, Michigan (1998–2003) Robin Douthitt, Wisconsin (2003–2008)		
USDA representative	Nancy Valentine (1998–2003) Caroline Crocoll (2003–2008)		

[a] Ph.D. dissertation from the RFS data
[b] Master's thesis from the RFS data
[c] Undergraduate honors thesis from the RFS data
[d] Data were processed for the RFS study at Oregon State. Dr. Richards trained many students to assist with this work. Research assistants (both graduate and undergraduate) were supported by the grants and individual state payments

co-project leaders in many of the states. In all, more than 50 researchers (faculty, research scientists, and graduate students) worked together on the RFS project. In addition, many states had undergraduate student interns involved in the research teams.

More people participated in the larger project than were involved in the data collection. The lead researchers for each state, and the students involved over the 10 years of the NC223/1011 project are included in Appendix Table A.1.

The publications from the research project that have been cited in the book are included in Further Reading. The list includes only those papers that were cited in the chapters and it is not, therefore, an inclusive list.

One of the goals of the RFS project was to support and to produce future scholars. Overall, 14 Ph.D. dissertations, 20 master's theses, and six undergraduate honors theses were written from the RFS data. These can be found on the website for the project. In addition, two documents are available that give general information about the entire project. They are a basebook and report of the grant funding for the NRICGP 2004–2006 projects. These are available at http://www.cehd.umn.edu/fsos/Centers/RuralFamiliesSpeak/pub.asp or www.ruralfamiliesspeak will redirect you to the main site and you can click on publications.

The project was funded by each state total or with a combination of funds from the states' Agricultural Experiment Stations, Cooperative Extension, as well as specific funding sources for researchers in some states. Three grants for the overall support of the project were obtained from USDA, National Research Initiative Cooperative Grant Program (2001-35401-10215, 2002-35201-11591, 2004-35401-14938-J.W. Bauer, P.I.)

Further Reading

Rural Families Speak Work Cited

Bauer, J. W. (2004). *Basebook report: Rural families speak project.* http://www.ched.umn.edu/
fsos/assets/centers/RuralFamiliesSpeak/pub.asp.

Bauer, J. W., & Dolan, E. (2003). The impact of financial life skills and knowledge of community
resources on food security [Abstract]. *Proceedings of the Fifth Conference of the International
Society for Quality-of-Life Studies* (p. 151). Frankfurt, Germany.

Bauer, J. W., Braun, B., & Olson, P. D. (2000). Welfare to well-being framework for research, education, and outreach. *Journal of Consumer Affairs, 34*(1), 62–81. doi:10.1111/j.1745-6606.2000.
tb00084.x.

Berry, A. A., Katras, M. J., Sano, Y., Lee, J., & Bauer, J. W. (2008). Job volatility of rural, low-
income mothers: A mixed methods approach. *Journal of Family and Economic Issues, 29,*
5–22. doi:1007/s10834-007-9096-1.

Bird, C. L., & Bauer, J. W. (2009). Understanding the factors that influence the opportunity for
education and training. *Consumer Interests Annual, 55,* 83–85. http://www.consumerinterests.
org/2000-2009Proceedings.php.

Bok, M., & Simmons, L. (2002). Post-welfare reform, low-income families and the dissolution of the safety net. *Journal of Family and Economic Issues, 23,* 217–238.
doi:10.1023/A:1020391009561.

Bove, C. F., & Olson, C. M. (2006). Obesity in low-income rural women: Qualitative insights
about physical activity and eating patterns. *Women & Health, 44*(1), 57–78. doi:10.1300/
J013v44n01_04.

Braun, B. (n.d.). *Barriers to mental health access for rural residents.* (Maryland Family Policy
Impact Seminar). http://www.sph.umd.edu/fmsc/fis/_docs/MentalHealthTaskForceBrief.pdf.

Braun, B. (2007). *Livin' on the byways—Rural families speak.* [Dramatization]. http://www.sph.
umd.edu/fmsc/people/documents/LivinOnLifesByWays11-15-07.pdf.

Braun, B. (2009). Advancing rural family resiliency research, education, and policy. *Journal of
Family & Consumer Sciences, 101*(4), 27–32.

Braun, B., & Bauer, J. (1998). Welfare reform: An opportunity to engage universities in community and economic development. *Journal of Public Service and Outreach, 3,* 33–37.

Braun, B., & Benning, L. (2001). Welfare reform 4 years later: The mobilization of the land-grant
system. *Journal of Extension, 39*(3). http://www.joe.org/joe/2001june/comm1.php.

Braun, B., & Philogene, M. (2001). *Employability task force welfare to work survey.* Washington,
DC: National Association of State Universities and Land-Grant Colleges.

Braun, B., & Waldman, J. (2006). *Engaging unheard voices*. Final Report to the Kettering Foundation. http://www.sph.umd.edu/fmsc/fis/_docs/Engaging_Unheard_Voices.pdf.

Braun, B., Lawrence, F. C., Dyk, P. H., & Vandergriff-Avery, M. (2002). Southern rural family economic well-being in the context of public assistance. *Southern Rural Sociology Research Journal, 18*, 259–295. http://www.ag.auburn.edu/auxiliary/srsa/pages/Articles/SRS%202002%2018%201%2020259-293.pdf.

Brewton, K. E. (2008). *Qualitative analysis of the stress and coping experiences of low-income rural mothers raising a child with a disability.* Unpublished master's thesis, University of Minnesota, St. Paul.

Brewton, K., Walker, S., & Bauer, J. (2008, November). *Stress and coping experiences of low income rural mothers raising a child with a disability.* Paper session presented at the annual conference of the National Council on Family Relations, Little Rock.

Corson, C. M. (2001). *Health, well-being, and financial self-sufficiency of low-income families in the context of welfare reform.* Unpublished master's thesis, Oregon State University, Corvallis.

Dolan, E. M. (2009). Policy implications. *Consumer Interests Annual, 55*, 91–92. http://www.consumerinterests.org/2000-2009Proceedings.php.

Dolan, E. M., Braun, B., Prochaska-Cue, K., & Varcoe, K. P. (2002). *Conceptualizing the interface among family, community and labor force participation for rural limited resource families.* Paper session presented at the 42nd Annual Workshop, National Association for Welfare Research and Statistics, Albuquerque, NM. http://www.nawrs.org/NewMexico/papers/t5b1.pdf.

Dolan, E. M., Richards, L. N., Sano, Y., Bauer, J., & Braun, B. (2005). Linkages between employment patterns and depression over time: The case of low-income rural mothers. *Consumer Interest Annual, 51*, 225–229. http://www.consumerinterests.org/2000-2009Proceedings.php.

Dolan, E. M., Seiling, S. B., & Glesner, T. (2006). Making it work: Rural low-income women in service jobs. In B. J. Cude (Ed.), *Proceedings of the Eastern Family Economics and Resource Management Association Conference* (pp. 38–46) Knoxville. http://mrupured.myweb.uga.edu/conf/5.pdf.

Dolan, E. M., Braun, B., Katras, M. J., & Seiling, S. (2008). Getting off TANF: Experiences of rural mothers. *Families in Society, 89*, 456–465. doi:10.1606/1044-3894.3771.

Dolan, E. M., Seiling, S., & Harris, S. (2009a). Work constraints of rural, low income mothers and their partners. *Consumer Interests Annual, 55*, 83–85. http://www.consumerinterests.org/2000-2009Proceedings.php.

Dolan, E. M., Seiling, S., & Harris, S. (2009b, November). *Rural, low-income dual earner parents—flexibility in work/family roles.* Poster session presented at the National Council on Family Relations 71st Annual Conference. Burlingame.

Frazer, M. S. (2011). *Poverty measurement and depression symptomology in the context of welfare reform.* Unpublished doctoral dissertation, University of Minnesota, St. Paul.

Garrison, M. E. B., Marks, L. D., Lawrence, F. C., & Braun, B. (2004). Religious beliefs, faith community involvement and depression: A study of rural, low-income mothers. *Women & Health, 40*(3), 51–62. doi:10.1300/J013v0n03_04.

Greder, K., Brotherson, M. J., & Garasky, S. (2004). Listening to the voices of marginalized families. In C. L. Anderson (Ed.), *Family and community policy: Strategies for civic engagement* (pp. 95–116). Alexandria: American Association of Family and Consumer Sciences.

Greder, K., Cook, C., Garasky, S., Sano, Y., & Randall, B. (2008). Rural Latino immigrant families: Hunger, housing, and social support. In R. L. Dalla, J. DeFrain, J. Johnson, & D. A. Abbott (Eds.), *Strengths and challenges of new immigrant families: Implications for research, policy, education and service* (pp. 345–367). Lanham: Lexington Books.

Gudmunson, C. G., Son, S., Lee, J., & Bauer, J. W. (2010). EITC participation and association with financial distress among rural low-income families. *Family Relations, 59*, 369–382. doi:10.1111/j.1741-3729.2010.00609x.

Guyer, A. (2003). *Depression risk: An examination of rural low-income mothers.* Unpublished master's thesis, Oregon State University, Corvallis.

Huddleston-Casas, C., & Braun, B. (2006, May). *Laboring towards economic self-sufficiency: A research perspective.* (RFS Research Brief). http://www.cehd.umn.edu/fsos/assets/pdf/RuralFamSpeak/May_ResearchBrief.pdf.

Huddleston-Casas, C., Charnigo, R., & Simmons, L. A. (2008). Food insecurity and maternal depression in rural, low-income families: A longitudinal investigation. *Public Health Nutrition, 12,* 1133–1140. doi:10.1017/S136890008003650.

Katras, M. J., Zuiker, V. S., & Bauer, J. W. (2004). Private safety net: Childcare resources from the perspective of rural low-income families. *Family Relations, 53,* 201–209. doi:10.1111/j.0022-2445.2004.00010.x.

Katras, M. J., Dolan, E. M., Seiling, S. B., & Braun, B. (2009). The bumpy road off TANF for rural mothers. *Family Science Review, 14*(1). http://www.familyscienceassociation.org/archived%20journal%20articles/FSR_vol14_2008/1Mary%20Jo_Katras.pdf.

Kim, E.-J., Geistfeld, L. V., & Seiling, S. B. (2003). Factors affecting health care decisions of rural poor women. *Asian Women, 16,* 73–85.

Kim, E.-J., Seiling, S., Stafford, K., & Richards, L. (2005). Rural low-income women's employment and mental health. *Journal of Rural Community Psychology, E8*(2). http://www.marshall.edu/jrcp/8_2_Eun.htm.

Ko, J., & Manoogian, M. (2005, April). *Commitment to parenting and personal outcomes for rural, low-income Appalachian mothers.* Paper session presented at the annual meeting of the Ohio Association of Family and Consumer Sciences, Perrysburg.

Lee, J., Katras, M. J., & Bauer, J. W. (2010). Values underlying U. S. low-income mothers' voices about welfare and welfare reform: An inductive analysis. *International Journal of Human Ecology, 11*(2), 63–75.

Mammen, S., & Dolan, E. M. (2005). *Employment and obstacles to employment for rural, low-income mothers in the Northeast.* Paper session presented at the Rural Poverty in the Northeast: Strengthening the Regional Research Effort Conference. College Park. http://nercrd.psu.edu/publications/rdppapers/rdp28.pdf.

Mammen, S., & Lawrence, F. C. (2006). How rural working families use the earned income tax credit: A mixed method analysis. *Financial Counseling and Planning, 17,* 51–63. http://www1067.ssldomain.com/afcpe/doc/Vol1715.pdf.

Mammen, S., Bauer, J. W., & Lass, D. (2009). Life satisfaction among rural low-income mothers: The influence of health, human, personal, and social capital. *Applied Research Quality of Life, 4,* 365–386. doi:.1007/s11482-009-9086-6.

Mammen, S., Bauer, J. W., & Richards, L. N. (2009). Understanding persistent food insecurity: A paradox of place and circumstance. *Social Indicators Research, 92,* 151–168. doi:.1007/s11205-008-9294-8.

Mammen, S., Lass, D., & Seiling, B. (2009). Labor force supply decisions of rural low-income mothers. *Journal of Family and Economic Issues, 30,* 67–79. doi:1007/s10834-008-9136-5.

Mammen, S., Lawrence, F. C., St. Marie, P., Berry, A. A., & Knight, S. E. (2011). The earned income tax credit and rural families: Differences between non-participants and participants. *Journal of Family and Economic Issues, 32,* 461–472. doi:1007/s10834-010-9238-8.

Manoogian, M., Richards, L., & Peters, C. (2003, November). *Negotiating poverty and family ties: Adult daughters' ambivalent relationships with mothers in rural, low-income families.* Symposium paper presented at annual meeting of National Council on Family Relations, Vancouver, Canada.

Maring, E. F., & Braun, B. (2006). Drug, alcohol and tobacco use in rural, low-income families: An ecological risk and resilience perspective. *Journal of Rural Community Psychology, E9*(2). http://www.marshall.edu/jrcp/Maring%20and%20Braun.pdf.

Olson, C. M. (1999). Nutrition and health outcomes associated with food insecurity and hunger. *Journal of Nutrition, 129,* 521S–524S. http://jn.nutrition.org/cgi/content/full/129/2/521S.

Olson, C. M. (2006). *Food insecurity in poor rural families with children: A human capital perspective.* (RFS Policy Brief). http://www.cehd.umn.edu/fsos/assets/pdf/RuralFamSpeak/RFS_March_FoodSecurity_policy%20brief_final2.pdf.

Olson, C. M., Anderson, K., Kiss, E., Lawrence, F. C., & Seiling, S. B. (2004). Factors protecting against and contributing to food insecurity among rural families. *Family Economics and Nutrition Review, 16*(1), 12–20. http://www.cnpp.usda.gov/Publications/FENR/V16N1/FENRV16N1.pdf.

Olson, C. M., Bove, C. F., & Miller, E. O. (2007). Growing up poor: Long-term implications for eating patterns and body weight. *Appetite, 49,* 198–207. doi:10.1016/j.appet.2007.01.012.

Piescher, K. N. (2004). *Economic, social, and community factors indicating depressive symptomatology in rural, low-income mothers.* Unpublished master's thesis, University of Minnesota, St. Paul.

Powell, S. E., & Bauer, J. W. (2010). Examining the resource use of rural low-income families caring for children with disabilities. *Journal of Children & Poverty, 16*(1), 67–83. doi:10.1080/10796120903575101.

Reschke, K. L., & Walker, S. K. (2006). Mothers' child caregiving and employment commitments and choices in the context of rural poverty. *Affilia: Journal of Women and Social Work, 21,* 306–319. doi:10.1177/086709906288970.

Reschke, K. L., Manoogian, M. M., Richards, L. N., Walker, S. K., & Seiling, S. B. (2006). Maternal grandmothers as child care providers for rural, low-income mothers. A unique child care arrangement. *Journal of Children & Poverty, 12,* 159–174. doi:10.1080/10796120600879590.

Richards, L., Manoogian, M., Seiling, S., & Bird, C. (2002, November). *Providing support and presenting challenge: Adult daughters and their mothers in rural, low-income families.* Paper session presented at the annual meeting of the National Council on Family Relations, Houston.

Sano, Y., Dolan, E. M., Richards, L. N., Bauer, J., & Braun, B. (2008). Employment patterns, family resources, and perception: Examining depressive symptoms among rural low-income mothers. *Journal of Rural Community Psychology. E11*(1). http://www.marshall.edu/jrcp/V11%20N1/Sano.pdf.

Sano, Y., Katras, M. J., Lee, J., Bauer, J. W., & Berry, A. A. (2010). Working toward sustained employment: A closer look on intermittent employment of rural low-income mothers. *Families in Society, 91*(4), 342–349. doi:10.1606/1044-3894.4039.

Sano, Y., Garasky, S., Greder, K., Cook, C. C., & Browder, D. E. (2011). Understanding food security among Latino immigrant families in rural America. *Journal of Family and Economic Issues, 32.* Advance on-line publication. doi:10.1007/s10834-010-9219-y.

Seiling, S. B. (2006). Changes in the lives of rural low-income mothers: Do resources play a role in stress? *Journal of Human Behavior in the Social Environment, 13,* 19–42. doi:10.1300/J137v13n01-02.

Seiling, S. B., Dolan, E. M., & Glesner, T. (2005, June). *Rural low-income women who work in service jobs tell about their lives.* Paper session presented at the Gender, Work and Organization 4th International Conference, Keele University, Staffordshire, United Kingdom.

Seiling, S. B., Stafford, K., McCabe, S., & Reschke, K. (2006, February). Social support as a means to well-being for rural low-income mothers. In B. J. Cude (Ed.), *Proceedings of the Eastern Family Economics and Resource Management Association Conference* (pp. 88–100), Knoxville. http://mrupured.myweb.uga.edu/conf/20.pdf.

Simmons, L. A. (2006, March). *Health: An essential to rural, low-income mother's economic well-being.* (RFS Policy Brief). http://www.cehd.umn.edu/fsos/assets/pdf/RuralFamSpeak/March_Health_PolicyBrief.pdf.

Simmons, L. A. (2006). *Health: Essential to rural, low-income mothers' economic well-being.* (RFS Fact Sheet). http://www.cehd.umn.edu/fsos/assets/pdf/RuralFamSpeak/March_Health_FactSheet.pdf.

Simmons, L. A., & Braun, B. (2005). *Income matters: Understanding health in rural, low-income women.* Paper session presented at the 8th International Women's Policy Research Conference of Institute for Women's Policy Research, Washington, DC.

Simmons, L. A., & Havens, J. R. (2007). Comorbid substance and mental disorders among rural Americans: Results from the national comorbidity survey. *Journal of Affective Disorders, 99,* 265–271. doi:10.1016/j.jad.2006.08.016.

Simmons, L. A., Braun, B., Wright, D. W., Miller, S. R. (2007). Human capital, social support, and economic wellbeing among rural, low-income mothers: A latent growth curve analysis. *Journal of Family and Economic Issues, 28,* 635–652. doi:.1007/s10834-007-9079-2.

Simmons, L. A., Dolan, E. M., & Braun, B. (2007). Rhetoric and reality of economic self-sufficiency among rural, low-income families: A longitudinal study. *Journal of Family and Economic Issues, 28*(3), 489–505. doi:10.1007/s10834-007-9071-x.

Simmons, L. A., Huddleston-Casas, C., & Berry, A. A. (2007). Low-income rural women and depression: Factors associated with self-reporting. *American Journal of Health Behavior, 31,* 657-666. http://www.atypon-link.com/PNG/doi/pdf/10.5555/ajhb.2007.31.6.657.

Simmons, L. A., Braun, B., Carnigo, R., Havens, J. R., & Wright, D. W. (2008). Depression and poverty among rural women: A relationship of social causation or social selection? *Journal of Rural Health, 24,* 292–298. doi:10.1111/j.1748-0361.2008.00171.x.

Simpson, E. (2007). *Oral health among low-income rural families: Implications for policy and programs.* Paper session presented at the Maryland Family Policy Impact Seminar. University of Maryland: College Park. http://www.csrees.usda.gov/nea/food/pdfs/oral_health.pdf.

Son, S., & Bauer, J. W. (2009, November). *The capability approach for research on families in poverty.* Paper session presented at the National Council on Family Relations 71st Annual Conference, Burlingame.

Son, S., & Bauer, J. W. (2010). Employed rural, low-income, single mothers' family and work over time. *Journal of Family and Economic Issues, 31,* 107–120. doi:.1007/s10834-009-9173-8.

Swanson, J., Lawrence, F., Anderson, K., & Olson, C. M. (2004). Low-income rural families: How formal and informal supports address food needs. In J. Fox (Ed.), *Proceedings of the Eastern Family Economics-Resource Management Association Conference* (pp. 27–29). Tampa.

Swanson, J. A., Olson, C. M., Miller, E. O. & Lawrence, F. C. (2008). Rural mothers' use of formal programs and informal social supports of meet family food needs: A mixed methods study. *Journal of Family Economic Issues, 29,* 674–690. doi:.1007/s10834-008-9127-6.

Tatum, J. M. (2006). *Comparing the health and healthcare needs of poor rural Hispanics and non-Hispanic Whites.* Unpublished honors thesis, Oregon State University, Corvallis.

Vandergriff-Avery, M. (2001). Rural families speak: A qualitative investigation of stress protective and crisis recovery strategies utilized by rural low-income women and their families. UMI Microform (3035864).

Vandergriff-Avery, M., Anderson, E. A., & Braun, B. (2004). Resiliency capacities among rural low-income families. *Families in Society, 85,* 562–570. doi:10.1606/1044-3894.1841.

Varcoe, K. P., Lees, N. B., & López, M. L. (2004). Rural Latino families in California are missing earned income tax benefits. *California Agriculture, 58,* 24–27. doi:10.3733/ca.v058n01p24.

Walker, S. K., & Reschke, K. L. (2004). Child care use by low-income families in rural areas: A contemporary look at the influence of women's work and partner availability. *Journal of Children & Poverty, 10,* 149–167. doi:10.1080/179612042000271585.

Waybright, L., Morrison, P., Seiling, S., Meek, J., & Manoogian, M. (2004). *The informal and formal support networks of rural, low-income Appalachian families.* Paper session presented at the annual conference of the National Association of Extension Family and Consumer Sciences, Nashville.

Author Index

Index includes sole authors and first authors citations only.

J. W. Bauer, E. M. Dolan (eds.), *Rural Families and Work*, International Series on Consumer Science 1,
DOI 10.1007/978-1-4614-0382-1, © Springer Science+Business Media, LLC 2011

Subject Index

J. W. Bauer, E. M. Dolan (eds.), *Rural Families and Work*, International Series on
Consumer Science 1,
DOI 10.1007/978-1-4614-0382-1, © Springer Science+Business Media, LLC 2011

CPSIA information can be obtained at www.ICGtesting.com
Printed in the USA
LVOW100104070112

262837LV00004B/34/P